CLYMER®

KAWASAKI

KZ400, KZ/Z440, EN450 & EN500
1974-1995

The world's finest publisher of mechanical how-to manuals

PRIMEDIA
Business Magazines & Media

P.O. Box 12901, Overland Park, Kansas 66282-2901

Copyright ©1996 PRIMEDIA Business Magazines & Media Inc.

FIRST EDITION
First Printing February, 1977

SECOND EDITION
Updated by Ed Scott to include 1978-1979 models
First Printing May, 1979

THIRD EDITION
Revised by Anton Vesely to include 1980 models
First Printing April, 1981

FOURTH EDITION
Revised by Anton Vesely to include 1981-1982 models
First Printing January, 1983

FIFTH EDITION
First Printing September, 1983
Second Printing June, 1984

SIXTH EDITION
Revised by Ed Scott
First Printing August, 1985

SEVENTH EDITION
Revised by Ron Wright to include 1984-1987 models
First Printing May, 1987
Second Printing October, 1987
Third Printing June, 1988
Fourth Printing April, 1990

EIGHTH EDITION
Updated by Ed Scott to include 1988-1990 models
First Printing June, 1991
Second Printing November, 1992

NINTH EDITION
Updated to include 1991-1994 models
First Printing July, 1994

TENTH EDITION
Updated to include 1995 models
First Printing May, 1996
Second Printing December, 1997
Third Printing January, 2000
Fourth Printing November, 2001

Printed in U.S.A.

CLYMER and colophon are registered trademarks of PRIMEDIA Business Magazines & Media Inc.

ISBN: 0-89287-679-4

Library of Congress: 96-75542

MEMBER
MOTORCYCLE INDUSTRY COUNCIL, INC.

Technical assistance by Action Fours, Inc., Santa Ana, California. Technical illustrations by Steve Amos.

COVER: Photography and motorcycle courtesy of Pieter Herremans. Special thanks to the Vintage Japanese Motorcycle Club (www.vjmc.org).

The following books and guides are published by PRIMEDIA Business Directories & Books.

More information available at *primediabusiness.com*

CONTENTS

QUICK REFERENCE DATA

ENGINE OIL CAPACITY

	Liters	U.S. qt.
1974-1977	3.0	3.2
1978-1983		
Without filter change	2.5	2.6
With filter change	2.9	3.1
1985-on		
Without filter change	2.8	2.9
With filter change	3.0	3.2

FRONT FORK OIL CAPACITY

Model	Dry capacity cc	Oil level* in.	mm
1974-1976	160	I 13.6	I 350
1977	160	I 13.5	I 343
1978	150	R 17.1	R 435
1979-1981 B, C	150	R 17.1	R 435
1979-1981 A, D, H	150	R 18.7	R 475
1982-1983 A, D	150	R 18.5	R 470
1982-1983 G, H	175	R 16.8	R 426
1985-1990 EN450	355	RC 6.4	RC 162
1990-on EN500	385	RC 5.04	RC 128

*On 1974-1983 models, fork oil level is checked with forks fully extended. On 1985-on models, fork oil level is checked with forks fully compressed:
I: Fork springs installed.
R: Fork springs removed.
RC: Fork springs removed, forks fully compressed.

FRONT FORK AIR PRESSURE

	psi	kg/cm^2
KZ440		
Standard	8.5	0.6
Usable range	7-10	0.5-0.7
Maximum	36	2.5
EN450		
Standard	0	0
Usable range	*	*
Maximum	*	*

*Not specified.

TIRES AND TIRE PRESSURE (1985-ON)

Model/tire size	Pressure @ load 0-215 lb. (0-97.5 kg)	Over 215 lb. (Over 97.5 kg)
Front		
EN500—100/90-19 57S	28 psi (196 kPa)	28 psi (196 kPa)
All others—100/90-10 57S	28 psi (196 kPa)	28 psi (196 kPa)
Rear—140/90-15 70S	28 psi (196 kPa)	32 psi (221 kPa)

TUNE-UP SPECIFICATIONS

Spark plugs (standard heat range)

Type	
1974-1977*	NGK B8ES or ND W24ES
1978-1983	NGK B7ES or ND 22ES-U
1985-on**	NGK D9EA or ND X27ES-U
1985-on***	NGK DR8ES-L or ND X27ESR-U
Gap	
1974-1983	0.7-0.8 mm (0.028-0.032 in.)
1985-on	0.6-0.7 mm (0.024-0.028 in.)
Breaker points	
Gap	0.35 mm (0.014 in.)
Dwell	53% (193°)
Valve clearance (cold)	
1974-1976	0.10-0.15 mm (0.004-0.006 in.)
1977*	0.13-0.15 mm (0.005-0.006 in.)
1978-1983	0.17-0.22 mm (0.007-0.009 in.)
1985-on	
Intake	0.13-0.18 mm (0.005-0.007 in.)
Exhaust	0.18-0.23 mm (0.007-0.009 in.)
Idle speed	
1974-1983	1,100-1,300 rpm
1985-on	1,150-1,250 rpm
Idle mixture (turns out from seated)	
1974	7/8
1975	1 1/2
1976	1 5/8
1977*	1 1/2
1978	1 1/4
1979 B	1 1/4
1979 H	2 1/4
1980-1981	2 1/4
1982-1983	2 3/4
1985-on	—
Compression	
1974-1977*	
Standard	142-156 psi (10-11 kg/cm^2)
Limit	107 psi (7.5 kg/cm^2)
1978-1983	
Standard	156 psi (11 kg/cm^2)
Limit	109 psi (7.7 kg/cm^2)
1985-1990 EN450	119-185 psi (8.4-13 kg/cm^2)
1990-on EN500	129-213 psi (9.1-15 kg/cm^2)

*Includes 1977-1978 Deluxe A models.
**U.S. and Swiss models.
***Other than above.

CLUTCH WEAR LIMITS

	mm	in.
Clutch spring free length		
1974-1977	32.3	1.271
1978-1983	*	*
1985-1990 EN450	32.2	1.267
1990-on EN500	33.1	1.303
Friction plate thickness		
1974-1977	2.5	0.098
1978-1983	2.7	0.106
1985-on	2.75	0.108

(continued)

CLUTCH WEAR LIMITS (continued)

	mm	in.
Clutch plate warpage		
1974-1977		
Friction	0.30	0.012
Steel	0.40	0.016
1978-1981 KZ400	0.40	0.016
1980-1983 KZ440	0.30	0.012
1985-on	0.30	0.012
Friction plate tangs/clutch housing		
finger clearance		
1974-1977	0.60	0.023
1978-1983	0.70	0.027
1985-on	*	*

*Not specified by Kawasaki.

MODEL YEAR/SUFFIX EQUIVALENTS

1974	1975	1976
KZ400	KZ400S	KZ400-S2
	KZ400D	KZ400-D3

1977	1978	1979
KZ400-S3	KZ400-C1	KZ400-B2
KZ400-D4	KZ400-B1	KZ400-H1
KZ400-A1 (Deluxe A)	KZ400-A2 (Deluxe A)	KZ400-G1

1980	1981	1982-1983
KZ440-A1	KZ440-A2	KZ440-A3
KZ440-B1	KZ440-B2	KZ440-D4
KZ440-D1	KZ440-C2	KZ440-G1
Z440-A1	KZ440-D2	KZ440-H1
Z440-C1	KZ440-D3 (late 1981)	
KZ400-B3	Z440-C	
KZ400-G2	KZ400-G3	
	KZ400-H3	

1985-1990	1990-ON
EN450-A1	EN500-A1

COOLING SYSTEM SPECIFICATIONS (1985-ON)

Capacity	1.4 L (1.5 qt.)
Coolant type	Antifreeze suited for aluminum engines
Mix ratio	50% purified water:50% coolant
Radiator cap pressure	0.75-1.05 kg/cm^2 (11-15 psi)
Thermostat	
Opening temperature	157.1-162.5° F (69.5-72.5° C)
Valve opening lift	Not less than 8 mm (0.315 in.) @ 203° F (95° C)

REAR SUSPENSION WEAR LIMITS (KZ400 AND KZ440)

	mm	ft.-lb.
Rim runout	2	0.078
Axle runout	0.7	0.027
Swing arm (1974-1977)		
Sleeve diameter	21.95	0.864
Bushing inside diameter	22.26	0.876
Pivot shaft runout	0.14	0.005
Swing arm (1978-1981 KZ400; KZ440)		
Sleeve diameter	21.96	0.864

DRIVE CHAIN SPECIFICATIONS

Number of links	
KZ400	100
KZ440	
1980, A	104
1980-1982, B and C	100
1982-1983, H	102

PULLEY DIAMETER WEAR LIMITS

	mm	in.
KZ440		
1980, D		
Front	95	3.740
Rear	264.0	10.393
1981-1983, D		
Front	103.85	4.088
Rear	286.25	11.269
EN450		
Front pulley tooth height	6.3	0.248
Rear pulley diameter	299.63	11.796
EN500		
Front pulley tooth height	6.1	0.240
Rear pulley tooth height	6.3	0.248

CLYMER®

KAWASAKI

KZ400, KZ/Z440, EN450 & EN500
1974-1995

INTRODUCTION

This detailed, comprehensive manual covers all 1974-1995 Kawasaki KZ400, KZ/Z440, EN450 and EN500 models. The *Supplement* contains all procedures and specifications unique to the 1990-1995 EN500.

The expert text gives complete information on maintenance, repair and overhaul. Hundreds of photos and drawings guide you through every step. The book includes all you need to know to keep your bike running right.

Where repairs are practical for the owner/mechanic, complete procedures are given. Equally important, difficult jobs are pointed out. Such operations are usually more economically performed by a dealer or independent garage.

A shop manual is a reference. You want to be able to find information fast. As in all Clymer books, this one is designed with this in mind. All chapters are thumb tabbed. Important items are extensively indexed at the rear of the book. All the most frequently used specifications and capacities are summarized on the *Quick Reference Data* pages at the front of the book.

Keep the book handy in your tool box and take it with you on long trips. It will help you to understand your Kawasaki better, lower repair and maintenance costs and generally improve your satisfaction with your bike.

CHAPTER ONE

GENERAL INFORMATION

This detailed, comprehensive manual covers Kawasaki KZ400, KZ/Z440, EN450 and EN500 models from 1974-on. **Table 1** lists the different models and their suffix designations.

The manual is written simply and clearly enough for owners who have never worked on a motorcycle, but is complete enough for use by experienced mechanics.

Troubleshooting, tune-up, maintenance and repair are not difficult if you know what tools and equipment to use and what to do. Anyone of average intelligence and with some mechanical ability can perform most of the procedures in this manual.

Some of the procedures require the use of special tools. Using an inferior substitute tool for a special tool is not recommended as it can be dangerous to you and may damage the part.

Metric and U.S. standards are used throughout this manual. Metric to U.S. conversion is given in **Table 2**.

MANUAL ORGANIZATION

This chapter provides general information and discusses equipment and tools useful both for preventive maintenance and troubleshooting.

Chapter Two provides methods and suggestions for quick and accurate diagnosis and repair of problems. Troubleshooting procedures discuss typical symptoms and logical methods to pinpoint the trouble.

Chapter Three explains all periodic lubrication and routine maintenance necessary to keep your Kawasaki operating well. Chapter Three also includes recommended tune-up procedures, eliminating the need to constantly consult other chapters on the various assemblies.

Subsequent chapters describe specific systems such as the engine, clutch, primary drive, transmission, fuel, exhaust, suspension, steering and brakes. Each chapter provides disassembly, repair and assembly procedures in simple step-by-step form. If a repair is impractical for a home mechanic, it is so indicated. It is usually faster and less expensive to take such repairs to a dealer or competent repair shop. Specifications concerning a particular system are included at the end of the appropriate chapter.

NOTES, CAUTIONS AND WARNINGS

The terms NOTE, CAUTION and WARNING have specific meanings in this manual. A NOTE provides additional information to make a step or procedure easier or clearer. Disregarding a NOTE could cause inconvenience, but would not cause damage or personal injury.

A CAUTION emphasizes areas where equipment damage could occur. Disregarding a CAUTION could cause permanent mechanical damage; however, personal injury is unlikely.

A WARNING emphasizes areas where personal injury or even death could result from negligence. Mechanical damage may also occur. WARNINGS *are to be taken seriously.* In some cases, serious injury and death have resulted from disregarding similar warnings.

SAFETY FIRST

Professional mechanics can work for years and never sustain a serious injury. If you observe a few rules of common sense and safety, you can enjoy many safe hours servicing your own machine. If you ignore these rules you can hurt yourself or damage the equipment.

1. Never use gasoline as a cleaning solvent.
2. Never smoke or use a torch in the vicinity of flammable liquids, such as cleaning solvent, in open containers.
3. If welding or brazing is required on the machine, remove the fuel tank and rear shocks to a safe distance, at least 50 feet away. Welding on a gas tank requires special safety precautions and must be performed by someone skilled in the process. Do not attempt to weld or braze a leaking gas tank.
4. Use the proper sized wrenches to avoid damage to fasteners and injury to yourself.
5. When loosening a tight or stuck nut, be guided by what would happen if the wrench should slip. Be careful; protect yourself accordingly.
6. When replacing a fastener, make sure to use one with the same measurements and strength as the old one. Incorrect or mismatched fasteners can result in damage to the vehicle and possible personal injury. Beware of fastener kits that are filled with cheap and poorly made nuts, bolts, washers and cotter pins. Refer to *Fasteners* in this chapter for additional information.
7. Keep all hand and power tools in good condition. Wipe greasy and oily tools after using them. They are difficult to hold and can cause injury. Replace or repair worn or damaged tools.
8. Keep your work area clean and uncluttered.
9. Wear safety goggles during all operations involving drilling, grinding, the use of a cold chisel or anytime you feel unsure about the safety of your eyes. Safety goggles should also be worn anytime compressed air is used to clean a part.

10. Keep an approved fire extinguisher nearby. Be sure it is rated for gasoline (Class B) and electrical (Class C) fires.
11. When drying bearings or other rotating parts with compressed air, never allow the air jet to rotate the bearing or part; the air jet is capable of rotating them at speeds far in excess of those for which they were designed. The bearing or rotating part is very likely to disintegrate and cause serious injury and damage.

SERVICE HINTS

Most of the service procedures covered are straightforward and can be performed by anyone reasonably handy with tools. It is suggested, however, that you consider your own capabilities carefully before attempting any operation involving major disassembly of the engine or transmission.

1. "Front," as used in this manual, refers to the front of the motorcycle; the front of any component is the end closest to the front of the motorcycle. The "left-" and "right-hand" sides refer to the position of the parts as viewed by a rider sitting on the seat facing forward. For example, the throttle control is on the right-hand side. These rules are simple, but confusion can cause a major inconvenience during service.
2. Whenever servicing the engine or transmission, or when removing a suspension component, the bike should be secured in a safe manner. If the bike is to be parked on its sidestand, check the stand to make sure it is secure and not damaged. Block the front and rear wheels if they remain on the ground. A small hydraulic jack and a block of wood can be used to raise the chassis. If the transmission is not going to be worked on and the drive chain or drive belt is connected to the the rear wheel, shift the transmission into first gear.
3. Disconnect the negative battery cable when working on or near the electrical, clutch or starter systems and before disconnecting any wires. On most batteries, the negative terminal will be marked with a minus (-) sign and the positive terminal with a plus (+) sign.
4. When disassembling a part or assembly, it is a good practice to tag the parts for location and mark all parts which mate together. Small parts, such as bolts, can be identified by placing them in plastic sandwich bags. Seal the bags and label them with masking tape and a marking pen. When reassembly will take place immediately, an accepted practice is to place nuts and bolts in a cupcake tin or egg carton in the order of disassembly.

5. Finished surfaces should be protected from physical damage or corrosion. Keep gasoline and brake fluid off painted surfaces.

6. Use penetrating oil on frozen or tight bolts, then strike the bolt head a few times with a hammer and punch (use a screwdriver on screws). Avoid the use of heat where possible, as it can warp, melt or affect the temper of parts. Heat also ruins finishes, especially paint and plastics.

7. Keep flames and sparks away from a charging battery or flammable fluids and do not smoke near them. It is a good idea to have a fire extinguisher handy in the work area. Remember that many gas appliances in home garages (water heater, clothes drier, etc.) have pilot lights.

8. No parts removed or installed (other than bushings and bearings) in the procedures given in this manual should require unusual force during disassembly or assembly. If a part is difficult to remove or install, find out why before proceeding.

9. Cover all openings after removing parts or components to prevent dirt, small tools, etc. from falling in.

10. Read each procedure *completely* while looking at the actual parts before starting a job. Make sure you *thoroughly* understand what is to be done and then carefully follow the procedure, step by step.

11. Recommendations are occasionally made to refer service or maintenance to a Kawasaki dealer or a specialist in a particular field. In these cases, the work will be done more quickly and economically than if you performed the job yourself.

12. In procedural steps, the term "replace" means to discard a defective part and replace it with a new or exchange unit. "Overhaul" means to disassemble, inspect, measure, repair or replace defective parts and reassemble.

13. Some operations require the use of a hydraulic press. It would be wiser to have these operations performed by a shop equipped for such work, rather than to try to do the job yourself with makeshift equipment that may damage your machine.

14. Repairs go much faster and easier if your machine is clean before you begin work. There are many special cleaners on the market, like Bel-Ray Degreaser, for washing the engine and related parts. Follow the manufacturer's directions on the container for the best results. Clean all oily or greasy parts with cleaning solvent as you remove them.

WARNING
Never use gasoline as a cleaning agent.
It presents an extreme fire hazard. Be
sure to work in a well-ventilated area
when using cleaning solvent. Keep a fire
extinguisher, rated for gasoline fires,
handy in any case.

15. Much of the labor charged for by dealers is to remove, disassemble, assemble and reinstall other parts in order to reach the defective part. It is frequently possible to perform the preliminary operations yourself and then take the defective unit to the dealer for repair at considerable savings.

16. If special tools are required, make arrangements to get them before you start. It is frustrating and time-consuming to get partly into a job and then be unable to complete it.

17. Make diagrams (or take a Polaroid picture) wherever similar-appearing parts are found. For instance, crankcase bolts are often not the same length. You may think you can remember where everything came from—but mistakes are costly. There is also the possibility that you may be sidetracked and not return to work for days or even weeks—in which time carefully laid out parts may have become disturbed.

18. When assembling parts, be sure all shims and washers are replaced exactly as they came out.

19. Whenever a rotating part butts against a stationary part, look for a shim or washer. Use new gaskets if there is any doubt about the condition of the old ones. A thin coat of oil on non-pressure type gaskets may help them seal more effectively.

20. If it is necessary to make a gasket, and you do not have a suitable old gasket to use as a guide, apply engine oil to the gasket surface of the part. Then place the part on the new gasket material and press the part slightly. The oil will leave a very accurate outline on the gasket material that can be cut around. Be sure to use the same gasket material thickness as the original gasket.

21. Heavy grease can be used to hold small parts in place if they tend to fall out during assembly. However, keep grease and oil away from electrical and brake components.

22. A carburetor is best cleaned by disassembling it and soaking the parts in a commercial carburetor cleaner. Never soak gaskets and rubber parts in these cleaners. Never use wire to clean out jets and air passages unless otherwise instructed to do so in Chapter Six. They are easily damaged. Use compressed air to blow out the carburetor only if the float has been removed first.

23. Take your time and do the job right. Do not forget that a newly rebuilt engine must be broken in just like a new one.

TORQUE SPECIFICATIONS

Torque specifications throughout this manual are given in Newton Meters (N•m) and foot-pounds (ft.-lb.).

Table 3 lists general torque specifications for nuts and bolts that are not listed in the respective chapters. To use the table, first determine the size of the nut or bolt. **Figure 1** and **Figure 2** show how this is done.

FASTENERS

The materials and designs of the various fasteners used on your Kawasaki are not arrived at by chance or accident. Fastener design determines the type of tool required to work the fastener. Fastener material is carefully selected to decrease the possibility of physical failure.

Threads

Nuts, bolts and screws are manufactured in a wide range of thread patterns. To join a nut and bolt, the diameter of the bolt and the diameter of the hole in the nut must be the same. It is just as important that the threads on both be properly matched.

The best way to tell if the threads on 2 fasteners are matched is to turn the nut on the bolt (or the bolt into the threaded hole in a piece of equipment) with fingers only. Be sure both pieces are clean. If much force is required, check the thread condition on each fastener. If the thread condition is good but the fasteners jam, the threads are not compatible. A thread pitch gauge can also be used to determine pitch. Kawasaki manufactures using metric standard fasteners. The threads are cut differently than those of American fasteners (**Figure 3**).

Most threads are cut so that the fastener must be turned clockwise to tighten it. These are called right-hand threads. Some fasteners have left-hand threads; they must be turned counterclockwise to be tightened. Left-hand threads are used in locations where normal rotation of the equipment would tend to loosen a right-hand threaded fastener.

Machine Screws

There are many different types of machine screws. **Figure 4** shows a number of screw heads requiring different types of turning tools. Heads are also designed to protrude above the metal (round) or to be slightly recessed in the metal (flat). See **Figure 5**.

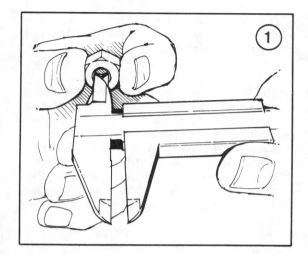

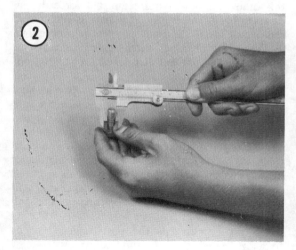

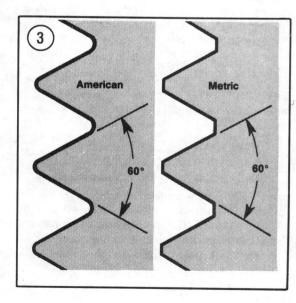

1

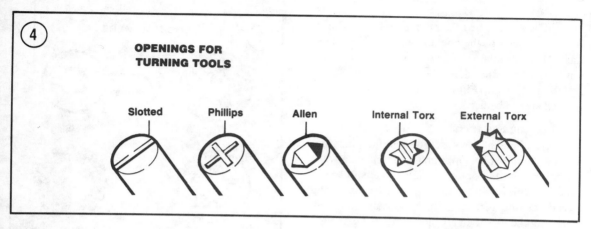

④ OPENINGS FOR TURNING TOOLS

Slotted   Phillips   Allen   Internal Torx   External Torx

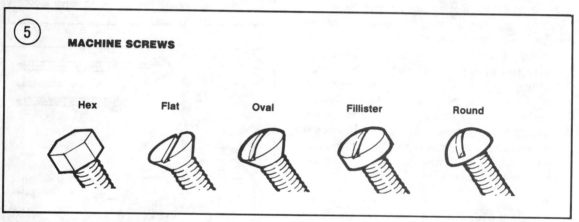

⑤ MACHINE SCREWS

Hex   Flat   Oval   Fillister   Round

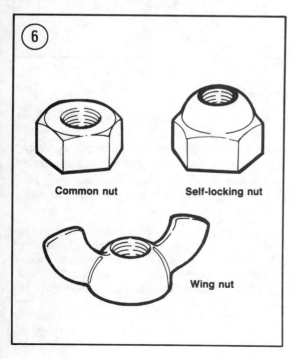

⑥

Common nut   Self-locking nut

Wing nut

Bolts

Commonly called bolts, the technical name for these fasteners is cap screw. Metric bolts are described by the diameter and pitch (or the distance between each thread). For example, a M8×1.25 bolt is one that has a diameter of 8 millimeters with a distance of 1.25 millimeters between each thread. The measurement across 2 flats on the head of the bolt indicates the proper wrench size to be used. **Figure 2** shows how to determine bolt diameter.

Nuts

Nuts are manufactured in a variety of types and sizes. Most are hexagonal (6-sided) and fit on bolts, screws and studs with the same diameter and pitch.

Figure 6 shows several types of nuts. The common nut is generally used with a lockwasher. Self-locking nuts have a nylon insert which prevents the nut from loosening; no lockwasher is required. Wing nuts are designed for fast removal by hand. Wing nuts are used for convenience in non-critical locations.

To indicate the size of a nut, manufacturers specify the diameter of the opening and the threads per inch. This is similar to bolt specifications, but without the length dimension. The measurement across 2 flats on the nut (**Figure 1**) indicates the proper wrench size to be used.

Self-Locking Fasteners

Several types of bolts, screws and nuts incorporate a system that develops an interference between the bolt, screw, nut or tapped hole threads. Interference is achieved in various ways: by distorting threads, coating threads with dry adhesive or nylon, distorting the top of an all-metal nut, using a nylon insert in the center or at the top of a nut, etc.

Self-locking fasteners offer greater holding strength and better vibration resistance. Some self-locking fasteners can be reused if in good condition. Others, like the nylon insert nut, form an initial locking condition when the nut is first installed; the nylon forms closely to the bolt thread pattern, thus reducing any tendency for the nut to loosen. When the nut is removed, the locking efficiency is greatly reduced. For greatest safety, it is recommended that you install new self-locking fasteners whenever they are removed.

Washers

There are 2 basic types of washers: flat washers and lockwashers. Flat washers are simple discs with a hole to fit a screw or bolt. Lockwashers are designed to prevent a fastener from working loose due to vibration, expansion and contraction. **Figure 7** shows several types of washers. Washers are also used in the following functions:

    a. As spacers.
    b. To prevent galling or damage of the equipment by the fastener.
    c. To help distribute fastener load during torquing.
    d. As seals.

Note that flat washers are often used between a lockwasher and a fastener to provide a smooth bearing surface. This allows the fastener to be turned easily with a tool.

Cotter Pins

Cotter pins (**Figure 8**) are used to secure special kinds of fasteners. The threaded stud must have a hole in it; the nut or nut lockpiece has castellations around which the cotter pin ends wrap. Cotter pins should not be reused after removal.

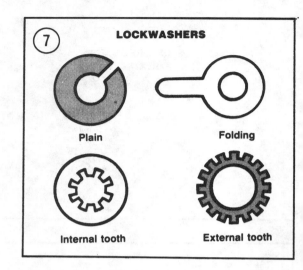

LOCKWASHERS

Plain

Folding

Internal tooth

External tooth

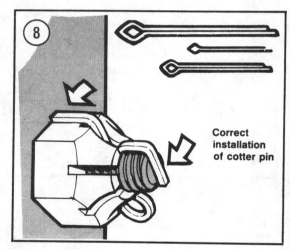

Correct installation of cotter pin

Snap Rings

Snap rings can be internal or external design. They are used to retain items on shafts (external type) or within tubes (internal type). In some applications, snap rings of varying thicknesses are used to control the end play of parts assemblies. These are often called selective snap rings. Snap rings should be replaced during installation as removal weakens and deforms them.

Two basic styles of snap rings are available; machined and stamped snap rings. Machined snap rings (**Figure 9**) can be installed in either direction (shaft or housing) because both faces are machined, thus creating two sharp edges. Stamped snap rings (**Figure 10**) are manufactured with one sharp edge and one rounded edge. When installing stamped snap rings in a thrust situation (transmission shafts, fork tubes, etc.), the sharp edge must face away from the part

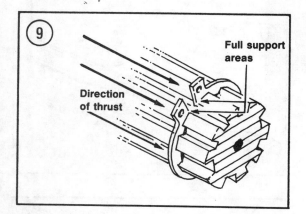

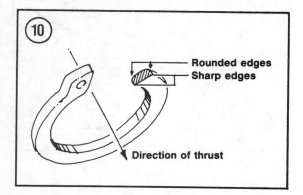

producing the thrust. When installing snap rings, observe the following:

   a. Compress or expand snap rings only enough to install them.

   b. After the snap ring is installed, make sure it is completely seated in its groove.

LUBRICANTS

Periodic lubrication assures long life for any type of equipment. The *type* of lubricant used is just as important as the lubrication service itself, although in an emergency the wrong type of lubricant is better than none at all. The following paragraphs describe the types of lubricants most often used on motorcycle equipment. Be sure to follow the manufacturer's recommendations for lubrication types.

Generally, all liquid lubricants are called "oil." They may be mineral-based (including petroleum bases), natural-based (vegetable and animal bases), synthetic-based or emulsions (mixtures). "Grease" is an oil to which a thickening base has been added so that the end product is semi-solid. Grease is often classified by the type of thickener added; lithium soap is commonly used.

Engine Oil

Oil for motorcycle and automotive engines is classified by the American Petroleum Institute (API) and the Society of Automotive Engineers (SAE) in several categories. Oil containers display these classifications on the top or label.

API oil classification is indicated by letters; oils for gasoline engines are identified by an "S". The engines covered in this manual require SE or SF oil.

Viscosity is an indication of the oil's thickness. The SAE uses numbers to indicate viscosity; thin oils have lower numbers while thick oils have higher numbers. A "W" after the number indicates that the viscosity testing was done at low temperature to simulate cold-weather operation. Engine oils fall into the 5W-30 and 20W-50 range.

Multi-grade oils (for example 10W-40) are less viscous (thinner) at low temperatures and more viscous (thicker) at high temperatures. This allows the oil to perform efficiently across a wide range of engine operating conditions. The lower the number, the better the engine will start in cold climates. Higher numbers are usually recommended for engine running in hot weather conditions.

Grease

Greases are graded by the National Lubricating Grease Institute (NLGI). Greases are graded by number according to the consistency of the grease; these range from No. 000 to No. 6, with No. 6 being the most solid. A typical multipurpose grease is NLGI No. 2. For specific applications, equipment manufacturers may require grease with an additive such as molybdenum disulfide (MOS2).

PARTS REPLACEMENT

Kawasaki makes frequent changes during a model year; some minor, some relatively major. When you order parts from the dealer or other parts distributor always order by engine and frame number. Write the numbers down and carry them with you. Compare new parts to old before purchasing them. If they are not alike, have the parts manager explain the difference to you.

BASIC HAND TOOLS

Many of the procedures in this manual can be carried out with simple hand tools and test equipment familiar to the average home mechanic. Keep your tools clean and in a tool box. Keep them organized with the sockets and related drives together, the open-end and combination wrenches together, etc. After using a tool, wipe off dirt and grease with a clean cloth and return the tool to its correct place.

Top quality tools are essential; they are also more economical in the long run. If you are now starting to build your tool collection, stay away from the "advertised specials" featured at some parts houses, discount stores and chain drug stores. These are usually a poor grade tool that can be sold cheaply. They are usually made of inferior material, and are thick, heavy and clumsy. Their rough finish makes them difficult to clean and they usually don't last very long. If it is ever your misfortune to use such tools you will probably find out that the wrenches do not fit the heads of bolts and nuts correctly and damage fasteners.

Quality tools are made of alloy steel and are heat treated for greater strength. They are lighter and better balanced than cheap ones. Their surface is smooth making them a pleasure to work with and easy to clean. The initial cost of good quality tools may be more, but they are cheaper in the long run. Don't try to buy everything in all sizes in the beginning; do it a little at a time until you have the

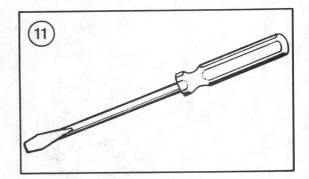

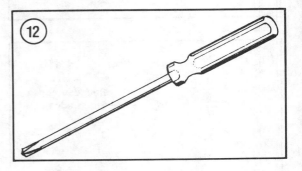

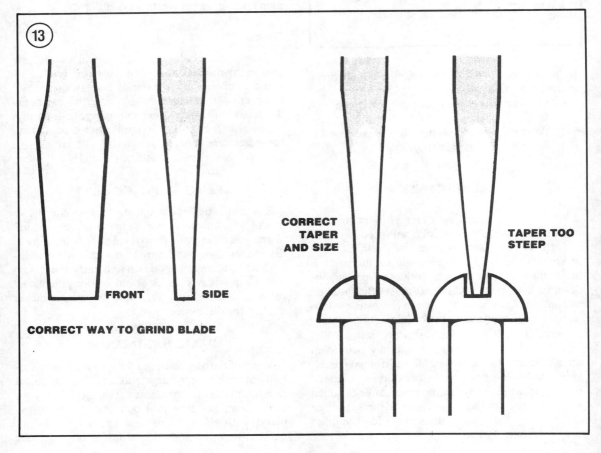

CORRECT WAY TO GRIND BLADE

FRONT   SIDE

CORRECT TAPER AND SIZE

TAPER TOO STEEP

screws and a large one for large screws or the screw head will be damaged.

Two basic types of screwdriver are required: common (flat-blade) screwdrivers (**Figure 11**) and Phillips screwdrivers (**Figure 12**).

Screwdrivers are available in sets which often include an assortment of common and Phillips blades. If you buy them individually buy, at least, the following:

    a. Common screwdriver—5/16×6 in. blade.
    b. Common screwdriver—3/8×12 in. blade.
    c. Phillips screwdriver—size 2 tip, 6 in. blade.

Use screwdrivers only for driving screws. Never use a screwdriver for prying or chiseling metal. Do not try to remove a Phillips or Allen head screw with a common screwdriver (unless the screw has a combination head that will accept either type); you can damage the head so that the proper tool will be unable to remove it.

Keep screwdrivers in the proper condition and they will last longer and perform better. Always keep the tip of a common screwdriver in good condition. **Figure 13** shows how to grind the tip to the proper shape if it becomes damaged. Note the symmetrical sides of the tip.

Pliers

Pliers come in a wide range of types and sizes. Pliers are useful for cutting, bending and crimping. They should never be used to cut hardened objects or to turn bolts or nuts. **Figure 14** shows several pliers useful in motorcycle repairs.

Each type of pliers has a specialized function. Gas pliers are general purpose pliers and are used mainly for holding things and for bending. Locking pliers, such as Vise-grips, are used either as pliers or to hold objects very tightly like a vise. Needlenose pliers are used to hold or bend small objects. Channel lock pliers can be adjusted to hold various sizes of objects; the jaws remain parallel to grip around objects such as pipe or tubing. There are many more types of pliers.

Box and Open-end Wrenches

Box and open-end wrenches are available in sets or separately in a variety of sizes. The size number stamped near the end refers to the distance between 2 parallel flats on the hex head bolt or nut.

Box wrenches are usually superior to open-end wrenches (**Figure 15**). Open-end wrenches grip the nut on only 2 flats. Unless a wrench fits well, it may slip and round off the points on the nut. The box wrench grips on all 6 flats. Both 6-point and 12-point openings on box wrenches are available. The 6-point gives superior holding power; the 12-point allows a shorter swing.

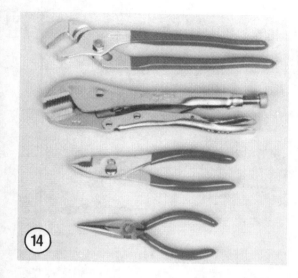

(14)

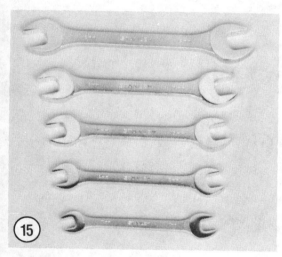

(15)

necessary tools. To sum up tool buying, "...the bitterness of poor quality lingers long after the sweetness of low price has faded."

The following tools are required to perform virtually any repair job. Each tool is described and the recommended size given for starting a tool collection. Additional tools and some duplicates may be added as you become familar with the vehicle. Kawasaki motorcycles are built with metric fasteners—so if you are starting your collection now, buy metric sizes.

Screwdrivers

The screwdriver is a very basic tool, but if used improperly it will do more damage than good. The slot on a screw has a definite dimension and shape. A screwdriver must be selected to conform with that shape. Use a small screwdriver for small

Combination wrenches which are open on one side and boxed on the other are also available. Both ends are the same size. See **Figure 16**.

Adjustable Wrenches

An adjustable wrench can be adjusted to fit a variety of nuts or bolt heads (**Figure 17**). However, it can loosen and slip, causing damage to the nut and perhaps to your knuckles. Use an adjustable wrench only when other wrenches are not available.

Adjustable wrenches come in sizes ranging from 4-18 in. overall. A 6 or 8 in. wrench is recommended as an all-purpose wrench.

Socket Wrenches

This type is undoubtedly the fastest, safest and most convenient to use. Sockets which attach to a ratchet handle (**Figure 18**) are available with 6-point or 12-point openings and 1/4, 3/8, 1/2 and 3/4 inch drives. The drive size indicates the size of the square hole which mates with the ratchet handle.

Torque Wrench

A torque wrench (**Figure 19**) is used with a socket to measure how tightly a nut or bolt is installed. They come in a wide price range and with either 3/8 or 1/2 in. square drive. The drive size indicates the size of the square drive which mates with the socket. Purchase one that measures 0-140 N•m (0-100 ft.-lb.).

Impact Driver

This tool makes removal of tight fasteners easy and eliminates damage to bolts and screw slots. Impact drivers and interchangeable bits (**Figure 20**) are available at most large hardware and motorcycle dealers. Sockets can also be used with a hand impact driver. However, make sure the socket is designed for impact use. Do not use regular hand type sockets as they may shatter.

Hammers

The correct hammer is necessary for repairs. Use only a hammer with a face (or head) of rubber or plastic or the soft-faced type that is filled with buckshot. These are sometimes necessary in engine teardowns. *Never* use a metal-faced hammer as severe damage will result in most cases. You can always produce the same amount of force with a soft-faced hammer.

Feeler Gauge

This tool has both flat and wire measuring gauges and is used to measure spark plug gap. See

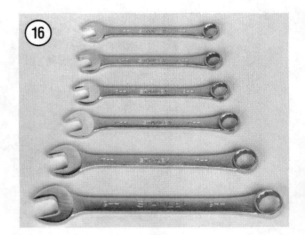

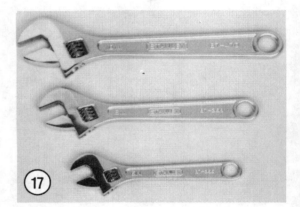

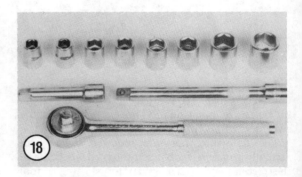

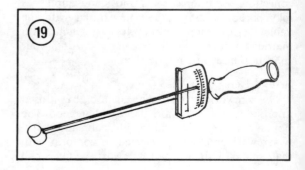

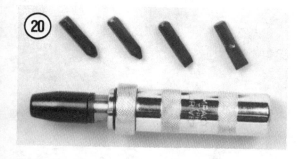

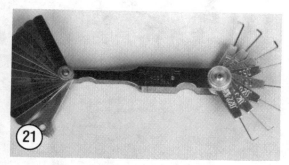

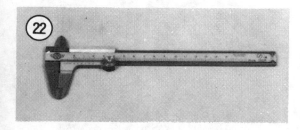

Figure 21. Wire gauges are used to measure spark plug gap; flat gauges are used for all other measurements.

Vernier Caliper

This tool is invaluable when reading inside, outside and depth measurements to close precision. The vernier caliper can be purchased from large dealers or mail order houses. See **Figure 22**.

Special Tools

A few special tools may be required for major service. These are described in the appropriate chapters and are available either from Kawasaki dealers or other manufacturers as indicated.

TEST EQUIPMENT

Voltmeter, Ammeter and Ohmmeter

A good voltmeter is required for testing ignition and other electrical systems. Voltmeters are available with analog meter scales or digital readouts. An instrument covering 0-20 volts is satisfactory. It should also have a 0-2 volt scale for testing points or individual contacts where voltage drops are much smaller. Accuracy should be ±1/2 volt.

An ohmmeter measures electrical resistance. This instrument is useful in checking continuity (for open and short circuits) and testing lights. A self-powered 12-volt test light can often be used in its place.

The ammeter measures electrical current. These are useful for checking battery starting and charging currents.

Some manufacturers combine the 3 instruments into one unit called a multimeter or VOM. See **Figure 23**.

Compression Gauge

An engine with low compression cannot be properly tuned and will not develop full power. A compression gauge measures the amount of pressure present in the engine's combustion chambers during the compression stroke. This indicates general engine condition.

The easiest type to use has screw-in adaptors that fit into the spark plug holes (**Figure 24**). Press-in rubber-tipped types (**Figure 25**) are also available.

Dial Indicator

Dial indicators (**Figure 26**) are precision tools used to check dimension variations on machined parts such as transmission shafts and axles and to check crankshaft and axle shaft end play. Dial indicators are available with various dial types for different measuring requirements.

Strobe Timing Light

This instrument is necessary for checking ignition timing. By flashing a light at the precise

instant the spark plug fires the position of the
timing mark can be seen. The flashing light makes
a moving mark appear to stand still opposite a
stationary mark.

Suitable lights range from inexpensive neon bulb
types to powerful xenon strobe lights. See **Figure
27**. A light with an inductive pickup is
recommended to eliminate any possible damage to
ignition wiring.

Portable Tachometer

A portable tachometer is necessary for tuning.
See **Figure 28**. Ignition timing and carburetor
adjustments must be performed at the specified
idle speed. The best instrument for this purpose is
one with a low range of 0-1,000 or 0-2,000 rpm and
a high range of 0-4,000 rpm. Extended range
(0-6,000 or 0-8,000 rpm) instruments lack accuracy
at lower speeds. The instrument should be capable
of detecting changes of 25 rpm on the low range.

Expendable Supplies

Certain expendable supplies are also required.
These include grease, oil, gasket cement, shop rags
and cleaning solvent. Ask your dealer for the
special locking compounds, silicone lubricants and
lube products which make vehicle maintenance
simpler and easier. Cleaning solvent is available at
some service stations.

MECHANIC'S TIPS

Removing Frozen Nuts and Screws

When a fastener rusts and cannot be removed,
several methods may be used to loosen it. First,
apply penetrating oil such as Liquid Wrench or
WD-40 (available at hardware or auto supply
stores). Apply it liberally and let it penetrate for

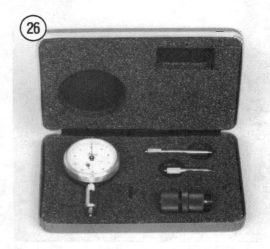

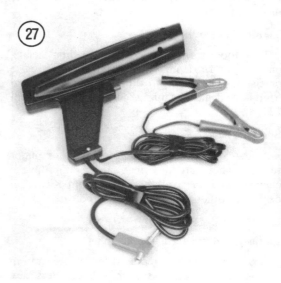

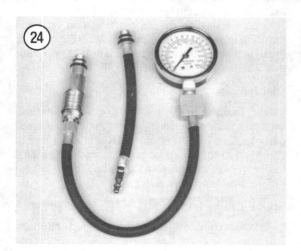

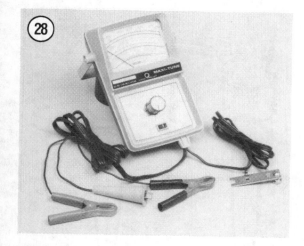

10-15 minutes. Rap the fastener several times with a small hammer; do not hit it hard enough to cause damage. Reapply the penetrating oil if necessary.

For frozen screws apply penetrating oil as described, then insert a screwdriver in the slot and rap the top of the screwdriver with a hammer. This loosens the rust so the screw can be removed in the normal way. If the screw head is too chewed up to use this method grip the head with locking pliers and twist the screw out.

Avoid applying heat unless specifically instructed as it may melt, warp or remove the temper from parts.

Remedying Stripped Threads

Occasionally, threads are stripped through carelessness or impact damage. Often the threads can be cleaned up by running a tap (for internal threads on nuts) or die (for external threads on bolts) through the threads. See **Figure 29**. To clean or repair spark plug threads a spark plug tap can be used (**Figure 30**).

Removing Broken Screws or Bolts

When the head breaks off a screw or bolt, several methods are available for removing the remaining portion.

If a large portion of the remainder projects out, try gripping it with locking pliers. If the projecting portion is too small, file it to fit a wrench or cut a slot in it to fit a screwdriver. See **Figure 31**.

If the head breaks off flush use a screw extractor. To do this centerpunch the exact center of the remaining portion of the screw or bolt. Drill a small hole in the screw and tap the extractor into the hole. Back the screw out with a wrench on the extractor. See **Figure 32**.

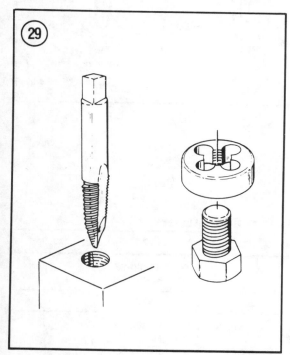

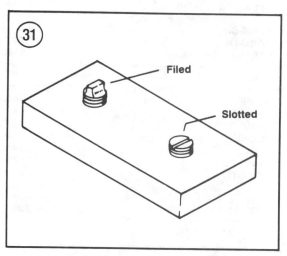

Filed

Slotted

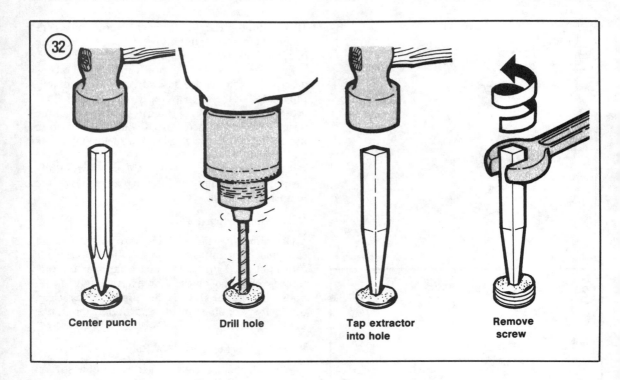

Center punch   Drill hole   Tap extractor   Remove
                                          into hole   screw

Table 1 MODEL YEAR/SUFFIX EQUIVALENTS

1974	1975	1976
KZ400	KZ400S KZ400D	KZ400-S2 KZ400-D3
1977	**1978**	**1979**
KZ400-S3 KZ400-D4 KZ400-A1 (Deluxe A)	KZ400-C1 KZ400-B1 KZ400-A2 (Deluxe A)	KZ400-B2 KZ400-H1 KZ400-G1
1980	**1981**	**1982-1983**
KZ440-A1 KZ440-B1 KZ440-D1 Z440-A1 Z440-C1 KZ400-B3 KZ400-G2	KZ440-A2 KZ440-B2 KZ440-C2 KZ440-D2 KZ440-D3 (late 1981) Z440-C KZ400-G3 KZ400-H3	KZ440-A3 KZ440-D4 KZ440-G1 KZ440-H1
1985-1990	**1990-ON**	
EN450-A1	EN500-A1	

Table 2 DECIMAL AND METRIC EQUIVALENTS

Fractions	Decimal in.	Metric mm	Fractions	Decimal in.	Metric mm
1/64	0.015625	0.39688	33/64	0.515625	13.09687
1/32	0.03125	0.79375	17/32	0.53125	13.49375
3/64	0.046875	1.19062	35/64	0.546875	13.89062
1/16	0.0625	1.58750	9/16	0.5625	14.28750
5/64	0.078125	1.98437	37/64	0.578125	14.68437
3/32	0.09375	2.38125	19/32	0.59375	15.08125
7/64	0.109375	2.77812	39/64	0.609375	15.47812
1/8	0.125	3.1750	5/8	0.625	15.87500
9/64	0.140625	3.57187	41/64	0.640625	16.27187
5/32	0.15625	3.96875	21/32	0.65625	16.66875
11/64	0.171875	4.36562	43/64	0.671875	17.06562
3/16	0.1875	4.76250	11/16	0.6875	17.46250
13/64	0.203125	5.15937	45/64	0.703125	17.85937
7/32	0.21875	5.55625	23/32	0.71875	18.25625
15/64	0.234375	5.95312	47/64	0.734375	18.65312
1/4	0.250	6.35000	3/4	0.750	19.05000
17/64	0.265625	6.74687	49/64	0.765625	19.44687
9/32	0.28125	7.14375	25/32	0.78125	19.84375
19/64	0.296875	7.54062	51/64	0.796875	20.24062
5/16	0.3125	7.93750	13/16	0.8125	20.63750
21/64	0.328125	8.33437	53/64	0.828125	21.03437
11/32	0.34375	8.73125	27/32	0.84375	21.43125
23/64	0.359375	9.12812	55/64	0.859375	21.82812
3/8	0.375	9.52500	7/8	0.875	22.22500
25/64	0.390625	9.92187	57/64	0.890625	22.62187
13/32	0.40625	10.31875	29/32	0.90625	23.01875
27/64	0.421875	10.71562	59/64	0.921875	23.41562
7/16	0.4375	11.11250	15/16	0.9375	23.81250
29/64	0.453125	11.50937	61/64	0.953125	24.20937
15/32	0.46875	11.90625	31/32	0.96875	24.60625
31/64	0.484375	12.30312	63/64	0.984375	25.00312
1/2	0.500	12.70000	1	1.00	25.40000

Table 3 GENERAL TIGHTENING TORQUES*

Nut	Bolt	ft.-lb.	N·m
10 mm	6 mm	4.5	6
12 mm	8 mm	11	15
14 mm	10 mm	22	30
17 mm	12 mm	40	55
19 mm	14 mm	51	85
22 mm	16 mm	94	130

* This table lists general torque for standard fasteners with standard ISO pitch threads. Use these specifications only if specific values are not provided for a given fastener.

CHAPTER TWO

TROUBLESHOOTING

Every motorcycle engine requires an uninterrupted supply of fuel and air, proper ignition and adequate compression. If any of these are lacking, the engine will not run.

Diagnosing mechanical problems is relatively simple if you use orderly procedures and keep a few basic principles in mind.

The troubleshooting procedures in this chapter analyze typical symptoms and show logical methods of isolating causes. These are not the only methods. There may be several ways to solve a problem, but only a systematic approach can guarantee success.

Never assume anything. Do not overlook the obvious. If you are riding along and the bike suddenly quits check the easiest, most accessible problem spots first. Is there gasoline in the tank? Has a spark plug wire fallen off?

If nothing obvious turns up in a quick check, look a little further. Learning to recognize and describe symptoms will make repairs easier for you or a mechanic at the shop. Describe problems accurately and fully. Saying that "it won't run" isn't the same thing as saying "it quit at high speed and won't start," or that "it sat in my garage for 3 months and then wouldn't start."

Gather as many symptoms as possible to aid in diagnosis. Note whether the engine lost power gradually or all at once. Remember that the more complicated a machine is the easier it is to troubleshoot because symptoms point to specific problems.

After the symptoms are defined, areas which could cause problems are tested and analyzed. Guessing at the cause of a problem may provide the solution, but it can easily lead to frustration, wasted time and a series of expensive, unnecessary parts replacements.

You do not need fancy equipment or complicated test gear to determine whether repairs can be attempted at home. A few simple checks could save a large repair bill and lost time while the bike sits in a dealer's service department. On the other hand, be realistic and don't attempt repairs beyond your abilities. Service departments tend to charge heavily for putting together a disassembled engine that may have been abused. Some won't even take on such a job—so use common sense and don't get in over your head.

OPERATING REQUIREMENTS

An engine has 3 basic needs to run properly: correct fuel/air mixture, compression and a spark at the correct time. If one or more are missing, the engine will not run. Four-stroke engine operating principles are illustrated in **Figure 1**. The electrical

(1)

4-STROKE OPERATING PRINCIPLES

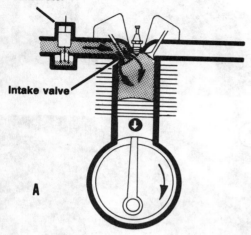

Carburetor

Intake valve

A

As the piston travels downward, the exhaust valve is closed and the intake valve opens, allowing the new air-fuel mixture from the carburetor to be drawn into the cylinder. When the piston reaches the bottom of its travel (BDC), the intake valve closes and remains closed for the next 1 1/2 revolutions of the crankshaft.

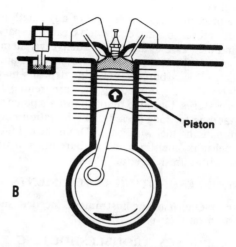

Piston

B

While the crankshaft continues to rotate, the piston moves upward, compressing the air-fuel mixture.

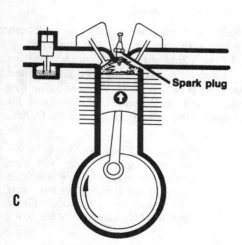

Spark plug

C

As the piston almost reaches the top of its travel, the spark plug fires, igniting the compressed air-fuel mixture. The piston continues to top dead center (TDC) and is pushed downward by the expanding gases.

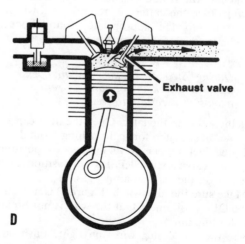

Exhaust valve

D

When the piston almost reaches BDC, the exhaust valve opens and remains open until the piston is near TDC. The upward travel of the piston forces the exhaust gases out of the cylinder. After the piston has reached TDC, the exhaust valve closes and the cycle starts all over again.

system is the weakest link of the 3 basics. More problems result from electrical breakdowns than from any other source. Keep that in mind before you begin tampering with carburetor adjustments and the like.

If the machine has been sitting for any length of time and refuses to start, check and clean the spark plugs and then look to the gasoline delivery system. This includes the fuel tank, fuel shutoff valve and fuel line to the carburetor. Gasoline deposits may have formed and gummed up the carburetor jets and air passages. Gasoline tends to lose its potency after standing for long periods. Condensation may contaminate the fuel with water. Drain the old fuel from fuel tank, fuel lines and carburetors and try starting with a fresh tankful.

TROUBLESHOOTING INSTRUMENTS

Chapter One lists the instruments needed and instruction on their use.

EMERGENCY TROUBLESHOOTING

When the bike is difficult to start, or won't start at all, it doesn't help to wear down the battery using the electric starter or your leg on kickstart models. Check for obvious problems even before getting out your tools. Go down the following list step by step. Do each one; you may be embarrassed to find the kill switch off, but that is better than wearing down the battery. If the bike still will not start, refer to the appropriate troubleshooting procedures which follow in this chapter.

> *WARNING*
> *During Step 1, do not use an open flame to check in the tank. A serious explosion is certain to result.*

1. Is there fuel in the tank? Open the filler cap and rock the bike. Listen for fuel sloshing around.
2. Is the fuel supply valve in the ON position? Turn the valve to the RESERVE position to be sure you get the last remaining gas.
3. Make sure the kill switch (**Figure 2**) is not stuck in the OFF position or that the wire is not broken and shorting out.
4. Are the spark plug wires on tight? Push both spark plugs on (**Figure 3**) and slightly rotate them to clean the electrical connection between the plug and the connector.
5. Is the choke in the right position?

ENGINE STARTING

An engine that refuses to start or is difficult to start is very frustrating. More often than not, the

problem is very minor and can be found with a simple and logical troubleshooting approach.

The following items will help isolate engine starting problems.

Engine Fails to Start

Perform the following spark test to determine if the ignition system is operating properly.
1. Remove one of the spark plugs.
2. Connect the spark plug wire and connector to the spark plug and touch the spark plug base to a good ground like the engine cylinder head. Position the spark plug so you can see the electrodes.

> *WARNING*
> *During the next step, do not hold the spark plug, spark plug wire or connector with fingers. The high voltage generated by the ignition system could produce serious or fatal shocks. Use a pair of insulated pliers to hold the spark plug or wire.*

3. Crank the engine over with the starter. A fat blue spark should be evident across the spark plug electrodes.
4. If the spark is good, check for one or more of the following possible malfunctions:
   a. Obstructed fuel line or fuel filter.
   b. Leaking head gasket.
   c. Low compression.

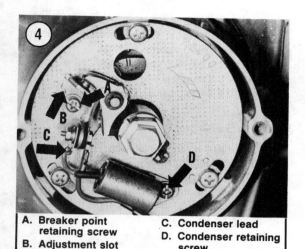

| A. Breaker point retaining screw | C. Condenser lead |
| B. Adjustment slot | D. Condenser retaining screw |

5. If the spark is not good, check for one or more of the following:
   a. Loose electrical connections.
   b. Dirty electrical connections.
   c. Loose or broken ignition coil ground wire.
   d. Broken or shorted high tension lead to the spark plug (**Figure 3**).
   e. Discharged battery.
   f. Disconnected or damaged battery connection.
   g. Breaker points oxidized (1974-1980). See **Figure 4**.

Engine is Difficult to Start

Check for one or more of the following possible malfunctions:
   a. Fouled spark plug(s).
   b. Improperly adjusted choke.
   c. Intake manifold air leak.
   d. Contaminated fuel system.
   e. Improperly adjusted carburetor.
   f. Weak ignition unit.
   g. Weak ignition coil(s).
   h. Poor compression.
   i. Timing advance weight sticking in advanced position (1974-1983 models only).
   j. Engine and transmission oil too heavy.

Engine Will Not Crank

Check for one or more of the following possible malfunctions:
   a. Blown fuse.
   b. Discharged battery.
   c. Defective starter motor or kickstarter assembly.
   d. Seized piston(s).
   e. Seized crankshaft bearings.
   f. Broken connecting rod.

ENGINE PERFORMANCE

In the following checklist, it is assumed that the engine runs, but is not operating at peak performance. This will serve as a starting point from which to isolate a performance malfunction.

The possible causes for each malfunction are listed in a logical sequence and in order of probability.

Engine Will Not Idle

   a. Carburetor incorrectly adjusted.
   b. Fouled or improperly gapped spark plug(s).
   c. Leaking head gasket.
   d. Obstructed fuel line or fuel shutoff valve.
   e. Obstructed fuel filter.
   f. *1974-1980:* Ignition timing incorrect.
   g. *1981-on:* Ignition timing incorrect due to defective ignition component(s).
   h. Valve clearance incorrect.

Engine Misses at High Speed

   a. Fouled or improperly gapped spark plugs.
   b. Improper carburetor main jet selection.
   c. *1974-1980:* Ignition timing incorrect.
   d. *1981-on:* Ignition timing incorrect due to defective ignition component(s).
   e. Weak ignition coil(s).
   f. Obstructed fuel line or fuel shutoff valve.
   g. Obstructed fuel filter.
   h. Clogged carburetor jets.

Engine Overheating

   a. Incorrect carburetor adjustment or jet selection.
   b. Ignition timing retarded due to improper adjustment or defective ignition component(s).
   c. Improper spark plug heat range.
   d. Damaged or blocked cooling fins.
   e. Oil level low.
   f. Oil not circulating properly.
   g. Valves leaking.
   h. Heavy engine carbon deposits.

Engine Overheating (Water-cooled Models)

Note the above, then proceed with the following items:
   a. Cloggged radiator.
   b. Damaged thermostat.
   c. Worn or damaged radiator cap.
   d. Water pump worn or damaged.

e. Fan relay damaged.
f. Thermostatic fan switch damaged.
g. Damaged fan blade(s).

Smoky Exhaust and Engine Runs Roughly

a. Clogged air filter element.
b. Carburetor adjustment incorrect—mixture too rich.
c. Choke not operating correctly.
d. Water or other contaminants in fuel.
e. Clogged fuel line.
f. Spark plugs fouled.
g. Ignition coil defective.
h. Breaker point models: points worn, dirty or out of adjustment. Loose condenser connections. Defective condenser.
i. Electronic ignition models: IC igniter or pickup coil defective.
j. Loose or defective ignition circuit wire.
k. Short circuit from damaged wire insulation.
l. Loose battery cable connection.
m. Valve timing incorrect.
n. Intake manifold or air cleaner air leak.

Engine Loses Power at Normal Riding Speed

a. Carburetor incorrectly adjusted.
b. Engine overheating.

c. *1974-1980:* ignition timing incorrect.
d. *1981-on:* ignition timing incorrect due to defective ignition component(s).
e. Incorrectly gapped spark plugs.
f. Obstructed muffler.
g. Dragging brake(s).

Engine Lacks Acceleration

a. Carburetor mixture too lean.
b. Clogged fuel line.
c. *1974-1980:* ignition timing incorrect.
d. *1981-on:* ignition timing incorrect due to defective ignition component(s).
e. Dragging brake(s).

ENGINE NOISES

Often the first evidence of an internal engine problem is a strange noise. That knocking, clicking or tapping sound which you never heard before may be warning you of impending trouble.

While engine noises can indicate problems, they are difficult to interpret correctly; inexperienced mechanics can be seriously misled by them.

Professional mechanics often use a special stethoscope (which looks like a doctor's stethoscope) for isolating engine noises. You can do nearly as well with a "sounding stick" which can

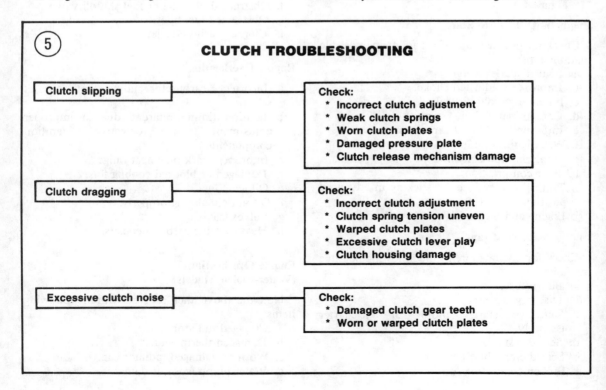

be an ordinary piece of doweling, a length of broom handle or a section of small hose. By placing one end in contact with the area to which you want to listen and the other end near your ear, you can hear sounds emanating from that area. The first time you do this, you may be horrified at the strange sounds coming from even a normal engine. If possible, have an experienced friend or mechanic help you sort out the noises. Consider the following when troubleshooting engine noises:

1. *Knocking or pinging during acceleration*— caused by using a lower octane fuel than recommended. May also be caused by poor fuel. Pinging can also be caused by a spark plug of the wrong heat range. Refer to *Correct Spark Plug Heat Range* in Chapter Three.

2. *Slapping or rattling noises at low speed or during acceleration*—may be caused by piston slap, i.e., excessive piston-cylinder wall clearance.

3. *Knocking or rapping while decelerating*—usually caused by excessive rod bearing clearance.

4. *Persistent knocking and vibration*—usually caused by worn main bearing(s).

5. *Rapid on-off squeal*—compression leak around cylinder head gasket or spark plug(s).

6. *Valve train noise*—check for the following:
   a. Valves adjusted incorrectly.
   b. Loose valve adjuster.
   c. Valve sticking in guide.
   d. Low oil pressure.
   e. Damaged rocker arm or shaft. Rocker arm may be binding on shaft.

ENGINE LUBRICATION

An improperly operating engine lubrication system will quickly lead to engine seizure. The engine oil level should be checked weekly and the tank refilled, as described in Chapter Three. Oil pump service is described in Chapter Four or Chapter Five.

Oil Consumption High or Engine Smokes Excessively

   a. Worn valve guides.
   b. Worn or damaged piston rings.

Excessive Engine Oil Leaks

   a. Clogged air cleaner breather hose.
   b. Loose engine parts.
   c. Damaged gasket sealing surfaces.

CLUTCH

The three basic clutch troubles are:
a. Clutch noise.
b. Clutch slipping.
c. Improper clutch disengagement or dragging.

All clutch troubles, except adjustments, require partial clutch disassembly to identify and cure the problem. The troubleshooting chart in **Figure 5** lists clutch troubles and checks to make. Refer to Chapter Six for clutch service procedures.

TRANSMISSION

The basic transmission troubles are:
a. Excessive gear noise.
b. Difficult shifting.
c. Gears pop out of mesh.
d. Incorrect shift lever operation.

Transmission symptoms are sometimes hard to distinguish from clutch symptoms. The troubleshooting chart in **Figure 6** lists transmission troubles and checks to make. Refer to Chapter Seven for transmission service procedures. Be sure that the clutch is not causing the trouble before working on the transmission.

CHARGING SYSTEM

Charging system testing procedures are described in Chapter Nine.

STARTING SYSTEM

The basic starter-related troubles are:

   a. The starter does not crank.
   b. The starter cranks, but the engine does not start.

Testing

Starting system problems are relatively easy to find. In most cases, the trouble is a loose or dirty electrical connection. Use the troubleshooting chart in **Figure 7** with the following tests.

Starter does not crank

1. Turn on the headlight and push the starter button. Check for one of the following conditions.

2. *Starter does not crank and headlight does not come on:* The battery is dead or there is a loose battery connection. Check the battery charge as described in Chapter Three. If the battery is okay, check the starter connections at the battery, solenoid and at the starter switch. Clean and tighten all connections.

3. *Headlight comes on, but goes out when the starter button is pushed:* There may be a bad connection at the battery. Wiggle the battery terminals and recheck. If the starter starts cranking, you've found the problem. Remove and clean the battery terminal clamps. Clean the battery posts also. Reinstall the terminal clamps and tighten securely.

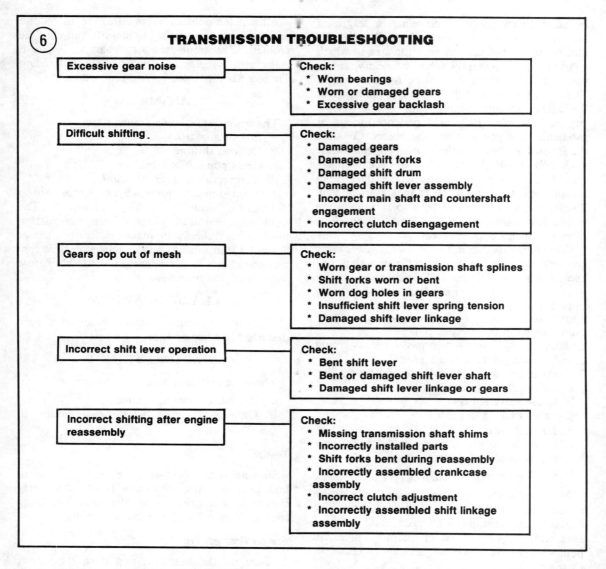

(6) **TRANSMISSION TROUBLESHOOTING**

Excessive gear noise

Check:
* Worn bearings
* Worn or damaged gears
* Excessive gear backlash

Difficult shifting

Check:
* Damaged gears
* Damaged shift forks
* Damaged shift drum
* Damaged shift lever assembly
* Incorrect main shaft and countershaft engagement
* Incorrect clutch disengagement

Gears pop out of mesh

Check:
* Worn gear or transmission shaft splines
* Shift forks worn or bent
* Worn dog holes in gears
* Insufficient shift lever spring tension
* Damaged shift lever linkage

Incorrect shift lever operation

Check:
* Bent shift lever
* Bent or damaged shift lever shaft
* Damaged shift lever linkage or gears

Incorrect shifting after engine reassembly

Check:
* Missing transmission shaft shims
* Incorrectly installed parts
* Shift forks bent during reassembly
* Incorrectly assembled crankcase assembly
* Incorrect clutch adjustment
* Incorrectly assembled shift linkage assembly

4. *Headlight comes on, but dims slightly when the starter button is pushed:* The problem is probably in the starter. Remove and test the starter as described in Chapter Nine.

5. *Headlight comes on, but dims severely when the starter button is pushed:* Either the battery is nearly dead or the starter or engine is partially seized. Check the battery as described in Chapter Three. Check the starter as described in Chapter Nine before checking for partial engine seizure.

6. *Headlight comes on and stays bright when the starter button is pushed:* The problem is in the starter button, starter button-to-solenoid wiring or in the starter itself. Check the starter switch, kill switch, starter relay and the starter circuit relay (1985-on). Check each switch by bypassing it with

a jumper wire. Check the starter as described in Chapter Nine.

***Starter spins but
engine does not crank***

If the starter spins at normal or high speed but the engine fails to crank, the problem is in the starter drive mechanism.

NOTE
Depending upon battery condition, the battery will eventually run down as the starter button is continually pressed. Remember that if the starter cranks normally, but the engine fails to start, the starter is working properly. It's time to start checking other engine systems. Don't wear the battery down.

⑦ STARTER TROUBLESHOOTING

Symptom	Probable Cause	Remedy
Starter does not work	Low battery	Recharge battery
	Worn brushes	Replace brushes
	Defective relay	Repair or replace
	Defective switch	Repair or replace
	Defective wiring or connection	Repair wire or clean connection
	Internal short circuit	Repair or replace defective component
Starter action is weak	Low battery	Recharge battery
	Pitted relay contacts	Clean or replace
	Worn brushes	Replace brushes
	Defective connection	Clean and tighten
	Short circuit in commutator	Replace armature
Starter runs continuously	Stuck relay	Replace relay
Starter turns; does not turn engine	Defective starter clutch	Replace starter clutch

⑧ IGNITION TROUBLESHOOTING

Symptom	Probable Cause	Remedy
No spark or weak spark, both cylinders	Discharged battery	Charge battery
	Defective fuse	Replace fuse
	Defective points	Clean or replace
	Defective coil	Replace coil
	Defective condenser	Replace condenser
	Broken wire	Repair wire
	Loose or corroded connection	Clean and tighten
Misfires	Fouled spark plug	Clean or replace
	Spark plugs too hot	Put in colder plugs
	Spark plugs too cold	Put in hotter plugs
	Defective points	Service or replace
	Defective coil	Replace
	Defective condenser	Replace
	Incorrect timing	Adjust timing

ELECTRICAL PROBLEMS

If bulbs burn out frequently, the cause may be excessive vibration, loose connections that permit sudden current surges or the installation of the wrong type of bulb.

Most light and ignition problems are caused by loose or corroded ground connections. Check these before replacing a bulb or electrical component.

IGNITION SYSTEM

The ignition system may be either a breaker point or breakerless type. See Chapter Nine. Most problems involving failure to start, poor driveability or rough running are caused by trouble in the ignition system, particularly in breaker point systems.

Note the following symptoms:
 a. Engine misses.
 b. Stumbles on acceleration (misfiring).
 c. Loss of power at high speed (misfiring).
 d. Hard starting (or failure to start).
 e. Rough idle.

Most of the symptoms can also be caused by a carburetor that is worn or improperly adjusted. But considering the law of averages, the odds are far better that the source of the problem will be found in the ignition system rather than the fuel system.

BREAKER POINT IGNITION TROUBLESHOOTING

The following basic tests are designed to quickly pinpoint and isolate problems in the primary circuit of a breaker point ignition. Before starting, make sure the battery is in good condition. See Chapter Three. If the primary circuit checks out satisfactorily, refer to *Tune-up* in Chapter Three and check the circuit breaker, spark plug wires and spark plugs. **Figure 8** lists common causes and remedies for breaker point ignition malfunctions.

NOTE
Before starting, connect a voltmeter between the battery terminals (positive to positive; negative to negative) and write down the reading. This is battery voltage.

1. Remove the circuit breaker point cover.
2. Rotate the engine until the points are closed (**Figure 4**).
3. Disconnect the high-voltage lead from one of the spark plugs.
4. Insert a metal adapter in the plug boot and hold it about 3/16 in. from a clean engine ground with insulated pliers.
5. Turn the ignition switch to the ON position.
6. Pry the points aparts with an insulated tool made of wood. A fat, blue-white spark should jump from the spark plug lead to the engine. If the spark is good, the ignition system is good but ignition timing may be incorrect. Check as described in Chapter Three.
7. Turn the ignition switch to the OFF position and let the points close.

8. Connect the positive lead of a voltmeter to the wire on the points (**Figure 9**) and the negative lead to a good ground. Turn the ignition switch to the ON position. If the voltmeter indicates more than 0.125 volts, the points are defective. Replace them as described in Chapter Three.

9. Open the points with the same tool used in Step 6. The voltmeter should indicate battery voltage. If not, the following may be the problem:

    a. Shorted points.

    b. Shorted condenser.

    c. Open coil primary winding.

Perform Steps 10-12 to isolate the problem.

10. With the ignition switch in the ON position, disconnect the condenser and the wire from the points (C, **Figure 4**). Connect the voltmeter positive lead to the wire which was connected to the points. Connect the voltmeter negative lead to a good ground (bare metal). The voltmeter should indicate battery voltage. If not, current is not reaching points.

    a. Check the ignition primary circuit wiring for breaks or bad connections. Repair as needed and retest.

    b. If current does not reach the points with the wiring in good condition, the primary winding inside the ignition coil may be defective. Substitute a known good ignition coil and retest.

11. If the voltmeter indicated battery voltage in Step 9, the coil primary circuit and primary winding are okay. Connect the positive voltmeter lead to the wire which goes from the coil to the points. Block the points open as in Step 6. Connect the negative voltmeter lead to the movable point. If the voltmeter indicates any voltage, the points are shorted and must be replaced.

12. If the preceding checks are satisfactory the problem is in the coil or condenser. Replace each of these separately with a known good one to determine which is defective.

Ignition Coil

Ignition coil testing is described in Chapter Nine.

BREAKERLESS IGNITION TROUBLESHOOTING

The following basic tests are designed to quickly pinpoint and isolate problems in the primary circuit of the breakerless inductive discharge ignition system.

Spark Test

Perform the following spark test to determine if the ignition system is operating properly.

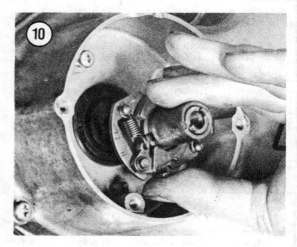

1. Remove one of the spark plugs.

2. Connect the spark plug wire and connector to the spark plug and touch the spark plug base to a good ground like the engine cylinder head. Position the spark plug so you can see the electrodes.

WARNING

During the next step, do not hold the spark plug, spark plug wire or connector. The high voltage generated by the ignition system could produce serious or fatal shocks. If necessary, use a pair of insulated pliers to hold the spark plug or wire.

3. Crank the engine over with the starter. A fat blue spark should be evident across the spark plug electrodes.

4A. If a spark is obtained in Step 3, the problem is not in the breakerless ignition or coil. Check the fuel system and spark plugs. On 1974-1980 models, check the ignition advance mechanism (**Figure 10**) as described in Chapter Nine.

4B. If no spark is obtained, proceed with the following tests for your model.

Testing

Test procedures for troubleshooting the ignition system for 1981-on models are found in the diagnostic chart in **Figure 11** (1981-1983 models) or **Figure 12** (1985-on models). A multimeter, as described in Chapter One, is required to perform the test procedures.

Before beginning actual troubleshooting, read the entire test procedure (**Figure 11** or **Figure 12**). When required, the diagnostic chart will refer you to a certain chapter for test procedures.

EXCESSIVE VIBRATION

Usually this is caused by loose engine mounting hardware. If not, it can be difficult to find without disassembling the engine. High speed vibration may be due to a bent axle shaft or loose or faulty suspension components. Vibration can also be caused by the following conditions:
a. Broken frame.
b. Severely worn primary chain.
c. Worn drive chain or belt.
d. Primary chain links tight due to improper lubrication.
e. Improperly balanced wheels.
f. Defective or damaged wheels.
g. Defective or damaged tires.
h. Internal engine wear or damage.

FRONT SUSPENSION AND STEERING

Poor handling may be caused by improper tire pressure, a damaged or bent frame or front steering components, worn wheel bearings or dragging brakes. Possible causes of suspension and steering malfunctions are listed below.

Irregular or Wobbly Steering

a. Loose wheel axle nuts.
b. Loose or worn steering head bearings.
c. Excessive wheel hub bearing play.
d. Damaged cast wheel.
e. Spoke wheel out of alignment.
f. Unbalanced wheel assembly.
g. Worn hub bearings.
h. Incorrect wheel alignment.
i. Bent or damaged steering stem or frame (at steering neck).
j. Tire incorrectly seated on rim.
k. Excessive front end loading from non-standard equipment.

Stiff Steering

a. Low front tire air pressure.
b. Bend or damaged steering stem or frame (at steering neck).
c. Loose or worn steering head bearings.

Stiff or Heavy Fork Operation

a. Incorrect fork springs.
b. Incorrect fork oil viscosity.
c. Excessive amount of fork oil.
d. Bent fork tubes.

Poor Fork Operation

a. Worn or damaged fork tubes.
b. Fork oil level low due to leaking fork seals.
c. Bent or damaged fork tubes.
d. Contaminated fork oil.
e. Incorrect fork springs.
f. Heavy front end loading from non-standard equipment.

Poor Rear Shock Absorber Operation

a. Weak or worn springs.
b. Damper unit leaking.
c. Shock shaft worn or bent.
d. Incorrect rear shock springs.
e. Rear shocks adjusted incorrectly.
f. Heavy rear end loading from non-standard equipment.
g. Incorrect loading.

BRAKE PROBLEMS

Sticking disc brakes may be caused by a stuck piston(s) in a caliper assembly, warped pad shim(s) or improper rear brake adjustment. See **Figure 13** for disc brake troubles and checks to make.

A sticking drum brake may be caused by worn or weak return springs, dry pivot and cam bushings or improper adjustment. Grabbing brakes may be caused by greasy linings which must be replaced. Brake grab may also be due to an out-of-round drum. Glazed linings will cause loss of stopping power. See **Figure 14** for drum brake troubles and checks to make.

CARBURETOR TROUBLESHOOTING

Basic carburetor troubleshooting procedures are found in **Figure 15**.

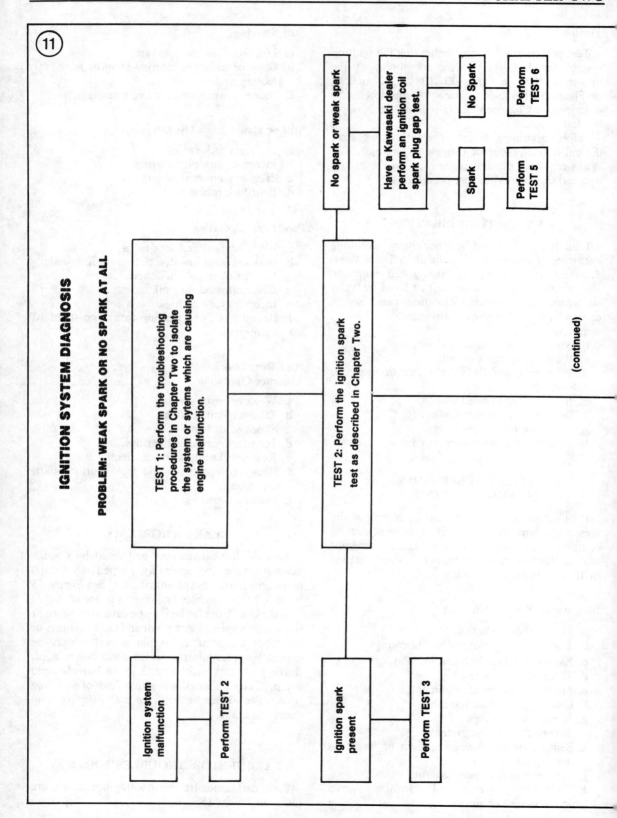

11

IGNITION SYSTEM DIAGNOSIS

PROBLEM: WEAK SPARK OR NO SPARK AT ALL

TEST 1: Perform the troubleshooting procedures in Chapter Two to isolate the system or sytems which are causing engine malfunction.

Ignition system malfunction

Perform TEST 2

Ignition spark present

Perform TEST 3

TEST 2: Perform the ignition spark test as described in Chapter Two.

No spark or weak spark

Have a Kawasaki dealer perform an ignition coil spark plug gap test.

Spark

Perform TEST 5

No Spark

Perform TEST 6

(continued)

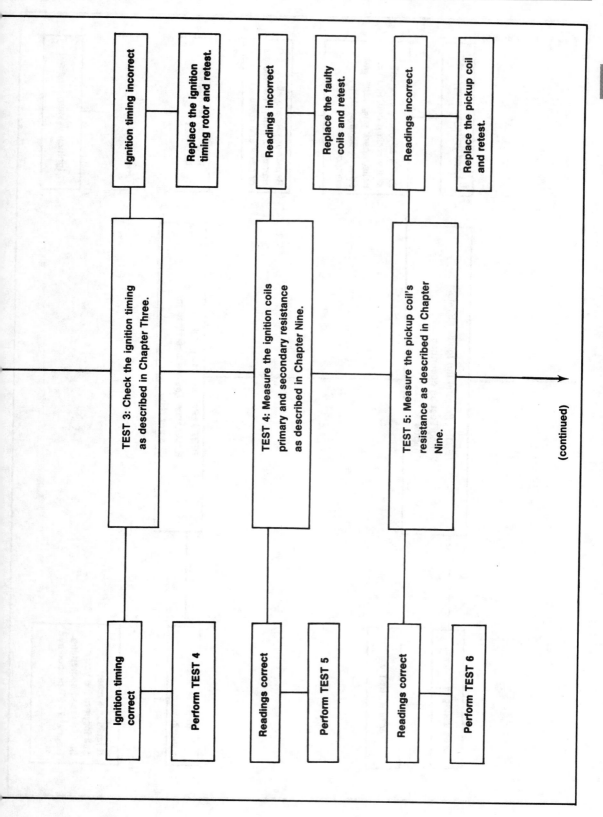

2

Ignition timing incorrect → **Replace the ignition timing rotor and retest.**

TEST 3: Check the ignition timing as described in Chapter Three.

Ignition timing correct → **Perform TEST 4**

Readings incorrect → **Replace the faulty coils and retest.**

TEST 4: Measure the ignition coils primary and secondary resistance as described in Chapter Nine.

Readings correct → **Perform TEST 5**

Readings incorrect. → **Replace the pickup coil and retest.**

TEST 5: Measure the pickup coil's resistance as described in Chapter Nine.

Readings correct → **Perform TEST 6**

(continued)

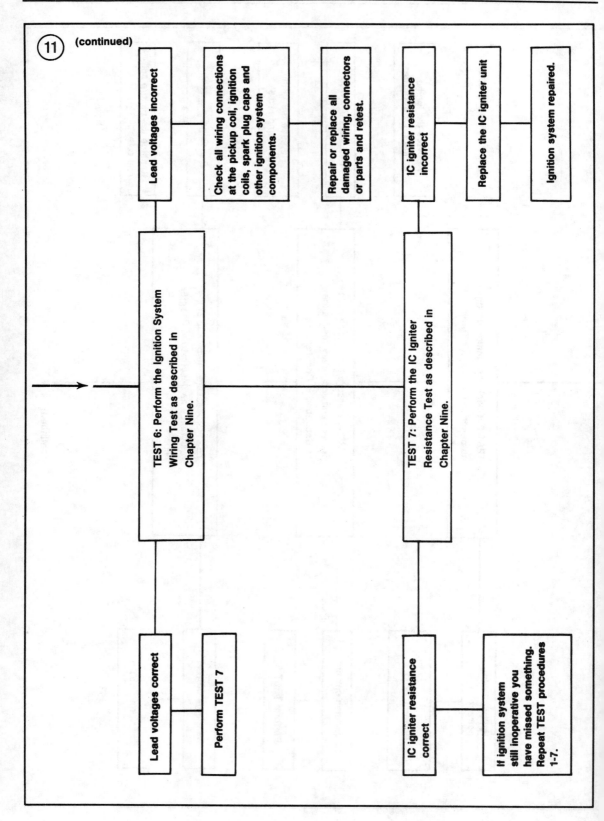

(11) (continued)

Lead voltages incorrect

Check all wiring connections at the pickup coil, ignition coils, spark plug caps and other ignition system components.

Repair or replace all damaged wiring, connectors or parts and retest.

IC igniter resistance incorrect

Replace the IC igniter unit

Ignition system repaired.

TEST 6: Perform the Ignition System Wiring Test as described in Chapter Nine.

TEST 7: Perform the IC Igniter Resistance Test as described in Chapter Nine.

Lead voltages correct

Perform TEST 7

IC igniter resistance correct

If ignition system still inoperative you have missed something. Repeat TEST procedures 1-7.

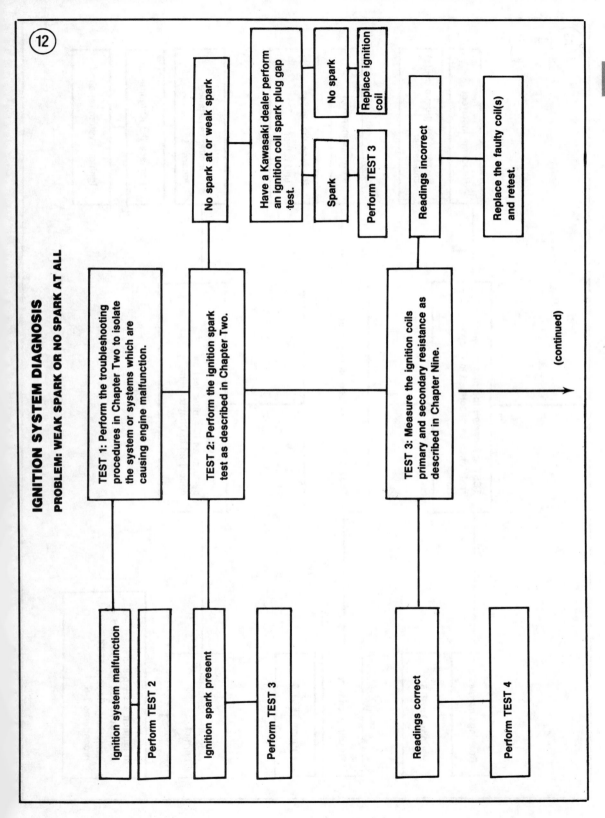

⑫

IGNITION SYSTEM DIAGNOSIS
PROBLEM: WEAK SPARK OR NO SPARK AT ALL

TEST 1: Perform the troubleshooting procedures in Chapter Two to isolate the system or systems which are causing engine malfunction.

Ignition system malfunction

Perform TEST 2

TEST 2: Perform the ignition spark test as described in Chapter Two.

Ignition spark present

Perform TEST 3

No spark at or weak spark

Have a Kawasaki dealer perform an ignition coil spark plug gap test.

Spark

Perform TEST 3

No spark

Replace ignition coil

TEST 3: Measure the ignition coils primary and secondary resistance as described in Chapter Nine.

Readings correct

Perform TEST 4

Readings incorrect

Replace the faulty coil(s) and retest.

(continued)

2

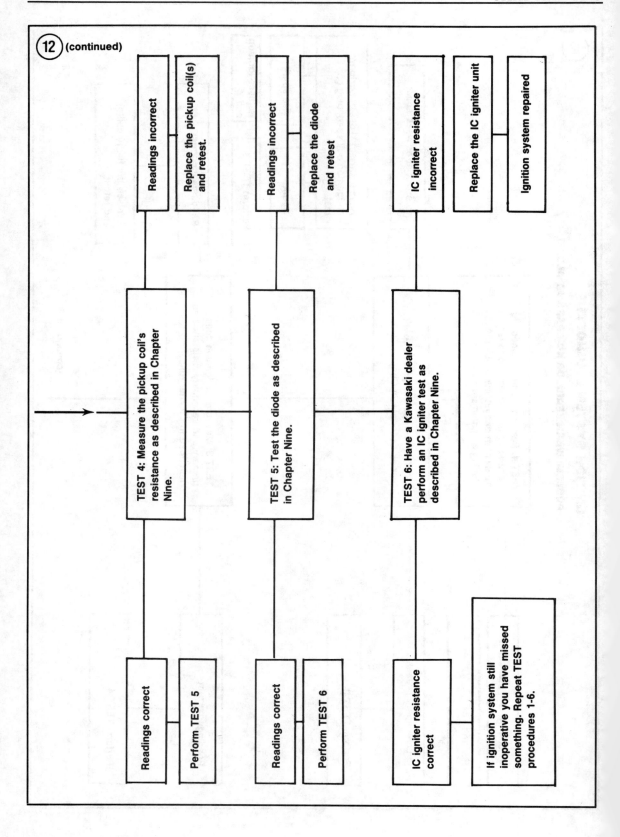

12 (continued)

TEST 4: Measure the pickup coil's resistance as described in Chapter Nine.

Readings incorrect — Replace the pickup coil(s) and retest.

Readings correct — Perform TEST 5

TEST 5: Test the diode as described in Chapter Nine.

Readings incorrect — Replace the diode and retest

Readings correct — Perform TEST 6

TEST 6: Have a Kawasaki dealer perform an IC igniter test as described in Chapter Nine.

IC igniter resistance incorrect — Replace the IC igniter unit — Ignition system repaired

IC igniter resistance correct — If ignition system still inoperative you have missed something. Repeat TEST procedures 1-6.

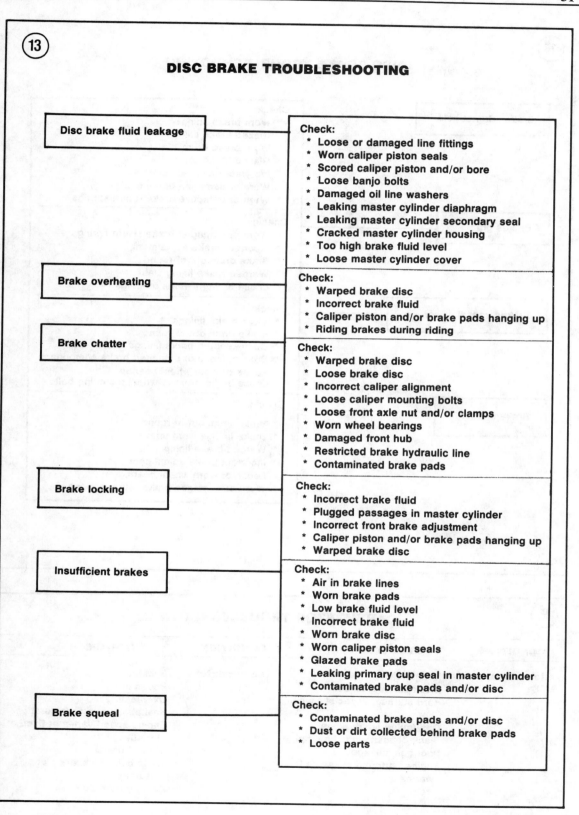

⑬

2

DISC BRAKE TROUBLESHOOTING

Disc brake fluid leakage

Check:
* Loose or damaged line fittings
* Worn caliper piston seals
* Scored caliper piston and/or bore
* Loose banjo bolts
* Damaged oil line washers
* Leaking master cylinder diaphragm
* Leaking master cylinder secondary seal
* Cracked master cylinder housing
* Too high brake fluid level
* Loose master cylinder cover

Brake overheating

Check:
* Warped brake disc
* Incorrect brake fluid
* Caliper piston and/or brake pads hanging up
* Riding brakes during riding

Brake chatter

Check:
* Warped brake disc
* Loose brake disc
* Incorrect caliper alignment
* Loose caliper mounting bolts
* Loose front axle nut and/or clamps
* Worn wheel bearings
* Damaged front hub
* Restricted brake hydraulic line
* Contaminated brake pads

Brake locking

Check:
* Incorrect brake fluid
* Plugged passages in master cylinder
* Incorrect front brake adjustment
* Caliper piston and/or brake pads hanging up
* Warped brake disc

Insufficient brakes

Check:
* Air in brake lines
* Worn brake pads
* Low brake fluid level
* Incorrect brake fluid
* Worn brake disc
* Worn caliper piston seals
* Glazed brake pads
* Leaking primary cup seal in master cylinder
* Contaminated brake pads and/or disc

Brake squeal

Check:
* Contaminated brake pads and/or disc
* Dust or dirt collected behind brake pads
* Loose parts

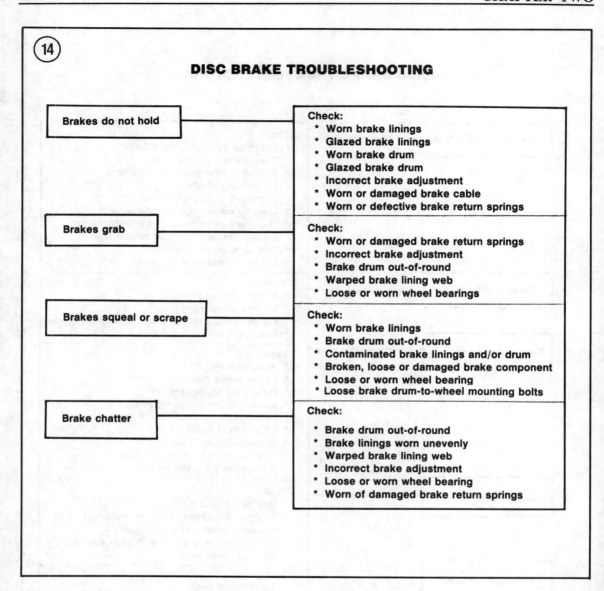

DISC BRAKE TROUBLESHOOTING

Brakes do not hold	Check: * Worn brake linings * Glazed brake linings * Worn brake drum * Glazed brake drum * Incorrect brake adjustment * Worn or damaged brake cable * Worn or defective brake return springs
Brakes grab	Check: * Worn or damaged brake return springs * Incorrect brake adjustment * Brake drum out-of-round * Warped brake lining web * Loose or worn wheel bearings
Brakes squeal or scrape	Check: * Worn brake linings * Brake drum out-of-round * Contaminated brake linings and/or drum * Broken, loose or damaged brake component * Loose or worn wheel bearing * Loose brake drum-to-wheel mounting bolts
Brake chatter	Check: * Brake drum out-of-round * Brake linings worn unevenly * Warped brake lining web * Incorrect brake adjustment * Loose or worn wheel bearing * Worn of damaged brake return springs

CARBURETOR TROUBLESHOOTING

CONDITION	SYMPTOM	CONDITION	SYMPTOM
Rich mixture	Rough idle Black exhaust smoke Hard starting, especially when hot Gas-fouled spark plugs Black deposits in exhaust pipe Poor gas mileage Engine performs worse as it warms up	Lean mixture	Backfiring Rough idle Overheating Hesitation upon accecleration Engine speed varies at fixed throttle Loss of power White color on spark plug insulator Poor acceleration

NOTE: If you own an EN500 model, first check the Supplement at the back of this book for any specific service information.

CHAPTER THREE

PERIODIC LUBRICATION, MAINTENANCE AND TUNE-UP

Your bike can be cared for in two ways: preventive and corrective maintenance. Because a motorcycle is subjected to tremendous heat, stress and vibration—even in normal use—preventive maintenance prevents costly and unexpected corrective maintenance. When neglected, any bike becomes unreliable and actually dangerous to ride. When properly maintained, your Kawasaki is one of the most reliable bikes available and will give many miles and years of dependable, fast and safe riding. By maintaining a routine service schedule as described in this chapter, costly mechanical problems and unexpected breakdowns can be prevented.

The procedures presented in this chapter can be easily performed by anyone with average mechanical skills. **Tables 1-3** show suggested factory maintenance schedules. **Tables 1-12** are located at the end of this chapter.

ROUTINE CHECKS

The following simple checks should be carried out at each fuel stop.

Engine Oil Level

Refer to *Periodic Lubrication* in this chapter.

Coolant Level (EN450)

Check the coolant level when the engine is cool.

Check the level in the coolant reserve tank. The level should be between the FULL and LOW marks (**Figure 1**). If necessary, add coolant to the reserve tank (not to the radiator) so the level is to the FULL mark. See **Figure 2**.

General Inspection

1. Examine the engine for signs of oil or fuel leakage.
2. Check the tires for imbedded stones. Pry them out with your ignition key.
3. Make sure all lights work.

NOTE
At least check the brake light. It can burn out anytime. Motorists cannot stop as quickly as you and need all the warning you can give.

Tire Pressure

Tire pressure must be checked with the tires cold. Correct tire pressure depends on the load you are carrying. See **Table 4** (1974-1983) or **Table 5** (1985-on).

Battery

Remove the left-hand side cover and check the battery electrolyte level. The level must be between the upper and lower level marks on the case (**Figure 3**).

For complete details see *Battery Removal/Installation and Electrolyte Level Check* in this chapter.

Lights and Horn

With the engine running, check the following.
1. Pull the front brake lever and check that the brake light comes on.
2. Push the rear brake pedal and check that the brake light comes on soon after you have begun depressing the pedal.
3. With the engine running, check to see that the headlight and taillight are on. On early models, operate the light switch.
4. Move the dimmer switch up and down between the high and low positions, and check to see that both headlight elements are working.
5. Push the turn signal switch to the left position and the right position and check that all 4 turn signal lights are working.
6. Push the horn button and note that the horn blows loudly.
7. If the horn or any light failed to work properly, refer to Chapter Nine.

MAINTENANCE INTERVALS

The services and intervals shown in **Tables 1-3** are recommended by the factory. Strict adherence to these recommendations will insure long life from your Kawasaki. If the bike is run in an area of high humidity, the lubrication services must be done more frequently to prevent possible rust damage.

For convenience when maintaining your motorcycle, most of the services shown in **Tables 1-3** are described in this chapter. Those procedures which require more than minor disassembly or adjustment are covered elsewhere in the appropriate chapter.

TIRES

Tire Pressure

Tire pressure should be checked and adjusted to accommodate rider and luggage weight. A simple, accurate gauge (**Figure 4**) can be purchased for a few dollars and should be carried in your motorcycle tool kit. The appropriate tire pressures are shown in **Table 4** and **Table 5**.

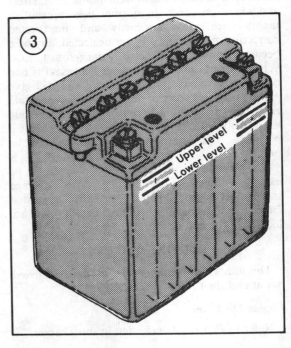

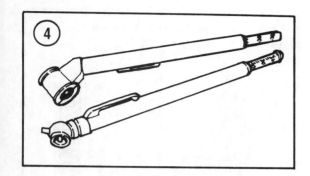

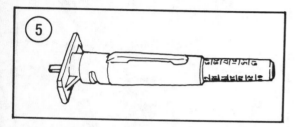

NOTE
After checking and adjusting the air pressure, make sure to reinstall the air valve cap. The cap prevents small pebbles and/or dirt from collecting in the valve stem; these could allow air leakage or result in incorrect tire pressure readings.

Tire Inspection

Check tire tread for excessive wear, deep cuts, imbedded objects such as stones, nails, etc. If you find a nail in a tire, mark its location with a light crayon before pulling it out. This will help locate the hole for repair. Refer to Chapter Eleven for tire changing and repair information.

Check local traffic regulations concerning minimum tread depth. Measure with a tread depth gauge (**Figure 5**) or small ruler. Kawasaki recommends replacement when the front tread

depth is 1 mm (0.04 in.) or less. For the rear tire, the recommended limit is 2 mm (0.08 in.).

Wheel Spoke Tension

On spoked wheels, tap each spoke with a screwdriver. The higher pitch of sound it makes, the tighter the spoke. The lower the sound frequency, the looser the spoke. A "ping" is good; a "clunk" says the spoke is loose.

If one or more spokes are loose, tighten them as described in Chapter Eleven.

Rim Inspection

Frequently inspect the wheel rims. If a rim has been damaged it might have been knocked out of alignment. Improper wheel alignment can cause severe vibration and result in an unsafe riding condition. If the rim portion of an alloy wheel is damaged the wheel must be replaced as it cannot be repaired.

BATTERY

CAUTION
If it becomes necessary to remove the battery vent tube when performing any of the following procedures, make sure to route the tube correctly during installation to prevent acid from spilling on parts.

Removal/Installation and Electrolyte Level Check

The battery is the heart of the electrical system. It should be checked and serviced as indicated (**Tables 1-3**). Most electrical system troubles can be attributed to neglect of this vital component.

In order to correctly service the electrolyte level it is necessary to remove the battery from the frame. The electrolyte level should be maintained between the two marks on the battery case (**Figure 3**). If the electrolyte level is low, it's a good idea to completely remove the battery so that it can be thoroughly cleaned, serviced and checked.

1. Remove the left-hand side cover and raise or remove the seat.
2. Disconnect the negative battery cable from the battery.
3. Disconnect the positive battery cable.
4. Disconnect the battery vent tube.
5. Lift the battery (**Figure 6**) out of the battery box and remove it.

WARNING
Protect your eyes, skin and clothing. If electrolyte gets into your eyes, flush your eyes thoroughly with clean water and get prompt medical attention.

6. Remove the caps from the battery cells and add distilled water. Never add electrolyte (acid) to correct the level. Fill only to the upper battery level mark (**Figure 3**). Reinstall the battery caps and gently shake the battery for several minutes to mix the existing electrolyte with the new water. Remove the battery caps.

7. After the level has been corrected and the battery allowed to stand for a few minutes, check the specific gravity of the electrolyte in each cell with a hydrometer (**Figure 7**). Follow the manufacturer's instructions for reading the instrument. See *Battery Testing* in this chapter.

8. After the battery has been refilled, recharged or replaced, install it by reversing these removal steps.

Testing

Hydrometer testing is the best way to check battery condition. Use a hydrometer with numbered graduations from 1.100 to 1.300 rather than one with color-coded bands. To use the hydrometer, squeeze the rubber ball, insert the tip in the cell and release the ball. Draw enough electrolyte to float the weighted float inside the hydrometer. Note the number in line with the surface of the electrolyte; this is the specific gravity for this cell. Return the electrolyte to the cell from which it came.

The specific gravity of the electrolyte in each battery cell is an excellent indication of that cell's condition (**Table 6**). A fully charged cell will read 1.260-1.280, while a cell in good condition reads from 1.230-1.250. Anything below 1.140 is discharged.

NOTE
Specific gravity varies with tempera-
ture. For each 10° that electrolyte tem-
perature exceeds 80° F, add 0.004 to
reading indicated on hydrometer. Sub-
tract 0.004 for each 10° below 80° F.

If the cells test in the poor range, the battery requires recharging. The hydrometer is useful for checking the progress of the charging operation. **Table 6** shows approximate state of charge.

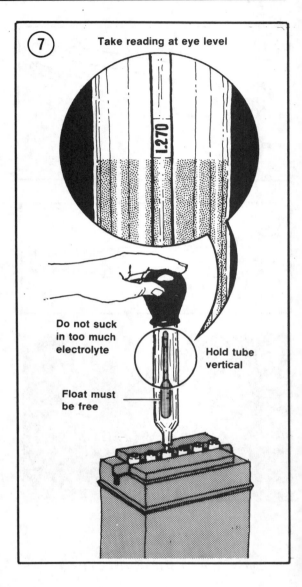

Take reading at eye level

1.270

Do not suck in too much electrolyte

Hold tube vertical

Float must be free

Charging

CAUTION
Always remove the battery from the motorcycle before connecting charging equipment.

WARNING
During charging, highly explosive hydrogen gas is released from the battery. The battery should be charged only in a well-ventilated area, and open flames and cigarettes should be kept away. Never check the charge of the battery by arcing across the terminals; the resulting spark can ignite the hydrogen gas.

1. Connect the positive (+) charger lead to the positive battery terminal and the negative (-) charger lead to the negative battery terminal.

2. Remove all vent caps from the battery, set the charger at 12 volts, and switch it on. If the output of the charger is variable, it is best to select a low setting – 1 1/2 to 2 amps.

CAUTION
The electrolyte level must be maintained at the upper level during the charging cycle; check and refill as necessary.

3. After battery has been charged for about 8 hours, turn the charger off, disconnect the leads and check the specific gravity. It should be within the limits

specified in **Table 6**. If it is, and remains stable for one hour, the battery is charged.

4. To ensure good electrical contact, cables must be clean and tight on the battery's terminals. If the cables terminals are badly corroded, even after performing the above cleaning procedures, the cables should be disconnected, removed from the bike and cleaned separately with a wire brush and a baking soda solution. After cleaning, apply a very thin coating of petroleum jelly (Vaseline) to the battery terminals before reattaching the cables. After connecting the cables, apply a light coating to the connections also – this will delay future corrosion.

New Battery Installation

When replacing the old battery with a new one, be sure to charge it completely (specific gravity, 1.260-1.280) before installing it in the bike. Failure to do so, or using the battery with a low electrolyte level will permanently damage the battery.

PERIODIC LUBRICATION

Engine Oil Level Check

Engine oil level is checked through the inspection window located at the bottom of the clutch cover on the right-hand side (**Figure 8**).

1. Place the bike on the centerstand. Start the engine and let it reach normal operating temperature.

2. Stop the engine and allow the oil to settle.

3. The oil level should be between the maximum and minimum window marks (**Figure 8**). If necessary, remove the oil fill cap (**Figure 9**) and add the recommended oil (**Table 7**) to raise the oil to the proper level. Do not overfill. Install the oil fill cap.

Engine Oil and Filter Change

The factory-recommended oil and filter change interval is specified in **Tables 1-3**. This assumes that the motorcycle is operated in moderate climates. The time interval is more important than the mileage interval because combustion acids, formed by gasoline and water vapor, will contaminate the oil even if the motorcycle is not run for several months. If a motorcycle is operated under dusty conditions, the oil will get dirty more quickly and should be changed more frequently than recommended.

Use only a detergent oil with an API classification of SE or SF. The classification is stamped on top of the can (**Figure 10**). Try always to use the same brand of oil. Use of oil additives is not recommended. Refer to **Table 7** for correct weight of oil to use under different temperatures.

To change the engine oil and filter you will need the following:

   a. Drain pan.
   b. Funnel.
   c. Can opener or pour spout.
   d. Wrench or socket to remove drain plug.
   e. Oil (see **Table 8**).
   f. Oil filter element.

NOTE
Never dispose of motor oil in the trash, on the ground, or down a storm drain. Many service stations accept used motor oil and waste haulers provide curbside used motor oil collection. Do not combine other fluids with motor oil to be recycled. To locate a recycler, contact the American Petroleum Institute (API) at www.recycleoil.org.

1. Place the motorcycle on the centerstand.
2. Start the engine and run it until it is at normal operating temperature, then turn it off.
3. Place a drip pan under the crankcase and remove the drain plug. See **Figure 11** for 1974-1977 and 1977-1987 Deluxe A models or **Figure 12** for 1978-1983 and 1985-on models.
4A. *1974-1983:* To service the oil filter, perform the following:

   a. To remove the oil filter, unscrew the filter cover bolt (**Figure 11** or **Figure 12**). Remove the spring and washer.
   b. Remove the cover and filter. Discard the filter.
   c. Clean the cover and bolt.
   d. Inspect the O-rings on the cover and on the filter bolt. Replace if damaged.
   e. Wipe the crankcase gasket surface with a clean, lint-free cloth.
   f. Insert the bolt into the cover and install the spring and washer. Insert the filter and reinstall into the crankcase.
   g. Torque the filter bolt to 30N•m (14.5 ft.-lb.).
4B. *1985-on:* These models use an automotive type spin-on filter. Service the oil filter as follows:

   a. Remove the filter (**Figure 13**) with a filter wrench.
   b. Discard the oil filter.
   c. Wipe the crankcase gasket surface with a clean, lint-free cloth.
   d. Coat the neoprene gasket on the new filter with clean oil (**Figure 14**).
   e. Screw the new filter onto the crankcase *by hand* until the filter gasket just touches the base. Stop when you feel the slightest

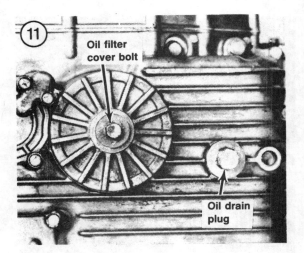

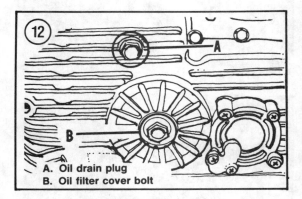

A. Oil drain plug
B. Oil filter cover bolt

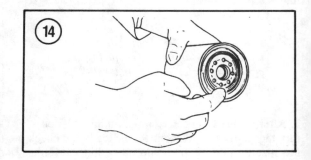

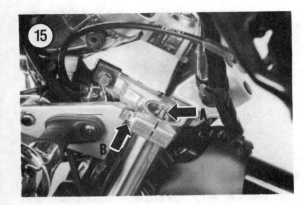

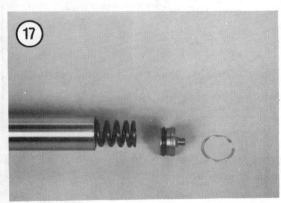

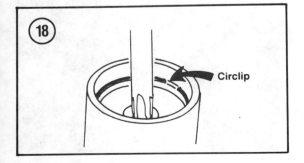

Circlip

resistance in turning the filter. Then tighten the filter *by hand* 2/3 more turn.

CAUTION
Do not overtighten and do not use a filter wrench or the filter may leak.

5. Reinstall the oil drain plug and tighten it securely.
6. Remove the oil filler cap (**Figure 9**) and fill the crankcase with the correct weight (**Table 7**) and quantity of oil (**Table 8**).
7. Screw in the oil fill plug securely.
8. After completing Step 7, start the engine and allow it to idle. Check for leaks.
9. Turn the engine off and check for correct oil level (**Figure 8**); adjust if necessary.

Front Fork Oil Change

1. Place the bike on the centerstand. Support the front end so that the front tire is clear of the ground.
2. Remove the rubber cap from the top of the fork tube.
3. *Air fork models:* Remove the air valve cap and depress the valve stem (A, **Figure 15**) with a screwdriver to release all air from the fork tube.
4. Loosen the upper triple clamp bolt (B, **Figure 15**).
5A. *1974-1977 and 1977-1978 Deluxe A models:* Unscrew the fork cap (**Figure 16**) and remove the fork spring.
5B. *1978-on:* The fork cap and and spring are held in position by a circlip (**Figure 17**). To remove the circlip, have an assistant depress the fork cap (**Figure 18**) using a suitable size drift or socket. Then pry the circlip (**Figure 18**) out of its groove in the fork with a small screwdriver. When the circlip is removed, release tension from the fork cap and remove it together with the fork spring (**Figure 17**).
6. Place a drip pan under the fork and remove the drain screw (**Figure 19**). Allow the oil to drain for at least 5 minutes.

WARNING
Do not allow the fork oil to come in contact with any of the brake components.

7. With both of the bike's wheels on the ground, have an assistant steady the bike. Then push the front end down and allow it to return. Perform this procedure until all the oil is expelled from the fork tube.
8. Install the drain screw (**Figure 19**).
9. Fill the fork tube with slightly less than the specified quantity of oil. See **Table 9**.

NOTE
In order to measure the correct amount of fluid, use a baby bottle. These bottles have measurements in fluid ounces (oz.) and cubic centimeters (cc) imprinted on the side.

NOTE
The amount of oil poured in is not as accurate a measurement as the actual level of the oil. You may have to add more oil later in this procedure.

10. After filling the fork tube, slowly pump the forks up and down to distribute the oil throughout the fork damper.

11. Refer to **Table 9**. If your model's fork oil level must be measured with the fork springs installed, install them. Measure the distance from the top of the fork tube to the surface of the oil (**Figure 20**).

12. Add oil, if required, to bring the level up to specifications (**Table 9**). Do not overfill the fork tube.

CAUTION
An excessive amount of oil can cause a hydraulic locking of the forks during compression, destroying the oil seals.

13A. *1974-1977 and 1977-1978 Deluxe A models:* Install the fork spring (if necessary) and fork cap.

13B. *1978-on:* Install the fork spring (if necessary) and fork cap. Have an assistant compress the fork cap and install a *new* circlip. Make sure the circlip seats fully in the groove in the fork tube before releasing the fork cap. See **Figure 18**.

14. Repeat Steps 2-13 for the opposite side.

NOTE
If the handlebar clamps have arrows stamped on them, the arrows must face towards the front of the bike.

15. *Air fork models:* Fill the forks with air as described in this chapter.

16. Install all components that were removed.

17. Tighten the upper triple clamp bolts to 20 N•m (14.5 ft.-lb.).

18. Road test the bike and check for oil and air leaks.

Control Cables

The control cables should be lubricated at the intervals specified in **Tables 1-3**. At this time, they should also be inspected for fraying, and the cable sheath should be checked for chafing. The cables are relatively inexpensive and should be replaced when found to be faulty.

They can be lubricated with a cable lubricant and a cable lubricator.

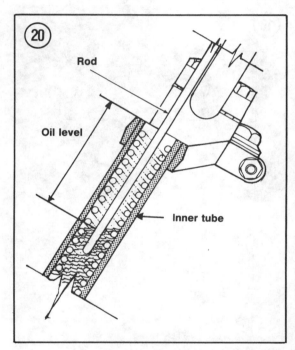

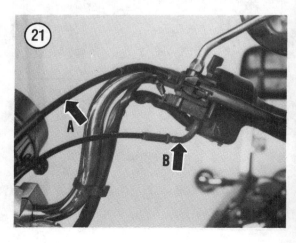

NOTE
The main cause of cable breakage or cable stiffness is improper lubrication. Maintaining the cables as described in this section will assure long service life.

1. Disconnect the clutch (A, **Figure 21**) and choke (B, **Figure 21**) cables from the left-hand side handlebar. Disconnect the throttle cables from the throttle grip (**Figure 22**).

NOTE
On the throttle cable, it is necessary to remove the screws that clamp the housing together to gain access to the cable ends.

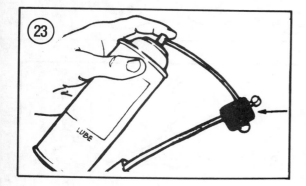

2. Attach a lubricator (**Figure 23**) to the cable following the manufacturer's instructions.

NOTE
Cable lubricators can be purchased at most motorcycle dealers.

3. Insert the nozzle of the lubricant can into the lubricator, press the button on the can and hold it down until the lubricant begins to flow out of the other end of the cable.

NOTE
Place a shop cloth at the end of the cable(s) to catch all excess lubricant that will flow out.

NOTE
If lubricant does not flow out the end of the cable, check the entire cable for fraying, bending or other damage.

4. Remove the lubricator, reconnect and adjust the cable(s) as described in this chapter.

Swing Arm Bearings

The rear swing arm bearings should be packed with a lithium-base, waterproof wheel bearing grease at the intervals specified in **Tables 1-3**. Refer to Chapter Twelve for complete details.

Brake Cam Lubrication

The brake cam (**Figure 24**) on front and rear drum brakes should be lubricated according to the maintenance schedule given in **Tables 1-3**. Refer to Chapter Thirteen.

Speedometer/Tachometer Cable Lubrication

Lubricate the cables every year or whenever needle operation is erratic.

1. Remove the cables from the instrument cluster (**Figure 25**).

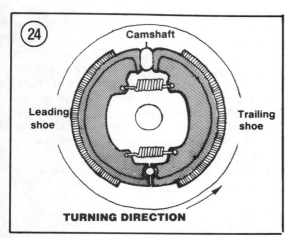

Camshaft

Leading shoe

Trailing shoe

TURNING DIRECTION

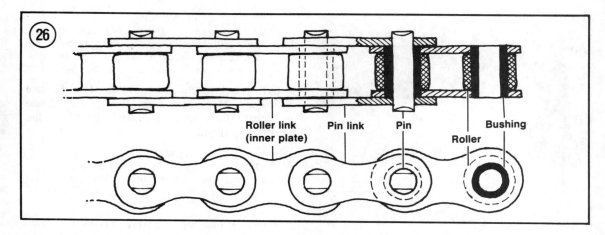

Roller link (inner plate)   Pin link   Pin   Roller   Bushing

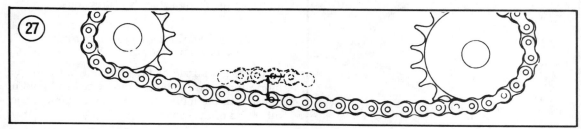

2. Pull the cable from the sheath.

3. If the grease is contaminated, thoroughly clean off all old grease.

4. Thoroughly coat the cable with a good grade of multi-purpose grease and reinstall into the sheath.

5. Make sure the cable is correctly seated into the drive unit.

> *NOTE*
> *If the cable does not seat into the drive unit, it will be necessary to disconnect the cable at its lower connection.*

PERIODIC MAINTENANCE

Drive Chain Lubrication

Kawasaki recommends SAE 90 gear oil for chain lubrication; it is less likely to be thrown off the chain than lighter oils. Many commercial drive chain lubricants are also available that do an excellent job.

1. Place the bike on the centerstand.

2. Oil the bottom chain run with SAE 90 gear oil or a commercial chain lubricant. Concentrate on getting the oil down between the side plates of the chain links (**Figure 26**).

3. Rotate the chain and continue until the entire chain has been lubricated.

4. Occasionally, the drive chain should be removed from the bike for a thorough cleaning and soak lubrication. Perform the following:

a. Brush off excess dirt and grit.

b. Remove the drive chain as described in Chapter Twelve.

c. Soak the chain in solvent for about half an hour and clean it thoroughly. Then hang the chain from a piece of wire and allow it to dry.

d. Soak the chain in heavy oil or hot grease and shake the chain around in the oil/grease to ensure thorough penetration of the lubricant.

e. Install the chain on the motorcycle as described in Chapter Twelve.

f. Adjust the drive chain as described in this chapter.

Drive Chain
Inspection/Adjustment

> *NOTE*
> *As drive chain stretches and wears in use, the chain will become tighter at one point. The chain must be checked and adjusted at this point.*

1. Turn the rear wheel and check the chain for its tightest point. Mark this spot and turn the wheel so that the mark is located on the chain's lower run, midway between both drive sprockets. Check and adjust the drive chain as follows.

2. With thumb and forefinger, lift up and press down the chain at that point, measuring the distance the chain moves vertically.

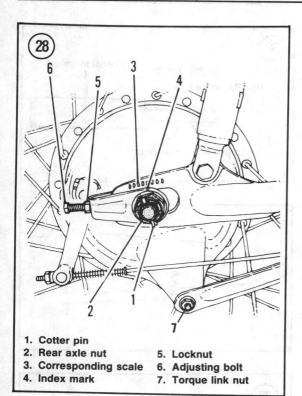

1. Cotter pin
2. Rear axle nut
3. Corresponding scale
4. Index mark
5. Locknut
6. Adjusting bolt
7. Torque link nut

3A. *Bike on centerstand:* The chain should have about 1 1/4 in. (30 mm) of vertical travel at midpoint (**Figure 27**).

3B. *Bike on side stand:* The chain should have about 1 in. (25 mm) of vertical travel at midpoint (**Figure 27**).

4. If necessary, adjust the chain as follows.

5. Loosen the rear torque link nut and the axle nut (**Figure 28**).

6. Loosen the axle adjuster locknut (5) on both sides of the wheel.

7. Turn each adjuster bolt clockwise to take up slack in the chain. To loosen the chain, turn each adjuster bolt counterclockwise. Be sure to turn each adjuster stud equally to maintain rear wheel alignment. Adjust the chain until the correct amount of free play is obtained (Step 3). See **Figure 27**.

8. Check rear wheel alignment by sighting along the chain as it runs over the rear sprocket. It should not appear to bend sideways. See **Figure 29**.

9. Partially tighten the axle nut, spin the wheel and stop it forcefully with the brake pedal, then tighten the axle nut. This centers the brake shoes in the drum and prevents a "spongy" feeling brake.

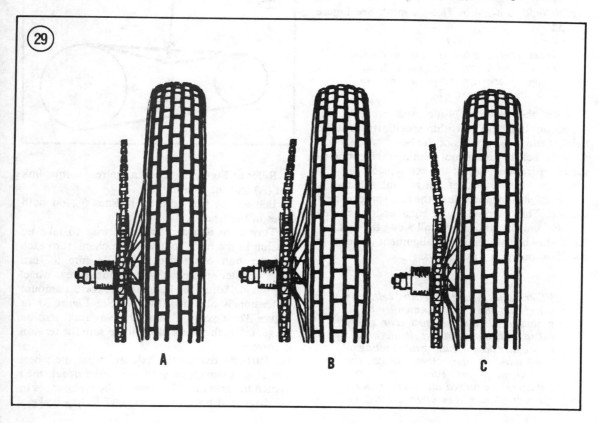

10. Tighten the chain adjuster locknuts and the rear torque link nut (**Figure 28**).
11. Recheck chain play.
12. Adjust the rear brake as described in this chapter.

Final Drive Belt Inspection/Adjustment

The final drive belt stretches very little after the first 500 miles of operation, but it should be inspected for tension and alignment according to the maintenance schedule (**Table 2** or **Table 3**).

NOTE
Some models come equipped with a Kawasaki belt tension gauge in the bike's tool kit (Figure 30). If you have such a gauge, follow the instructions provided with the gauge. The procedure given here applies to all models and can be used if the gauge has been lost or damaged.

1. Put the motorcycle on its centerstand.
2. Apply 10 lb. (4.5 kg) of force to the middle of the belt run. Deflection of the belt should be as follows:
   a. *KZ440:* 3/8-5.8 in. (8.5-17 mm). See **Figure 31**.
   b. *EN450:* 3/8-3/4 in. (8.5-18 mm). See **Figure 32**.

NOTE
When checking belt tension on EN450 models with the Kawasaki tension gauge, place the gauge at the point indicated in Figure 33.

3. Turn the wheel a little and recheck belt deflection. It should be within specifications at the tightest and loosest parts of the belt.
4. If the belt tension is not within specification as the belt is rotated, adjust the belt tension.
5. Check the sprocket alignment. Place a straightedge along the side of the rear sprocket near the top. There should be an equal space between the belt and the straightedge all along the belt.
6. If the belt tension or alignment is out of specification, adjust as follows.

NOTE
When adjusting the final drive belt, rear wheel and sprocket alignment must be maintained. A misaligned rear wheel will drastically shorten belt life and it may cause poor handling and pulling to one side or the other. Once the alignment is set correctly, if both adjusters are moved an equal amount, the rear wheel will be aligned correctly.

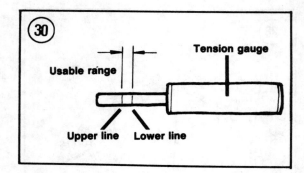

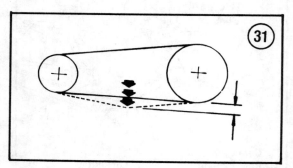

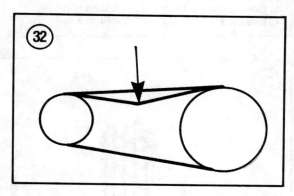

7. Refer to **Figure 34**. Loosen the rear torque link nut (A) and the axle nut (B).
8. Loosen the belt adjuster locknut (C) on both sides of the wheel.
9. Turn each adjuster bolt clockwise to take up tension in the belt. To loosen the chain, turn each adjuster bolt counterclockwise. Be sure to turn each adjuster stud equally to maintain rear wheel alignment. Adjust the belt until the correct amount of tension is obtained (Step 2). See **Figure 31** or **Figure 32**. If you are using the Kawasaki tension gauge, insert the gauge again to be sure the tension is correct.
10. Partially tighten the axle nut, spin the wheel and stop it forcefully with the brake pedal, then tighten the axle nut. This centers the brake shoes in the drum and prevents a "spongy" feeling brake.

11. Tighten the belt adjuster locknuts and the rear torque link nut. See **Figure 34**.

12. Recheck belt tension.

13. Adjust the rear brake as described in this chapter.

Disc Brake Inspection

The hydraulic brake fluid in the disc brake master cylinder should be checked every month. The disc brake pads should be checked at the intervals specified in **Table 1**. Replacement is described in Chapter Twelve.

Disc Brake Fluid
Level Inspection

On models with translucent reservoirs or transparent windows, check that the fluid level is between the upper and lower level lines (**Figure 35**). Remove the reservoir cap if you cannot see the fluid level.

Adding Brake Fluid

1. Clean the outside of the reservoir cap thoroughly with a dry rag and remove the reservoir cap. Remove the washer and diaphragm under the cap.

2. The fluid level in the reservoir should be up to the upper level line. Add fresh brake fluid as required.

> *WARNING*
> *Use only brake fluid clearly marked DOT 3 and specified for disc brakes. Others may vaporize and cause brake failure.*

> *CAUTION*
> *Be careful not to spill brake fluid on painted or plated surfaces as it will destroy the surface. Wash immediately with soapy water and thoroughly rinse it off.*

3. Reinstall all parts. Make sure the cap is tightly secured.

> *NOTE*
> *If the brake fluid was so low as to allow air in the hydraulic system, the brakes will have to be bled. Refer to **Bleeding The System** in Chapter Thirteen.*

Disc Brake Lines and Seals

Check brake lines between the master cylinder and the brake caliper. If there is any leakage, tighten the connections and bleed the brakes as described in Chapter Thirteen. If this does not stop the leak or if a line is obviously damaged, cracked or chafed, replace the line and seals and bleed the brake.

Disc Brake Pad Inspection

Inspect the disc brake pads for wear according to the maintenance schedule.

1. Apply the front brake.

2. Shine a light between the caliper and the disc (from in front of the fork leg) and inspect the brake pads.

3A. *KZ400 and KZ440:* If either pad is worn to the bottom of the first step (1974-1977) or to the bottom of the notch (1978-1983), replace both pads as a set. See **Figure 36**.

3B. *EN450:* If either pad lining thickness is 1/32 in. (1 mm) or less, replace both pads as a set. See **Figure 37.**

4. Replace brake pads as described in Chapter Thirteen.

Disc Brake Fluid Change

Every time you remove the reservoir cap a small amount of dirt and moisture enters the brake fluid. The same thing happens if a leak occurs or when any part of the hydraulic system is loosened or disconnected. Dirt can clog the system and cause unnecessary wear. Water in the fluid vaporizes at high temperatures, impairing the hydraulic action and reducing brake performance.

To change brake fluid, follow the *Bleeding the Brake System* procedure in Chapter Thirteen. Continue adding new fluid to the master cylinder and bleeding at the caliper until the fluid leaving the caliper is clean and free of contaminants and air bubbles.

> *WARNING*
> *Use brake fluid clearly marked DOT 3 only. Others may vaporize and cause brake failure.*

Front Brake Lever Adjustment (Disc Brake)

1974-1977

Periodic adjustment of the front disc brake is not required because because disc pad wear is automatically compensated. However, the front brake lever is equipped with an adjuster to remove excessive lever play from lever wear or when the lever is removed. If the lever play is in excess of 5 mm (3/16 in.), perform the following.

> *NOTE*
> *Free play is the distance the lever travels from the at-rest position to the applied position, when the master cylinder is depressed by the lever adjuster.*

1. Slide back the rubber shield.
2. Straighten the adjuster bolt lockwasher.
3. Loosen the lock nut and turn the adjusting bolt until the front brake lever free play is less than 5 mm (3/16 in.).
4. Tighten the locknut and bend the lockwasher over the adjuster bolt.
5. Rotate the front wheel and check for brake drag.

Also operate the brake lever several times to make sure it returns to the at-rest position immediately after release. Reposition the rubber shield.

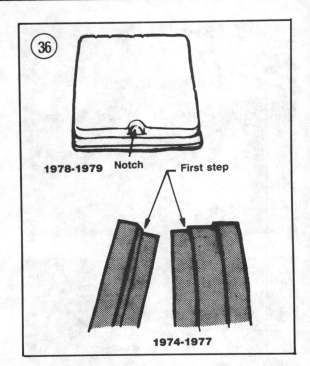

1978-1979   Notch   First step

1974-1977

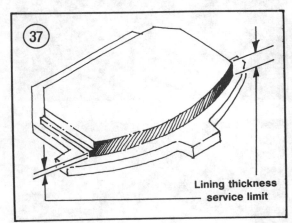

Lining thickness
service limit

> *WARNING*
> *If the brake lever adjustment is less than specified, brake drag could cause excessive heat bulidup and possible front brake lockup.*

> *WARNING*
> *Do not ride the bike until you are sure the front brake is adjusted and operating correctly.*

1978-on

Periodic adjustment of the front disc brake is not required because disc pad wear is automatically compensated. If there is excessive play in the front

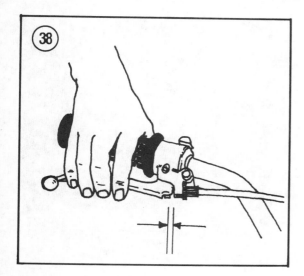

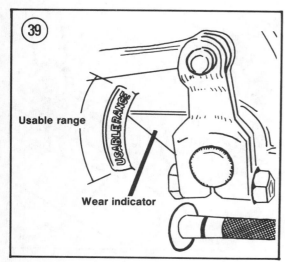

Usable range

Wear indicator

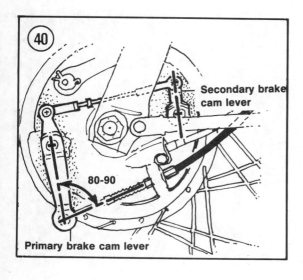

Secondary brake cam lever

80-90

Primary brake cam lever

brake lever, check the lever pivot hole and bolt for excessive wear. Replace worn parts.

Front Brake Lever Adjustment (Drum Brake)

Normal free play is approximately 4-5 mm (3/16 in.) at the cable end of the lever (**Figure 38**).

1. To adjust lever play, loosen the large knurled locknut on the brake lever and turn the adjuster until the desired brake cable free play is achieved. If the adjustment at the hand lever is used up, turn the adjuster at the lower end of the cable until brake lever free play is desired. Tighten the locknut by hand.

> *NOTE*
> *If the cable adjustment is difficult to make, the cable may be stretched or the brake shoes are worn and require replacement.*

2. Raise the bike's front end and spin the front wheel. If the wheel does not spin freely, the front brake lever adjustment is too tight. Loosen the locknut and readjust until the front wheel spins freely.

> *WARNING*
> *If the brake lever adjustment is less than specified, the front brake could lock when the lever is applied.*

> *WARNING*
> *Do not ride the bike until you are sure the front brake is adjusted and operating correctly.*

Front Brake Lining Wear Inspection (Drum Brake)

Inspect the brake linings for wear according to the maintenance schedule in **Table 1** and **Table 2**.

1. Apply the front brake fully.

2. Check the brake lining wear indicator on the backing plate (**Figure 39**). When the wear indicator pointer moves out of the USABLE RANGE, disassemble the brake and inspect the linings. See Chapter Thirteen.

Brake Shoe Synchronization

The front brake's double leading shoes must be synchronized for effective braking. Normally, synchronization will not be required unless the front wheel is removed or the brake is disassembled.

1. Apply the front brake fully.

2. Both brake cam levers should form an angle of 80-90° with the brake rod (**Figure 40**). If either

lever's angle exceeds 100°, remove the front wheel and inspect the brake linings (Chapter Thirteen). If the brake linings are okay, reinstall the front wheel and synchronize the brake as follows.

3. Loosen the locknut on the brake lever connecting link (B, **Figure 41**) and lengthen the connecting link (back it out) one turn to loosen the rear shoe.

4. Support the bike with the front wheel off the ground and spin it. Turn the adjuster (A, **Figure 41**) until the wheel just begins to drag.

5. Spin the wheel again and shorten the connecting link (turn it in) until the drag from the rear shoe just becomes noticeable. Tighten the locknut (B, **Figure 41**).

6. Adjust free play at the lower cable adjuster (A, **Figure 41**).

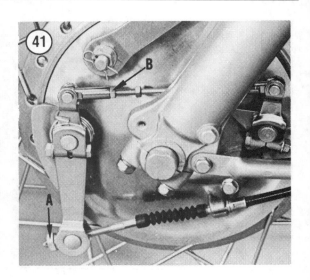

Rear Brake

Brake drum and lining wear will increase brake pedal play and decrease braking effectiveness. Proper brake adjustment consists of the following inspections and adjustments:

    a. Brake shoe inspection.
    b. Brake pedal height adjustment.
    c. Brake pedal travel adjustment.
    d. Rear brake light switch adjustment.

> *WARNING*
> *Do not ride the bike until you are sure the rear brake is adjusted and operating correctly.*

Rear Brake Shoe Inspection

Before adjusting the rear brake or at the specified maintenance intervals (**Tables 1-3**), inspect the rear brake shoes as follows:

1. Apply the rear brake fully.

2. Check the brake lining wear indicator on the backing plate (**Figure 42**). When the wear indicator pointer moves out of the USABLE RANGE, disassemble the brake and inspect the linings. See Chapter Thirteen.

3. The brake cam lever should form an angle of 80-90° with the brake rod (**Figure 43**). If the angle exceeds 100°, disassemble the brake and inspect the linings and cam (Chapter Thirteen).

Rear Brake Pedal Height Adjustment

1. Place the motorcycle on the centerstand.

2. Check to be sure the brake pedal is in the at-rest position.

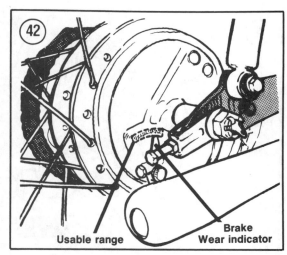

Usable range — Brake Wear indicator

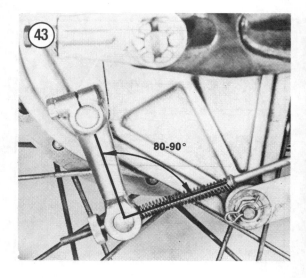

80-90°

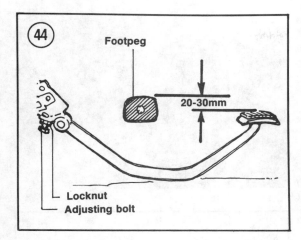

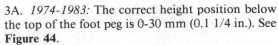

3A. *1974-1983:* The correct height position below the top of the foot peg is 0-30 mm (0.1 1/4 in.). See **Figure 44**.

3B. *EN450:* See **Figure 45**. The correct height positon from the center of the footpeg (A) to the center of the brake pedal (B) is 50-60 mm (2-2 3/8 in.).

4. To adjust, proceed to Step 5.

5. Loosen the locknut and turn the adjusting bolt to achieve the correct height. See **Figure 46** (1973-1983) or **Figure 47** (EN450). Tighten the locknut securely and adjust the rear brake free play and brake light switch.

Rear Brake Pedal Free Play

Adjust the brake pedal to the correct height as described earlier. Then turn the adjustment nut on the end of the brake rod (**Figure 48**) until the brake pedal has 20-30 mm (3/4-1 1/4 in.) free play. Free play is the distance the pedal travels from the at-rest position to the applied position when the pedal is depressed lightly.

Rotate the rear wheel and check for brake drag. Also operate the pedal several times to make sure it returns to the at-rest position immediately after release.

Rear Brake Light Switch Adjustment

1. Turn the ignition switch to the ON position.
2. Depress the brake pedal. The brake light should come on just as the rear brake begins to work.
3A. *1974-1983:* To make the light come on earlier, hold the switch body (**Figure 49**) and turn the adjusting locknut to move the switch body *up*. To delay the light, move the switch body *down*. Tighten the locknuts.

3B. *EN450:* To make the light come on earlier, hold the switch body (C, **Figure 45**) and turn the adjusting locknut to move the switch body *rearward.* To delay the light, move the switch body *forward.* Tighten the locknuts.

Clutch Lever Adjustment

Pull the clutch lever until resistance is felt. Then measure the distance from the adjuster locknut and the clutch lever (**Figure 50**). This is clutch cable free play. The clutch cable should have about 2-3 mm (3/32-1/8 in.) free play. Minor adjustment can be made at the hand lever. Loosen the locknut, turn the adjuster as required and tighten the locknut.

> *NOTE*
> *If sufficient free play cannot be obtained at the hand lever, additional adjustment can be made at the clutch mechanism adjuster.*

Clutch Mechanism Adjustment

1974-early 1981

1. In front of the engine, loosen the clutch mid-cable adjuster locknut and shorten the adjuster all the way (**Figure 51**).
2. At the clutch lever, loosen the locknut and turn the adjuster until 5-6 mm (3/16-1/4 in.) of threads are showing between the locknut and the adjuster body (**Figure 52**).
3. Remove the 2 clutch adjuster cover screws and the cover.
4. Loosen the locknut (A, **Figure 53**).
5A. *1974-1977 and 1977-1978 Deluxe A models:* Turn the screw (B, **Figure 53**) out until it turns freely. Then turn the adjuster in until it becomes hard to turn. Then turn the screw out 1/2 turn.
5B. *1978-early 1981:* Turn the screw (B, **Figure 53**) in until it turns freely. Then turn the screw out until it becomes hard to turn. Then turn the screw in 1/4 turn.
6. Hold the screw in this position and tighten the locknut.
7. In front of the engine, lengthen the mid-cable adjuster until it has just taken all the slack out of the cable and the clutch lever has no free play. Tighten the locknut.
8. Check that the lower end of the clutch cable (below the engine) is fully seated in its socket.
9. At the clutch lever, turn the adjuster as required to get about 2-3 mm (3/32-1/8 in.) of cable play at the clutch lever.
10. Install the clutch adjuster cover. Tighten the locknuts securely.

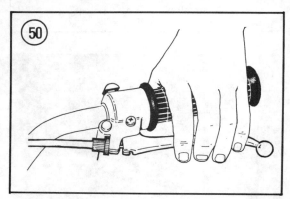

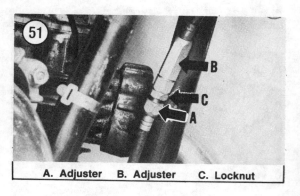

A. Adjuster　　B. Adjuster　　C. Locknut

Late 1981-on

1. Loosen the clutch cable adjuster nuts (**Figure 54**) at the crankcase as far as they will go.
2. At the clutch lever, loosen the locknut and turn the adjuster until 5-6 mm (3/16-1/4 in.) of threads are showing between the locknut and the adjuster body (**Figure 52**).
3. At the crankcase, pull the clutch cable forward and tighten the adjuster nuts.
4. At the clutch lever, turn the adjuster as required to get about 2-3 mm (3/32-1/8 in.) of cable play at the clutch lever.
5. Tighten all locknuts.

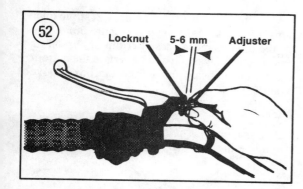

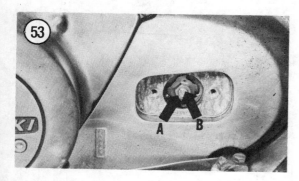

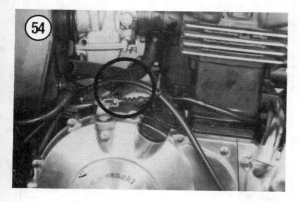

> *WARNING*
> *If idle speed increases when the handlebar is turned to right or left, check throttle cable routing. Do not ride the motorcycle in this unsafe condition.*

Dual cables

1. Loosen both throttle grip cable adjuster locknuts (**Figure 55**) and shorten both adjusters fully for maximum cable play.
2. Lengthen the return cable (rear cable) by backing the adjuster out 3 full turns.
3. Lengthen the open cable (front cable) adjuster until all play is removed. Tighten the open cable locknut.
4. Go back to the return cable adjuster and shorten it to get your desired free play. Tighten the return cable locknut.

> *NOTE*
> *If the adjustment range is entirely used up at the throttle grip, use the adjusters at the carburetor end of the throttle cables.*

Single cable

1. Loosen the locknut at the throttle grip and turn the adjuster as required to obtain the correct amount of free play.
2. Tighten the locknut and recheck the free play.

> *NOTE*
> *If the adjustment range is entirely used up at the throttle grip, use the adjuster at the carburetor end of the throttle cable.*

Fuel Shutoff Valve/Filter

At the intervals specified in **Tables 1-3**, remove and drain the fuel tank. Remove the fuel shutoff valve and clean it of all dirt and debris. Replace worn or damaged O-rings and gaskets.

Fuel and Vacuum Line Inspection

Inspect all fuel and vacuum lines for cracks or deterioration; replace if necessary. Make sure the hose clamps are in place and holding securely.

Exhaust System

Check for exhaust leakage at all fittings. Do not forget the crossover pipe connections. Tighten all bolts and nuts; replace any gaskets as necessary.

Air Filter Removal/Installation

A clogged air filter can decrease the efficiency and life of the engine. Never run the bike without

Throttle Cable Play

Always check the throttle cables before you make any carburetor adjustments. Too much free play causes delayed throttle response; too little free play will cause unstable idling.

Check the throttle cable from grip to carburetors. Make sure they are not kinked or chafed. Replace them if necessary.

Make sure that the throttle grip rotates smoothly from fully closed to fully open. Check at center, full left, and full right position of steering.

Check free play at the throttle grip flange. Kawasaki specifies about 2-3 mm (3/32-1/8 in.). If adjustment is required proceed as follows.

the air filter installed; even minute particles of dust can cause severe internal engine wear.

The service intervals specified in **Tables 1-3** should be followed with general use. However, the air cleaner should be serviced more often if the bike is ridden in dusty areas.

1974-1977 and 1977-1978 deluxe A model

1. Remove the left side cover.
2. Remove the air filter housing cover screw. Then remove the side cover.
3. Remove the air filter.
4. Tap the filter element against a solid surface to remove heavy particles, then blow it clean with compressed air, if available.
5. Clean the paper-type filter in a non-oily solvent, then allow to air dry or use compressed air directed from inside the filter.
6. Install by reversing these steps. Install the filter element so that the holes align with the air filter duct holes.

1978-1981 KZ400 and 1980-1981 KZ440B and C

1. Open the seat and prop it open.
2. Remove the tool kit. Then remove the tool tray bolt and lift the tray out.
3. Remove the filter element.
4. Tap the filter element against a solid surface to remove heavy particles, then blow it clean with compressed air (directed from the inside), if available.
5. Clean the paper-type filter in a non-oily solvent, then allow to air dry or use compressed air directed from inside the filter.
6. Install by reversing these steps, noting the following.
7. Install the filter element so that the open side faces *up*.
8. When installing the filter element into the housing, take care not to force the sponge gasket on the end of the element out of position.

All KZ440 models except B and C

1. Raise the seat and prop it open.
2. Remove the filter housing screws (**Figure 56**) and remove the housing.
3. Pull out the filter element (**Figure 57**).
4. Pull the foam element off its frame. Clean the element in solvent and let it dry. Inspect the element and replace it if it has any holes or tears.
5. Soak the foam element with SAE 30 motor oil, then wrap it in a rag and carefully squeeze it as dry as possible.

6. When installing the filter element, seat the filter against the back of the air box (**Figure 58**). Make sure the filter element doesn't crimp or slip off its frame when you install it and be certain the bottom ridge of the housing fits in the air box groove (**Figure 58**).

EN450

1. Slide the air filter holder down (A, **Figure 59**).
2. Remove the cover (B, **Figure 59**).

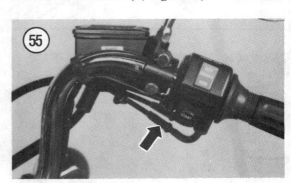

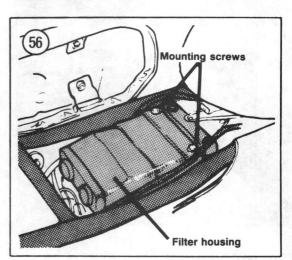

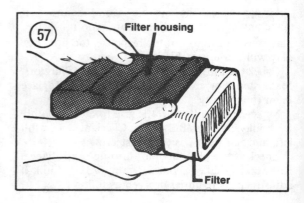

3. Remove the air filter element.

4. Tap the filter element against a solid surface to remove heavy particles, then blow it clean with compressed air (directed from the inside), if available.

CAUTION
Do not clean the filter element in any type of solvent or cleaner.

5. Install by reversing these steps.

Wheel Bearings

The wheel bearings should be cleaned and repacked at the service intervals specified in **Tables 1-3**. Refer to Chapter Eleven or Chapter Twelve for complete service procedures.

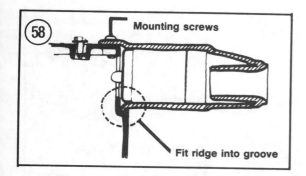

Mounting screws
Fit ridge into groove
58

59

60

Steering Play

The steering head should be checked for looseness at the intervals specified in **Tables 1-3**.

1. Prop up the motorcycle so that the front tire clears the ground.

2. Center the front wheel. Push lightly against the left handlebar grip to start the wheel turning to the right, then let go. The wheel should continue turning under its own momentum until the forks hit their stop.

3. Center the wheel, and push lightly against the right handlebar grip.

4. The steering adjustment is not too tight if the front wheel will turn all the way to the stop with a light push in either direction.

5. Center the front wheel and kneel in front of it. Grasp the bottoms of the 2 front fork slider legs. Try to pull the forks toward you, and then try to push them toward the engine. If no play is felt, the steering adjustment is not too loose.

6. If the steering adjustment is too tight or too loose, readjust it as described under *Steering Stem Installation* in Chapter Eleven.

Front Fork Air Adjustment

Air forks are standard equipment on some models. Both the fork springs and air pressure support the motorcycle and rider. Air pressure should be measured with the forks at normal room temperature.

The air pressure can be varied to suit the load and your ride preference, but it is very important to have the same pressure in both forks to prevent an unbalanced suspension with poor handling. The maximum allowable air pressure difference between the forks is 1.5 psi. Don't use a high-pressure hose or bottle to pressurize the forks; a tire pump is a lot closer to the scale you need. Note the following when adjusting the front fork air pressure:

   a. Increase air pressure for heavy loads.

   b. If the suspension is too hard, reduce air pressure.

   c. If the suspension is too soft, increase air pressure.

1. Support the bike with the front wheel off the ground.

2. Remove the air valve caps.

CAUTION
Do not exceed 36 psi or the fork seals will be damaged.

3. Connect a pump to the valve (**Figure 60**) and pump the forks to about 20 psi.

4. Slowly bleed off the air pressure to reach the desired pressure. The standard pressure is listed in **Table 10**. Kawasaki recommends balancing light fork air pressure with light rear shock preload; heavy fork air pressure with heavy rear shock preload.

> *NOTE*
> *Each application of a pressure gauge bleeds off some air pressure in the process of applying and removing the gauge.*

5. Install the valve caps.

Rear Shock Spring Adjustment

The rear shock absorbers feature adjustable spring preload. To adjust spring preload, use the spanner or screwdrivers in your motorcycle tool kit to turn both preload adjusters to the same setting (**Figure 61**). You will feel the adjuster become harder to turn as you set it for heavy preload.

> *WARNING*
> *Both rear shock absorbers must be set at the same preload settings for safe handling.*

On models with air forks, Kawasaki recommends balancing light fork air pressure with light rear shock preload; heavy fork air pressure with heavy rear shock preload.

Cooling System Inspection (EN450)

At the intervals indicated in **Table 3**, the following items should be checked. If you do not have the test equipment, the tests can be done by a Kawasaki dealer, radiator shop or service station.

> *WARNING*
> *Do not remove the radiator cap when the engine is hot.*

1. Have the radiator cap pressure tested (**Figure 62**). The specified radiator cap relief pressure is 11-15 psi (0.75-1.05 kg/cm^2). The cap must be able to sustain this pressure for 6 seconds. Replace the radiator cap if it does not hold pressure or if the relief pressure is too high or too low.

> *CAUTION*
> *If test pressure exceeds the specifications the radiator may be damaged.*

2. Leave the radiator cap off and have the entire cooling system pressure tested (**Figure 63**). The entire cooling system should be pressurized up to, but not exceeding, 15 psi (1.5 kg/cm^2). The system

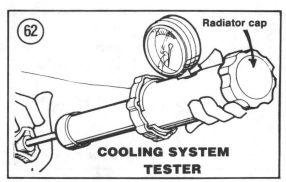

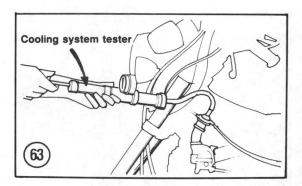

must be able to sustain this pressure for 6 seconds. Replace or repair any components that fail this test.

3. Check all cooling system hoses for damage or deterioration. Replace any hose that is questionable. Make sure all hose clamps are tight.

4. Carefully clean any road dirt, bugs, mud, etc. from the radiator core. Use a whisk broom, compressed air or low-pressure water aimed at the backside of the radiator core. If the radiator has been hit by a small rock or other item, *carefully* straighten out the fins with a screwdriver.

Coolant Change

The cooling system should be completely drained and refilled at the interval indicated in **Table 3**.

> *CAUTION*
> *Use only a high quality ethylene glycol antifreeze specifically labeled for use with aluminum engines. Do not use an alcohol-based antifreeze.*

In areas where freezing temperatures occur, add a higher percentage of antifreeze to protect the system in temperatures far below those likely to occur. **Table 11** lists the recommended amount of antifreeze. The following procedure must be performed when the engine is cool.

> *CAUTION*
> *Be careful not to spill antifreeze on painted surfaces as it will destroy the surface. Wash immediately with soapy water and rinse thoroughly with clean water.*

1. Place the bike on the centerstand.
2. Remove the fuel tank.
3. Remove the radiator and coolant reservoir covers (**Figure 64**).

> *WARNING*
> *Do not remove the radiator cap when the engine is hot.*

4. Remove the radiator cap (**Figure 65**).
5. Place a drain pan under the frame on the right-hand side of the bike under the water pump. Remove the drain screw (**Figure 66**) and sealing washer on the water pump cover. Do not install the drain screw yet.
6. Take the bike off the centerstand and tip the bike from side to side to drain any residual coolant from the cooling system. Place the bike back onto the centerstand.
7. Install the drain screw and sealing washer on the water pump cover.
8. Remove the reservoir tank (**Figure 67**) and drain it of all coolant. Reinstall the reservoir tank.
9. Refill the radiator. Add the coolant through the radiator filler neck (**Figure 65**), not the reservoir tank. Use the recommended mixture of antifreeze and purified water (**Table 11**). Do not install the radiator cap at this time.
10. Start the engine and let it run at idle speed until the engine reaches normal operating temperature. Make sure there are no air bubbles in the coolant and that the coolant level stabilizes at the correct level. Add coolant as necessary.
11. Install the radiator cap (**Figure 65**).
12. Add coolant to the reservoir tank to correct the level.
13. Add the radiator and coolant reservoir covers (**Figure 64**).

14. Install the fuel tank.

15. Test ride the bike and readjust the coolant level in the reserve tank if necessary.

Steering Head Bearings

The steering head bearings should be repacked at the intervals specified in **Tables 1-3**. See Chapter Eleven.

Front Suspension Check

1. Apply the front brake and pump the fork up and down as vigorously as possible. Check for smooth operation and check for any oil leaks.

2. Make sure the upper and lower fork bridge bolts are tight.

3. Check that the front axle pinch bolt is tight.

4. Check that the front axle nut cotter pin is in place and that the axle nut is tight.

> *WARNING*
> *If any of the previously mentioned bolts and nuts are loose, refer to Chapter Eleven for correct procedures and torque specifications.*

Rear Suspension Check

1. Place the bike on the centerstand.

2. Push hard on the rear wheel sideways to check for side play in the rear swing arm bushings or bearings.

3. Check the tightness of the upper and lower shock absorber mounting nuts and bolts.

4. Check the tightness of the rear brake torque arm bolts.

5. Make sure the rear axle nut is tight and the cotter pin is still in place.

> *WARNING*
> *If any of the previously mentioned nuts or bolts are loose, refer to Chapter Twelve for correct procedures and torque specifications.*

Nuts, Bolts and Other Fasteners

Constant vibration can loosen many fasteners on a motorcycle. Check the tightness of all fasteners, especially those on:

  a. Engine mounting hardware.
  b. Engine crankcase covers.
  c. Handlebar and front forks.
  d. Gearshift lever.
  e. Sprocket bolts and nuts.
  f. Brake pedal and lever.
  g. Exhaust system.
  h. Lighting equipment.

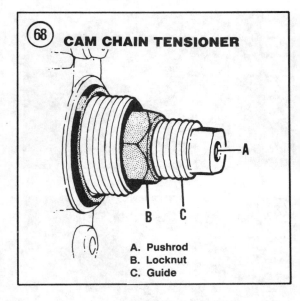

68 CAM CHAIN TENSIONER

A. Pushrod
B. Locknut
C. Guide

TUNE-UP

A complete tune-up restores performance and power that is lost due to normal wear and deterioration of engine parts. Because engine wear occurs over a combined period of time and mileage, the engine tune-up should be performed at the intervals specified in **Tables 1-3**. More frequent tune-ups may be required if the bike is ridden primarily in stop-and-go traffic.

Table 12 summarizes tune-up specifications.

Before starting a tune-up procedure, make sure to have all the necessary new parts on hand.

Because different systems in an engine interact, the procedures should be done in the following order:

  a. Clean or replace the air filter element.
  b. Adjust cam chain tension.
  c. Adjust valve clearances.
  d. Check engine compression.
  e. Check or replace the spark plugs.
  f. Check the ignition timing.
  g. Synchronize carburetors and set idle speed.

Tools

To perform a tune-up on your Kawasaki, you will need the following tools:

  a. Spark plug wrench.
  b. Socket wrench and assorted sockets.
  c. Flat feeler gauge.
  d. Compression gauge.
  e. Spark plug wire feeler gauge and gapper tool.
  f. Ignition timing light.
  g. Carburetor synchronization tool—to measure manifold vacuum.

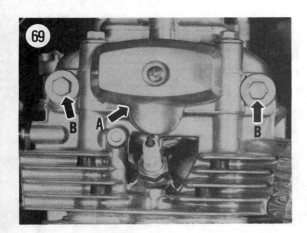

Air Filter Element

The air filter element should be cleaned or replaced before doing other tune-up procedures. Refer to *Air Filter Cleaning* in this chapter.

Cam Chain Tension
(1974-1979 KZ400)

In time the cam chain and guides will wear and develop slack. If neglected too long, the cam chain could break and cause serious damage to the engine.

When the chain tensioner adjustment no longer quiets the cam chain, the cam chain guides and tensioner may require replacement.

1. Check that the ignition switch is in the OFF position.
2. Remove the spark plugs.
3. Remove the ignition timing cover and gasket from the lower right side of the engine.
4. Remove the cam chain tensioner cap.

CAUTION
When performing step 5, do not use the small inner bolt to turn the engine or you will damage the ignition advance mechanism.

5. Turn the crankshaft counterclockwise with the 17 mm bolt on the right end of the crankshaft. At the same time, watch the tensioner pushrod move into the end of the tensioner (A, **Figure 68**).
6. Watch the pushrod move in and out as you turn the engine; stop turning when the pushrod moves to its innermost position.
7. Loosen the locknut (B, **Figure 68**). Then turn the pushrod guide (C) by its flats until the end of the guide is flush with the end of the pushrod inside it.
8. Tighten the locknut and install the tensioner cap and O-ring.

NOTE
If you are going to adjust the valves, leave the ignition timing cover and gasket off the engine.

Cam Chain Tension
(KZ440 and EN450)

The cam chain tensioner on these models is automatic and cannot be adjusted.

Valve Adjustment
(1974-1977)

1. Check that the ignition switch is in the OFF position.
2. Remove the spark plugs.
3. Remove the ignition timing cover and gasket from the lower right side of the engine.
4. See **Figure 69**. Remove the cylinder head side cover (A) and the valve adjuster plugs (B) from the engine.

CAUTION
In Step 5, do not use the small inner bolt to turn the engine or you will damage the ignition advance mechanism.

5. Positon the right piston at top dead center (TDC) on its compression stroke. To do this, turn the crankshaft to the left (counterclockwise) with the 17 mm bolt on the end of the crankshaft and at the same time watch the right cylinder intake (rear) valve through the side cover. After that valve has opened and closed (moved down then up), continue to turn the crankshaft about 1/4 turn until the "T" mark on the ignition advance mechanism aligns with the index pointer (**Figure 70**).

6. Insert a feeler gauge between each right cylinder valve stem and its rocker arm. The correct clearance is listed in **Table 12**. The clearance is measured correctly when there is slight drag on the feeler gauge when it is inserted and withdrawn. If the clearance is within tolerance, go on to Step 9. If adjustment is required, continue with Step 7.

7. Loosen the locknut (A, **Figure 71**), then turn the shaft (B) with a screwdriver as required to obtain the proper clearance.

8. Hold the shaft (B) steady and torque the locknut to 28 N•m (20 ft.-lb.).

NOTE
When adjusting the valve clearance, always keep the punch mark on each shaft facing inward, toward the (+) and (–) marks.

9. Turn the crankshaft one full turn counterclockwise, so that the "T" mark again lines up with the index pointer and repeat Steps 6-8 for the left cylinder.

10. Reinstall all parts previously removed.

**Valve Clearance
(1978-1983)**

1. Check that the ignition switch is in the OFF position.

2. Remove the fuel tank.

3. Remove the spark plugs.

4. Remove the ignition timing cover and gasket from the lower right side of the engine.

5. Remove the 4 valve adjusting caps (**Figure 72**).

CAUTION

In Step 6, do not use the small inner bolt to turn the engine or you will damage the ignition advance mechanism.

6. Positon the right piston at top dead center (TDC) on its compression stroke. To do this, turn the crankshaft counterclockwise with the 17 mm bolt on the end of the crankshaft and at the same time watch the right cylinder intake (rear) valve through the side cover. After that valve has opened and closed (moved down then up), continue to turn the crankshaft about 1/4 turn until the "T" mark on the ignition advance mechanism aligns with the index pointer (**Figure 70**).

7. Insert a feeler gauge between each right-hand cylinder valve stem and its rocker arm. The correct clearance is listed in **Table 12**. The clearance is measured correctly when there is a slight drag on the feeler gauge when it is inserted and withdrawn.

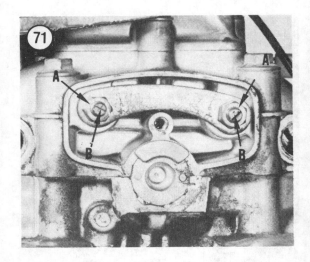

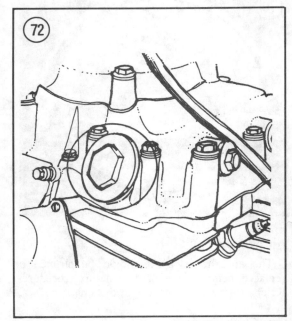

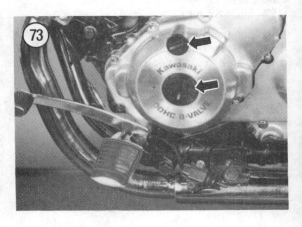

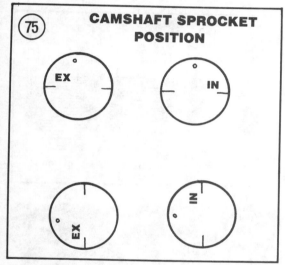

CAMSHAFT SPROCKET POSITION

If the clearance is within tolerance, go on to Step 9. If adjustment is required, continue with Step 8.

8. Adjust by loosening the adjuster locknut and turning the adjuster as required to get the proper clearance. Hold the adjuster steady and tighten the locknut securely. Check that the locknut is tightened to 15 N•m (11 ft.-lb.).

9. Turn the crankshaft one full turn counterclockwise, so that the "T" mark again lines up with the index pointer and repeat Steps 7 and 8 for the left cylinder.

10. Install all parts previously removed.

Valve Clearance (1985-on)

1. Place the motorcycle on the centerstand.
2. Remove the cylinder head cover. Refer to *Cylinder Head Cover Removal/Installation* in Chapter Five.
3. Remove the 2 alternator cover caps (**Figure 73**).
4. Positon the right piston at top dead center (TDC) on its compression stroke. To do this, turn the crankshaft to the right (clockwise) with the bolt on the end of the crankshaft (A, **Figure 74**) and at the same time watch the right-hand side cylinder

intake and exhaust valves. After valves have opened and closed (moved down then up), continue to turn the crankshaft until the "C" mark on the rotor aligns with the notch in the edge of the upper hole in the alternator cover (B, **Figure 74**). When the right piston is at TDC, the camshaft lobes will be facing away from the rocker arms and both camshaft sprockets will be positioned as shown in **Figure 75**.

5. Insert a feeler gauge between the right cylinder's intake and exhaust valve stem and rocker arm. The correct clearance is listed in **Table 12**. The clearance is measured correctly when there is a slight drag on the feeler gauge when it is inserted and withdrawn. If the clearance is within tolerance, go on to Step 8. If adjustment is required, continue with Step 7.

6. Adjust by loosening the adjuster locknut and turning the adjuster as required to get the proper clearance. Hold the adjuster steady and tighten the locknut securely. Check that the locknut is tightened to 15 N•m (11 ft.-lb.).

7. Turn the crankshaft one full turn clockwise, so that the "T" mark for the left cylinder lines up with the index pointer and both camshaft sprockets are aligned as shown in **Figure 75**. Repeat Steps 6 and 7 for the left cylinder.

8. Install the cylinder head cover. Refer to *Cylinder Head Cover Removal/Installation* in Chapter Five.

Compression Test

At every tune-up, check cylinder compression. Record the results and compare them at the next check. A running record will show trends in deterioration so that corrective action can be taken before complete failure can occur.

The results, when properly interpreted, can indicate general cylinder, piston ring and valve condition.

NOTE
The valves must be properly adjusted to correctly interpret the results of this test.

1. Warm the engine to normal operating temperature. Ensure that the choke valve and throttle valve are completely open.
2. Remove the spark plugs.
3. Connect a compression tester (**Figure 76**) to one cylinder following manufacturer's instructions.
4. Have an assistant crank the engine over until there is no further rise in pressure.
5. Remove the tester and record the reading.
6. Repeat Steps 3-5 for the other cylinder.

7. When interpreting the results, actual readings are not as important as the difference between the readings. Readings should be from about 170 ± 15 psi $(12 \pm 2.0 \text{ kg/cm}^2)$. A maximum difference of 57 psi (4 kg/cm^2) between any 2 cylinders is acceptable. Greater differences indicate worn or broken rings, leaky or sticky valves, blown head gasket or a combination of all.

If compression reading does not differ between cylinders by more than 10 percent, the rings and valves are in good condition.

If a low reading (10% or more) is obtained on one of the cylinders, it indicates valve or ring trouble. To determine which, pour about a teaspoon of engine oil through the spark plug hole onto the top of the piston. Turn the engine over once to clear some of the excess oil, then take another compression test and record the reading. If the compression increases significantly, the valves are good but the rings are defective on that cylinder. If compression does not increase, the valves require servicing. A valve could be hanging open but not burned or a piece of carbon could be on a valve seat.

> *NOTE*
> *If the compression is low, the engine cannot be tuned to maximum performance. The worn parts must be replaced and the engine rebuilt.*

Correct Spark Plug Heat Range

Spark plugs are available in various heat ranges that are hotter or colder than the spark plugs originally installed at the factory.

Select plugs in a heat range designed for the loads and temperature conditions under which the engine will operate. Using incorrect heat ranges, however, can cause piston seizure, scored cylinder walls or damaged piston crowns.

In general, use a hotter plug for low speeds, low loads and low temperatures. Use a colder plug for high speeds, high engine loads and high temperatures.

> *NOTE*
> *In areas where seasonal temperature variations are great the factory recommends a "two-plug system"—a cold plug for hard summer riding and a hot plug for slower winter operation. This may prevent spark plug and engine problems.*

The reach (length) of a plug is also important. A longer than normal plug could interfere with the valves and pistons, causing permanent and severe

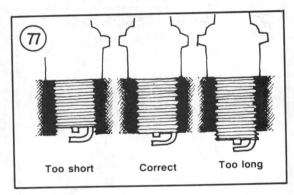

Too short   Correct   Too long

damage (**Figure 77**). The standard heat range spark plugs are listed in **Table 12**.

Spark Plug Removal/Cleaning

1. Grasp the spark plug leads (**Figure 78**) as near to the plug as possible and pull them off the plugs.
2. Blow away any dirt that has accumulated in the spark plug wells.

> *CAUTION*
> *The dirt could fall into the cylinders when the plugs are removed, causing serious engine damage.*

3. Remove the spark plugs with a spark plug wrench.

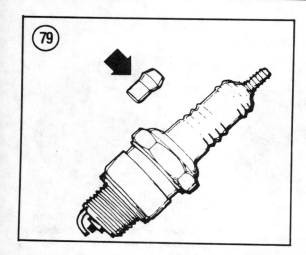

NOTE
If plugs are difficult to remove, apply penetrating oil, like WD-40 or Liquid Wrench, around base of plugs and let it soak in (about 10-20 minutes).

4. Inspect spark plug carefully. Look for plugs with broken center porcelain, excessively eroded electrodes and excessive carbon or oil fouling. Replace such plugs.

NOTE
Spark plug cleaning with the use of a sand-blast type device is generally not recommended. While this type of cleaning is thorough, the plug must be perfectly free of all abrasive cleaning material when done. If not, it is possible for the cleaning material to fall into the engine during operation and cause damage.

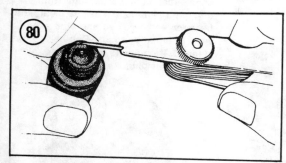

Gapping and Installing the Plugs

New plugs should be carefully gapped to ensure a reliable, consistent spark. You must use a special spark plug gapping tool with a wire gauge.

1. Remove the new plugs from the box. Do *not* screw in the small pieces that are loose in each box (**Figure 79**); they are not used.

2. Insert a wire gauge between the center and the side electrode of each plug (**Figure 80**). The correct gap is found in **Table 12**. If the gap is correct, you will feel a slight drag as you pull the wire through. If there is no drag, or the gauge won't pass through, bend the side electrode *with the gapping tool* (**Figure 81**) to set the proper gap (**Table 12**).

3. Put a small drop of oil on the threads of each spark plug.

4. Screw each spark plug in by hand until it seats. Very little effort is required. If force is necessary, you have the plug cross-threaded; unscrew it and try again.

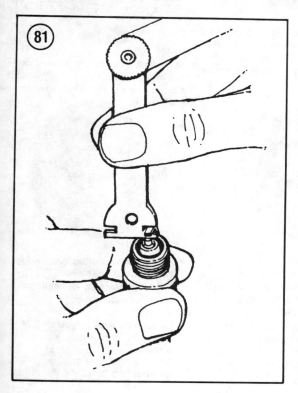

NOTE
If a spark plug is difficult to install, the cylinder head threads may be dirty or slightly damaged. To clean the threads, apply grease to the threads of a spark plug tap and screw it carefully into the cylinder head. Turn the tap slowly until it is completely installed. If the tap cannot be installed, the threads are severely damaged.

5. Tighten the spark plugs to a torque of 20 N•m (14 ft.-lb.). If you don't have a torque wrench, an additional 1/4 to 1/2 turn is sufficient after the gasket has made contact with the head. If you are

SPARK PLUG CONDITION

NORMAL
- Identified by light tan or gray deposits on the firing tip.
- Can be cleaned.

GAP BRIDGED
- Identified by deposit buildup closing gap between electrodes.
- Caused by oil or carbon fouling. If deposits are not excessive, the plug can be cleaned.

OIL FOULED
- Identified by wet black deposits on the insulator shell bore and electrodes.
- Caused by excessive oil entering combustion chamber through worn rings and pistons, excessive clearance between valve guides and stems, or worn or loose bearings. Can be cleaned. If engine is not repaired, use a hotter plug.

CARBON FOULED
- Identified by black, dry fluffy carbon deposits on insulator tips, exposed shell surfaces and electrodes.
- Caused by too cold a plug, weak ignition, dirty air cleaner, too rich a fuel mixture or excessive idling. Can be cleaned.

LEAD FOULED
- Identified by dark gray, black, yellow or tan deposits or a fused glazed coating on the insulator tip.
- Caused by highly leaded gasoline. Can be cleaned.

WORN
- Identified by severely eroded or worn electrodes.
- Caused by normal wear. Should be replaced.

FUSED SPOT DEPOSIT
- Identified by melted or spotty deposits resembling bubbles or blisters.
- Caused by sudden acceleration. Can be cleaned.

OVERHEATING
- Identified by a white or light gray insulator with small black or gray brown spots and with bluish-burnt appearance of electrodes.
- Caused by engine overheating, wrong type of fuel, loose spark plugs, too hot a plug or incorrect igntion timing. Replace the plug.

PREIGNITION
- Identified by melted electrodes and possibly blistered insulator. Metallic deposits on insulator indicate engine damage.
- Caused by wrong type of fuel, incorrect ignition timing or advance, too hot a plug, burned valves or engine overheating. Replace the plug.

A. Breaker point retaining screw
B. Adjustment slot
C. Condenser lead
D. Condenser retaining screw

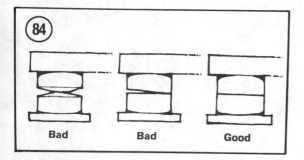

Bad   Bad   Good

reinstalling old, regapped plugs and are reusing the old gasket, tighten only an additional 1/4 turn.

CAUTION
Do not overtighten. Besides making the plug difficult to remove, the excessive torque will squash the gasket and destroy its sealing ability.

6. Install each spark plug wire. Make sure it goes to the correct spark plug.

Reading Spark Plugs

Much information about engine and spark plug performance can be determined by careful examination of the spark plugs. This information is more valid after performing the following steps.

1. Ride bike a short distance at full throttle in any gear.
2. Turn off kill switch before closing throttle, and simultaneously, pull in clutch and coast to a stop. Do not downshift transmission in stopping.
3. Remove spark plugs and examine them. Compare them to **Figure 82**.

If the insulator tip is white or burned, the plug is too hot and should be replaced with a colder one.

A too-cold plug will have sooty deposits ranging in color from dark brown to black. Replace with a

hotter plug and check for too-rich carburetion or evidence of oil blow-by at the piston rings.

If either plug is found unsatisfactory, replace them both.

BREAKER POINT IGNITION

The breaker points are shown in **Figure 83**. During normal operation, the contact surfaces of the points gradually erode and become contaminated. The point rubbing block also wears, retarding ignition timing. Periodic cleaning and gap adjustment are required to keep the engine operating at peak efficiency.

Contact Point Inspection

1. Turn the ignition switch to the OFF position.
2. Remove the ignition timing cover and gasket from the lower right-hand side of the engine.
3. Inspect the contact surfaces. If the points are not badly pitted they can be removed and dressed with a few strokes from a point file. If the contact surfaces are badly pitted, replace the breaker point assembly and the condenser.

CAUTION
Don't use sandpaper or emery cloth for dressing the points. They will leave abrasive particles embedded in the points and cause arcing.

4. Clean the contact surfaces by closing the points on a piece of clean paper, such as a business card, and pulling the paper through the points. Do this until no discoloration or residue remains on the card. Check the points when closed. If they do not meet squarely (**Figure 84**), replace them.
5. Inspect the breaker spring tension by hand. A weak breaker spring will allow the points to bounce at high engine speeds and cause misfiring. Usually the spring will last for the life of the contacts.
6. Apply a small amount of point cam lubricant or high temperature grease to the felt that bears against the point cam. If you use too much grease, the cam will sling it onto the contacts, fouling them.
7. Check the point gap and ignition timing.

Contact Point Gap
(With Feeler Gauge)

1. Turn the ignition switch to the OFF position.
2. Remove the ignition timing cover and gasket from the lower right-hand side of the engine.

CAUTION
When performing Step 3, do not use the small inner bolt to turn the engine or you will damage the ignition advance mechanism.

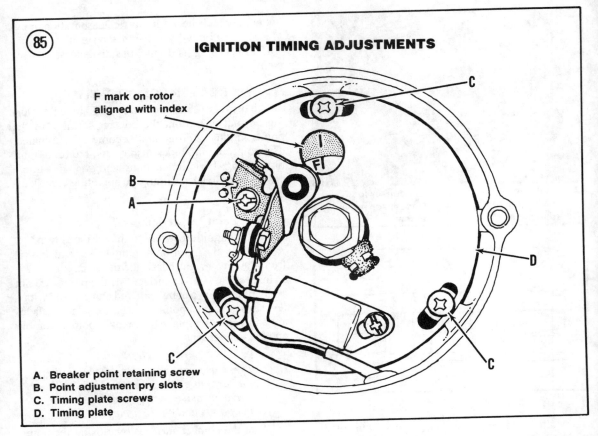

IGNITION TIMING ADJUSTMENTS

F mark on rotor aligned with index

A. Breaker point retaining screw
B. Point adjustment pry slots
C. Timing plate screws
D. Timing plate

3. Turn the crankshaft to the left (counterclockwise) with the 17 mm bolt on the end of the crankshaft until the points are open to their widest gap.

4. Measure the point gap with a clean feeler gauge. The gap should be as specified in **Table 12**.

NOTE
There should be a slight drag on the feeler gauge as it is inserted and removed. Hold the gauge loosely in your fingers to make sure you're not prying the points open.

5. To adjust the point gap, loosen the locking screw slightly (A, **Figure 83**), then insert a screwdriver into the pry slots (B) and move the base contact as required to set the gap. Tighten the locking screw (A) and recheck the gap.

6. Check the ignition timing.

Contact Point Gap
(With Dwell Angle Meter)

The dwell angle is the number of degrees (or the percentage of 360°) of point cam rotation during which the points are closed and current can flow

through them to the primary winding of the ignition coil. The breaker point gap can be adjusted with greater accuracy with a dwell angle meter than with a feeler gauge.

1. Connect a dwell angle meter according to the manufacturer's instructions.

2. Start the engine and allow it to idle.

3. Note the reading on the meter. The reading for the correct gap on a meter calibrated in percentages is 53 percent; the correct reading for a meter calibrated in degrees is 190° when set for "2 cylinders."

4. If the reading is incorrect, adjust the point gap. Loosen the retaining screw slightly (A, **Figure 83**). Then insert a screwdriver into the pry slots (B) and move the stationary contact as required to obtain the correct meter reading. Tighten the screw (A) and recheck the meter reading.

5. Check the ignition timing.

Contact Point and
Condenser Replacement

It is a good idea to replace the condenser every time you replace the points.

1. Turn the ignition switch to the OFF position.

2. Remove the ignition timing cover and gasket from the lower right-hand side of the engine.

3. Remove the screw that mounts the breaker point assembly to its backing plate (A, **Figure 83**).

4. Lift the point assembly from its pivot, loosen the nut and remove the ignition coil wire and condenser wire from the point terminal (C, **Figure 83**).

5. To remove the condenser, remove its retaining screw from the backing plate (D, **Figure 83**). Remove all old lubricant from the point cam.

6. Install a new condenser and set of points. Make sure the new contacts are clean and that the backing plate is clean for a good ground connection.

7. Apply a small amount of point cam lubricant or high temperature grease to the felt that bears against the point cam. If you use too much grease, the cam will sling it onto the contacts, fouling them.

8. Adjust the point gap and set the ignition timing.

Ignition Timing

Periodic inspection and adjustment of ignition timing is necessary to compensate for point and rubbing block wear. Failure to do so will result in incorrect ignition timing which in turn may cause poor performance, overheating, knocking or engine damage.

Clean the contact points and adjust their gap before inspecting ignition timing.

There are 2 ways to inspect ignition timing: "static" (engine not running) and "dynamic" (engine running). Dynamic timing inspection is preferable if a stobe timing light is available, because it checks timing under actual operating conditions and allows inspection of the ignition advance function.

Dynamic ignition timing

1. Connect a tachometer and a stroboscopic timing light according to the manufacturer's instructions.

2. Start the engine and allow it to idle. If idle speed is not within the specifications listed in **Table 12**, adjust it as described in this chapter.

3. Shine the light at the timing inspection hole. The "F" mark should align with the index mark at idle (**Figure 85**). If the "F" mark does not align at idle, loosen the timing plate screws (C, **Figure 85**) and rotate the timing plate as required to align the marks. Tighten the timing plate screws.

NOTE
*On some 1977 models, unstable idle may result if the timing marks are aligned as shown in **Figure 85**. A more stable idle is possible if the left edge of the "F" mark is aligned with the index mark. This sets timing at 15° BTDC at idle and 45° BTDC at full advance. Premium fuel may be required to prevent spark knock.*

4. Increase the engine speed to 3,500 rpm and check that the double line advance mark aligns with the index mark (**Figure 86**). If the advance does not work correctly, refer to Chapter Nine.

5. Stop the engine and install the timing cover and gasket.

Static ignition timing

1. Turn the ignition switch and kill switch to OFF.

2. Connect a timing tester, points checker or ohmmeter between the contact point terminal and the engine case for a good ground.

CAUTION
When performing Step 3, do not use the inner bolt to turn the engine or you will damage the ignition advance mechanism.

3. Using the 17 mm bolt on the end of the crankshaft, slowly turn the crankshaft to the left (counterclockwise) until the "F" mark aligns with the index mark (**Figure 85**). The timing tester should indicate the breaker points are just beginning to open when the marks align (the tone will change, the bulb will light or the ohmmeter needle will flicker).

4. If the ignition timing is incorrect, continue turning the crankshaft until the "F" mark aligns with the index mark again. Loosen the timing plate

screws (C, **Figure 85**) and rotate the timing plate as required so the points are just beginning to open.
5. Tighten the timing plate screws and recheck timing as described in Step 3.

> *NOTE*
> *On 1977 models, unstable idle may result if the timing marks are aligned as shown in **Figure 85**. A more stable idle is possible if the left edge of the "F" mark is aligned with the index mark. This sets the timing at 15° BTDC at idle and 45° BTDC at full advance. Premium fuel may be required to prevent spark knock.*

6. Install the timing cover and gasket.

ELECTRONIC IGNITION
(1980-1983)

Transistorized ignition timing is very stable and once it is set properly it should last the life of the motorcycle without adjustment. This optional procedure is provided in case of suspected trouble.

The ignition advance mechanism is a mechanical device that must be lubricated according to the maintenance schedule (**Table 2**). If not maintained properly, the advance mechanism could stick and cause low power, overheating, spark knock or detonation.

> *NOTE*
> *Transistorized ignition cannot be checked statically. It must be inspected dynamically (engine running) with a strobe timing light.*

1. Remove the timing cover and gasket from the lower right-hand side of the engine.
2. Connect a portable tachometer according to the manufacturer's instructions.
3. Hook up a stroboscopic timing light to either spark plug lead acording to the manufacturer's instructions.
4. Start the engine and allow it to idle. Check that the idle speed is within specifications before inspecting dynamic timing; a very high idle speed will begin the ignition advance process and give a faulty reading.
5. Shine the timing light at the timing inspection marks. The "F" mark on the advancer should align with the index mark at idle (**Figure 87**).
6. If the "F" mark does not align at idle, stop the engine and remove and inspect the ignition advance assembly. See *Ignition Advance Unit* in Chapter Nine. Recheck the ignition timing.

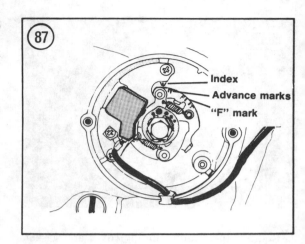

Index
Advance marks
"F" mark

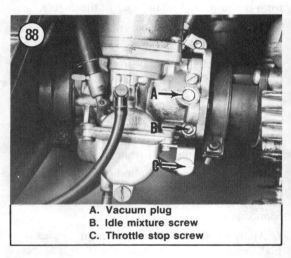

A. Vacuum plug
B. Idle mixture screw
C. Throttle stop screw

7. Increase the engine speed to 4,000 rpm and check that the index mark falls between the double line advance mark (**Figure 87**). If the ignition timing is incorrect, the advancer may not be operating correctly; refer to *Ignition Advance Unit* in Chapter Nine. If the advancer is okay, refer to Chapter Two for further testing information.
8. Stop the engine and disconnect the portable tachometer and timing light. Install the timing cover and gasket.

ELECTRONIC IGNITION
(1985-ON)

The ignition system on these models is completely electronic; no mechanical advance unit is used. The ignition timing is fixed; no adjustment is provided. If the engine is running poorly and the trouble has been traced to the ignition system, refer to Chapter Two for troubleshooting procedures.

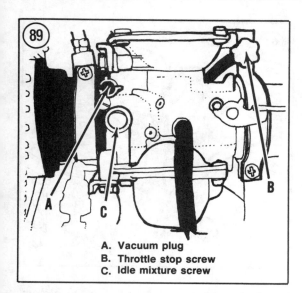

A. Vacuum plug
B. Throttle stop screw
C. Idle mixture screw

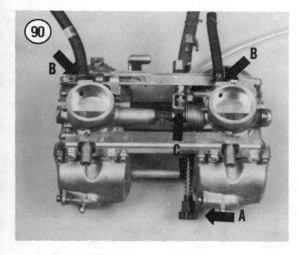

CARBURETOR

Idle Speed

Proper idle speed setting is necessary to prevent stalling and to provide adequate engine compression braking. It cannot be set accurately with the bike's tachometer. A portable tachometer is strongly recommended for this procedure.

1. Attach a portable tachometer, following the manufacturer's instructions.
2. Start the engine and warm it to normal operating temperature.
3. Turn the throttle stop screw (**Figure 88**, **Figure 89** or **A, Figure 90**) to set the idle speed as specified in **Table 12**. If you do not have a portable tachometer, set the idle at the lowest speed at which the engine will idle smoothly.

NOTE
Figure 90 shows the throttle stop screw with the carburetor removed for clarity.

4. Rev the engine a couple of times to see if it settles down to the set speed. Readjust, if necessary.
5. Disconnect the portable tachometer.

Idle Mixture

The idle/fuel mixture affects low-speed emissions, as well as idling stability and response off idle. The range of adjustment is limited by a limiter cap on 1978-1979 U.S. models. Do not remove the limiter caps from the mixture screws; no standard specification of idle mixture screw initial setting is available for 1980-on U.S. models. On 1980-1985 U.S models, the idle mixture screw is sealed; periodic adjustment is not required.

Idle mixture adjustment (1974-1978)

1. Adjust the idle speed.
2. Turn each idle mixture screw (**Figure 88** or **Figure 89**) in or out to the setting that gives the highest stable idle speed.
3. Turn each mixture screw slightly again and see if the idle speed increases. Readjust idle speed, if necessary.

Idle mixture adjustment (1979)

1. Adjust the idle speed.
2. Turn each idle mixture screw (**Figure 89**) to the right (clockwise) against its stop.
3. Turn each idle mixture screw to the left (counterclockwise) against its stop, observing the idle speed. Interpret results as follows:
   a. If the idle speed rose as the screw was turned counterclockwise, turn it back in to the point just before the idle speed increased.
   b. If the idle speed did not increase as the screw was turned counterclockwise, turn it all the way to the right (clockwise) against its stop.

Idle mixture (1980-on)

On 1980 and later models, the idle mixture screw is set and sealed at the factory and requires no adjustment.

Carburetor Synchronization

Synchronizing the carburetors ensures that one cylinder doesn't try to run faster than the other, resulting in cut power and lower gas mileage. You can check for a rough balance by listening to the exhaust noise at idle and feeling pressure at the mufflers, but the only accurate way to synchronize the carburetors is to use a set of vacuum gauges that measure the intake vacuum of both cylinders at the same time.

1. Start the engine and warm it to normal operating temperature.

2. Adjust the idle speed as described in this chapter.

3. Remove the vacuum port plug screws or covers.

   a. **Figure 88**: 1974-1977 and 1977-1978 Deluxe A models.

   b. **Figure 89**: 1978-1979 models.

   c. **Figure 91**: On 1980-1983 models, the left-hand carburetor vacuum tap is plugged with a rubber cap and the right-hand tap is attached to the fuel tap vacuum line. Turn the automatic fuel tap to PRI (prime) after connecting the vacuum gauges.

   d. B, **Figure 90**: 1985-on.

Attach the vacuum gauges, following the manufacturer's instructions.

4. Start the engine and check that the difference between the cylinders is less than 1.2 in. (3 cm) Hg. Identical readings are desirable.

5. If the difference is greater, loosen the locknut and turn the synchronizing screw located between the carburetors (C, **Figure 90**) as required to equalize the vacuum in both cylinders. Tighten the locknut. You may have to remove the fuel tank to get at the synchronizing screw. If you can synchronize the carburetors before the float bowls

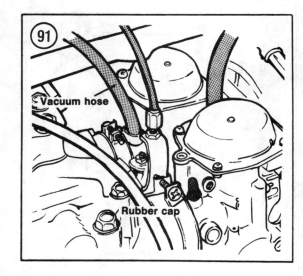

run dry, fine; if not, you'll have to supply fuel from a temporary hookup.

WARNING
When supplying fuel by temporary means, make sure the fuel tank is secure and that all fuel lines are tight—no leaks.

6. Reset the idle speed, stop the engine and disconnect the vacuum gauges. Install the vacuum plug screws and rubber covers. When installing vacuum plug screws, make sure the sealing gaskets are in good condition; replace them if necessary.

Table 1 MAINTENANCE SCHEDULE (1974-1979)

Weekly/gas Stop	•Check tire pressure cold; adjust to suit load and speed •Check brakes for a solid feel •Check brake lever play (1974-1977); adjust if necessary •Check brake pedal play; adjust if necessary •Check throttle grip for smooth opening and return •Check clutch lever play; adjust if necessary •Check for smooth but not loose steering •Lubricate drive chain every 200 miles (300 km); check and adjust play if necessary. •Inspect drive belt tension with tension gauge •Check axle, suspension, controls and linkage nuts, bolts, fasteners; tighten if necessary •Check engine oil level; add oil if necessary •Check lights and horn operation, especially brake light •Check engine for abnormal noise and leaks •Check kill switch operation
Monthly/3,000 miles (5,000 km)	•Check battery electrolyte level (check more frequently in warm weather); add distilled water if necessary •Check disc brake fluid and add if necessary

(continued)

Table 1 MAINTENANCE SCHEDULE (1974-1979) (continued)

6 months/3,000 miles (5,000 km)

- All above checks and the following:
- Clean or replace air filter
- Drain float bowls; clean fuel tap
- Clean spark plugs; adjust gap and replace if necessary
- Adjust cam chain tension (1974-1979)
- Check valve clearance; adjust if necessary
- Clean contact points; adjust gap and lube cam
- Check ignition timing; adjust if necessary
- Check throttle cables; adjust free play
- Adjust and synchronize carburetor idle
- Change engine oil and filter (filter every other time)
- Lube cables, levers, pedals, pivots, throttle grip
- Adjust clutch release
- Check tires for wear
- Check wire spokes and rim runout
- Check drive chain for wear
- Check brake pad/lining for wear
- Check steering play; adjust if necessary
- Check suspension

Yearly/6,000 mile (10,000 km)

- All above checks and the following:
- Change fork oil
- Change brake fluid
- Replace air filter
- Lubricate ignition advance
- Check and tighten all nuts, bolts, fasteners
- Lubricate swing arm pivot

2 Years/12,000 miles (20,000 km)

- All above checks and the following:
- Grease speedometer gear housing
- Grease wheel bearings
- Grease steering bearings
- Grease drum brake cam and pivot post

Table 2 MAINTENANCE SCHEDULE (1980-1983)

Weekly/gas stop

- Check tire pressure cold; adjust to suit load and speed
- Check brakes for a solid feel
- Check brake lever play; adjust if necessary
- Check brake pedal play; adjust if necessary
- Check throttle grip for smooth opening and return
- Check clutch lever play; adjust if necessary
- Check for smooth but not loose steering
- Lubricate drive chain every 200 miles (300 km); check and adjust play if necessary[1]
- Check axles, suspension, controls and linkage nuts, bolts and fasteners; tighten if necessary
- Check engine oil level; add oil if necessary
- Check lights and horn operation, especially brake light
- Check for any abnormal engine noise and leaks
- Check kill switch operation

(continued)

Table 2 MAINTENANCE SCHEDULE (1980-1983) (continued)

Monthly/3,000 miles (5,000 km)

- Check battery electrolyte level (more frequently in hot weather); add distilled water if necessary
- Check disc brake fluid level; add if necessary

6 month/3,000 miles (5,000 km)

- All above checks and the following:
- Clean or replace air filter
- Drain float bowls; clean fuel tap
- Clean spark plugs, set gap; replace if necessary
- Clean contact breaker points, adjust gap; replace if necessary[2]
- Check ignition timing; adjust if necessary[2]
- Check valve clearance; adjust if necessary
- Check and adjust carburetor cable play, idle speed mixture;
- synchronize if necessary
- Change engine oil and filter (filter @ every other oil change)
- Lube cables, levers, pedals, pivots and throttle grip
- Adjust clutch release
- Check tire wear
- Check drive chain wear[1]
- Check drive belt tension, adjust if necessary; inspect for wear[3]
- Check brake lining wear
- Check steering play; adjust if necessary
- Check suspension

Yearly/6,000 miles (10,000 km)

- All above checks and the following:
- Replace air filter element
- Change disc brake fluid
- Change fork oil
- Lubricate ignition advance
- Check and tighten all nuts, bolts and fasteners
- Grease swing arm pivot

2 years/12,000 miles (20,000 km)

- All above checks and the following:
- Grease speedometer gear housing
- Grease wheel bearings
- Grease steering bearings
- Grease drum brake camshaft
- Replace disc brake master cylinder cup and dust seal
- Replace disc brake caliper piston seal and dust seal

Every 4 years

- Replace brake hoses
- Replace fuel hoses

1. Chain-driven models.
2. Breaker-point models.
3. Belt-driven models.

Table 3 MAINTENANCE SCHEDULE (1985-ON)

Weekly/gas stop

- Check tire pressure cold; adjust to suit load and speed
- Check brakes for a solid feel
- Check brake lever play; adjust if necessary
- Check brake pedal play; adjust if necessary
- Check throttle grip for smooth opening and return

(continued)

Table 3 MAINTENANCE SCHEDULE (1985-ON) (continued)

Weekly gas stops (continued)	• Check clutch lever play; adjust if necessary • Check for smooth but not loose steering • Check axles, suspension, controls and linkage nuts, bolts and fasteners; tighten if necessary • Check engine oil level; add oil if necessary • Check lights and horn operation, especially brake light • Check for any abnormal engine noise and leaks • Check kill switch operation
Monthly/3,000 miles (5,000 km)	• Check battery electrolyte level (more frequently in hot weather); add distilled water if necessary • Check disc brake fluid level; add if necessary
6 months/3,000 miles (5,000 km)	• All above checks and the following: • Clean or replace air filter • Check and adjust carburetor cable play • Check carburetor synchronization; adjust if necessary • Check carburetor idle speed; adjust if necessary • Check spark plugs, set gap; replace if necessary • Check air suction valve • Check evaporative emission control system • Check brake lining wear • Check brake light switch operation; adjust if necessary • Check rear brake pedal free play; adjust if necessary • Adjust clutch • Check steering play; adjust if necessary • Check drive belt tension, adjust if necessary; inspect for wear • Change engine oil and filter (filter @ every other oil change) • Check tire wear • Lubricate all pivot points • Check and tighten all nuts, bolts and fasteners
Yearly/6,000 miles (10,000 km)	• Check valve clearance; adjust if necessary • Check cylinder head bolt torque • Change front fork oil • Lubricate swing arm pivot shaft • Check radiator hoses • Check fuel system hoses, clamps and all fittings
2 years/12,000 miles (20,000 km)	• Change brake fluid • Lubricate drum brake camshaft • Change coolant • Lubricate steering stem bearings • Replace master cylinder cups and seals • Replace caliper piston seal and dust seal • Replace brake cable
Every 4 years	• Replace hydraulic brake hoses • Replace fuel hoses

Table 4 TIRES AND TIRE PRESSURE (1974-1983)

Model/Tire Size	Pressure @ Load		
	0-215 lb. (0-97.5 kg)	Over 215 lb. (Over 97.5 kg)	
1982-on G, H			
Front - 3.60S-19 4PR	25 psi (175 kpa)	25 psi (175 kpa)	
Rear - 4.10S-18 4PR	28 psi (200 kpa)	32 psi (225 kpa)	
1980-on A, D and			
1979 A, D, H			
Front - 3.25S-19 4PR	25 psi (175 kpa)	25 psi (175 kpa)	
Rear - 130/90-16 67S	21 psi (150 kpa)	25 psi (175 kpa)	
1979-on B, C			
Front - 3.00S-18 4PR	25 psi (175 kpa)	25 psi (175 kpa)	
Rear - 3.50S-18 4PR	28 psi (200 kpa)	36 psi (250 kpa)	
	Pressure @ Load		
	0-280 lb. (0-127 kg)	280-330 lb. (127-150 kg)	Over 330 lb. (Over 150 kg)
1977-1978 A			
Front - 3.25S-18 4PR	32 psi (225 kpa)	32 psi (225 kpa)	32 psi (225 kpa)
Rear - 3.50S-18 6PR	32 psi (225 kpa)	36 psi (250 kpa)	40 psi (276 kpa)
	Pressure @ Load		
	0-215 lb. (0-97.5 kg)	Over 215 lb. (97.5 kg)	
1974-1977 D, S			
Front - 3.25S-18 4PR	25 psi (175 kpa)	25 psi (175 kpa)	
Rear - 3.50S-18 4PR	28 psi (200 kpa)	36 psi (250 kpa)	

Table 5 TIRES AND TIRE PRESSURE (1985-ON)

Model/tire size	Pressure @ load 0-215 lb. (0-97.5 kg)	Over 215 lb. (Over 97.5 kg)
Front-100/90-10 57S	28 psi (196 kpa)	28 psi (196 kpa)
Rear-140/90-15 70S	28 psi (196 kpa)	32 psi (221 kpa)

Table 6 STATE OF CHARGE

Specific gravity	State of charge
1.110-1.130	Discharged
1.140-1.160	Almost discharged
1.170-1.190	One-quarter charged
1.200-1.220	One-half charged
1.230-1.250	Three-quarters charged
1.260-1.280	Fully charged

3

Table 7 RECOMMENDED LUBRICANTS AND FUEL

Engine oil	Rated SE or SF
	10W-40—20° F and above*
	10W-50—20° F and above*
	20W-50—32° F and above*
Front fork oil	SAE 10W-20
Brake fluid	DOT 3
Fuel	87 pump octane (RON + MON)/2
	91 research octane (RON)
Battery	Distilled water
Cooling system	Permanent type antifreeze compounded for aluminum engines and radiator

*50 weight oil should be used when engine is operated under high ambient temperatures and heavy loads.

Table 8 ENGINE OIL CAPACITY

	Liter	U.S. qt.
1974-1977	3.0	3.2
1978-1983		
Without filter change	2.5	2.6
With filter change	2.9	3.1
1985-on		
Without filter change	2.8	2.9
With filter change	3.0	3.2

Table 9 FRONT FORK OIL CAPACITY

	Dry capacity	Oil level*	
Model	cc	in.	mm
1974-1976	160	I 13.6	I 350
1977	160	I 13.5	I 343
1978	150	R 17.1	R 435
1979-1981 B, C	150	R 17.1	R 435
1979-1981 A, D, H	150	R 18.7	R 475
1982-1983 A, D	150	R 18.5	R 470
1982-1983 G, H	175	R 16.8	R 426
1985-on	355	RC 6.4	RC 162

*On 1974-1983 models, fork oil level is checked with forks fully extended. On 1985-on models, fork oil level is checked with forks fully compressed:
  I: fork springs installed.
  R: fork springs removed.
  RC: fork springs removed, forks fully compressed.

Table 10 FRONT FORK AIR PRESSURE

	psi	kg/cm^2
KZ440		
Standard	8.5	0.6
Usable range	7-10	0.5-0.7
Maximum	36	2.5
EN450		
Standard	0	0
Usable range	*	*
Maximum	*	*

*Not specified.

Table 11 COOLING SYSTEM SPECIFICATIONS (1985-ON)

Capacity	1.4 L (1.5 qt.)
Coolant type	Antifreeze suited for aluminum engines
Mix ratio	50% purified water:50% coolant
Radiator cap pressure	0.75-1.05 kg/cm^2 (11-15 psi)
Thermostat	
Opening temperature	157.1-162.5° F (69.5-72.5° C)
Valve opening lift	Not less than 8 mm (0.315 in.) @ 203° F (95° C)

Table 12 TUNE-UP SPECIFICATIONS

Spark plugs (standard heat range)	
Type	
1974-1977*	NGK B8ES or ND W24ES
1978-1983	NGK B7ES or ND 22ES-U
1985-on**	NGK D9EA or ND X27ES-U
1985-on***	NGK DR8ES-L or ND X27ESR-U
Gap	
1974-1983	0.7-0.8 mm (0.028-0.032 in.)
1985-on	0.6-0.7 mm (0.024-0.028 in.)
Breaker points	
Gap	0.35 mm (0.014 in.)
Dwell	53% (193°)
Valve clearance (cold)	
1974-1976	0.10-0.15 mm (0.004-0.006 in.)
1977*	0.13-0.15 mm (0.005-0.006 in.)
1978-1983	0.17-0.22 mm (0.007-0.009 in.)
1985-on	
Intake	0.13-0.18 mm (0.005-0.007 in.)
Exhaust	0.18-0.23 mm (0.007-0.009 in.)
Idle speed	
1974-1983	1,100-1,300 rpm
1985-on	1,150-1,250 rpm
Idle mixture (turns out from seated)	
1974	7/8
1975	1 1/2
1976	1 5/8
1977*	1 1/2
1978	1 1/4
1979 B	1 1/4
1979 H	2 1/4
1980-1981	2 1/4
1982-1983	2 3/4
1985-on	—
Compression	
1974-1977*	
Standard	142-156 psi (10-11 kg/cm^2)
Limit	107 psi (7.5 kg/cm^2)
1978-1983	
Standard	156 psi (11 kg/cm^2)
Limit	109 psi (7.7 kg/cm^2)
1985-on	
Standard	119-185 psi (8.4-13 kg/cm^2)

*Includes 1977-1978 Deluxe A models.
**U.S. and Swiss models.
***Other than above.

CHAPTER FOUR

ENGINE (KZ400 AND KZ440)

The Kawasaki KZ400 and KZ440 are equipped with a vertical twin engine. Valves are operated by a chain-driven overhead camshaft. The crankshaft and pistons are so arranged that cylinders fire alternately; while either piston is at firing position on its compression stroke, the other piston is on its exhaust stroke.

This chapter provides complete service and overhaul procedures, including information for removal, disassembly, inspection, service and reassembly of the engine. Before starting any work, read the service hints in Chapter One. You will do a better job with this information fresh in your mind.

Tables 1-6 at the end of this chapter provide complete engine specifications.

ENGINE

Removal/Installation

1. Place motorcycle on centerstand.
2. Disconnect the negative battery cable.
3. Remove the fuel tank.
4. Disconnect the spark plug cables.
5. Disconnect the tachometer cable at the cylinder head.
6. Remove both side covers.
7. Disconnect the starter cable at the starter relay.

8. Disconnect the breather hose at the breather cover on top of the engine.
9. Remove the carburetors as described in Chapter Eight.
10. Remove the exhaust system.
11. Remove the cylinder head as described in this chapter.
12. Remove the cylinders and pistons as described in this chapter.
13. Remove the clutch as described in Chapter Six.
14. Disconnect the drive chain by removing the master link.
15. Disconnect all electrical connectors as required to remove the engine.
16. Remove the engine mount bolts (**Figure 1**, typical). Note any spacers and their position.
17. Remove the front engine mount brackets (**Figure 1**, typical).
18. Lift the engine upward and remove it from the left-hand side of the frame.
19. Installation is the reverse of these steps.
20. Tighten the engine mount bolts to the torque specifications in **Tables 4-6**.
21. Refill the engine oil as described in Chapter Three.
22. Adjust the clutch as described in Chapter Three.

CYLINDER HEAD AND CYLINDER HEAD COVER (1974-1977 AND 1977-1978 DELUXE A MODELS)

Refer to **Figure 2** when performing procedures in this section.

Cylinder Head Cover
Removal/Installation

1. Disconnect the negative battery cable.
2. Remove the fuel tank.
3. Disconnect the tachometer cable at the cylinder head.
4. Disconnect the breather hose at the breather cover.
5. Remove the ignition coils.
6. Remove the upper engine mount brackets.
7. Remove the cylinder head cover nuts (**Figure 3**). Then tap the cover lightly and lift the cover from the cylinder head (**Figure 4**).
8. Installation is the reverse of these steps, noting the following.
9. Replace the cylinder head cover gasket, if necessary.
10. Remove both spark plugs.

> *CAUTION*
> *Do not use the small inner bolt to turn the engine in Step 3 or you will damage the ignition advance mechanism.*

11. Remove the breaker points cover. Then turn the engine to the left (counterclockwise) until the "T" mark on the advance mechanism aligns with the pointer.
12. Make sure that all small O-rings are in place in the cylinder head cover. Apply gasket sealer to the large O-ring.
13. Tighten the cylinder head cover nuts in the order shown in **Figure 3** to 23 N•m (16 ft.-lb.).

Rocker Arm
Removal/Installation

1. Remove the cylinder head cover as described in this chapter.
2. Remove the side cover (**Figure 5**).
3. Remove the rocker arm locknuts, then remove the plates (**Figure 6**).
4. Carefully tape the jaws of a pair of pliers, then pull out the rocker arm shafts slightly. Remove the rocker arms as the rocker arm shafts are pulled out. See **Figure 7**.
5. Installation is the reverse of these steps, noting the following.
6. Replace all O-rings.

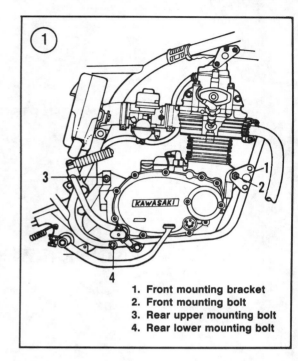

1. **Front mounting bracket**
2. **Front mounting bolt**
3. **Rear upper mounting bolt**
4. **Rear lower mounting bolt**

7. Apply engine oil to all O-ring and bearing surfaces.
8. Install the rocker arms so that their large ends face toward the camshaft. Turn each rocker arm shaft so that the punch mark on its end faces inward.
9. Tighten the rocker arm locknuts to 30 N•m (23 ft.-lb.).

Rocker Arm Inspection

1. Inspect both contact surfaces of each rocker arm for damage or uneven wear. Replace any rocker arm that exhibits such defects.
2. Measure the inside diameter of each rocker arm with a snap gauge. Replace any arm that is worn to the wear limit (**Table 1**).
3. Measure each rocker arm shaft diameter where it passes through the rocker arm. Replace any shaft excessively worn (**Table 1**).

Camshaft
Removal/Installation

1. Remove the cylinder head cover as described in this chapter.
2. Remove the chain tensioner cover, then remove the cam chain tensioner mechanism (**Figure 8**).

> *CAUTION*
> *Do not use the small inner bolt to turn the engine in Step 3 or you will damage the ignition advance mechanism.*

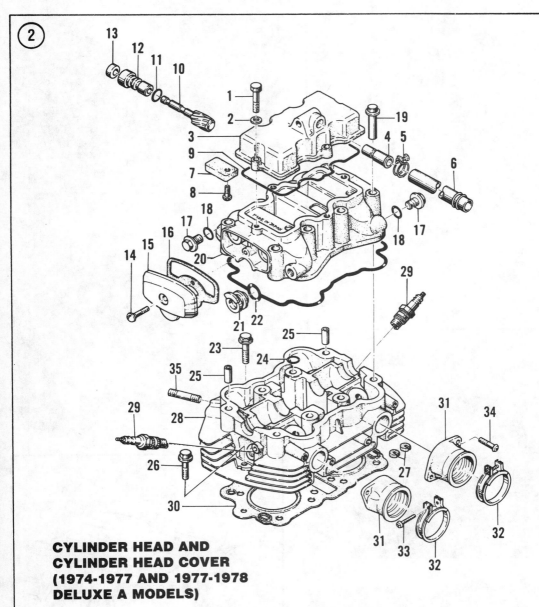

CYLINDER HEAD AND CYLINDER HEAD COVER (1974-1977 AND 1977-1978 DELUXE A MODELS)

1. Bolt
2. Washer
3. Breather cover
4. Connector
5. Clamp
6. Hose
7. Plate
8. Screw
9. O-ring
10. Tachometer gear
11. O-ring
12. Guide
13. Oil seal

14. Screw
15. Cap
16. Gasket
17. Plug
18. O-ring
19. Nut
20. Cylinder head cover
21. Plug
22. O-ring
23. Bolt
24. O-ring
25. Dowel
26. Bolt

27. Damper
28. Cylinder
29. Spark plug
30. Gasket
31. Duct
32. Clamp
33. Screw
34. Screw
35. Stud

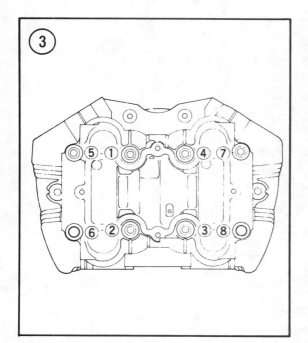

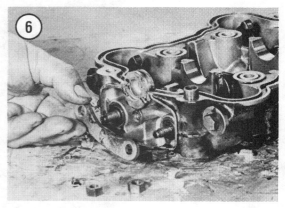

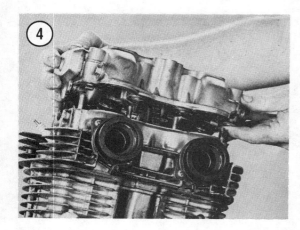

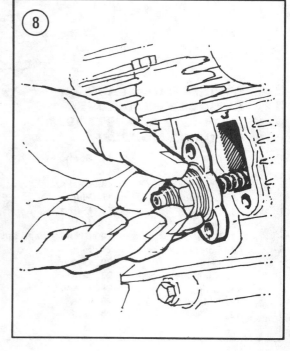

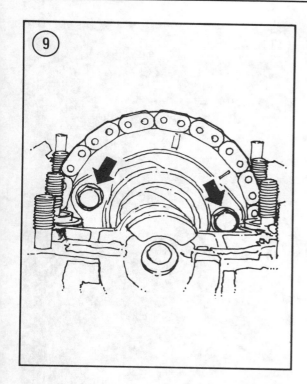

4

3. Remove the cam sprocket bolts (**Figure 9**). Turn the engine, as necessary to gain access to the bolts, with a 17 mm wrench on the large bolt under the breaker cover.

4. Slide the cam sprocket along the camshaft until the chain can be removed from the sprocket.

CAUTION
Tie a piece of wire to the cam chain to prevent it from falling into the crankcase.

5. Remove the camshaft and sprocket together (**Figure 10**).

6. Hold the cylinder head in place with the cylinder head cover nuts and several washers of suitable thickness until the camshaft is installed.

7. Lubricate all moving parts liberally with engine oil.

8. With the cylinder head in position, install the camshaft and its sprocket.

CAUTION
Follow all camshaft installation steps exactly. Severe engine damage will result if the camshaft is installed incorrectly.

9. Slide the sprocket over the camshaft so that its marked side faces to the right-hand side of the engine.

10. Slide the camshaft through the loop in the cam chain from the right-hand side of the engine, then loop the chain over the sprocket. Remove the wire from the cam chain.

11. Turn the engine until the "T" mark on the ignition advance mechanism aligns with the index pointer (**Figure 11**). Then verify engine positioning by turning engine exactly 90° counterclockwise. Angle on centrifugal advance mechanism will align with index pointer (**Figure 12**).

12. Remove chain from sprocket, then turn camshaft until notch on right end points upward (**Figure 13**).

13. Turn sprocket until arrow which has no letter adjoining it is parallel to the cylinder head surface and pointing toward the front of the engine (**Figure 14**).

14. Fit the cam chain over the sprocket. Then slide the sprocket into position on the camshaft. It is normal that the bolt holes are not aligned at this time.

15. Hold the camshaft in position, then turn the engine until the camshaft sprocket holes align with corresponding holes in camshaft. Note that sprocket will fit only one way.

16. Apply Loctite 242 (blue) to the sprocket bolts, then tighten them to 14-16 N•m (10-11.5 ft.-lb.).

17. Turn the engine counterclockwise until the "T" mark on the advance mechanism aligns with the index pointer. Check that the arrow next to the "T" mark points to the front of the engine and is parallel to the cylinder head surface. Notch on the right end of the cam must face up.

18. Remove the cylinder head cover bolts and the temporary spacer washers installed in Step 6.

19. Remove the tachometer gear and caps from the cylinder head cover.

20. Turn the engine counterclockwise until the "T" mark on the ignition advance unit aligns with its index pointer (**Figure 11**).

21. Be sure that all O-rings are in place. Apply gasket sealer to the large outer O-ring to hold it in position.

22. Place the cylinder head cover in position.

23. Tighten the cylinder head cover bolts as described in this chapter.

24. If removed, apply a small quantity of grease to the tachometer gear, then install gear.

25. Install the cam chain tensioner. Tighten the bolts securely.

26. Adjust the cam chain tensioner as described in Chapter Three.

27. Adjust the valves as described in Chapter Three.

Camshaft Inspection

1. Measure the height of each cam lobe with a micrometer (**Figure 15**). Replace the camshaft if any lobe is worn beyond the service limits in **Table 1**.

2. Measure the diameter of each camshaft journal. Replace the camshaft if any journal is worn beyond the service limits in **Table 1**.

3. Place the camshaft outer bearings in V-blocks or some other suitable centering device, then measure runout at its center (**Figure 16**). Replace the camshaft if runout exceeds the service limit (**Table 1**).

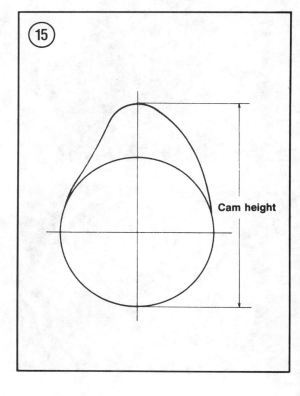

Cam height

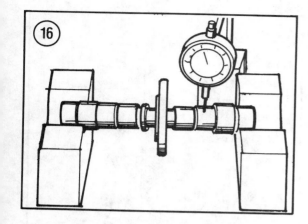

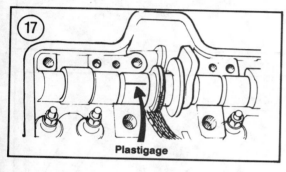

Plastigage

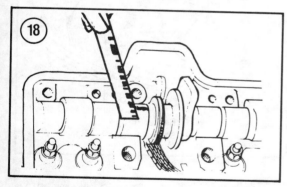

Camshaft Bearing
Clearance Measurement

This procedure requires the use of a Plastigage set. The camshaft must be installed into the cylinder head. Before installation, wipe all oil residue from each cam bearing journal and bearing surface in the cylinder head and all camshaft holders.

1. Install the camshaft into the cylinder head.
2. Wipe all oil from cam bearing journals before using the Plastigage material.
3. Place a strip of Plastigage material on top of each cam bearing journal, parallel to the cam, as shown in **Figure 17**.
4. Install and tighten the cylinder head cover as described in this chapter.

NOTE
Do not rotate the camshaft with the Plastigage material in place.

5. Remove the cylinder head cover bolts in the crisscross pattern shown in **Figure 3**. Remove the cylinder head cover carefully.
6. Measure the width of the flattened Plastigage according to manufacturer's instructions (**Figure 18**).
7. Standard clearance is 0.033 mm (0.0013 in.). Replace the camshaft and/or cylinder head and cylinder head cover if clearance exceeds the service limit in **Table 1**.

CAUTION
Remove all particles of Plastigage material from all cylinder head cover bearing journals and camshaft bearing journals. This material must not be left in the engine as it can plug up a small oil control orifice and cause severe engine damage.

Cylinder Head
Removal/Installation

1. Remove the exhaust pipes.
2. Remove the carburetors as described in Chapter Eight.
3. Remove the camshaft as described in this chapter.
4. Remove the cylinder head mounting bolts. Then tap the cylinder head with a plastic tipped hammer and remove it (**Figure 19**).
5. Secure the cam chain with a piece of wire to keep it from falling into the crankcase.
6. Remove the cylinder head gasket and 2 O-rings.
7. Installation is the reverse of these steps, noting the following.

8. Clean the cylinder head and cylinder mating surfaces of all gasket material.

9. Make sure the 2 dowel pins are installed at their correct position (large arrows, **Figure 20**).

10. Install a new cylinder head gasket and 2 new O-rings. See **Figure 20**.

11. Align the cylinder head with the cylinder studs. Then guide the cam chain up through the cylinder head and lower the cylinder head onto the cylinder.

12. Install the camshaft as described in this chapter.

> *NOTE*
> *Secure the cam chain with a piece of wire until the engine is reassembled.*

Cylinder Head Inspection

1. Clean the cylinder head mating surfaces thoroughly.

2. Place a straightedge across the cylinder head-to-cylinder mating surface at several points. Measure warpage by inserting a feeler gauge between the straightedge and cylinder head at each location (**Figure 21**). If the cylinder head warpage exceeds the service limit (**Table 1**), replace the cylinder head.

**CYLINDER HEAD
AND CYLINDER HEAD COVER
(1978-1983)**

**Cylinder Head Cover
Removal/Installation**

1. Remove the fuel tank.

2. Remove the ignition coils.

3. Remove the upper engine mount brackets.

4. Slip the breather hose out of its fitting on the cylinder head cover.

5. Remove the breather cover bolts and remove the breather cover.

6. Remove the contact breaker cover from the right-hand side.

> *CAUTION*
> *Do not use the small inner bolt to turn the engine or you will damage the ignition advance mechansim.*

7. Rotate the engine using a 17 mm wrench on the bolt on the end of the crankshaft (A, **Figure 22**). Rotate the crankshaft until the "T" mark on the ignition advance mechanism aligns with the index pointer (B, **Figure 22**). This indicates that one of the cylinders is at top dead center (TDC).

8. Remove the screw securing the tachometer pinion holder and remove the pinion and holder from the cylinder head.

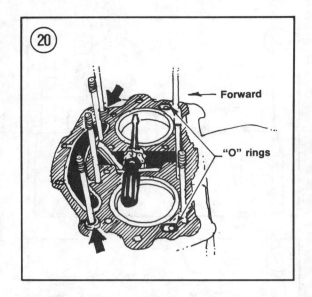

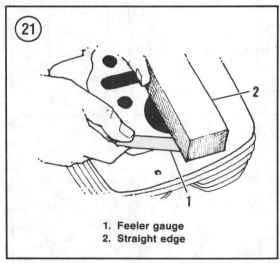

1. Feeler gauge
2. Straight edge

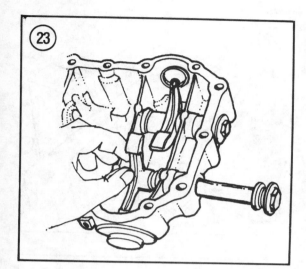

9. Remove the cylinder head cover bolts.

10. Tap the cover with a plastic tipped hammer. Lift the cover off the cylinder head.

11. Installation is the reverse of these steps, noting the following.

12. Clean the cylinder head and cover mating surfaces.

13. Make sure the tachometer pinion is still removed from the cylinder head cover and that the 2 dowel pins are in position.

14. Check that the crankshaft is still positioned at TDC. Refer to Step 7.

15. Apply a non-hardening gasket cement to both mating surfaces and install the cylinder head cover and its bolts.

16. Finger-tighten all bolts at first, then tighten the 8 mm bolts to 25 N•m (18 ft.-lb.). Tighten the 6 mm bolts to 10 N•m (7 ft.-lb.).

17. Apply a small amount of high temperature grease to the tachometer pinion shaft and install it and the holder into the cylinder head. Install the holder stop screw.

18. Install all parts previously removed.

Rocker Arm
Removal/Inspection/Installation

1. Remove the cylinder head cover as described in this chapter.

> *NOTE*
> *Before removal, mark each rocker arm and shaft with an R or L (right- or left-hand cylinder) and an I or E (intake and exhaust). This will avoid any mixup of parts upon installation.*

2. Unscrew the rocker arm shaft and withdraw it and the flat washer (**Figure 23**).

3. Lift up on the rocker arms as the shaft is withdrawn and remove them.

4. Wash all parts in solvent and allow to dry.

5. Inspect both contact surfaces of each rocker arm for damage or uneven wear. Replace any rocker arm that exhibits such defects. Measure the inside diameter of each rocker arm. Replace any rocker arm that is worn to the service limit (**Table 2** or **Table 3**).

6. Measure diameter of each rocker arm shaft where it passes through the rocker arm. Replace any shaft worn to the service limit in **Table 2** or **Table 3**.

> *NOTE*
> *Don't forget the flat washer under the head of the rocker arm shaft.*

7. Apply assembly oil to all bearing surfaces. Correctly position the rocker arm (refer to identification marks made during removal), and slide the rocker arm shaft into it. Screw the rocker arm shaft in and tighten to 25 N•m (18 ft.-lb.). Repeat for all shafts.

8. Install the cylinder head cover as described in this chapter.

Camshaft/Cylinder Head
Removal

1. Remove the cylinder head cover as described in this chapter.

2. Remove the cam chain tensioner as described in this chapter.

> *CAUTION*
> *Do not use the small inner bolt to turn the engine or you will damage the ignition advance mechanism.*

3. Remove the cam sprocket bolts (**Figure 24**). Turn the engine, as necessary to expose the bolts, with the 17 mm bolt on the end of the crankshaft under the contact breaker cover.

4. Slide the cam sprocket along the camshaft until the chain can be removed from the sprocket.

5. Remove the bolts securing the 3 cam bearing caps in a crisscross pattern and remove them.

> *NOTE*
> *Secure the cam chain with a piece of wire.*

6. Remove the cam and sprocket together.

7. Remove the banjo bolt securing the oil pipe upper end to the cylinder head (**Figure 25**). Hold the upper end of the pipe stationary with a wrench while removing the bolt.

8. Loosen the 8 cylinder head nuts a little at a time in the sequence shown in **Figure 26**. Remove all nuts and washers.

9. Tap around the cylinder head with a plastic or rubber mallet to free the cylinder head. Pull the head straight up and off the cylinder head crankcase studs.

Camshaft Inspection

1. Measure the height of each cam lobe with a micrometer (**Figure 15**). Replace the camshaft if any lobe is worn beyond the service limit in **Table 2** or **Table 3**.

2. Measure the diameter of each camshaft journal. Replace camshaft if any journal is worn (**Table 2** or **Table 3**).

3. Place the camshaft outer bearings in V-blocks or some other suitable centering device, then measure runout at its center (**Figure 16**). Replace the camshaft if runout is excessive (**Table 2** or **Table 3**).

Camshaft Bearing
Clearance Measurement

This procedure requires the use of a Plastigage set. The camshaft must be installed into the cylinder head. Before installation, wipe all oil residue from each cam bearing journal and bearing surface in the cylinder head and all camshaft holders.

1. Install the camshaft into the cylinder head.

2. Wipe all oil from cam bearing journals before using the Plastigage material.

3. Place a strip of Plastigage material on top of each cam bearing journal, parallel to the cam, as shown in **Figure 17**.

4. Place all cam bearing caps into their correct positions. The arrow on the caps must face forward (**Figure 27**). Tighten the cap bolts to 12 N•m (8.5 ft.-lb.) in the sequence shown in **Figure 27**.

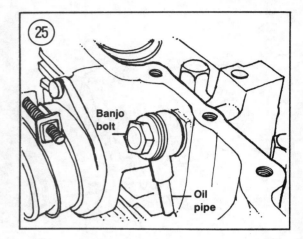

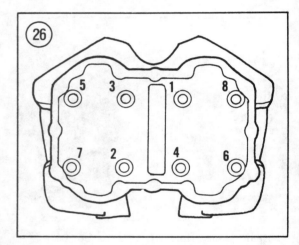

> *NOTE*
> *Do not rotate the camshaft with the Plastigage material in place.*

5. Remove the camshaft cap bolts in a crisscross pattern shown in **Figure 27**. Remove the caps carefully.

6. Measure the width of the flattened Plastigage according to manufacturer's instructions (**Figure 18**).

7. Replace the camshaft and/or cylinder head and camshaft caps if clearance exceeds the service limit in **Table 2** or **Table 3**.

> *CAUTION*
> *Remove all particles of Plastigage material from all cylinder head cover bearing journals and camshaft bearing journals. This material must not be left in the engine as it can plug up a small oil control orifice and cause severe engine damage.*

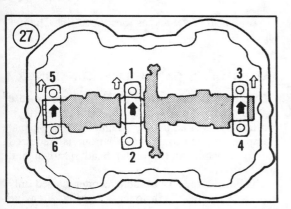

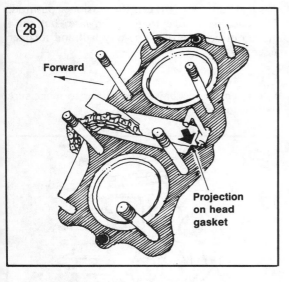

Projection
on head
gasket

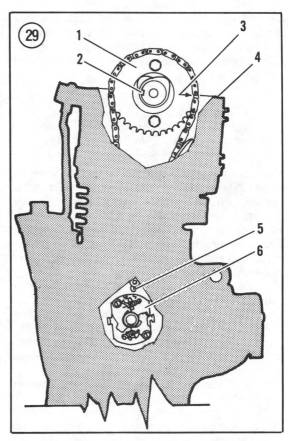

Cylinder Head Inspection

1. Clean the cylinder head mating surfaces thoroughly.

2. Place a straightedge across the cylinder head-to-cylinder mating surface at several points. Measure warpage by inserting a feeler gauge between the straightedge and cylinder head at each location (**Figure 21**). If the cylinder head warpage exceeds 0.25 mm (0.010 in.), replace the cylinder head.

Cylinder Head and Camshaft Installation

1. Install both cylinder head locating dowels and a new cylinder head gasket.

NOTE
*Install the cylinder head gasket with the projection, in the area of the cam chain opening, located at the rear left-hand side. See **Figure 28**.*

2. Install the cylinder head. Be careful not to bend the oil pipe. Pull the cam chain up through the opening in the head and secure it with wire to prevent it from falling into the crankcase.

3. Install the 8 copper washers and 8 cylinder head nuts. Tighten the nuts in 2 steps using the torque sequence shown in **Figure 26**. Tighten the first step to 20 N•m (14 ft.-lb.), then to 40 N•m (29 ft.-lb.).

4. Install the banjo bolt into the upper end of the oil pipe using new washers on each end of the pipe. Hold the upper end of the pipe with a wrench and tighten the banjo bolt to 20 N•m (14.5 ft.-lb.).

5. If the oil receiver was removed, reinstall it with the arrow facing toward the front of the bike. Apply Loctite 242 (blue) to the screw threads before installation.

6. Apply assembly oil to all bearing surfaces of the cam, cam bearing caps and bearing surfaces on the cylinder head.

7. Install the cam through the cam chain from the right-hand side. The end of the cam with the notch must be on the right-hand side of engine.

8. Install the cam sprocket (1, **Figure 29**) from the right-hand side so that the side with the arrow

faces the right-hand side of the engine. Do not slide the sprocket into its final position at this time.

9. Check to make sure that the engine is still at TDC. Refer to **Figure 29**, items 5 and 6, and readjust if necessary.

> *CAUTION*
> *Be sure to pull the cam chain taut when rotating the crankshaft to avoid damage to the chain and timing sprocket on the crankshaft.*

10. Position the cam sprocket so that its arrow (3, **Figure 29**) is pointing to the front of the bike and is aligned with the cylinder head surface (4, **Figure 29**). Install the cam chain onto the sprocket.

11. Slide the sprocket and chain up into its correct position. Turn the cam so that the notch on the right-hand end is facing toward the rear (2, **Figure 29**). Hold the sprocket stationary.

12. Apply Loctite 242 (blue) to the sprocket bolts and tighten to 15 N•m (11 ft.-lb.).

13. Install all 6 cam bearing cap dowel pins and install the 3 cam bearing caps. The arrow on the cap must face forward (**Figure 27**). Tighten the cap bolts to 12 N•m (8.5 ft.-lb.) in the sequence shown in **Figure 27**.

14. Install the cam chain tensioner assembly as described in this chapter.

15. Rotate the crankshaft *counterclockwise* until the cam sprocket arrow is again facing to the front of the engine. Check that all the timing marks (5 and 6, **Figure 29**) again align. If they do, cam timing is correct; if not, correct by repeating Steps 9-14 until the timing is correct.

> *CAUTION*
> *Follow all camshaft installation steps exactly. If the camshaft is installed incorrectly, it could cause engine failure or severe engine damage.*

16. Install the cylinder head cover as described in this chapter.

17. Adjust the valves as described in Chapter Three.

AUTOMATIC CAM CHAIN TENSIONER

Late KZ400 models and all KZ440 models use an automatic cam chain tensioner that is continually self-adjusting (**Figure 30**). Special attention to tensioner installation is required during camshaft and cylinder head removal and installation.

The bolt on the end of the tensioner is used only to lock the tensioner during engine disassembly/assembly. During normal operation, this lockbolt doesn't touch the tensioner pushrod. The pushrod is free to move inward, but can't move out because of a one-way ball and retainer assembly.

Removal

1. Loosen the lockbolt several turns to make sure the tensioner pushrod is free.

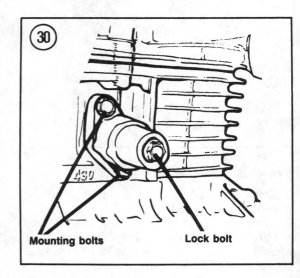

Mounting bolts   **Lock bolt**

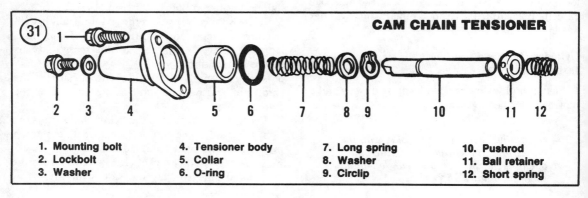

CAM CHAIN TENSIONER

1. Mounting bolt
2. Lockbolt
3. Washer
4. Tensioner body
5. Collar
6. O-ring
7. Long spring
8. Washer
9. Circlip
10. Pushrod
11. Ball retainer
12. Short spring

2. Remove the 2 tensioner mounting bolts and the tensioner assembly.

CAUTION
Do not loosen the tensioner mounting bolts without removing, resetting and locking the tensioner. If you don't reset the tensioner, the pushrod will overextend and lock, damaging the cam chain when the mounting bolts are tightened.

Resetting and Installation

1. See **Figure 31**. Loosen the lockbolt a few turns.
2. If disassembled, put the long spring and flat washer on the pushrod, then push the pushrod into the tensioner body, compressing the spring and aligning the flats on the end of the rod with the recess in the body. Thread the lockbolt into the pushrod to keep it in the compressed position (**Figure 32**).

WARNING
Do not loosen the lockbolt before installing the tensioner. The pushrod could spring out forcefully.

3. Hold the tensioner rod up and drop the retainer and ball assembly onto the pushrod, then install the short spring.
4. Install the locked tensioner assembly and O-ring on the cylinder block. Tighten the mounting bolts.
5. Listen carefully as you loosen the lockbolt. You should hear the tensioner rod spring out against the cam chain and take up the chain slack.
6. Tighten the lockbolt; it should turn freely all the way until the bolt head seats against the tensioner body. If it doesn't, you must remove, reset and re-install the tensioner as described in this section.

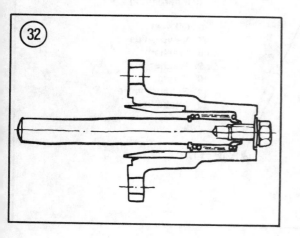

(32)

VALVES AND VALVE COMPONENTS

Refer to **Figure 33** or **Figure 34** for this procedure.
1. Remove the cylinder head as described in this chapter.
2. Install a valve spring compressor squarely over the valve retainer with other end of tool placed against valve head (**Figure 35**).
3. Tighten valve spring compressor until the split valve keepers separate. Lift out split keepers with needlenose pliers.
4. Gradually loosen valve spring compressor and remove from head.

CAUTION
*Remove any burrs from the valve stem grooves before removing the valve (**Figure 36**). Otherwise the valve guides will be damaged.*

CAUTION
All component parts of each valve assembly must be kept together. Do not mix with like components from other valves or excessive wear may result.

5. Remove the valve springs and valves in the order shown in **Figure 33** or **Figure 34**.
6. Repeat Steps 2-5 and remove remaining valve(s).

Inspection

1. Clean valves with a wire brush and solvent.
2. Inspect the contact surface of each valve for burning (**Figure 37**). Minor roughness and pitting can be removed by lapping the valve as described in this chapter. Excessive unevenness to the contact surface is an indication that the valve is not serviceable. The contact surface of the valve may be ground on a valve grinding machine, but it is best to replace a burned or damaged valve with a new one.
3. Inspect the valve stem for wear and roughness and measure the vertical runout of the valve stem as shown in **Figure 38**. The runout should not exceed specifications (**Tables 1-3**).
4. Measure valve stem for wear with a micrometer (**Figure 39**). Compare with specifications in **Tables 1-3**.
5. Remove all carbon and varnish from the valve guides with a stiff spiral wire brush.

NOTE
Step 6 requires special measuring equipment. If you do not have the required measuring devices, proceed to Step 7.

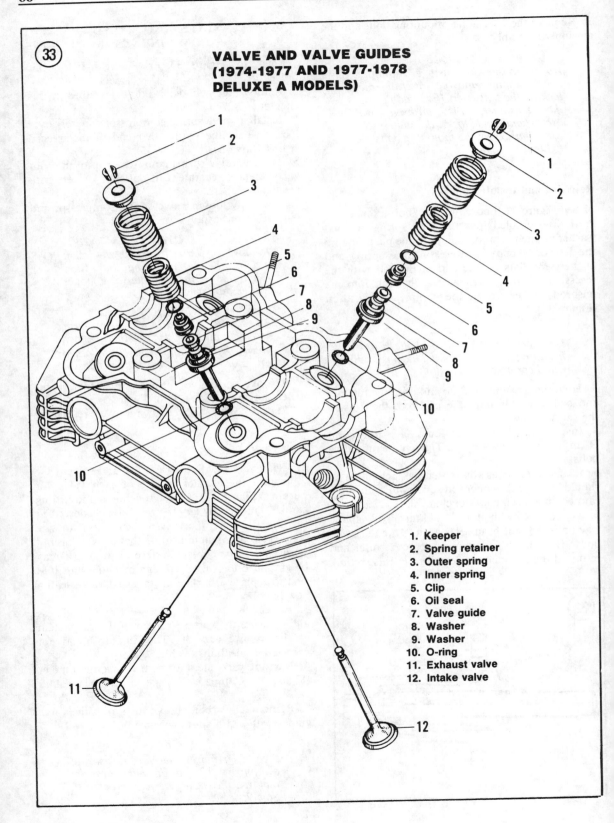

33

**VALVE AND VALVE GUIDES
(1974-1977 AND 1977-1978
DELUXE A MODELS)**

1. Keeper
2. Spring retainer
3. Outer spring
4. Inner spring
5. Clip
6. Oil seal
7. Valve guide
8. Washer
9. Washer
10. O-ring
11. Exhaust valve
12. Intake valve

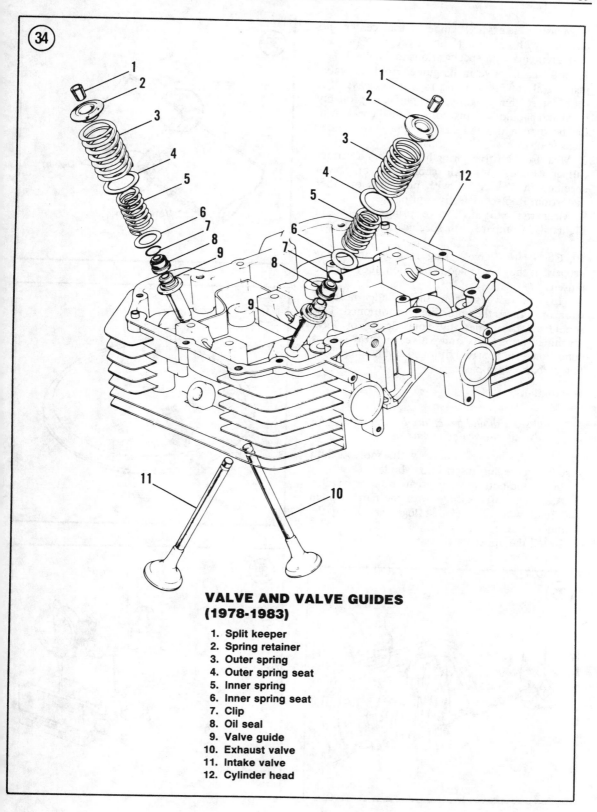

VALVE AND VALVE GUIDES
(1978-1983)

1. Split keeper
2. Spring retainer
3. Outer spring
4. Outer spring seat
5. Inner spring
6. Inner spring seat
7. Clip
8. Oil seal
9. Valve guide
10. Exhaust valve
11. Intake valve
12. Cylinder head

6. Measure each valve guide at top, center and bottom with a small hole gauge. Compare measurements with specifications in **Tables 1-3**.

7. Insert each valve in its guide. Hold the valve just slightly off its seat and rock it sideways. If it rocks more than slightly, the guide is probably worn and should be replaced. As a final check, take the head to a dealer and have the valve guides measured.

8. Measure the valve spring heights with a vernier caliper (**Figure 40**). All should be of length specified in **Tables 1-3** with no bends or other distortion. Replace defective springs.

9. Measure the tilt of all valve springs as shown in **Figure 41**. Compare with specifications in **Tables 1-3**.

10. Check the valve spring retainer and valve keepers. If they are in good condition, they may be reused.

11. Inspect valve seats in the cylinder head. If worn or burned, they must be reconditioned. This should be performed by your dealer or local machine shop. Seats and valves in near-perfect condition can be reconditioned by lapping with fine carborundum paste.

Installation

NOTE
Oil seals should be replaced whenever a valve is removed or replaced.

1. Coat the valve stems with molybdenum disulfide paste and insert into cylinder head.

2. Install the bottom spring seat and a new seal.

3. Assemble valve springs with the narrow pitch end (end with coils closest together) facing the cylinder head.

4. Install the upper valve seat.

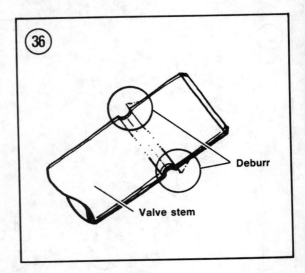

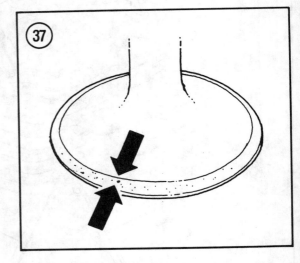

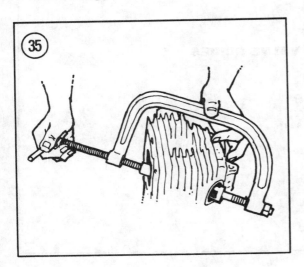

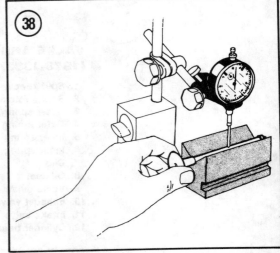

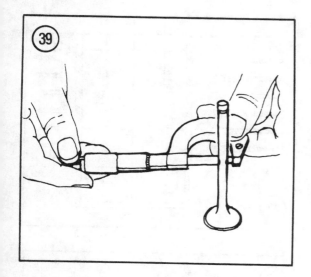

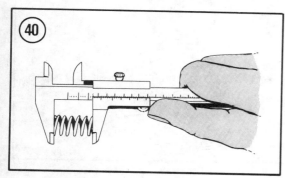

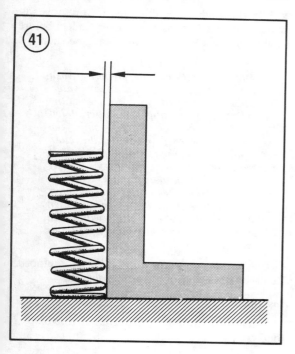

5. Push down on the upper valve seat with the valve spring compressor and install valve keepers. After releasing tension from compressor, examine valve keepers and make sure they are seated correctly.

6. Repeat Steps 1-5 for remaining valve(s).

Valve Guide Replacement

When guides are worn so that there is excessive stem-to-guide clearance or valve tipping, they must be replaced. Replace all, even if only one is worn. This job should only be done by a Kawasaki dealer or qualified specialist as special tools are required.

Valve Seat Reconditioning

This job is best left to your dealer or local machine shop. They have the special equipment and knowledge for this exacting job. You can still save considerable money by removing the cylinder head and taking just the head to the shop.

Valve Lapping

Valve lapping is a simple operation which can restore the valve seal without machining if the amount of wear or distortion is not too great.

1. Smear a light coating of fine grade valve lapping compound on seating surface of valve.

2. Insert the valve into the head.

3. Wet the suction cup of the lapping stick and stick it onto the head of the valve. Lap the valve to the seat by spinning the lapping stick in both directions. Every 5 to 10 seconds, rotate the valve 180° in the valve seat. Lap only enough to achieve a precise seating ring around valve head.

4. Closely examine valve seat in cylinder head. It should be smooth and even with a smooth, polished seating "ring."

5. Thoroughly clean the valves and cylinder head in solvent to remove all grinding compound. Any compound left on the valves or the cylinder head will end up in the engine and will cause excessive wear and damage.

6. After the lapping has been completed and the valve assemblies have been reinstalled into the head the valve seal should be tested. Check the seal of each valve by pouring solvent into each of the intake and exhaust ports. There should be no leakage past the seat. If leakage occurs, combustion chamber will appear wet. If fluid leaks past any of the seats, disassemble that valve assembly and repeat the lapping procedure until there is no leakage.

CYLINDER

Removal

1. Remove the cylinder head as described in this chapter.
2. Remove the head gaskets and dowel pins.
3. Loosen the cylinder by tapping around the perimeter with a rubber or plastic mallet.

> *CAUTION*
> *On models so equipped, be careful not to damage the oil pipe during cylinder removal.*

4. Pull the cylinder straight up and off the pistons and cylinder studs.

> *NOTE*
> *Be sure to keep the cam chain wired up to prevent it from falling into the lower crankcase.*

5. Stuff clean shop rags into the crankcase opening to prevent objects from falling into the crankcase.
6. If the cam chain guide requires replacement, perform the following:
   a. Push the camshaft chain guide up slightly and remove the upper guide pin (A, **Figure 42**).
   b. Withdraw the guide (B, **Figure 42**) from the bottom of the cylinder block.

Inspection

1. Wash the cylinder bore in solvent to remove any oil and carbon particles. The bore must be cleaned thoroughly before attempting any measurement as incorrect readings may be obtained.
2. Measure the cylinder bore, with a cylinder gauge or inside micrometer at the points shown in **Figure 43**.
3. Measure in 2 axes—in line with the piston pin and at 90° to the pin. If the taper or out-of-round is greater than specifications (**Tables 1-3**), the cylinders must be rebored to the next oversize and new pistons and rings installed. Rebore both cylinders even though only one may be worn.

> *NOTE*
> *The new pistons should be obtained first before the cylinders are bored so that the pistons can be measured; each cylinder must be bored to match one piston only. Piston-to-cylinder clearance is specified in **Tables 1-3**.*

4. If the cylinder(s) are not worn past the service limits, check the bore carefully for scratches or gouges. The bore still may require boring and reconditioning.

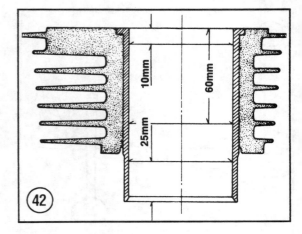

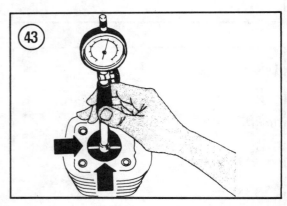

5. If the cylinders require reboring, remove all dowel pins and O-rings from the cylinders before leaving them with the dealer or machine shop.

> *NOTE*
> *After having the cylinders rebored, wash them thoroughly in hot soapy water. This is the best way to clean the cylinders of all fine grit material left from the bore job. After washing the cylinders, run a clean white cloth through them; the cloth should show no traces of dirt or other debris. If the rag is dirty, the cylinders are not clean and must be rewashed. After the cylinders are thoroughly cleaned, dry and then lubricate the cylinder walls with clean engine oil to prevent the cylinder liners from rust.*

6. Check the 2 cylinder O-rings, if so equipped. Replace the O-rings if worn or damaged.

Installation

1. If removed, install the camshaft chain guide as follows:

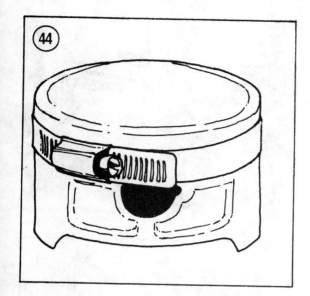

the cylinders and pistons liberally with engine oil before installation.

> *NOTE*
> *Once the cylinder is placed over the studs, run the chain and wire up through it.*

8. Compress each ring as it enters the cylinder with your fingers or by using aircraft type hose clamps of appropriate diameter. See **Figure 44**.

> *CAUTION*
> *Don't tighten the clamp any more than necessary to compress the rings. If the rings can't slip through easily, the clamp may gouge the rings.*

9. Remove the piston holding fixtures and push the cylinder all the way down.
10. Install the cylinder head and camshaft as described in this chapter.

PISTONS AND PISTON RINGS

Piston
Removal/Installation

1. Remove the cylinder head and cylinder as described in this chapter.
2. Stuff the crankcase with clean shop rags to prevent objects from falling into the crankcase.
3. Lightly mark the piston with a L (left) or R (right) so they will be installed into the correct cylinder.
4. Remove the piston rings as described in this chapter.
5. Remove the circlips from the piston pin bore (**Figure 45**).
6. Remove the piston pin by pushing it out (**Figure 46**). If the pin is difficult to push out, use a homemade tool as shown in **Figure 47**.
7. Inspect the piston as described in this chapter.
8. Coat the connecting rod bushing, piston pin and piston with assembly oil.
9. Place the piston over the connecting rod. If you are installing old parts, make sure the piston is installed on the correct rod as marked during removal. The arrow on the piston crown should face to the front of the engine.
10. Insert the piston pin and tap it with a plastic mallet until it starts into the connecting rod bushing. Hold the rod so that the lower end does not take any shock. If the pin does not slide easily, use the homemade tool (**Figure 47**) but eliminate the piece of pipe. Push the pin in until it is centered in the piston.
11. Install *new* circlips in the piston bore.

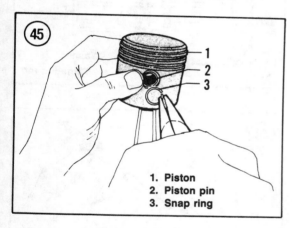

1. Piston
2. Piston pin
3. Snap ring

a. On 1978-on models, position the camshaft chain guide with the side projections facing toward the left-hand side of the engine.
b. Make sure the lower guide pins are on the guide.
c. Install the camshaft chain guide from the bottom and install the upper guide pin.
2. If the base gasket is stuck to the bottom of the cylinder it should be removed and the cylinder surface cleaned thoroughly.
3. Check that the top cylinder surface is clean of all old gasket material.
4. Install the 2 dowel pins onto the crankcase.
5. Install a new cylinder base gasket to the crankcase. Make sure all holes align.
6. Install a piston holding fixture under each piston.
7. Carefully install the cylinder onto the cylinder studs and slide it down over the pistons. Lubricate

12. Install rings as described in this chapter.

13. Repeat Steps 1-12 for the opposite piston.

Piston Inspection

1. Carefully clean the carbon from the piston crown with a soft scraper. Do not remove or damage the carbon ridge around the circumference of the piston above the top ring.

CAUTION
Do not wire brush piston skirts.

2. Examine each ring groove for burrs, dented edges and wide wear. Pay particular attention to the top compression ring groove, as it usually wears more than the others.

3. Measure piston-to-cylinder clearance as described under *Piston Clearance* in this chapter.

4. If damage or wear indicate piston replacement, select a new piston as described under *Piston Clearance* in this chapter.

Piston Clearance

1. Make sure the piston and cylinder walls are clean and dry.

2. Measure the inside diameter of the cylinder at a point 13 mm (1/2 in.) from the upper edge with a bore gauge.

3. Measure piston diameter at right angles to the piston pin (**Figure 48**). This measurement should be made 5 mm (0.2 in.) from the bottom of the piston.

4. Subtract the piston diameter from the bore diameter; the difference is piston-to-cylinder clearance. Compare to specifications in **Tables 1-3**. If clearance is excessive, both pistons should be replaced and the cylinders rebored.

NOTE
The new pistons should be obtained before the cylinders are rebored so the pistons can be measured individually; slight manufacturing tolerances must be taken into account to determine the actual bore size.

Piston Ring
Removal/Installation

WARNING
The edges of all piston rings are very sharp. Be careful when handling them to avoid cut fingers.

1. Measure the side clearance of each ring in its groove with a flat feeler gauge (**Figure 49**) and compare with the specifications listed in **Tables**

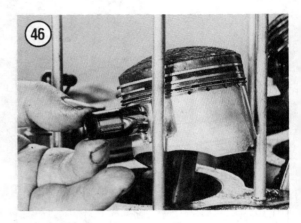

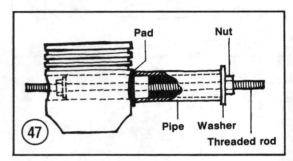

Pad   Nut
Pipe   Washer
Threaded rod

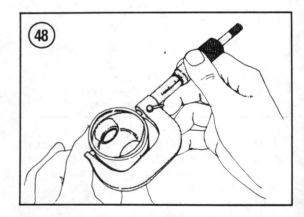

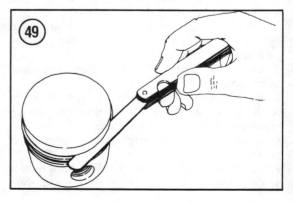

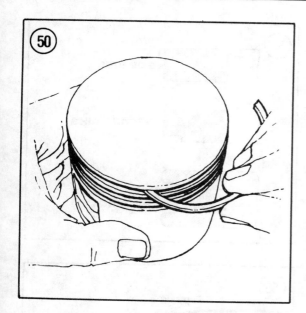

(50)

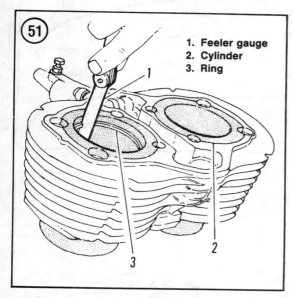

(51)

1. Feeler gauge
2. Cylinder
3. Ring

1-3. If the clearance is greater than specified, the rings must be replaced. If the clearance is still excessive with the new rings, the piston must be replaced.

2. Remove the old rings with a ring expander tool or by spreading the ring ends with your thumbs and lifting the rings up evenly.

3. Using a broken piston ring, remove all carbon from the piston ring grooves (**Figure 50**).

4. Inspect grooves carefully for burrs, nicks, or broken or cracked lands. Replace piston if necessary.

5. Check end gap of each ring. To check ring, insert the ring into the bottom of the cylinder bore and square it with the cylinder wall by tapping it with the piston. The ring should be pushed in about 15 mm (5/8 in.). Insert a feeler gauge as shown in **Figure 51** . Compare gap with **Tables 1-3**. Replace ring if gap is too large. If the gap on the new ring is smaller than specified, hold a small file in a vise, grip the ends of the ring with your fingers and enlarge the gap.

NOTE
The oil control ring expander spacer is unmeasurable. If the oil control ring rails show wear, both rails and the spacer should be replaced as a set.

6. Roll each ring around its piston groove as shown in **Figure 52** to check for binding. Minor binding may be cleaned up with a fine-cut file.

7. Check the oil control holes in the piston (**Figure 53**) for carbon or oil sludge buildup. Clean the holes with a small diameter drill bit.

8. Install the piston rings in the order shown in **Figure 54** (KZ400) or **Figure 55** (KZ440).

NOTE
Install all rings with the manufacturer's markings facing up.

9. Install the piston rings—first the bottom, then the middle, then the top ring—by carefully

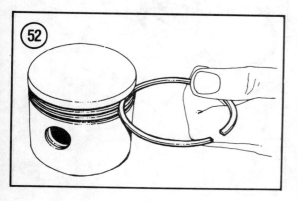

(52)

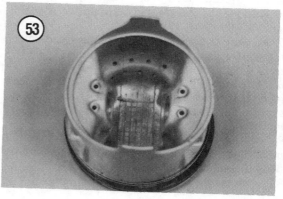

(53)

spreading the ends with your thumbs or with a ring expander tool (**Figure 56**) and slipping the rings over the top of the piston. Remember that the piston rings must be installed with the marks on them facing up toward the top of the piston or there is the possibility of oil pumping past the rings.

10. Install oil ring in oil ring groove with a ring expander tool or by spreading the ends with your thumbs.

11. Make sure the rings are seated completely in their grooves all the way around the piston and that the end gaps are distributed around the piston as shown in **Figure 57**. It is important that the ring gaps are not aligned with each other when installed to prevent compression pressures from escaping past them.

12. If installing oversize compression rings, check the number to make sure the correct rings are being installed. The ring numbers should be the same as the piston oversize number.

13. If new rings are installed, measure the side clearance of each ring (**Figure 49**) in its groove and compare to dimensions in **Tables 1-3**.

OIL PUMP (1974-1977 AND 1977-1978 DELUXE A MODELS)

Removal/Installation

Refer to **Figure 58** for this procedure.

1. Remove the clutch and primary chain as described in Chapter Six.

2. To remove the oil pump, remove its retaining screw and withdraw the pump assembly (**Figure 59**).

3. Installation is the reverse of these steps. Replace all O-rings during installation.

Inspection

1. Remove the clip (1, **Figure 58**) and washer (2).

2. Disassemble the outer (3) and inner (7) pump bodies.

3. Remove the inner (4) and outer (5) rotors.

4. Remove the pin (8) and separate the gear (9) and the inner body (7).

5. Measure clearance between the inner and outer rotors. If clearance exceeds specifications (**Table 1**), replace both rotors.

6. Place a straightedge across both rotors and the pump body. If clearance between the rotor and the straightedge exceeds specifications (**Table 1**), replace both rotors.

7. Measure clearance between the outer rotor and pump body. Replace the outer rotor or the pump body if clearance is excessive (**Table 1**).

8. Assemble the oil pump by reversing steps 1-4.

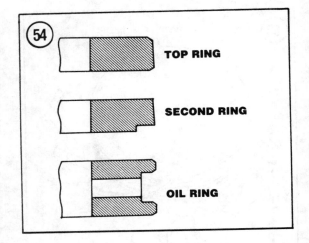

TOP RING

SECOND RING

OIL RING

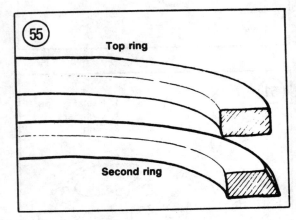

Top ring

Second ring

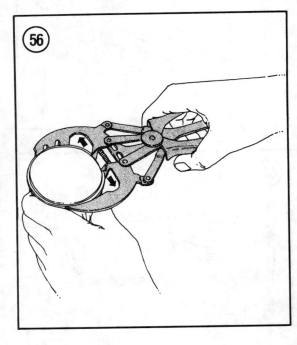

OIL PUMP (1978-1983)

Refer to **Figure 60** for this procedure.
1. Remove the clutch and primary chain as described in Chapter Six.
2. To remove the oil pump, remove the retaining screws and withdraw the pump assembly (**Figure 61**).
3. Installation is the reverse of these steps, noting the following:

   a. Fill the oil pump with new engine oil for initial lubrication.
   b. Make sure the 2 dowel pins are installed on the back of the pump before installation.
   c. Install a new oil pump gasket.

Inspection

1. Remove the bolt (7, **Figure 60**) and remove the cover plate (2).
2. Remove the outer rotor (4).
3. Measure clearance between the inner and outer rotors. If clearance exceeds specifications (**Table 2** or **Table 3**) replace both rotors.
4. Place a straightedge across both rotors and the pump body. If clearance between the rotor and the straightedge exceeds specifications (**Table 2** or **Table 3**), replace both rotors.
5. Measure clearance between the outer rotor and pump body. Replace the outer rotor or the pump body if clearance is excessive (**Table 2** or **Table 3**).
6. Reverse Step 1 and Step 2 to assemble the oil pump.

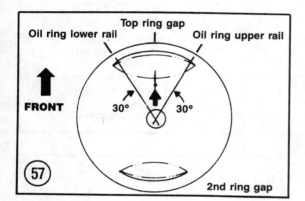

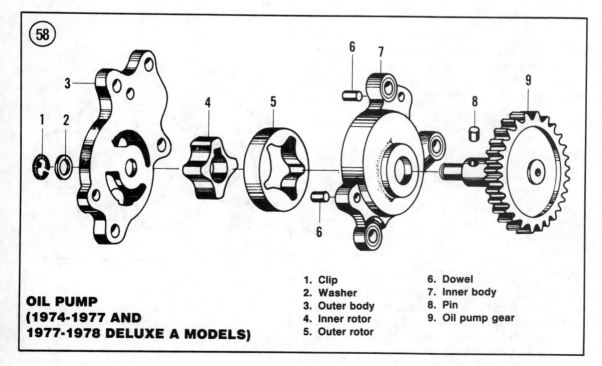

OIL PUMP (1974-1977 AND 1977-1978 DELUXE A MODELS)

1. Clip
2. Washer
3. Outer body
4. Inner rotor
5. Outer rotor
6. Dowel
7. Inner body
8. Pin
9. Oil pump gear

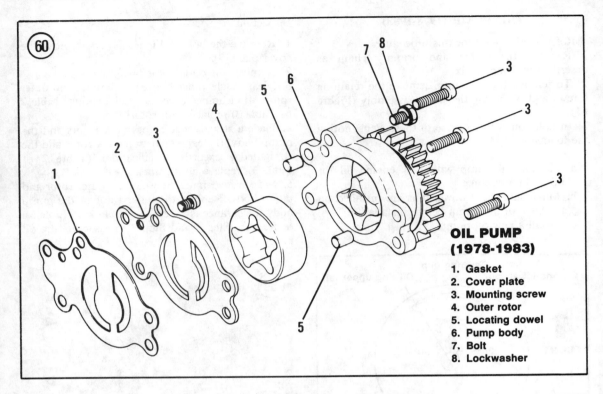

**OIL PUMP
(1978-1983)**

1. Gasket
2. Cover plate
3. Mounting screw
4. Outer rotor
5. Locating dowel
6. Pump body
7. Bolt
8. Lockwasher

Oil Pump Screen

To protect the oil pump, a screen is installed in the lower crankcase. It removes any small metal particles and other foreign matter that may otherwise damage the pump.

Remove the screws (**Figure 62**) securing the oil screen cover and remove it and the screen. Clean the screen with solvent and blow dry with compressed air. If the screen is damaged in any way, replace it with a new one.

OIL PRESSURE RELIEF VALVE
(1978-1983)

Removal/Installation

1. Remove the clutch and primary chain. See Chapter Six.
2. Remove the relief valve (**Figure 63**).
3. Apply Loctite 242 (blue) to the relief valve threads before installation. Tighten to 15 N•m (11 ft.-lb.).

Inspection

Push in on the ball with a small wood dowel or soft rod (**Figure 64**). Check to make sure the spring pushes the ball back into its seated position. If not, clean the valve assembly (intact) in solvent and blow dry with compressed air.

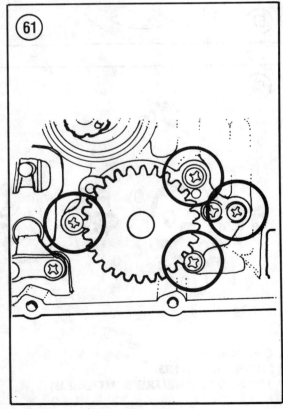

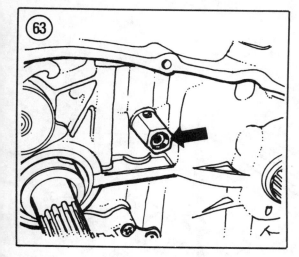

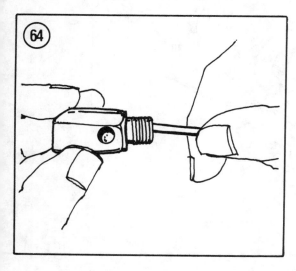

NOTE
Do not disassemble the valve as this may affect or change valve operation.

If the ball will not seat correctly, replace the entire unit. Replacement parts are not available.

ALTERNATOR AND STARTER

The alternator and starter are discussed together, because complete removal of one entails removal of the other. Refer to Chapter Nine for testing.

Removal/Installation
(1974-1977 and 1977-1978
Deluxe A Models)

Refer to **Figure 65** for this procedure.
1. Remove the field coil plug from the connector underneath the voltage regulator.
2. Remove the shift pedal.
3. Remove the left footpeg and kickstand spring.
4. Remove the engine sprocket cover.
5. Remove the wiring harness clip from above the engine sprocket.
6. Remove the starter cover (**Figure 66**).
7. Disconnect the oil pressure switch at the inline connector.
8. Disconnect the neutral indicator switch wire.
9. Remove the alternator cover. Do not remove the 3 Allen bolts from the center of the cover.
10. Remove the starter motor chain guide and sprocket guide (B, **Figure 67**).
11. Remove the stator retaining bolts (A, **Figure 67**). Remove the stator.
12. Remove the field coil retaining bolts (**Figure 68**), then pull out the field coil.
13. Remove the rotor retaining bolt. Note that this bolt uses a left-hand thread.
14. Using a rotor puller, remove the alternator rotor and starter clutch (**Figure 69**). Remove thrust washer if necessary.
15. Installation is the reverse of these steps, noting the following.
16. Apply Loctite 242 (blue) to the field coil and stator bolts. Tighten the bolts to 7-8 N•m (5-6 ft.-lb.).
17. Check the alternator rotor magnets (**Figure 70**) for any signs of metal debris, washers or nuts that may have collected.
18. Be sure there is no foreign material on the tapered portion of the crankshaft when installing the rotor.
19. Tighten the rotor bolt (left-hand threads) to 65-70 N•m (47-51 ft.-lb.).

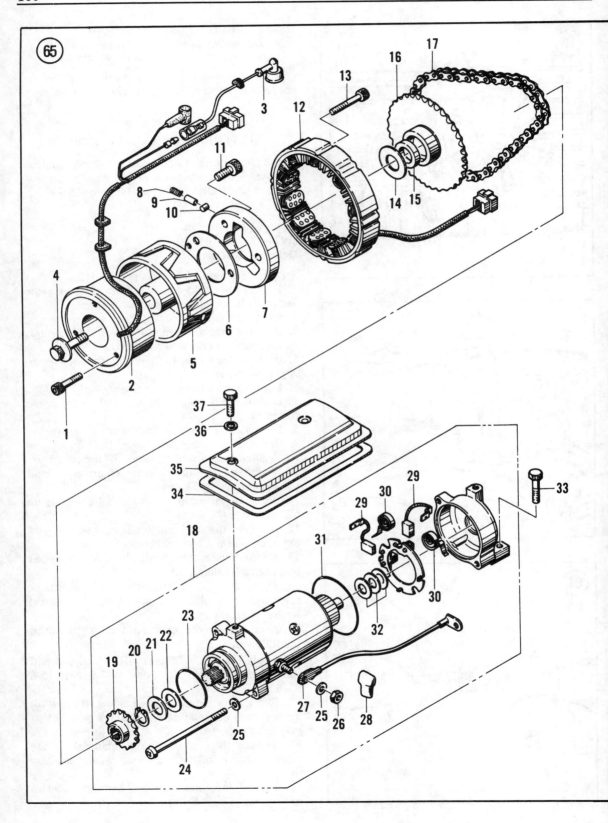

ALTERNATOR/STARTER
(1974-1977 AND 1977-1978
DELUXE A MODELS)

1. Bolt
2. Field coil
3. Wire
4. Bolt
5. Rotor
6. Plate
7. Starter clutch
8. Spring
9. Plug
10. Roller
11. Bolt
12. Stator
13. Bolt
14. Washer
15. Oil seal
16. Gear
17. Chain
18. Motor
19. Sprocket
20. Snap ring
21. Washer
22. Washer
23. O-ring
24. Screw
25. Washer
26. Nut
27. Wire
28. Terminal cap
29. Brush
30. Spring
31. O-ring
32. Washer
33. Bolt
34. Gasket
35. Cover
36. Washer
37. Bolt

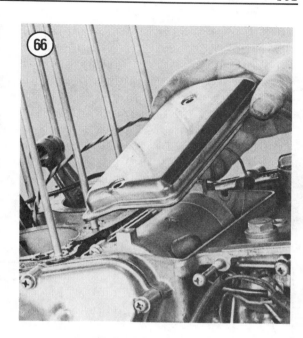

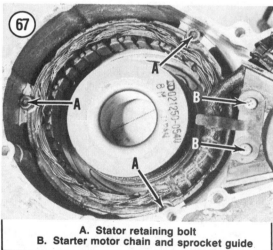

A. Stator retaining bolt
B. Starter motor chain and sprocket guide

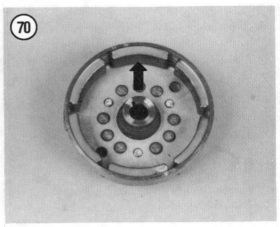

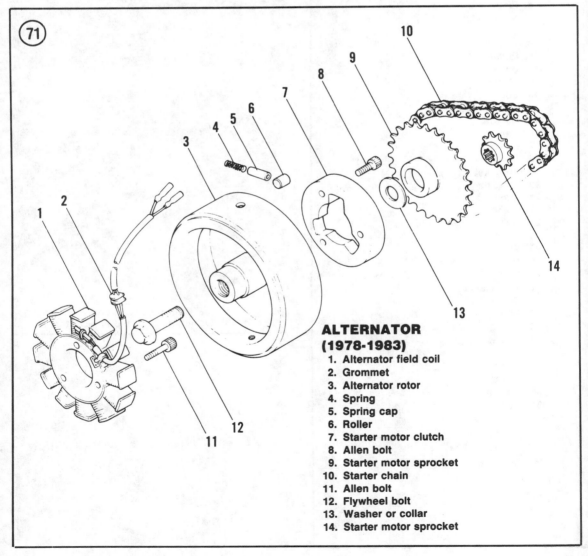

**ALTERNATOR
(1978-1983)**
1. Alternator field coil
2. Grommet
3. Alternator rotor
4. Spring
5. Spring cap
6. Roller
7. Starter motor clutch
8. Allen bolt
9. Starter motor sprocket
10. Starter chain
11. Allen bolt
12. Flywheel bolt
13. Washer or collar
14. Starter motor sprocket

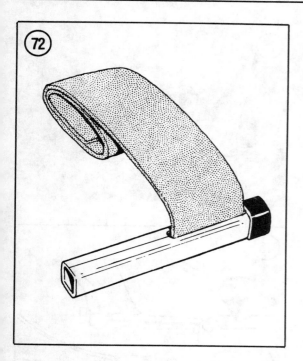

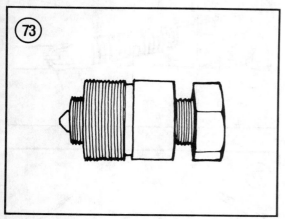

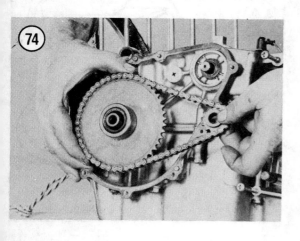

20. Install the shift pedal so that its end is level with the alternator cover lower screw.

Alternator Removal/Installation (1978-1983)

Refer to **Figure 71** for this procedure.
1. Remove the engine sprocket cover.
2. Disconnect the 2 yellow electrical leads coming from the alternator.
3. Place a drip pan under the alternator cover as some oil will drain out when the cover is removed.
4. Remove the screws securing the cover and remove it and the gasket.
5. Remove the rotor securing bolt.

NOTE
*If necessary, use a strap wrench (**Figure 72**) to secure the rotor from turning while removing the bolt.*

6. Screw in the flywheel puller (**Figure 73**) until it stops. Use a wrench on the puller and turn it until the rotor disengages. Remove the puller and the rotor/starter clutch assembly.

NOTE
There will either be a thrust washer or a collar behind the rotor/starter clutch assembly. Remove the part as necessary.

7. Install by reversing these removal steps. Thoroughly clean the crankshaft taper of any dirt or oil before installing the rotor.
8. Be sure to install either the thrust washer or collar onto the crankshaft, then install the rotor. Tighten the rotor bolt to 70 N•m (51 ft.-lb.).

Starter Chain and Sprockets (All Models)

Once the rotor and starter clutch have been removed, it is only necessary to pull off both starter sprockets and drive chain as an assembly (**Figure 74**). Installation is the reverse of removal.

Starter Motor (All Models)

1. Remove the alternator cover as described in this chapter.
2. Disconnect the cable from the terminal on the starter motor.
3. Remove the starter motor retaining bolts.
4. Tap the starter motor with a plastic mallet to free it, then lift it from the engine (**Figure 75**). Do not tap the starter shaft; doing so may result in damage.

5. Reverse the removal procedures to install the starter. Apply a little oil to the starter O-ring before installation.

ENGINE SPROCKET COVER
(1978-1983)

Removal/Installation

1. Remove the left-hand footpeg.
2. Remove the bolt securing the shift lever and remove it.
3. Remove the side stand drive lever pivot bolt (A, **Figure 76**) and lever (B, **Figure 76**).

> *NOTE*
> *Don't lose the lockwasher, flat washer and collar on the bolt.*

4. Slide the rod (C, **Figure 76**) to the rear.
5. Remove the screws securing the sprocket cover and remove it.
6. Remove the cotter pin from the clutch release lever (**Figure 77**). Remove the cable from the lever and remove the cable from the cover.
7. Install by reversing these removal steps. Be sure to use a new cotter pin on the clutch cable—never reuse an old cotter pin.
8. Be sure to install the collar, flat washer and lockwasher on the pivot shaft. Hook the rod onto the lever.

ENGINE SPROCKET OR PULLEY

Removal/Installation
(1974-1977 and 1977-1978
Deluxe A Models)

1. Remove the engine sprocket cover.
2. Using a blunted chisel, flatten the tab on the sprocket lockwasher.
3. If the engine is installed in the frame, apply the rear brake firmly, then remove the sprocket nut. If the engine has been removed, a suitable sprocket holder can be fabricated from the drive chain and a wooden board. Secure the chain to the board in such a manner that the assembly can be used much as a strap wrench.
4. Remove the sprocket (**Figure 78**).
5. Inspect the sprocket teeth or pulley for wear as described in Chapter Three.
6. Reverse these procedures to install the sprocket. Tighten the retaining nut to 120-150 N•m (87-108 ft.-lb.). Be sure to bend up a tab on the lockwasher to lock the nut.

> *NOTE*
> *Use a shifter shaft oil seal guide to protect the oil seal when the sprocket cover is installed.*

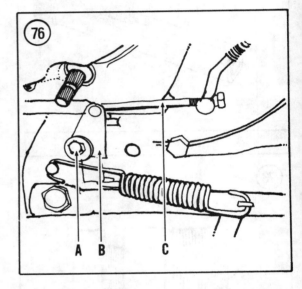

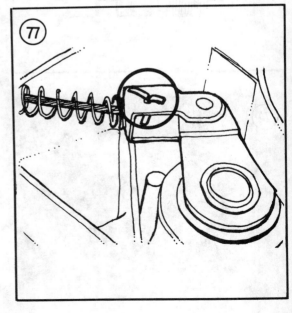

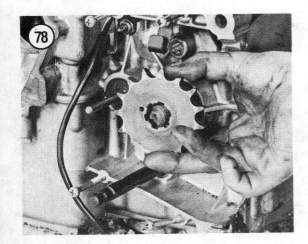

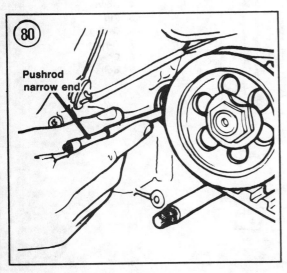

Pushrod
narrow end

Removal/Installation
(1978-1983)

1. Remove the engine sprocket cover as described in this chapter.

2. *Models with automatic side stand return mechanism:* Refer to **Figure 79**. Remove the pivot bolt (A), lever (B), rod (C) and return spring (D).

3. Straighten out the tab on the lockwasher.

4A. *Drive chain:* Perform the following:

  a. If the engine is installed in the frame, apply the rear brake firmly, then remove the sprocket nut. If the engine has been removed, a suitable sprocket holder can be fabricated from the drive chain and a wooden board. Secure the chain to the board in such a manner that the assembly can be used as a strap wrench.

  b. Loosen the rear axle and loosen the chain adjuster bolts. Push the rear wheel forward as far as possible.

  c. Remove the sprocket (**Figure 78**).

  d. Inspect the sprocket teeth for wear as described in Chapter Three.

  e. Reverse these procedures to install the sprocket. Tighten the retaining nut to 85 N•m (61 ft.-lb.). Be sure to bend up a tab on the lockwasher to lock the nut.

4B. *Drive belt:* Perform the following:

  a. On 1980-1981 models, pull out the clutch pushrod (**Figure 80**).

  b. If the engine is installed in the frame, apply the rear brake firmly, then remove the pulley nut. If the engine has been removed, a sprocket holder must be used.

  c. Loosen the rear axle and loosen the belt adjuster bolts. Push the rear wheel forward to obtain as much belt slack as possible.

  d. Slide the pulley off of the transmission countershaft. Then slip the pulley out of the belt and remove it.

  e. Reverse these procedures to install the pulley. Tighten the nut to 85 N•m (61 ft.-lb.).

5. Bend up one side of the toothed lockwasher against the side of the nut.

CRANKCASE

Service to the lower end requires that the crankcase assembly be removed from the motorcycle frame and disassembled (split).

Disassembly

1. Remove the engine as described in this chapter. Remove all exterior assemblies from the crankcase. Set the engine on the workbench.

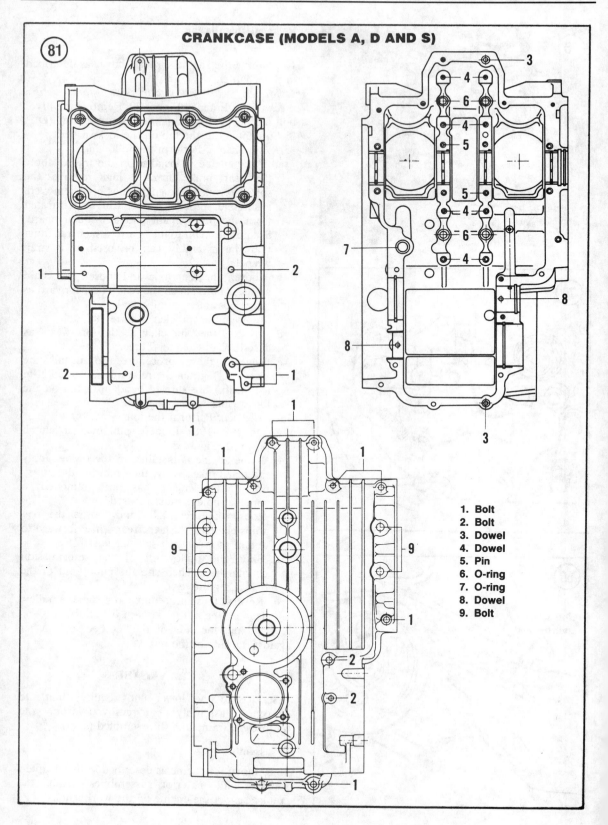

CRANKCASE (MODELS A, D AND S)

81

1. Bolt
2. Bolt
3. Dowel
4. Dowel
5. Pin
6. O-ring
7. O-ring
8. Dowel
9. Bolt

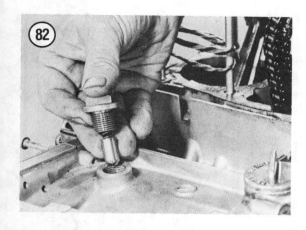

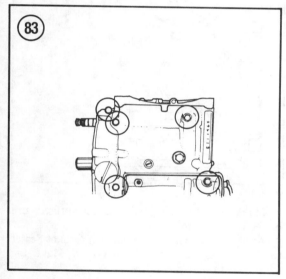

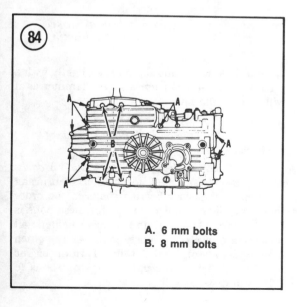

A. 6 mm bolts
B. 8 mm bolts

2A. *1974-1977 and 1977-1978 Deluxe A models:*
Perform the following:

   a. Remove the bolts from the upper crankcase, then invert the engine and remove the lower bolts. A few are longer than the others; note their locations. See **Figure 81**.

   b. Remove the neutral stop bolt, spring and plunger (**Figure 82**).

2B. *1978-1983:* Remove the upper crankcase bolts (**Figure 83**), then invert the engine and remove the lower bolts (**Figure 84**). The bolts vary in length; make note of their locations during removal.

3. Gently lift the lower crankcase away from the upper crankcase. There are 3 pry points where the crankcase halves mate. Use these points carefully with a broad tipped screwdriver to help split the case halves.

> *CAUTION*
> *Do not pry the cases apart between mating surfaces with any metal tool or an oil leak will develop.*

4. Be sure that all shafts remain in the upper crankcase half; tap them with a rubber or plastic mallet, if necessary, to loosen them from the lower half.

5. Remove the transmission, shift forks and shift drum assemblies from the upper crankcase half as described in Chapter Seven.

6. Remove the crankshaft and balancer shaft assemblies as described in this chapter.

7A. *1974-1977 and 1977-1978 Deluxe A models:* If the cam chain guide requires replacement, perform the following:

   a. Remove the crankshaft and camshaft chain as described in this chapter.

   b. At the front of the crankcase, push the pivot pin (A, **Figure 85**) out, then withdraw the pin.

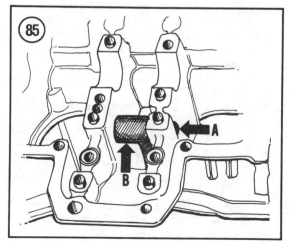

Remove the camshaft front chain guide (B, **Figure 85**). Note that the grooved end of the pin is on the left-hand side of the engine (alternator side). It must be reinstalled in the same position.

7B. *1978-on:* If the cam chain guide requires replacement, perform the following:

   a. Remove the crankshaft and camshaft chain as described in this chapter.

   b. At the front of the crankcase, remove the retaining pin, push the pivot pin out and then withdraw the pin (A, **Figure 85**). Remove the camshaft front chain guide (B, **Figure 85**).

Inspection

1. Thoroughly clean the inside and outside of both crankcase halves with cleaning solvent. Dry with compressed air. Make sure there is no solvent residue left in the cases as it will contaminate the engine oil. Lubricate the bearings with oil to prevent rust formation.

2. Make sure all oil passages are clean; blow them out with compressed air.

3. Check the crankcases for cracks or other damage. Inspect the mating surfaces of both halves. They must be free of gouges, burrs or any damage that could cause an oil leak.

4. Make sure the cylinder studs are not bent and the threads are in good condition. Make sure they are screwed into the crankcase tightly. Do not remove the covers from the cylinder studs.

5. Inspect the crankcase bearings as described in this chapter.

Assembly

1. If the cam chain guide was removed, perform the following:

   a. At the front of the crankcase, place the camshaft front chain guide into position.

   b. *1974-1977 and 1977-1978 Deluxe A Models:* Install the pivot pin so the grooved end of the pin is facing toward the left-hand side of the engine (alternator side).

   c. *1978-1983:* Install the pivot pin and the retaining pin.

2. Before installation of all parts, coat all parts with assembly oil or engine oil.

3. Install the crankshaft as described in this chapter.

4. Install the shift drum, shift forks and transmission assemblies as described in Chapter Seven.

5. Place the transmission in NEUTRAL.

6. Clean the crankcase mating surfaces of both halves with contact cleaner.

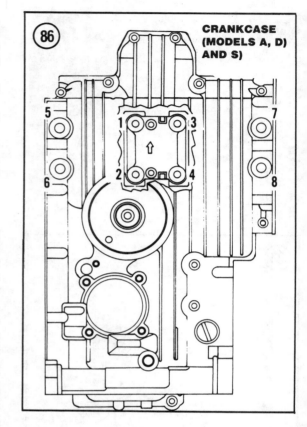

86 CRANKCASE (MODELS A, D) AND S)

7. Make sure the case half sealing surfaces are perfectly clean and dry.

8. Apply a light coat of Gasgacinch Gasket Sealer to the sealing surfaces of each half. Make the coating as thin as possible.

> *NOTE*
> *Always use the correct type of gasket sealer—avoid thick and hard-setting materials.*

9. Join both halves and tap together lightly with a plastic mallet—do not use a metal hammer as it will damage the cases.

> *NOTE*
> *Make sure the oil seals don't slip out of place.*

10A. *1974-1977 and 1977-1978 Deluxe A Models:* Set the lower crankcase into position, then install the 8 mm crankshaft bearings bolts in the order shown in **Figure 86**. The torque for these bolts is 25-30 N•m (18-22 ft.-lb.). Then tighten all remaining lower bolts snugly, and finally tighten them to 8-10 N•m (5.8-7.2 ft.-lb.). Turn the engine upright and tighten the upper crankcase bolts to 8-10 N•m (5.8-7.2 ft.-lb.).

10B. *1978-1983:* Install and finger-tighten the four lower crankcase 8 mm bolts (B, **Figure 84**) and the eleven 6 mm bolts (A, **Figure 84**). Then tighten all 8 mm bolts first to 15 N•m (11 ft.-lb.) and then to 25 N•m (18 ft.-lb.). Use the torque sequence indicated by the bolt number adjacent to the bolt hole. Tighten the 6 mm bolts to 10 N•m (7.2 ft.-lb.). Turn the engine upright and tighten the upper crankcase bolts to 10 N•m (ft.-lb.).

11. Install all engine assemblies that were removed.

12. Install the engine as described in this chapter.

KICKSTARTER (1974-1977 AND 1977-1978 DELUXE A MODELS)

Removal/Installation

Refer to **Figure 87** for this procedure.

1. Disassemble the crankcase assembly as described in this chapter.

2. Bend down the locking tabs, then remove the retaining bolts and stop plate (**Figure 88**).

3. Remove the snap ring, spring and spring guide (**Figure 89**).

4. Remove the retaining plate and collar.

5. Remove the kickstarter shaft from the engine.

6. Installation is the reverse of these steps, noting the following.

7. Turn the shaft fully clockwise before inserting the end of the return spring. Be sure that the mark on the ratchet gear aligns with the notch on the shaft (**Figure 90**).

Inspection

1. Measure the shaft diameter at the point where it passes through the kick gear. Replace if its diameter is less than 19.93 mm (0.785 in.).

2. Measure the inside diameter of the kick gear. Replace if its diameter is greater than 20.07 mm (0.790 in.).

3. Inspect the ratchet teeth on both gears for wear. Replace the gears if the ratchet teeth are badly worn.

4. Be sure that neither spring is cracked or bent. Replace them if their condition is doubtful.

BALANCER (1974-1977 AND 1977-1978 DELUXE A MODELS)

The balancer consists of a pair of chain driven weight assemblies, their associated bearings and a drive chain. Since it operates under conditions of high stress, check the balancer each time the engine is disassembled to catch and correct any problems.

Refer to **Figure 91** for these procedures.

Removal

1. Disassemble the crankcase as described in this chapter.

2. Remove the bearing cap (**Figure 92**). Note that the longer bolts go into holes 1 and 4.

3. Remove the balancer guide (**Figure 93**).

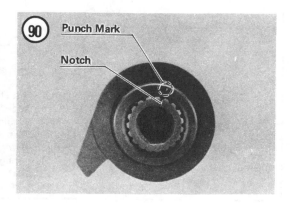

Punch Mark

Notch

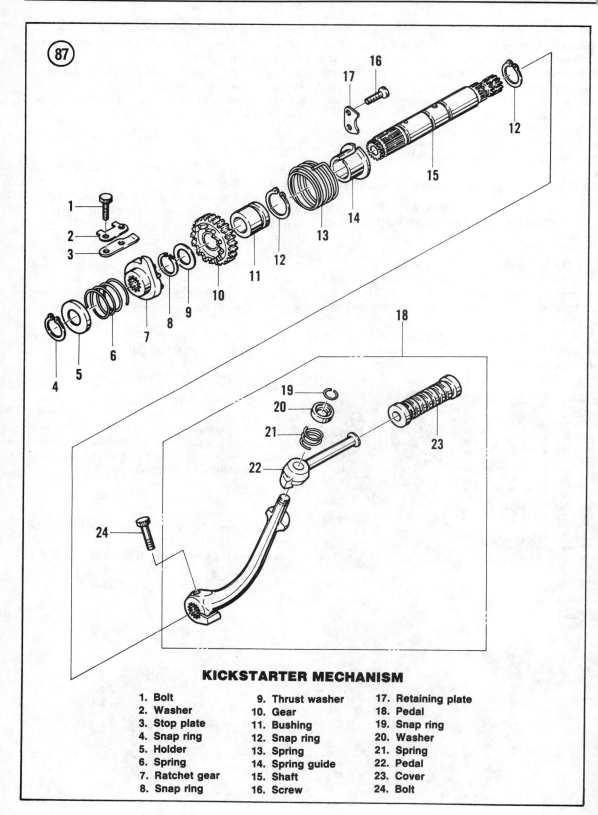

KICKSTARTER MECHANISM

1. Bolt	9. Thrust washer	17. Retaining plate
2. Washer	10. Gear	18. Pedal
3. Stop plate	11. Bushing	19. Snap ring
4. Snap ring	12. Snap ring	20. Washer
5. Holder	13. Spring	21. Spring
6. Spring	14. Spring guide	22. Pedal
7. Ratchet gear	15. Shaft	23. Cover
8. Snap ring	16. Screw	24. Bolt

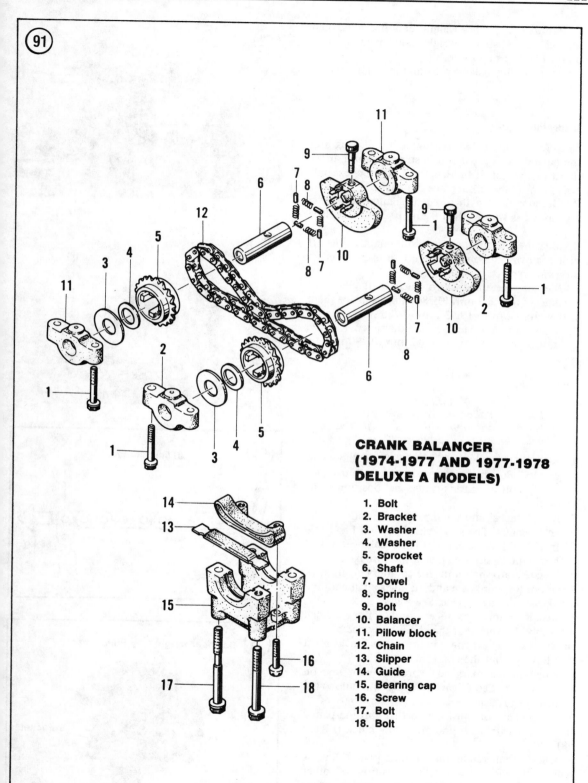

**CRANK BALANCER
(1974-1977 AND 1977-1978
DELUXE A MODELS)**

1. Bolt
2. Bracket
3. Washer
4. Washer
5. Sprocket
6. Shaft
7. Dowel
8. Spring
9. Bolt
10. Balancer
11. Pillow block
12. Chain
13. Slipper
14. Guide
15. Bearing cap
16. Screw
17. Bolt
18. Bolt

4. Remove all balance weight retaining bolts, then lift off each balance weight and its associated pillow blocks as an assembly.

5. Remove the balancer from the engine as an assembly.

Inspection

1. Refer to **Figure 94**. Measure a 20 link length of the balancer chain when it is stretched with an 11 lb. (5 kg) weight. If the length of 20 links exceeds 162.4 mm (6.39 in.), replace the chain.

2. Measure the length of each balancer spring. If any spring is shorter than 9 mm (0.35 in.), replace it.

3. Measure the thickness of both chain guides. If either is worn to 4 mm (0.16 in.), or is damaged in any way, replace it.

4. Measure the thickness of each shaft. Standard thickness is 19.967 mm (0.7861 in.). Replace them if they are worn to 19.93 mm (0.785 in.).

5. Measure pillow block inside diameter. Replace them if they are worn to 20.08 mm (0.790 in.).

Installation

> *CAUTION*
> *Follow installation instructions exactly. Engine vibration will result if the balancer is installed incorrectly.*

1. Assemble weights and sprockets as shown in **Figure 95**. Punch marks on sprockets must face outward, and sprockets must be positioned as shown.

2. Install the shims on the sprocket side of the balancer shafts. The small shim goes on first.

3. Install pillow blocks onto the balancer shafts with machined surfaces facing the sprocket.

4. Rotate crankshaft until the counterweights stick up out of the crankcase and oil holes align with the crankcase mating surface. See **Figure 96**.

5. Install either balancer and pillow block assembly. Be sure that the chain is looped around the sprocket. The arrows on the pillow blocks must point away from the crankshaft.

6. Align punch marks on sprocket with line on pillow block. See **Figure 97**. Do not allow the crankshaft to turn.

7. Loop chain on sprocket so that chrome-plated link aligns with with line on pillow block (**Figure 98**).

8. Check that remaining chrome-plated link is reasonably close to installed position of other sprocket. If not, repeat Step 7, but align the other chrome-plated link with the line.

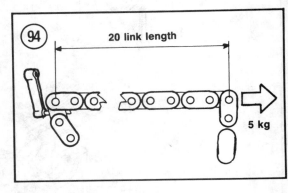

20 link length

5 kg

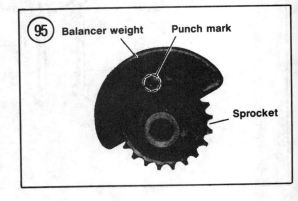

Balancer weight   Punch mark

Sprocket

9. Install remaining balance weight assembly. Punch mark, stamped line and chrome-plated links must all align.

10. Tighten balance weight bolts to 11-13 N•m (8-9.4 ft.-lb.). Use Loctite 242 (blue) on these bolts.

11. Install chain guide and bearing cap. Be sure that bearings are clean, then lubricate them with engine oil. Tighten bearing cap bolts, in the order marked on the cap, to 25-30 N•m (18-22 ft.-lb.).

Note that the longer bolts go into locations 1 and 4 (**Figure 92**). Use Loctite 242 (blue) on these bolts.

BALANCER
(1978-1983)

The balancer consists of a pair of chain-driven weight assemblies, their associated bearings and a drive chain.
Refer to **Figure 99**.

Removal

1. Disassemble the crankcase as described in this chapter.

2. Refer to **Figure 100**. Remove the four 10 mm bolts (A) and the four 8 mm bolts (B) securing the main bearing cap/balancer assembly and remove it.

Installation

1. Install the 4 assembly locating dowels into the upper crankcase.

2. Make sure that the 2 main bearing inserts are in place in the assembly.

3. Rotate the crankshaft until the oil holes in the crankshaft are centered on the mating surface of the upper crankcase (**Figure 101**). The crankshaft counterbalance weights will be positioned up.

4. Make sure that the balancer chain and sprockets are correctly positioned (**Figure 102**). On the front sprocket the plated link must be positioned on the punch marked sprocket tooth (**Figure 103**). The rear sprocket must have the 4th plated link (counting from the front of the chain) on the punch marked sprocket tooth (**Figure 103**). With the 2 plated links in the correct position, the 2 remaining plated links must be centered within the main bearing cap surface area as viewed from the bottom of the assembly.

5. Install the main bearing/cap balancer assembly onto the upper crankcase half. The arrow (C, **Figure 100**) must point toward the front of the engine. Engage the link between the 2nd and 3rd plated link onto the top tooth of the crankshaft sprocket (**Figure 102**).

6. Make sure that the painted line on each balancer weight aligns with the raised bar on the main bearing cap assembly (**Figure 104**). Also the

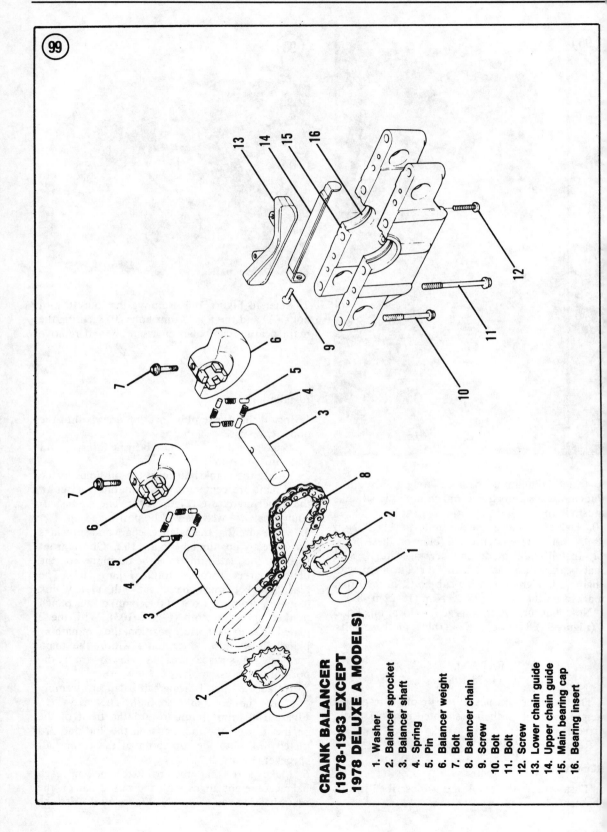

99

CRANK BALANCER
(1978-1983 EXCEPT
1978 DELUXE A MODELS)

1. Washer
2. Balancer sprocket
3. Balancer shaft
4. Spring
5. Pin
6. Balancer weight
7. Bolt
8. Balancer chain
9. Screw
10. Bolt
11. Bolt
12. Screw
13. Lower chain guide
14. Upper chain guide
15. Main bearing cap
16. Bearing insert

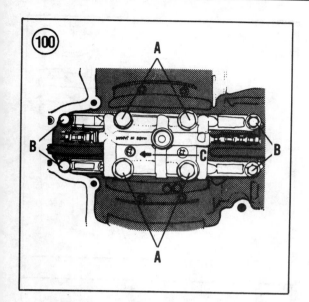

4

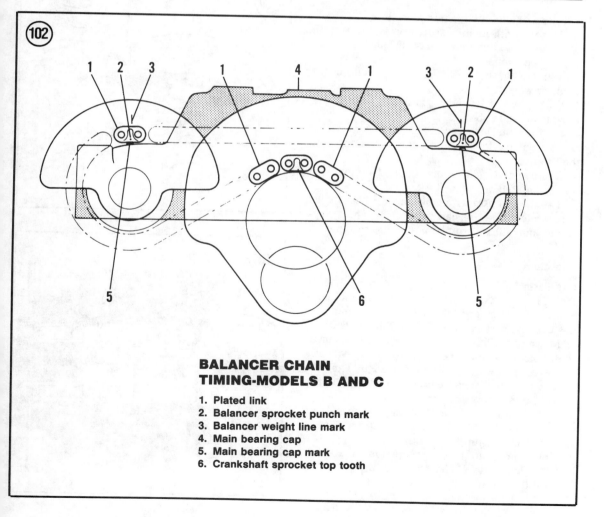

BALANCER CHAIN
TIMING-MODELS B AND C

1. Plated link
2. Balancer sprocket punch mark
3. Balancer weight line mark
4. Main bearing cap
5. Main bearing cap mark
6. Crankshaft sprocket top tooth

plated link must be positioned on the punch marked sprocket tooth (**Figure 103**).

> *CAUTION*
> *If any of the 4 alignment points is incorrect, remove the main bearing cap/balancer assembly and correct it. This alignment is necessary for proper engine operation. Engine vibration will result if the balancer is installed incorrectly.*

7. Install, and finger-tighten only, the four 10 mm and four 8 mm bolts. Tighten the bolts in two stages using the torque sequence shown in **Figure 105**. First tighten the 8 mm bolts to 15 N•m (11 ft.-lb.) and the 10 mm bolts to 25 N•m (18 ft.-lb.). Finally tighten the 8 mm bolts to 25 N•m (18 ft.-lb.) and the 10 mm bolts to 40 N•m (29 ft.-lb.).

Disassembly

Refer to **Figure 99** for this procedure.
1. Remove both main bearing inserts. Mark them right and left so that they will be installed into their original positions.
2. Remove the bolts (7, **Figure 99**) securing the balancer weights to the shaft.
3. Withdraw the balancer shafts (3), washers (1), weights (6) and sprockets (2).
4. Remove the balancer chain guide screws (12) and lift out the lower chain guide (13) along with the chain.
5. Remove the guide screw (9) and remove the upper chain guide (14).
6. Tap the sprocket with a plastic or rubber mallet to separate it from the balancer weight. The springs (4) and pins (5) will come off at the same time.

Inspection

1. Measure the outer diameter of the balancer shaft (3) at each end where it rotates in the main bearing cap. Replace the shaft if the diameter is less than the service limit (**Table 2 or Table 3**).
2. Measure the inside diameter of each balancer shaft hole in the main bearing cap. If any balancer hole exceeds the service limit (**Table 2 or Table 3**), replace both the main bearing cap and the upper crankcase assembly as a set.
3. Measure the free length of each spring (4) as shown in **Figure 106**. Replace any spring that is shorter than 9.3 mm (0.366 in.).
4. Hold the chain taut and measure a 20 link length (**Figure 107**). The standard dimension is 160.0-160.3 mm (6.299-6.311 in.). Replace the chain if it is longer than 162.4 mm (6.394 in.).

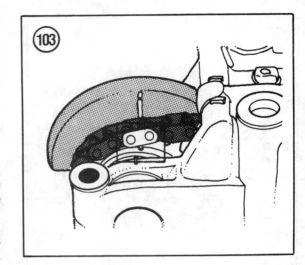

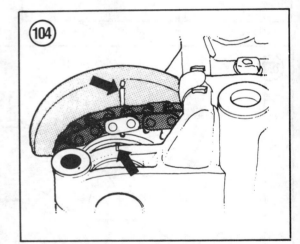

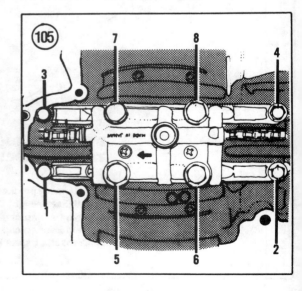

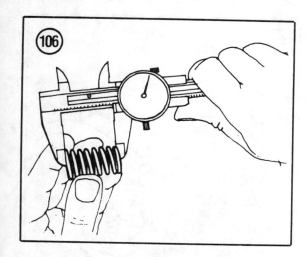

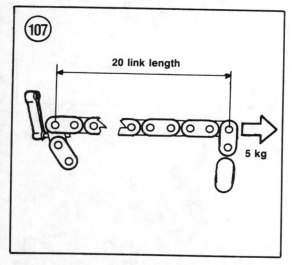

20 link length

5 kg

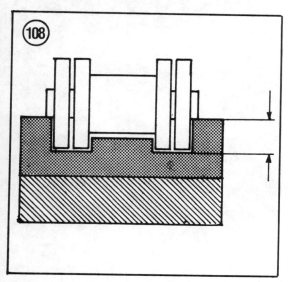

NOTE
If the chain has to be replaced, carefully inspect all sprockets (both balancers and crankshaft) for wear. If the sprockets are damaged or worn, they must be replaced. If the crankshaft sprocket is worn, the entire crankshaft must be replaced.

5. Inspect the chain guides for wear and deterioration. Measure the depth of the grooves where the chain links travel (**Figure 108**). The minimum thickness on the upper guide (14, **Figure 99**) is 1.0 mm (0.0395 in.) and 1.5 mm (0.0591 in.) for the lower guide (13). Replace either or both guides if the dimension is less than specified.

Assembly

1. Install the upper chain guide (14, **Figure 99**). Install the screw (9); apply Loctite 242 (blue) to the screws threads before installation.

NOTE
When installing a new guide, tighten the screw and bend the opposite end up and over the main bearing cap.

NOTE
Install the chain with the 4 plated links facing toward the left-hand side of the engine when installed.

2. Install the lower chain guide (13) and chain. Install the 2 screws (12); apply Loctite 242 (blue) to the threads before installation.
3. Install the 4 springs (4) and pins (5) into position in the inner circumference of the balancer weight (6). Install the sprocket (2) with the punch mark facing away from the balancer weight.

CAUTION
Align the punch mark on the sprocket with the painted line on the balancer weight (Figure 109).

4. After the sprocket is correctly positioned, move each spring and pin outward within its groove so that it will not interfere with the balancer shaft when it is inserted through the balancer weight.

5. Repeat Steps 3 and 4 for the other balancer weight assembly.

6. Install each balancer weight and sprocket assembly onto the chain and install the washer (1, **Figure 99**) onto each sprocket side (**Figure 110**).

7. Apply assembly oil to the balancer shafts; install them into the main bearing cap and balancer weight (keep the chain on the sprocket). Align the hole in the shaft with the hole in the balancer weight and instll the bolts (7). Apply Loctite 242 (blue) to the threads before installation. Tighten the bolts to 15 N•m (11 ft.-lb.).

> *NOTE*
> *Make sure the washer is in place between each sprocket and main bearing cap.*

8. Install the main bearing inserts (16). If old inserts are used, refer to the marks made during disassembly, and install them into their original positions.

9. Reassemble the crankcase as described in this chapter.

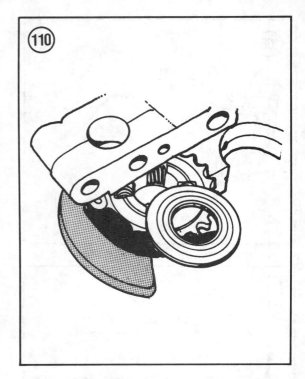

CRANKSHAFT AND CONNECTING RODS

Removal/Installation

1. Split the crankcase as described under *Crankcase Disassembly* in this chapter.

2. Remove the transmission assemblies as described in Chapter Seven.

3. Remove the kickstarter as described in this chapter.

4. Remove the balancer shaft assembly as described in this chapter.

5. Lift the crankshaft and camshaft chain assembly from the crankcase (**Figure 111**).

6. Remove the cam chain from the crankshaft.

> *NOTE*
> *If necessary, remove the connecting rods from the crankshaft as described in Step 7.*

7. See **Figure 112**. Remove the connecting rod cap bolts and separate the rods from the crankshaft. Mark each rod cap and bearing insert so that they can be reinstalled in their original position.

8. Install by reversing these removal steps, noting the following procedures.

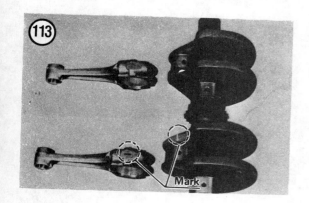

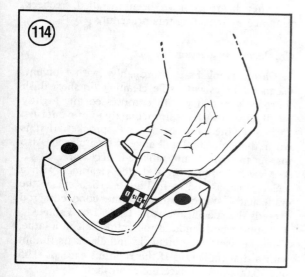

9. Install the bearing inserts into each connecting rod and cap. Make sure they are locked in place correctly.

CAUTION
If the old bearings are reused, be sure they are installed in their exact original positions.

10. Lubricate the bearings and crankpins with assembly oil and install the rods so that the weight marks on the cap and connecting rod (**Figure 113**) align. Apply molybdenum disulfide grease to the threads of the connecting rods. Install the caps and tighten the cap nuts evenly, in a couple of steps, to the torque specifications in **Table 5** or **Table 6**.
11. Install the crankshaft and cam chain.

Connecting Rod Inspection

1. Check each rod for obvious damage such as cracks and burns.
2. Check the piston pin bushing for wear or scoring.

3. Take the rods to a machine shop and have them checked for twisting and bending.
4. Examine the bearing inserts for wear, scoring or burning. They are reusable if in good condition. Make a note of the bearing size (if any) stamped on the back of the insert if the bearing is to be discarded; a previous owner may have used undersize bearings.
5. Check bearing clearance as described in this chapter.

Connecting Rod Bearing
and Clearance Measurement

CAUTION
If the old bearings are to be reused, be sure that they are installed in their exact original locations.

1. Wipe bearing inserts and crankpins clean. Install bearing inserts in rod and cap.
2. Place a piece of Plastigage on one crankpin parallel to the crankshaft.
3. Install rod and cap. Tighten nuts to specifications (**Tables 4-6**).

CAUTION
Do not rotate crankshaft or connecting rod while Plastigage is in place.

4. Remove rod cap.
5. Measure width of flattened Plastigage according to the manufacturer's instructions (**Figure 114**). Measure at both ends of the strip. A difference of 0.025 mm (0.001 in.) or more indicates a tapered crankpin; the crankshaft must be reground or replaced.
6. If the crankpin taper is within tolerance, measure the bearing clearance with the same strip of Plastigage. Correct bearing clearance is specified in **Table 2** and **Table 3**. Remove Plastigage strips.
7. If the bearing clearance is greater than specified, replace the bearings. Record the numbers off of the crankshaft and connecting rod and refer new bearing selection from a Kawasaki dealer.

Crankshaft Main Bearing
and Journal Inspection

1. Check the inside and outside surfaces of the bearing inserts for wear, bluish tint (burned), flaking, abrasion and scoring. If the bearings are good, they may be reused. If any insert is questionable, replace the entire set.
2. Clean the bearing surfaces of the crankshaft and the main bearing inserts. Measure the main bearing clearance by performing the following steps.
3. Set the crankcase upside down on the workbench on wood blocks.

4. Install the existing main bearing inserts in the upper crankcase.

5. Install the crankshaft into the upper crankcase.

6. Place a stip of Plastigage material over each main bearing journal parallel to the crankshaft. Do not place the Plastigage strip over an oil hole in the crankshaft.

NOTE
Do not rotate the crankshaft while the Plastigage strips are in place.

7. Install the existing bearing inserts into the lower crankcase.

8. Assemble the crankcase as described in this chapter. Install the crankcase bolts and tighten them to their correct torque specifications (**Table 5** or **Table 6**).

9. Remove the crankcase bolts in the reverse order of installation.

10. Carefully remove the lower crankcase and measure the width of the flattened Plastigage material following manufacturer's instructions. Measure both ends of the Plastigage strip (**Figure 114**). A difference of 0.025 mm (0.001 in.) or more indicates a tapered journal. Confirm with a micrometer. New bearing clearance and service limit dimensions are listed in **Table 2** or **Table 3**. Remove the Plastigage strips from all bearing journals.

11. If the bearing clearance is greater than specified, record the selection marks on the crankshaft and connecting rod and bearing inserts and refer them to a Kawasaki dealer for new bearing selection.

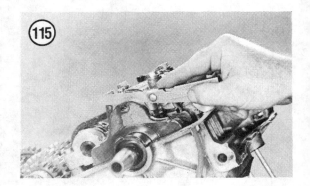

12. After bearings have been installed, recheck clearance by repeating this procedure.

Crankshaft Inspection

1. Clean crankshaft thoroughly with solvent. Clean oil holes with rifle cleaning brushes; flush thoroughly and dry with compressed air. Lightly oil all journal surfaces immediately to prevent rust.

2. Inspect the cam chain drive sprocket. If it is worn, the crankshaft will have to be replaced. Also inspect the cam chain; replace if necessary.

3. Measure connecting rod side clearance with a feeler gauge as shown in **Figure 115**. Replace the crankshaft if side clearance of either connecting rod exceeds the specifications in **Table 2** or **Table 3**.

4. Support both ends of the crankshaft in a lathe, V-blocks or an alignment jig and check its runout with a dial indicator. If the runout exceeds 0.05 mm (0.002 in.), replace the crankshaft.

Table 1 ENGINE SPECIFICATIONS
(1974-1977 AND 1977-1978 DELUXE A MODELS)

	Standard mm (in.)	Wear limit mm (in.)
Camshaft journal clearance	0.030-0.140 (0.001-0.005)	0.19 (0.007)
Camshaft journal diameter	27.94-27.96 (1.100-1.101)	27.92 (1.099)
Camshaft runout		0.1 (0.004)
Camshaft lobe height	38.339-38.479 (1.509-1.515)	38.25 1.506
Camshaft chain wear (20 links)	160 (6.299)	162.4 (6.394)
Chain guide wear		
Front		1.5 (0.059)
Rear		2 (0.079)
Rocker arm inside diameter	13.00-13.018 (0.512-0.513)	13.05 (0.514)
Rocker arm shaft outer diameter	12.966-12.984 (0.510-0.511)	12.94 (0.509)
Cylinder head warpage limit		0.05 (0.002)
Valve head thickness	0.75-1.25 (0.030-0.049)	0.5 (0.020)

(continued)

Table 1 ENGINE SPECIFICATIONS
(1974-1977 AND 1977-1978 DELUXE A MODELS) (continued)

	Standard mm (in.)	Wear limit mm (in.)
Valve stem bend		0.05 (0.020)
Valve stem diameter		
Intake	6.965-6.980 (0.274-0.275)	6.90 (0.272)
Exhaust	6.955-6.970 (0.274-0.275)	6.89 (0.271)
Valve guide inside diameter	7.000-7.015 (0.276-0.2761)	7.08 (0.2787)
Valve spring free length		
Inner	32.4 (1.275)	31.0 (1.220)
Outer	37.3 (1.468)	36.0 (1.417)
Cylinder inside diameter	63.984-64.004 (2.519-2.520)	64.08 (2.5228)
Piston diameter		63.8 (2.512)
Piston-to-cylinder clearance	0.034-0.054 (0.0013-0.0021)	— —
Piston ring thickness		
Top ring	1.460-1.475 (0.0574-0.0581)	1.38 (0.0543)
Second	1.475-1.490 (0.0581-0.0586)	1.40 (0.0551)
Oil ring	2.475-2.490 (0.0974-0.0980)	2.40 (0.0945)
Piston ring groove width		
Top/second ring	1.50-1.52 (0.0590-0.0598)	1.60 (0.063)
Oil ring	2.50-2.52 (0.0984-0.0992)	2.60 (2.6394)
Piston ring/groove clearance		
Top	0.025-0.060 (0.0009-0.0023)	0.160 (0.0063)
Second/oil control ring	0.010-0.045 (0.0004-0.0018)	0.145 (0.0057)
Piston ring end gap	0.2-0.4 (0.0078-0.0157)	0.7 (0.0275)
Connecting rod journal clearance	0.041-0.071 0.0016-0.0028)	0.1 (0.0039)
Connecting rod side clearance	0.15-0.25 (0.0059-0.0098)	0.45 (0.0177)
Crankshaft runout		0.05 (0.0019)
Crankshaft journal clearance	0.036-0.078 (0.0014-0.0030)	0.11 (0.0043)
Crankshaft journal diameter	35.984-36.00 (1.4166-1.4173)	35.96 (1.4157)
Crankshaft thrust clearance	0.10-0.20 (0.0039-0.0078)	0.45 (0.0017)
Balancer shaft		
Shaft diameter	19.967-19.980 (0.7861-0.7866)	19.93 (0.7846)
Holder inside diameter	20.007-20.028 (0.7876-0.7885)	20.08 (0.7905)
Oil pump		
Outer rotor/inner rotor side clearance		0.21 (0.008)
Rotor side wear		0.15 (0.006)
Pump body clearance		0.25 (0.009)

4

Table 2 ENGINE SPECIFICATIONS (1978-1981 KZ400)

	Standard mm (in.)	Wear limit mm (in.)
Camshaft journal clearance	0.130-0.240 (0.0051-0.0094)	0.29 (0.0114)
Camshaft journal diameter	24.950-24.970 (0.9823-0.9831)	24.93 (0.9815)
Camshaft runout		0.1 (0.004)
Camshaft chain wear (20 links)	160 (6.299)	162.4 (6.394)
Chain guide wear		
Front		1.5 (0.059)
Rear		2.5 (0.0984)
Camshaft lobe height	38.339-38.479 (1.509-1.515)	(38.25) (1.506)
Rocker arm inside diameter	13.00-13.018 (0.512-0.513)	13.05 (0.514)
Rocker arm shaft outer diameter	12.966-12.984 (0.510-0.511)	12.94 (0.509)
Cylinder head warpage limit		0.25 (0.010)
Valve head thickness	1.0 (0.03937)	0.5 (0.020)
Valve stem bend		0.05 (0.020)
Valve stem diameter		
Intake	6.965-6.980 (0.274-0.275)	6.90 (0.272)
Exhaust	6.955-6.970 (0.274-0.275)	6.90 (0.2716)
Valve guide inside diameter	7.000-7.018 (0.276-0.2763)	7.08 (0.2787)
Valve spring free length		
Inner	22.2 (0.8740)	—
Outer	25.7 (1.012)	—
Cylinder inside diameter	64.000-64.012 (2.5196-2.5201)	64.10 (2.5236)
Piston diameter		63.80 (2.512)
Piston-to-cylinder clearance	0.037-0.064 (0.0015-0.0025)	—
Piston ring thickness (1978)		
Top ring	1.170-1.190 (0.0460-0.0468)	1.10 (0.0433)
Second	1.475-1.490 (0.0581-0.0586)	1.40 (0.0551)
Oil ring	2.475-2.490 (0.0974-0.0980)	2.40 (0.0945)
Piston ring thickness (1979-1981)		
Top ring	1.160-1.180 (0.0456-0.0464)	1.09 (0.0429)
Second	1.475-1.490 (0.0581-0.0586)	1.40 (0.0551)
Oil ring	2.475-2.490 (0.0974-0.0980)	2.40 (0.0945)
Piston ring groove width		
Top ring	1.23-1.25 (0.0484-0.0492)	1.33 (0.0526)
Second	1.50-1.52 (0.0590-0.0598)	1.60 (0.063)
Oil ring	2.50-2.52 (0.0984-0.0992)	2.61 (0.1023)

(continued)

Table 2 ENGINE SPECIFICATIONS (1978-1981 KZ400) (continued)

	Standard mm (in.)	Wear limit mm (in.)
Piston ring/groove clearance (1978)		
Top	0.040-0.080 (0.0157-0.0031)	0.18 (0.0070)
Second	0.010-0.045 (0.0004-0.0018)	0.145 (0.0057)
Oil ring	0.020-0.055 (0.0007-0.0021	0.15 (0.1893)
Piston ring/groove clearance (1979-1981)		
Top	0.050-0.090 (0.0019-0.0035)	0.19 (0.0074)
Second	0.010-0.050 (0.0004-0.0019)	0.15 (0.0059)
Oil ring	0.020-0.055 (0.0007-0.0021)	0.15 (0.1893)
Piston ring end gap	0.2-0.4 (0.0078-0.0157)	0.7 (0.0275)
Connecting rod journal clearance	0.040-0.069 0.0016-0.0027)	0.1 (0.0039)
Connecting rod side clearance	0.15-0.25 (0.0059-0.0098)	0.45 (0.0177)
Crankshaft runout		0.05 (0.0019)
Crankshaft journal clearance		
1978-1980	0.034-0.076 (0.0013-0.0029)	0.11 (0.0043)
1981	0.034-0.076 (0.0013-0.0029)	0.08 (0.0031)
Crankshaft journal diameter	35.984-36.00 (1.4166-1.4173)	35.96 (1.4157)
Crankshaft thrust clearance	0.20-0.30 (0.0078-0.0118)	0.45 (0.0017)
Balancer shaft		
Shaft outer diameter	19.967-19.980 (0.7861-0.7866)	19.93 (0.7846)
Main bearing holder hole inside diameter	20.000-20.030 (0.7874-0.7992)	20.08 (0.7905)
Oil pump		
Outer rotor/inner rotor side clearance		0.21 (0.008)
Rotor side wear		0.15 (0.006)
Pump body clearance		0.25 (0.009)

4

Table 3 ENGINE SPECIFICATIONS (1980-1983 KZ440)*

	Wear limit mm (in.)
Camshaft journal clearance	0.29 (0.0114)
Camshaft journal diameter	24.93 (0.9815)
Camshaft runout	0.1 (0.004)
Camshaft chain wear (20 links)	128.8 (5.071)
Chain guide wear	
Front	3.6 (0.1417)
Rear	4.5 (0.1771)
Camshaft lobe height	38.25 (1.506)
Rocker arm inside diameter	13.05 (0.514)
Rocker arm shaft outer diameter	12.94 (0.509)
Cylinder head warpage limit	0.25 (0.010)
Valve head thickness	0.5 (0.020)
Valve stem bend	0.05 (0.002)
Valve stem diameter	
Intake	6.90 (0.272)
Exhaust	6.90 (0.272)
Valve guide inside diameter	7.08 (0.2787)
Valve spring free length	
Inner	22.2 (0.8740)
Outer	25.7 (1.012)
Cylinder inside diameter	67.60 (2.6614)
Piston diameter	67.30 (2.6496)
Piston-to-cylinder clearance	0.035-0.062 (0.0013-0.0024)
Piston ring thickness	
Top ring	1.10 (0.0433)
Second	1.40 (0.0551)
Piston ring groove width	
Top ring	1.33 (0.0526)
Second	1.60 (0.063)
Oil ring	2.61 (0.1023)
Piston ring/groove clearance	
Top	0.18 (0.0070)
Second	0.014 (0.0057)
Piston ring end gap	0.7 (0.0275)
Connecting rod journal clearance	0.1 (0.0039)
Connecting rod side clearance	0.45 (0.0177)
Crankshaft runout	0.05 (0.0019)
Crankshaft journal clearance	0.08 (0.0031)
Crankshaft journal diameter	35.96 (1.4157)
Crankshaft thrust clearance	0.45 (0.0017)
Balancer shaft	
Shaft diameter	19.93 (0.7846)
Main bearing holder	
hole inside diameter	20.08 (0.7905)
Oil pump	
Outer rotor/inner rotor	
side clearance	0.21 (0.008)
Rotor side wear	0.15 0.25 (0.009)

* Kawasaki provides wear limit specifications only for these models.

Table 4 ENGINE TIGHTENING TORQUES
(1974-1977 AND 1977-1978 DELUXE A MODELS)

	N•m	ft.-lb.
Breather cover	18-20	13-14.5
Cylinder head cover nuts	25-30	18-22
Cylinder head bolts		
8 mm	25-30	18-22
6 mm	11-13	8-9
Camshaft sprocket bolts	14-16	10-11.5
Rocker arm locknuts	24-26	18-22
Rotor bolt	65-70	47-51
Starter clutch Allen bolts	33-37	24-27
Sprocket nut	120-150	87-108
Crankcase bolts		
6 mm	8-10	6-7
8 mm	25-30	18-22
Balancer holder bolts	23-27	16.5-19.5
Balancer weight bolts	11-13	8-9
Crankshaft bushing cap bolts	25-30	18-22
Connecting rod nuts	35-38	25-27
Neutral indicator switch	15-20	11-14.5
Oil pressure switch	14-16	10-11.5
Engine mounting bolts	34-46	25-33
Engine mounting bracket bolts		
Front	20-28	14.5-20
Rear	16-22	11.5-16

Table 5 ENGINE TIGHTENING TORQUES (1978-1981 KZ400)

	N•m	ft.-lb.
Breather cover bolts	25	18
Camshaft cap bolts	12	8.7
Camshaft chain tensioner		
Cap	15	11
Locknut	15	11
Camshaft sprocket bolts	15	11
Connecting rod nuts	14	17.5
Crankcase bolts		
Lower (6 mm)	10	7.2
8 mm	25	18
Upper	10	7.2
Crankshaft main bearing cap bolts		
8 mm	25	18
10 mm	40	29
Balancer bearing cap/bolts		
8 mm	25	18
10 mm	40	29
Balancer weight bolt	15	11
Cylinder head nuts	40	29
Cylinder head cover bolts (6 mm)	7.2	10
8 mm	25	18
Rotor bolt	70	51
Neutral switch	15	11
Oil pressure switch	15	11
Oil pressure relief valve	15	11
Rocker arm shafts	25	18
Engine mounting bolts	40	29
Engine mounting bracket bolts		
Upper	18	13
Front and rear	24	17.5

Table 6 ENGINE TIGHTENING TORQUES (1981-1983 KZ440)

	N·m	ft.-lb.
Rotor bolt	70	51
Balancer bearing cap/bolts		
8 mm	25	18
10 mm	40	29
Balancer weight bolts	15	11
Breather cover bolts	25	18
Camshaft cap bolts	12	8.7
Camshaft chain tensioner bolt	10	7.2
Camshaft sprocket bolts	15	11
Connecting rod nuts	37	27
Crankcase bolts		
Upper	10	7.2
Lower		
6 mm	10	7.2
8 mm	25	18
Crankshaft main bearing cap bolts		
8 mm	25	18
10 mm	40	29
Cylinder head nuts	40	29
Cylinder head cover bolts		
6 mm	10	7.2
8 mm	25	18
Neutral switch	15	11
Oil pressure switch	15	11
Oil pressure relief valve	15	11
Rocker arm shaft	25	18
Engine mounting bolts		
10 mm	40	29
8 mm	25	18

CHAPTER FIVE

ENGINE (1985-ON EN450)

The engine is a liquid-cooled double overhead cam eight-valve parallel twin. Valves are operated by two chain-driven overhead camshafts. The crankshaft and pistons are so arranged that cylinders fire alternately; while either piston is at firing position on its compression stroke, the other piston is on the exhaust stroke.

This chapter provides complete service and overhaul procedures, including information for disassembly, removal, inspection, service and reassembly of the engine.

Before starting any work, read the service hints in Chapter One. You will do a better job with this information fresh in your mind.

Table 1 and **Table 2** at the end of the chapter list complete engine specifications.

SERVICING ENGINE IN FRAME

Many components can be serviced while the engine is mounted in the frame:
  a. Cylinder head.
  b. Cylinders and pistons.
  c. Gearshift mechanism.
  d. Clutch (partial disassembly).
  e. Carburetors.
  f. Starter motor and gears.
  g. Alternator and electrical systems.

ENGINE

Removal/Installation

1. Place the motorcycle on its centerstand. Remove the left- and right-hand side covers, and accessories such as fairings and crash bars.
2. Remove the seat and disconnect the negative battery terminal (**Figure 1**).
3. Remove the fuel tank.
4. Drain the engine oil as described in Chapter Three.
5. Drain the cooling system as described in Chapter Three.
6. Remove the following as described in Chapter Ten:
  a. Radiator and fan; refer to *Radiator and Fan Removal/Installation.*
  b. Thermostat housing; refer to *Thermostat Removal/Installation.*
7. Remove the coolant reservoir tank from the right-hand side.
8. Disconnect the spark plug wires. Then disconnect the ignition coil electrical connectors and remove the coils (**Figure 2**).
9. Remove the exhaust system.
10. Remove the carburetors as described in Chapter Eight.

11. Remove the air filter housing.

12. Loosen the clutch cable at the hand grip (**Figure 3**). Then disconnect the clutch cable at the crankcase (**Figure 4**).

13. Disconnect the crankcase breather hose.

14. Remove the right footpeg and brake pedal assembly (**Figure 5**).

15. Remove the gearshift lever (**Figure 6**).

16. Remove the engine pulley cover (**Figure 6**).

17. Disconnect the following wiring connectors:
    a. Starter motor (**Figure 7**).
    b. Neutral switch (**Figure 8**).
    c. Oil pressure switch (**Figure 9**).
    d. Rear brake switch (right-hand side).

18. Remove the following as described in this chapter:
    a. Cylinder head.
    b. Cylinder.
    c. Pistons.
    d. Alternator.
    e. Starter.

19. Remove the clutch plates as described in Chapter Six.

20. Remove the external shift mechanism. See Chapter Seven.

21. Remove the drive pulley and belt. See Chapter Twelve.

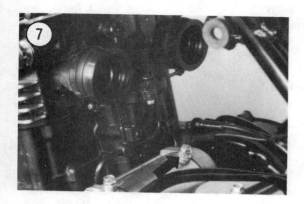

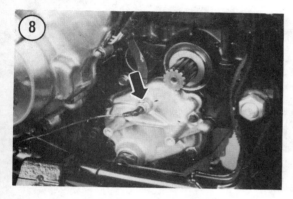

22. Examine the engine to make sure everything has been disconnected and positioned out of the way.

23. Place wooden blocks under the crankcase to support the engine once the mounting bolts are removed.

24. Loosen, but do not remove, all front (**Figure 10**) and rear (**Figure 11**) engine mount nuts.

25. Remove the front engine mount bolts, nuts and brackets (**Figure 10**).

26. Withdraw the lower and the upper rear engine mount through-bolts (**Figure 11**).

27. Lift the crankcase (**Figure 12**) up and remove it.

NOTE
If the engine is being removed with the cylinder and cylinder head assembly installed, remove the engine through the right-hand side.

28. While the engine is removed for service, check all of the frame engine mounts for cracks or other damage. If any cracks are detected, take the chassis assembly to a Kawasaki dealer for further examination.

29. Install by reversing the removal steps, noting the following.

30. After the engine is positioned correctly, install the engine mount brackets, bolts and nuts.

31. Tighten the engine mount nuts and bolts to the specifications in **Table 2**.

32. Fill the crankcase with the recommended type and quantity of engine oil. Refer to Chapter Three.

33. Refill the cooling system. Refer to Chapter Three.

34. Adjust the following as described in Chapter Three:

    a. Clutch.

    b. Drive belt.

    c. Rear brake.

    d. Throttle cable.

35. Start the engine and check for leaks.

CYLINDER HEAD AND CAMSHAFTS

This section describes removal, inspection and installation procedures for the cylinder head and camshaft components. Valves and valve components are described in a separate section.

Cylinder Head Cover
Removal/Installation

1. Place the motorcycle on the centerstand.

2. Drain the engine coolant as described in Chapter Three.

3. Remove the seat and fuel tank.

4. Remove the following as described in Chapter Ten:

    a. Radiator and fan.

    b. Thermostat housing.

5. Remove the coolant reservoir tank.

6. Unscrew the tachometer cable (A, **Figure 13**).

7. Disconnect the ignition coil wiring and remove the ignition coils (**Figure 2**).

8. *U.S. models:* Remove the air suction valves and hoses (B, **Figure 13**).

9. Remove the 2 cylinder head water pipes (**Figure 14**).

10. Remove the cylinder head cover bolts and remove the cover (A, **Figure 15**) and tachometer drive pin (**Figure 16**).

11. Installation is the reverse of these steps, noting the following.

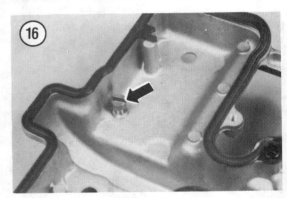

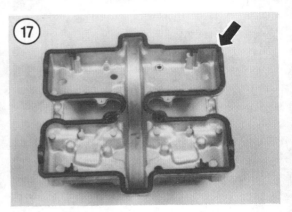

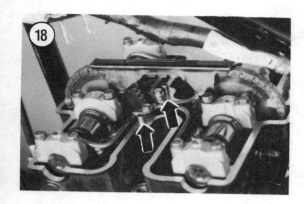

12. Replace the cylinder head cover gasket (**Figure 17**), if necessary.

13. Install the 2 cylinder head cover dowel pins (**Figure 18**).

14. Apply a non-hardening gasket sealer (such as RTV) to the mating areas indicated in B, **Figure 15**. Apply sealer to both left- and right-hand sides of the cylinder head.

CAUTION
Before installing the cylinder head cover in Step 15, note the tachometer pin protruding through the tachometer drive on the right-hand side of the cylinder head cover. Figure 16 shows the pin with the cover removed. If the tachometer pin (Figure 16) is loose in its mounting ring, it could fall into the engine as the cylinder head cover is installed. To prevent the pin from falling, pull up on the pin with a pair of pliers to make sure it is tight in its mounting ring. If the pin is loose and you feel it could fall out, have an assistant hold the pin with the pliers as you install the cylinder head cover.

15. Make sure the tachometer pin is installed in the cylinder head cover (**Figure 16**).

16. Tighten the cylinder head cover bolts to the specifications in **Table 2**.

Camshaft Removal

1. Remove the cylinder head cover as described in this chapter.

2. Loosen the valve adjuster locknuts and loosen the adjusters.

3. Remove the cam chain tensioner as described in this chapter.

4. Remove the cylinder head oil pipes (**Figure 19**).

CAUTION
The oil pipes can be easily damaged. Place them in a box until reassembly.

5. Remove the upper chain guide (**Figure 20**).

NOTE
Each camshaft cap is marked with an arrow (pointing forward) and with a letter representing position. See Figure 21 and Figure 22. If the camshaft cap markings on your bike differ from those in Figure 22 or there are no marks, label them for direction and position before performing Step 6.

6. Remove the camshaft cap bolts and remove the caps (**Figure 23**).

NOTE
*The camshaft cap labeled "G" houses the tachometer drive gear (**Figure 24**). Remove the camshaft cap and drive gear as as assembly.*

7. Secure the camshaft chain with wire. Then remove both camshafts with their sprockets (**Figure 25**).

Cylinder Head
Removal

1. Remove the 2 cylinder head oil line banjo bolts (**Figure 26**) and copper washers.
2. Remove the front (**Figure 27**) and rear (**Figure 28**) 6 mm cylinder head bolts.
3. Remove the 10 mm cylinder head bolts.
4. Loosen the cylinder head (**Figure 29**) by tapping around the perimeter with a rubber or plastic mallet.

CAUTION
Remember, the cooling fins are fragile and may be damaged if tapped on too hard. Never use a metal hammer.

5. Remove the cylinder head (**Figure 29**) by pulling straight up and off the cylinder. Place a clean shop rag into the cam chain opening in the cylinder to prevent the entry of foreign matter.

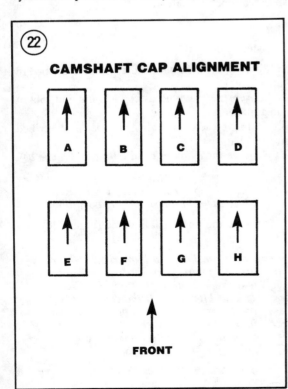

22

CAMSHAFT CAP ALIGNMENT

A	B	C	D
↑	↑	↑	↑

E	F	G	H
↑	↑	↑	↑

↑
FRONT

NOTE
After removing the cylinder head, check the top and bottom mating surfaces for any indication of leakage. Also check the head and base gaskets for signs of leakage. A blown gasket could indicate possible cylinder head warpage or other damage.

6. Remove the 2 dowel pins (A, **Figure 30**) and the cylinder head gasket (B, **Figure 30**). Discard the gasket.

Camshaft Inspection

1. Check cam lobes (A, **Figure 31**) for wear. The lobes should not be scored and the edges should be square. Slight damage may be removed with a silicon carbide oilstone. Use No. 100-120 grit initially, then polish with a No. 280-320 grit.
2. Even though the cam lobe surfaces appear to be satisfactory, with no visible signs of wear, they must be measured with a micrometer as shown in **Figure 32**. Replace the shaft(s) if worn beyond the service limits (measurements less than those given in **Table 1**).
3. Check the camshaft bearing journals (B, **Figure 31**) for wear and scoring.
4. Even though the camshaft bearing journal surface appears satisfactory, with no visible signs of wear, the camshaft bearing journals must be measured with a micrometer. Replace the shaft(s)

5

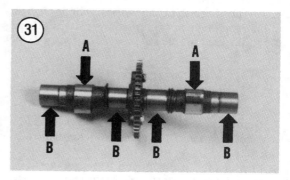

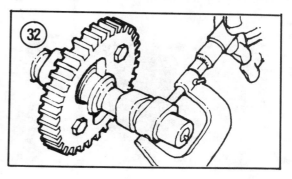

if worn beyond the service limits (measurements less than those given in **Table 1**).

5. Place the camshaft on a set of V-blocks and check its runout with a dial indicator. Replace the camshaft if runout exceeds specifications in **Table 1**. Repeat for the opposite camshaft.

6. Inspect the camshaft sprockets (**Figure 33**) for wear; replace if necessary.

7. Check the camshaft bearing journals in the cylinder head (**Figure 34**) and camshaft caps (**Figure 35**) for wear and scoring. They should not be scored or excessively worn. If necessary, replace the cylinder head and camshaft caps as a matched pair.

Camshaft Bearing Clearance Measurement

This procedure requires the use of a Plastigage set. The camshaft must be installed into the head. Before installation, wipe all oil residue from each cam bearing journal and bearing surface in the head and all camshaft caps.

1. Install the camshafts into the cylinder head.

2. Install all locating dowels into their camshaft caps.

3. Wipe all oil from the cam bearing journals before using the Plastigage material.

4. Place a strip of Plastigage material on top of each cam bearing journal (**Figure 36**), parallel to the cam.

5. Place the camshaft cap into position.

6. Install all camshaft cap bolts. Install finger-tight at first, then tighten in a crisscross pattern (**Figure 37**) to the final torque specification listed in **Table 2**.

> *CAUTION*
> *Do not rotate the camshaft with the Plastigage material in place.*

7. Gradually remove the camshaft cap bolts in a crisscross pattern. Remove the camshaft caps carefully.

8. Measure the width of the flattened Plastigage according to manufacturer's instructions (**Figure 38**).

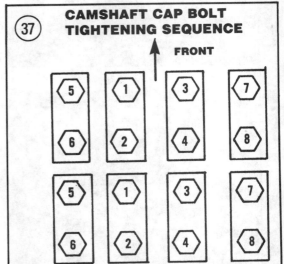

CAMSHAFT CAP BOLT TIGHTENING SEQUENCE

FRONT

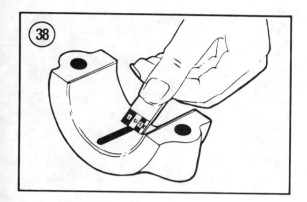

1. Straightedge
2. Feeler gauge

9. If the clearance exceeds the wear limits in **Table 1**, measure the camshaft bearing journals with a micrometer and compare to the limits in **Table 1**. If the camshaft bearing journal is less than dimension specified, replace the cam. If the cam is within specifications, the cylinder head and camshaft caps must be replaced as a matched set.

> *CAUTION*
> *Remove all particles of Plastigage from all camshaft bearing journals and the camshaft holder. Be sure to clean the camshaft holder groove. This material must not be left in the engine as it can plug up an oil control orifice and cause severe engine damage.*

Cylinder Head Inspection

1. Remove all traces of gasket from cylinder head and cylinder mating surfaces. Do not scratch the gasket surface.
2. Without removing valves, remove all carbon deposits from the combustion chambers (**Figure 39**) with a wire brush or wooden scraper. Take care not to damage the head, valves or spark plug threads.

> *CAUTION*
> *If the combustion chambers are cleaned while the valves are removed, make sure to keep the scraper or wire brush away from the valve seats to prevent damaging the seat surfaces. A damaged or even slightly scratched valve seat will cause poor valve seating.*

3. Examine the spark plug threads in the cylinder head for damage. If damage is minor or if the threads are dirty or clogged with carbon, use a spark plug thread tap to clean the threads following the manufacturer's instructions. If thread damage is severe, refer further service to a Kawasaki dealer or machine shop.
4. After all carbon is removed from combustion chambers, and valve ports and the spark plug thread holes are repaired, clean the entire head in solvent and blow dry with compressed air.
5. Clean away all carbon on the piston crowns. Do not remove the carbon ridge at the top of the cylinder bore (**Figure 40**).
6. Check for cracks in the combustion chamber and exhaust ports. A cracked head must be replaced.
7. After the head has been thoroughly cleaned, place a straightedge across the gasket surface at several points (**Figure 41**). Measure warp by inserting a feeler gauge between the straightedge and cylinder head at each location. Maximum

allowable warpage is listed in **Table 1**. If warpage exceeds this limit, the cylinder head must be replaced.

8. Check the valves and valve guides as described under *Valves and Valve Components* in this chapter.

Oil Pipes
Cleaning/Inspection

1. Examine the cylinder head (**Figure 42**) and main oil pipes (**Figure 43**) for damage. Check the brazed joints for cracking or other apparent damage. Check the cylinder oil pipe O-rings (**Figure 44**) for wear. If the O-ring surfaces are not perfectly smooth, replace them.
2. Flush the oil pipes with solvent and allow to dry.

Cylinder Head Installation

1. If removed, install the rear chain guide (**Figure 45**).
2. Clean the cylinder head (**Figure 46**) and cylinder (**Figure 45**) mating surfaces of all gasket residue.

> *NOTE*
> *The cylinder head gasket is marked with the word HEAD on one side. This side must face up.*

3. Install a new cylinder head gasket (B, **Figure 30**) and the 2 dowel pins (A, **Figure 30**).
4. Install the cylinder head (**Figure 29**).
5. Install the bolts securing the cylinder head. Tighten the 10 mm bolts in 2-3 stages in a crisscross pattern (**Figure 47**) to the torque specifications listed in **Table 2**.
6. Tighten the front (**Figure 27**) and rear (**Figure 28**) cylinder head 6 mm bolts to the torque specifications listed in **Table 2**.
7. Install the main oil pipe and banjo bolts, using new copper washers. Tighten the banjo bolts to the specifications listed in **Table 2**.

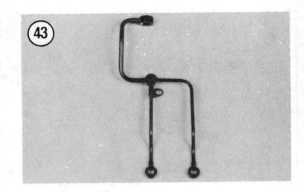

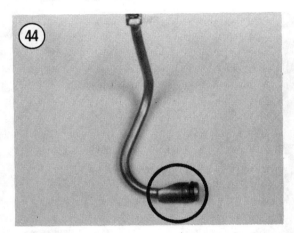

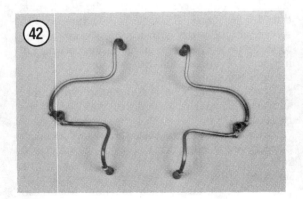

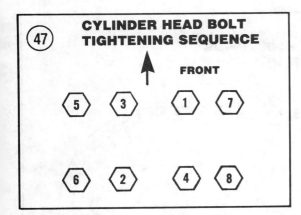

CYLINDER HEAD BOLT TIGHTENING SEQUENCE

FRONT

47

5 3 1 7

6 2 4 8

48

49

50

Camshaft Installation

1. The intake and exhaust sprockets are identical. If the sprockets were removed from the camshafts, install them as follows:

   a. Install the sprockets onto their camshafts so that the sides marked with an IN and EX face to the left.

   b. There are 4 holes drilled into each sprocket. On the intake camshaft (cam with tachometer gear threads), use the sprocket bolt holes marked IN. On the exhaust camshaft, use the sprocket bolt holes marked EX.

   c. Tighten the sprocket bolts to the specifications in **Table 2**.

2. Coat all camshaft lobes and bearing journals with molybdenum disulfide grease or assembly oil.

3. Also coat the bearing surfaces in the cylinder head and camshaft bearing caps.

NOTE
The intake cam has tachometer gear threads on one side (Figure 48). Install this cam toward the rear.

4. Lift up on the cam chain and slide the 2 camshafts through and seat them in the cylinder head. Engage the cam chain with the cam sprockets. Remove the wire from the cam chain.

5. Remove the 2 caps on the alternator cover (**Figure 49**).

6. Using a socket on the crankshaft bolt (A, **Figure 50**), turn the crankshaft clockwise until the "C" TDC mark for the No. 2 cylinder is aligned with the notch in the upper hole (B, **Figure 50**).

7. Lift the cam chain off the sprocket. Without turning the crankshaft, align the EX line on the exhaust cam sprocket and the IN on the intake cam sprocket with the upper cylinder head surface as shown in **Figure 51**.

8. Refer to **Figure 51**. Locate the punch mark on the intake sprocket. Beginning with this mark, count off 24 cam chain pins toward the exhaust sprocket. The 24th pin must align with the punch mark on the exhaust sprocket. If it does not, recheck your pin count and reposition the intake or exhaust camshaft as required.

9. Check that the cam chain is properly seated in the front and rear cam chain guides.

10. Check that the camshaft cap dowel pins are in place and loosely install the camshaft caps in their original positions. The arrow on each cap must face to the front of the bike and the alphabet lettering must be installed in the order shown in **Figure 52**.

11. Install the upper cam chain guide (**Figure 53**).

5

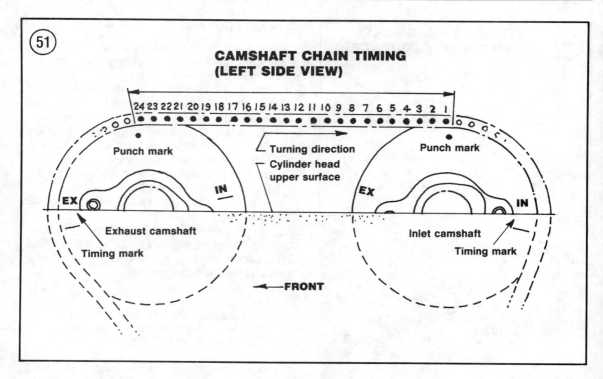

CAMSHAFT CHAIN TIMING (LEFT SIDE VIEW)

24 23 22 21 20 19 18 17 16 15 14 13 12 11 10 9 8 7 6 5 4 3 2 1

Punch mark

Turning direction
Cylinder head
upper surface

Punch mark

EX   IN

EX   IN

Exhaust camshaft

Inlet camshaft

Timing mark

Timing mark

FRONT

12. Tighten the camshaft cap bolts marked No. 1 and 2 (**Figure 54**) for the exhaust and intake cams. This will seat the camshafts in position. Then tighten all bolts in a crisscross pattern to the torque specification in **Table 2**.

13. Slowly turn the crankshaft clockwise 2 full turns, using the bolt (A, **Figure 50**) on the left end of the crankshaft. Check that all cam sprocket timing marks again align as shown in **Figure 51** when the "C" TDC mark on the rotor is aligned with the notch in the alternator cover upper hole (B, **Figure 50**). If all marks align as indicated, cam timing is correct. If not, readjust as necessary.

CAUTION
*If there is any binding while turning the crankshaft, **stop**. Recheck the camshaft timing marks. Improper timing can cause valve and piston damage.*

14. Position the oil pipes into the cylinder head. Then push both ends of one pipe into the head at the same time. Repeat for the opposite side. Install the oil pipe mounting bolts and tighten securely. See **Figure 55**.

15. Install the cam chain tensioner as described in this chapter.

16. Adjust the valves as described in Chapter Three.

17. Install the cylinder head cover as described in this chapter.

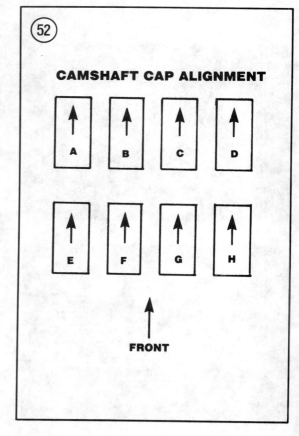

CAMSHAFT CAP ALIGNMENT

A   B   C   D

E   F   G   H

FRONT

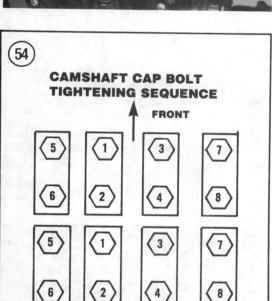

CAMSHAFT CAP BOLT
TIGHTENING SEQUENCE

FRONT

ROCKER ARM ASSEMBLIES

The rocker arms are identical (same Kawasaki part No.) but they will develop different wear patterns during use. It is recommended that all parts be marked during removal so that they can be assembled in their original positions.

Removal/Inspection/Installation

NOTE
The rocker arms can be removed with the cylinder head installed on the engine. The following procedure is shown with the cylinder removed for clarity.

1. *Cylinder head installed on engine:* Remove the camshafts as described in this chapter.
2. With an Allen wrench, loosen one of the rocker arm shafts (**Figure 56**) and remove it. See **Figure 57**.
3. Remove the rocker arm and spring (**Figure 58**).
4. Repeat Steps 2 and 3 for the remaining rocker arms.
5. Wash all parts in cleaning solvent and throughly dry.

6. Inspect the rocker arm pad (**Figure 59**) where it rides on the cam lobe and where the adjuster (**Figure 60**) rides on the valve stem. If the pad is scratched or unevenly worn, inspect the cam lobe for scoring, chipping or flat spots. Replace the rocker arm if defective.

NOTE
*If the rocker arm pad (**Figure 59**) is worn, also check the mating cam lobe for wear or damage. See **Figure 61**.*

7. Measure the inside diameter of the rocker arm bore (A, **Figure 62**) with an inside micrometer and check against dimension in **Table 1**. Replace if worn to the service limit or greater.
8. Inspect the rocker arm shaft for wear or scoring. Measure the outside diameter (B, **Figure 62**) with a micrometer and check against dimension in **Table 1**. Replace if worn to the service limit or greater.
9. Coat the rocker arm shaft and rocker arm bore with assembly oil.
10. Assemble the springs (**Figure 59**) onto each rocker arm so that the spring will face against the camshaft chain after installation. See **Figure 63**.
11. Install the rocker arm and spring (**Figure 58**).
12. Install the rocker arm shaft (**Figure 57**) and tighten it to the torque specifications in **Table 2**.

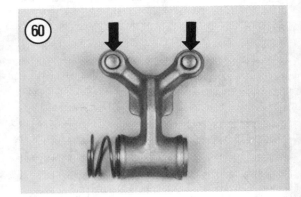

CAM CHAIN TENSIONER

The automatic tensioner is continuously self-adjusting. The tensioner pushrod is free to move inward, but can't move out. Whenever the cam chain tensioner bolts are loosened, the tensioner assembly must be completely removed and reset as described in this section.

Removal/Installation

1. Loosen the front cam chain tensioner cap bolt.
2. Remove the 2 tensioner mounting bolts (**Figure 64**) and the tensioner assembly.
3. Remove the tensioner cap bolt (**Figure 65**).

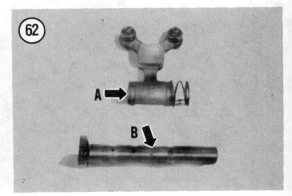

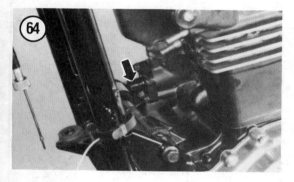

CAUTION
When performing step 4, do not turn
the tensioner counterclockwise as this
could cause the rod to disconnect.

4. Hold the tensioner in your hand as shown in
Figure 66 and insert a small screwdriver into the
end of the tensioner body. Turn the rod *clockwise*
while pushing it in until it protrudes approximately
10 mm through the rear of the tensioner body.

5. While holding the rod in position (**Figure 67**)
install the tensioner onto the cylinder. Then
remove the screwdriver and install and tighten the
mounting bolts to the specifications in **Table 2**.

NOTE
If the tensioner rod slips before
installing the mounting bolts, remove
the tensioner and repeat this procedure.

6. Install the tensioner cap bolt.

VALVES AND VALVE COMPONENTS

Refer to **Figure 68** for this procedure.

1. Remove the cylinder head as described in this
chapter.

2. Install a valve spring compressor squarely over
the valve retainer with other end of tool placed
against valve head (**Figure 69**).

3. Tighten valve spring compressor until the split
valve keepers separate. Lift out split keepers with
needlenose pliers.

4. Gradually loosen valve spring compressor and
remove from head. Lift off upper valve seat.

CAUTION
Remove any burrs from the valve stem
grooves before removing the valve
(Figure 70). Otherwise the valve guides
will be damaged.

5. Remove the inner and outer springs and valve.

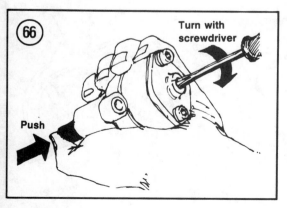

Turn with
screwdriver

Push

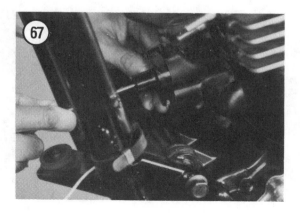

6. Remove the oil seal.

7. Remove the lower spring seat.

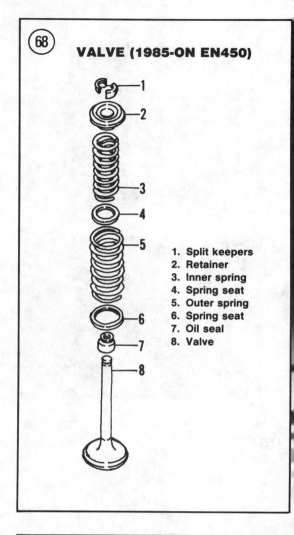

CAUTION
*All component parts of each valve
assembly must be kept together. Do not
mix with like components from other
valves or excessive wear may result.*

8. Repeat Steps 2-7 and remove remaining
valve(s).

Inspection

1. Clean valves with a wire brush and solvent.

2. Inspect the contact surface of each valve for
burning (**Figure 71**). Minor roughness and pitting
can be removed by lapping the valve as described
in this chapter. Excessive unevenness to the
contact surface is an indication that the valve is not
serviceable. The contact surface of the valve may
be ground on a valve grinding machine, but it is
best to replace a burned or damaged valve with a
new one.

3. Inspect the valve stems for wear and roughness
and measure the runout of the valve stem as shown
in **Figure 72**. The runout should not exceed the
wear limit specifications (**Table 1**).

4. Measure valve stems for wear using a
micrometer (**Figure 73**). Compare with
specifications in **Table 1**.

5. Remove all carbon and varnish from the valve
guides with a stiff spiral wire brush.

NOTE
*Step 6 and Step 7 require special
measuring equipment. If you do not
have the required measuring devices,
proceed to Step 8.*

6. Measure each valve guide at top, center and
bottom with a small hole gauge. Compare
measurements with specifications in **Table 1**.

7. Replace the valves (Step 4) or valve guides (Step
6) if they exceed the wear limits in **Table 1**.

VALVE (1985-ON EN450)

1. Split keepers
2. Retainer
3. Inner spring
4. Spring seat
5. Outer spring
6. Spring seat
7. Oil seal
8. Valve

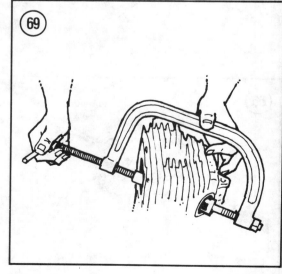

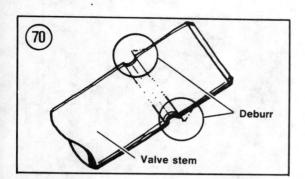

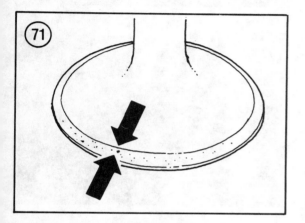

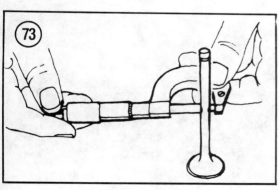

8. Insert each valve in its guide. Hold the valve just slightly off its seat and rock it sideways. If it rocks more than slightly, the guide is probably worn and should be replaced. As a final check, take the head to a dealer and have the valve guides measured.

9. Measure the valve spring length with a vernier caliper (**Figure 74**). All should be of length specified in **Table 1** with no bends or other distortion. Replace defective springs.

10. Measure the tilt of all valve springs as shown in **Figure 75**. Replace if tilt exceeds 1.5 mm (0.059 in.).

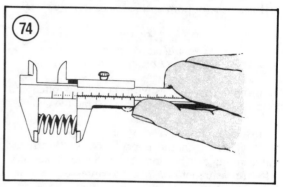

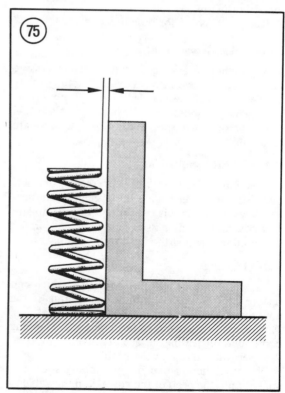

11. Check the valve spring retainer and valve keepers. If they are in good condition, they may be reused.

12. Inspect valve seats. If worn or burned, they must be reconditioned. This should be performed by your dealer or local machine shop. Seats and valves in near-perfect condition can be reconditioned by lapping with fine carborundum paste. Lapping, however, is always inferior to precision grinding.

Installation

1. Coat the valve stems with molybdenum disulfide paste and insert into cylinder head.

2. Install the bottom spring seat and a new seal.

> *NOTE*
> *Oil seals should be replaced whenever a valve is removed or replaced.*

3. Install valve springs with the narrow pitch end (end with coils closest together) facing the cylinder head.

4. Install the upper valve seat.

5. Push down on the upper valve seat with the valve spring compressor and install valve keepers. After releasing tension from compressor, examine valve keepers and make sure they are seated correctly (**Figure 76**).

6. Repeat Steps 1-5 for remaining valve(s).

Valve Guide Replacement

When guides are worn so that there is excessive stem-to-guide clearance or valve tipping, they must be replaced. Replace all, even if only one is worn. This job should only be done by a Kawasaki dealer or qualified specialist as special tools are required.

Valve Seat Reconditioning

This job is best left to your dealer or local machine shop. They have the special equipment and knowledge for this exacting job. You can still save considerable money by removing the cylinder head and taking just the head to the shop.

Valve Lapping

Valve lapping is a simple operation which can restore the valve seal without machining if the amount of wear or distortion is not too great.

1. Smear a light coating of fine grade valve lapping compound on seating surface of valve.

2. Insert the valve into the head.

3. Wet the suction cup of the lapping stick and stick it onto the head of the valve. Lap the valve to

the seat by spinning the lapping stick in both directions. Every 5 to 10 seconds, rotate the valve 180° in the valve seat. Lap only enough to achieve a precise seating ring around valve head.

4. Closely examine valve seat in cylinder head. It should be smooth and even with a smooth, polished seating "ring."

5. Thoroughly clean the valves and cylinder head in solvent to remove all grinding compound. Any compound left on the valves or the cylinder head will end up in the engine and will cause excessvie wear and damage.

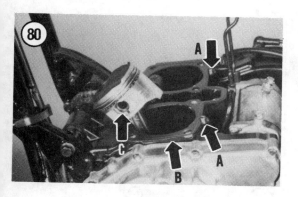

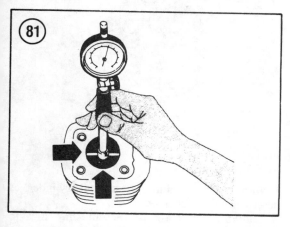

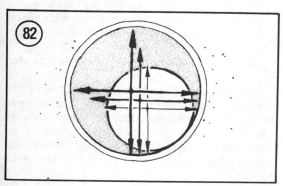

6. After the lapping has been completed and the valve assemblies have been reinstalled into the head the valve seal should be tested. Check the seal of each valve by pouring solvent into each of the intake and exhaust ports. There should be no leakage past the seat. If leakage occurs, combustion chamber will appear wet. If fluid leaks past any of the seats, disassemble that valve assembly and repeat the lapping procedure until there is no leakage.

CYLINDER

Removal

1. Remove the cylinder head as described in this chapter.

2. Remove the dowel pins (A, **Figure 77**) and head gasket (B, **Figure 77**).

3. Remove the rear chain guide (**Figure 78**).

4. Loosen the cylinder by tapping around the perimeter with a rubber or plastic mallet.

5. Pull the cylinder (**Figure 79**) straight up and off the piston and cylinder studs.

NOTE
Be sure to keep the cam chain wired up to prevent it from falling into the lower crankcase.

6. Stuff clean shop rags into the crankcase opening to prevent objects from falling into the crankcase.

7. Remove the dowel pins (A, **Figure 80**) and base gasket (B, **Figure 80**).

Inspection

1. Wash the cylinder bore in solvent to remove any oil and carbon particles. The bore must be cleaned thoroughly before attempting any measurement as incorrect readings may be obtained.

2. Measure the cylinder bores with a cylinder gauge (**Figure 81**) or inside micrometer at the points shown in **Figure 82**.

3. Measure in 2 axes—in line with the piston pin and at 90° to the pin. If the taper or out-of-round is greater than specifications (**Table 1**), the cylinders must be rebored to the next oversize and new pistons and rings installed. Rebore both cylinders even though only one may be worn.

NOTE
The new pistons should be obtained first before the cylinders are bored so that the pistons can be measured; each cylinder must be bored to match one piston only. Piston-to-cylinder clearance is specified in Table 1.

4. If the cylinder(s) are not worn past the service limits, check the bore carefully for scratches or gouges. The bore still may require boring and reconditioning.

5. If the cylinders require reboring, remove all dowel pins from the cylinder before leaving it with the dealer or machine shop.

CAUTION
After having the cylinders rebored, wash them thoroughly in hot soapy water. This is the best way to clean the cylinder of all fine grit material left from the bore job. After washing the cylinder, run a clean white cloth through the cylinder; it should show no traces of dirt or other debris. If the rag is dirty, the cylinder is not clean and must be rewashed. After the cylinder is thoroughly cleaned, dry and then lubricate the cylinder walls with clean engine oil to protect the cylinder liners from rust.

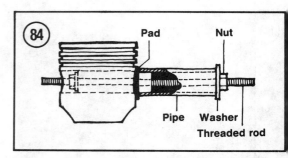

Installation

1. If the base gasket is stuck to the bottom of the cylinder it should be removed and the cylinder surface cleaned thoroughly.

2. Check that the top cylinder surface (**Figure 83**) is clean of all old gasket material.

3. Install the 2 dowel pins onto the crankcase (A, **Figure 80**).

4. Install a new cylinder base gasket (B, **Figure 80**) to the crankcase. Make sure all holes align.

5. Install a piston holding fixture under the pistons.

6. Lubricate cylinders and pistons liberally with engine oil before installation.

7. Carefully align the cylinder with the pistons.

NOTE
Once the cylinder is installed, run the chain and wire up through the cylinder.

8. Compress each ring as it enters the cylinder with your fingers or by using aircraft type hose clamps of appropriate diameter.

CAUTION
Don't tighten the clamp any more than necessary to compress the rings. If the rings can't slip through easily, the clamp may gouge the rings.

9. Remove the piston holding fixture and push the cylinder all the way down.

10. Install the cylinder head and camshafts as described in this chapter.

PISTONS AND PISTON RINGS

Piston
Removal/Installation

1. Remove the cylinder head and cylinder as described in this chapter.

2. Stuff the crankcase with clean shop rags to prevent objects from falling into the crankcase.

3. Lightly mark the piston crown with a L (left) or R (right) so they will be installed into the correct cylinder.

4. Remove the piston rings as described in this chapter.

5. Before removing the piston, hold the rod tightly and rock the piston. Any rocking motion (do not confuse with the normal sliding motion) indicates wear on the piston pin, rod bushing, pin bore, or more likely, a combination of all three. Mark the piston and pin so that they will be reassembled into the same set.

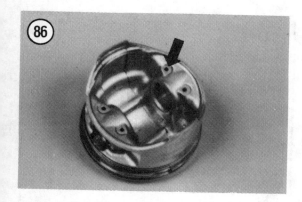

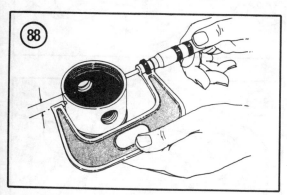

6. Remove the circlips from the piston pin bore (C, **Figure 80**).

7. Remove the piston pin. If the pin is tight, use a homemade tool as shown in **Figure 84**.

8. Inspect the piston as described in this chapter.

9. Coat the connecting rod bushing, piston pin and piston with assembly oil.

10. Place the piston over the connecting rod. If you are installing old parts, make sure the piston is installed on the correct rod as marked during removal. The arrow on each piston crown must face to the front of the engine.

11. Insert the piston pin and push it until it starts into the connecting rod bushing. If the pin does not slide easily, use the homemade tool (**Figure 84**),

but eliminate the piece of pipe. Push the pin in until it is centered in the piston.

12. Install *new* circlips in the piston bore.

13. Install rings as described in this chapter.

14. Repeat Steps 1-13 for the opposite piston.

Piston Inspection

1. Carefully clean the carbon from the piston crown (**Figure 85**) with a soft scraper. Do not remove or damage the carbon ridge around the circumference of the piston above the top ring. If the pistons, rings and cylinders are found to be dimensionally correct and can be reused, removal of the carbon ring from the top of the piston or the carbon ridges from the cylinders will promote excessive oil consumption.

CAUTION
Do not wire brush piston skirts.

2. Examine each ring groove for burrs, dented edges and wide wear. Pay particular attention to the top compression ring groove, as it usually wears more than the others.

3. Check the oil control holes in the piston (**Figure 86**) for carbon or oil sludge buildup. Clean the holes with a small diameter drill bit.

4. Check the piston skirts (**Figure 87**) for cracks or other damage.

5. Measure piston-to-cylinder clearance as described under *Piston Clearance* in this chapter.

6. If damage or wear indicate piston replacement, select a new piston as described under *Piston Clearance* in this chapter.

Piston Clearance

1. Make sure the piston and cylinder walls are clean and dry.

2. Measure the inside diameter of the cylinder at a point 13 mm (1/2 in.) from the upper edge with a bore gauge.

3. Measure the outside diameter of the piston at a point 5 mm (3/16 in.) from the lower edge of the piston at 90° to piston pin axis (**Figure 88**).

4. Subtract the piston diameter from the bore diameter; the difference is piston-to-cylinder clearance. Compare to specification in **Table 1**. If clearance is excessive, the piston should be replaced and the cylinder rebored. Purchase the new piston first; measure its diameter and add the specified clearance to determine the proper cylinder bore diameter.

NOTE
If one cylinder requires boring, the other cylinder must be bored also.

**Piston Ring
Removal/Installation**

> *WARNING*
> *The edges of all piston rings are very
> sharp. Be careful when handling them
> to avoid cut fingers.*

1. Measure the side clearance of each ring in its groove with a flat feeler gauge (**Figure 89**) and compare with the specifications in **Table 1**. If the clearance is greater than specified, the rings must be replaced. If the clearance is still excessive with the new rings, the piston must be replaced.
2. Remove the old rings with a ring expander tool or by spreading the ring ends with your thumbs and lifting the rings up evenly (**Figure 90**).
3. Using a broken piston ring, remove all carbon from the piston ring grooves.
4. Inspect grooves carefully for burrs, nicks or broken or cracked lands. Replace piston if necessary.
5. Check end gap of each ring. To check ring, insert the ring into the bottom of the cylinder bore and square it with the cylinder wall by tapping it with the piston. The ring should be pushed in about 15 mm (5/8 in.). Insert a feeler gauge as shown in **Figure 91** . Compare gap with **Table 1**. Replace ring if gap is too large. If the gap on the new ring is smaller than specified, hold a small file in a vise, grip the ends of the ring with your fingers and enlarge the gap.
6. Roll each ring around its piston groove as shown in **Figure 92** to check for binding. Minor binding may be cleaned up with a fine-cut file.
7. Install the piston rings in the order shown in **Figure 93**.

> *NOTE*
> *Install all rings with the manufacturer's
> markings facing up.*

8. Install the piston rings—first the bottom, then the middle, then the top ring—by carefully spreading the ends with your thumbs and slipping the rings over the top of the piston. Remember that the piston rings must be installed with the marks on them facing up toward the top of the piston or there is the possibility of oil pumping past the rings.
9. Install oil ring in oil ring groove with a ring expander tool or by spreading the ends with your thumbs.
10. Make sure the rings are seated completely in their grooves all the way around the piston and that the end gaps are distributed around the piston as shown in **Figure 93**. It is important that the ring

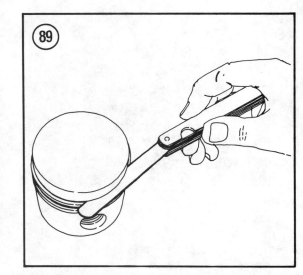

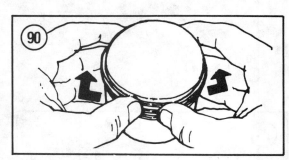

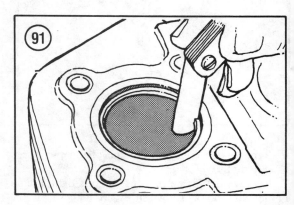

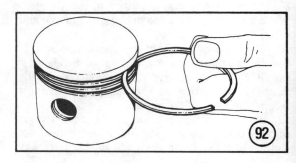

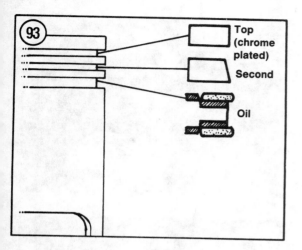

Top
(chrome
plated)

Second

Oil

gaps are not aligned with each other when installed to prevent compression pressures from escaping past them (**Figure 94**).

11. If installing oversize compression rings, check the number to make sure the correct rings are being installed. The ring numbers should be the same as the piston oversize number.

12. If new rings are installed, measure the side clearance of each ring (**Figure 89**) in its groove and compare to dimensions in **Table 1**.

OIL PUMP

The engine must be removed and the crankcase disassembled to remove the oil pump.

Removal/Installation

1. Remove the engine as described in this chapter.
2. Separate the crankcase as described in this chapter.
3. Remove the oil pan.
4. Remove the 3 O-rings (**Figure 95**).
5. Lift the oil pipe (**Figure 96**) out of the crankcase.
6. Remove the bolt (**Figure 97**) and lift the oil pipe (**Figure 98**) out of the crankcase.

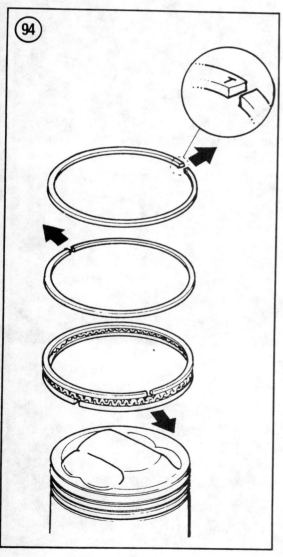

7. Remove the circlip securing the oil pump gear (**Figure 99**) and remove the gear.

8. Remove the oil pump screws (**Figure 100**) and lift the oil pump out of the crankcase.

9. Installation is the reverse of these steps, noting the following.

10. To prime the oil pump, add clean engine oil into the oil pump opening while turning the pump shaft (**Figure 101**).

11. Apply Loctite 242 (blue) to the oil pump screws before assembly. Tighten the screws securely.

12. Install new O-rings during assembly.

Disassembly/Inspection/Assembly

This procedure describes disassembly and inspection of the oil pump assembly. If any part is worn or damaged, the entire pump assembly must be replaced.

Refer to **Figure 102** for this procedure.

> *CAUTION*
> *An impact driver with a Phillips bit will be necessary to loosen the oil pump housing screws (**Figure 103**) in Step 1. Attempting to loosen the screws with a Phillips screwdriver may ruin the screw heads.*

1. Remove the oil pump screws and remove the cover.

2. Remove the outer and inner rotors from the housing.

3. Remove the rotor pin from the pump shaft.

4. Remove the oil pump shaft.

5. Clean all parts in solvent and dry thoroughly with compressed air.

6. Assemble the rotors and check the clearance between the rotors with a flat feeler gauge (**Figure 104**). The clearance should be within the specifications in **Table 1**. If the clearance is greater, replace the rotors as a set.

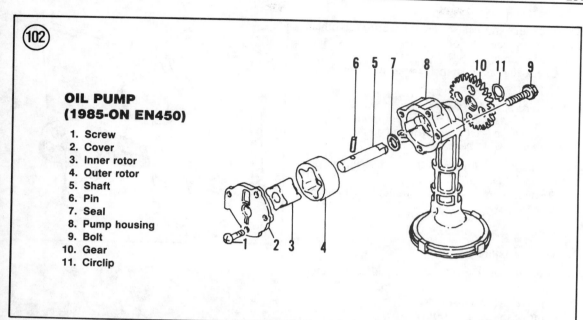

**OIL PUMP
(1985-ON EN450)**

1. Screw
2. Cover
3. Inner rotor
4. Outer rotor
5. Shaft
6. Pin
7. Seal
8. Pump housing
9. Bolt
10. Gear
11. Circlip

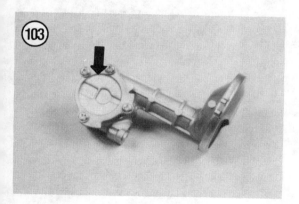

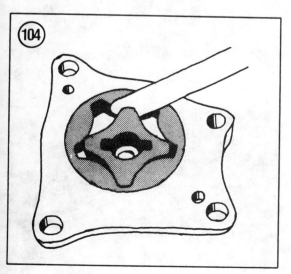

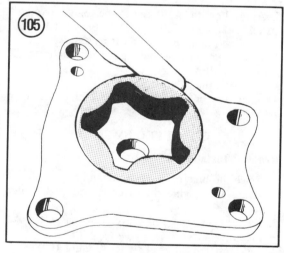

7. Measure the clearance between the outer rotor and the pump body with a flat feeler gauge (**Figure 105**). If the clearance is greater than the specification in **Table 1**, measure the rotor with a micrometer. If the rotor is less than the service limit in **Table 1**, replace the rotors as a set. If the rotor diameter is within specification, measure the oil pump body inside diameter with a bore or snap gauge. If the clearance is greater than the service limit, replace the oil pump assembly.

8. Check the rotor end clearance with a straightedge and flat feeler gauge (**Figure 106**). If the clearance is greater than the service limit in **Table 1** the oil pump must be replaced.

9. Check the strainer screen for tearing or other damage; replace the oil pump assembly if the strainer is damaged.

10. Check the pump shaft for wear or damage.

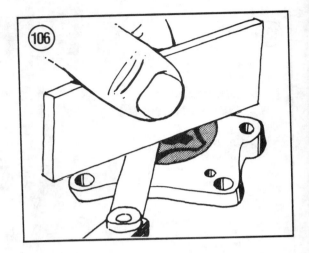

NOTE
Proceed with Step 11 only when the above inspection and measurement steps have been completed and all parts are known to be good.

11. Coat all parts (**Figure 102**) with fresh engine oil before assembly.

12. Reverse Steps 1-4 to reassemble the oil pump.

OIL PRESSURE RELIEF VALVE

Removal/Installation

1. Drain the engine oil as described in Chapter Three.
2. Remove the exhaust pipe.
3. Remove the oil pan (**Figure 107**).
4. Unscrew the relief valve (**Figure 108**) and remove it.
5. Apply Loctite 242 (blue) to the relief valve and install it. Tighten the valve to 15 N•m (11 ft.-lb.).
6. Replace the oil pan gasket if necessary.
7. Install the oil pan and tighten the bolts to 12 N•m (8.5 ft.-lb.).
8. Reinstall the exhaust pipes.
9. Refill the engine oil as described in Chapter Three.

OIL LEVEL SWITCH

Removal/Installation

1. Place the bike on the centerstand.
2. Drain the engine oil as described in Chapter Three.
3. Disconnect the oil level switch electrical connector.
4. Unscrew the oil level switch (**Figure 109**).
5. Installation is the reverse of these steps, noting the following.
6. Make sure the area around the switch mounting position is clean of all dirt and other debris. Tighten the switch securely.
7. Refill the engine oil as described in Chapter Three.

NEUTRAL SWITCH

Removal/Installation

1. Place the bike on the centerstand.
2. Remove the pulley cover.
3. Disconnect the electrical connector at the neutral switch (**Figure 110**).

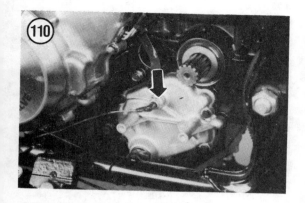

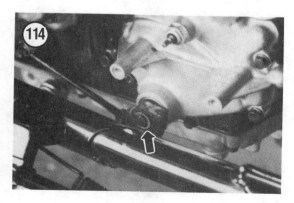

4. Remove the neutral switch.

5. Installation is the reverse of these steps, noting the following.

6. Install a new gasket on the switch.

7. Make sure the area around the switch mounting position is clean of all dirt and other debris.

8. Tighten the neutral switch to 15 N•m (11 ft.-lb.).

ALTERNATOR, STARTER DRIVE MECHANISM AND STARTER

The alternator and starter are discussed together, because complete removal of one entails removal of the other. Refer to Chapter Nine for alternator and starter service.

Alternator Cover
Removal/Installation

1. Raise the seat and disconnect the battery negative lead.

2. Remove the left-hand footpeg and the gearshift lever (**Figure 111**).

3. Remove the engine pulley cover.

4. Remove the circlip (**Figure 112**) and washer (**Figure 113**) from the front gearshift pivot shaft. Then remove the circlip from the shift lever shaft (**Figure 114**).

5. Disconnect the alternator electrical connectors.

6. Place an oil pan underneath the alternator cover.

7. Remove the alternator cover bolts and remove the cover (**Figure 115**). Note the path of the wire harness as it must be routed the same during installation.

8. Install by reversing these steps, noting the following.

9. Install a new alternator cover gasket and the 2 dowel pins. See A, **Figure 116**.

10. Apply silicone sealant, such as RTV, underneath the rubber wiring grommet in the cover (**Figure 117**).

11. Make sure the gearshift pivot shaft (**Figure 118**) is installed through the cover before installing it.

Rotor/Starter Gears
Removal

1. Raise the seat and disconnect the battery negative lead.
2. Remove the alternator cover as described in this chapter.

> *CAUTION*
> *The bolt securing the alternator rotor has **left-hand threads**. The bolt must be turned **clockwise** for removal.*

3. Remove the rotor bolt as follows:
   a. To keep the rotor from turning while removing the bolt, use a strap wrench (**Figure 119**) on the outer perimeter of the rotor.
   b. If the drive pulley is installed, shift the transmission into gear and hold the rear brake on.
   c. Turning a socket *clockwise*, remove the bolt securing the alternator rotor (B, **Figure 116**).
4. Screw in a rotor puller (**Figure 120**) until it stops. Use the Kawasaki rotor puller (part No. 57001-254 or 57001-1099), Honda rotor puller (part No. 07933-3330000) or equivalent.

> *CAUTION*
> *Don't try to remove the rotor without a puller; any attempt to do so will ultimately lead to some form of damage to the engine and/or rotor. Many aftermarket pullers are available from motorcycle dealers or mail order houses. If you can't buy or borrow one, have the dealer remove the rotor.*

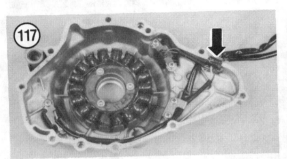

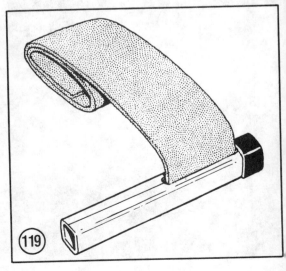

5. Secure the rotor with the puller used to remove the rotor bolt and turn the rotor puller with a wrench until the rotor is free.

NOTE
If the rotor is difficult to remove, strike the puller with a hammer a few times. This will usually break it loose.

CAUTION
If normal rotor removal attempts fail, do not force the puller as the threads may be stripped out of the rotor causing expensive damage. Take the bike to a dealer and have the rotor removed.

6. Remove the rotor and Woodruff key (**Figure 121**).

7. Remove the chain guide bolts and remove the guide (**Figure 122**).

8. Remove the washer (**Figure 123**).

9. Remove the starter driven gear, chain and the starter drive gear. See **Figure 124**.

Rotor/Starter Gears
Inspection

1. Inspect the teeth on the starter driven gear (A, **Figure 125**) and the starter drive gear (B, **Figure 125**). Check for chipped or missing teeth. Replace if necessary.

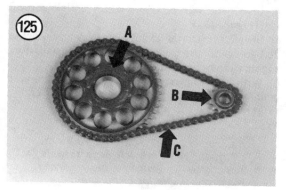

2. Check the drive chain (C, **Figure 125**) for worn or damaged links, pins and side plates. Replace if necessary.

3. Place the drive chain on the workbench and pull it tight. Measure the length of 21 pins (20 links) with a vernier caliper (**Figure 126**). Replace the starter chain if the specified length exceeds 159 mm (6.230 in.).

4. Check the rollers (**Figure 127**) in the starter clutch for uneven or excessive wear; replace as a set if any are bad.

5. To replace the rollers, perform the following:

   a. Remove the rollers (**Figure 127**).

   b. Remove the plungers (**Figure 128**).

   c. Remove the springs (**Figure 129**).

   d. If necessary, secure the rotor with a holding tool and remove the 3 Allen bolts (A, **Figure 130**) and remove the starter clutch housing (B, **Figure 130**).

   e. Check the rollers, plungers and springs for wear, cracks or other damage. Replace if necessary.

   f. If the starter clutch housing was removed, install it by applying Loctite 242 (blue) to the threads of the Allen bolts and torque them to 34 N•m (25 ft.-lb.).

   g. Install the spring, plunger and roller (**Figure 131**) into each receptacle in the starter clutch.

Rotor/Starter Gears
Installation

1. Inspect the inside of the rotor (**Figure 132**) for small bolts, washers or other metal "trash" that may have been picked up by the magnets. These small metal bits can cause severe damage to the alternator stator assembly.

2. Using electrical contact cleaner, clean the crankshaft taper and the rotor taper.

3. Assemble the starter driven gear, starter chain and the starter drive gear (**Figure 125**) and install them as shown in **Figure 124**.

4. Install the washer (**Figure 123**) and Woodruff key (**Figure 121**).

5. Install the starter chain guide. Apply Loctite 242 (blue) to the guide bolts before installation. Tighten the bolts securely.

6. With your fingers, rotate the starter driven gear *counterclockwise* and push the rotor assembly (**Figure 133**) all the way on until it seats.

> *CAUTION*
> *Remember, the bolt securing the alternator rotor has **left-hand threads**. The bolt must be turned **counterclockwise** for installation.*

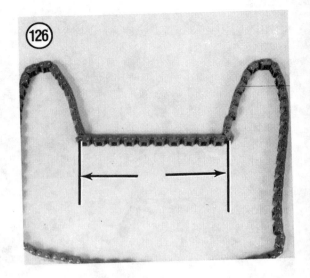

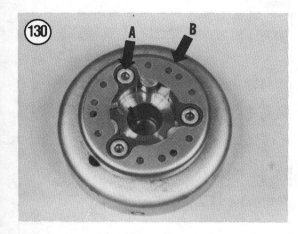

7. Install the alternator rotor bolt.

8. Use the same tool set-up used for removal and tighten the bolt *counterclockwise* to the torque specification listed in **Table 2**.

9. Install the alternator cover as described in this chapter.

10. Connect the battery negative lead and install the seat.

Starter
Removal/Installation

1. Remove the alternator cover as described in this chapter.

2. Remove the carburetors (Chapter Eight).

3. Disconnect the electrical cable from terminal on starter motor.

4. Remove the starter mounting bolts.

5. Carefully pry the starter towards the right-hand side and out of the starter sprocket and chain.

6. Install by reversing these steps. Apply oil to the starter O-ring before installation.

7. Adjust the throttle cables as described in Chapter Three.

CRANKCASE

Service to the lower end requires that the crankcase assembly be removed from the motorcycle frame and disassembled (split).

Disassembly

1. Remove the engine as described in this chapter. Remove all exterior assemblies from the crankcase as described in this chapter and other related chapters.

2. Remove the oil line (**Figure 134**).

3. Remove the drive shaft plug plate (**Figure 135**).

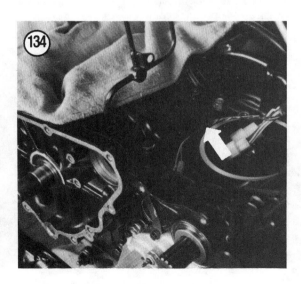

4. Remove the upper crankcase bolts (**Figure 136**) in the following order:
   a. 6 mm bolts.
   b. Allen bolts.
   c. 8 mm bolt.
5. Turn the engine so that the bottom end faces up. Remove the following parts:
   a. Oil pan.
   b. Oil pump outer pipe.
   c. Main oil pipe.
6. Loosen the lower crankcase bolts in the following order by reversing the bolt tightening sequence in **Figure 137**:
   a. 6 mm bolts.
   b. 8 mm bolts.
   c. Remove the bolts.
7. Lift the breather pipe (**Figure 138**) out of the upper crankcase and leave it in place.
8. Using a soft-faced mallet, tap around the perimeter of the crankcase and remove the lower crankcase half.
9. After separating the crankcase halves, the transmission and crankshaft and balancer shaft assemblies will stay in the upper crankcase half.
10. Remove the 2 dowel pins. See **Figure 139** and **Figure 140**.
11. Remove the chain guide locking pin (**Figure 141**).
12. Remove the transmission, shift forks and shift drum assemblies as described in Chapter Seven.
13. Remove the crankshaft assembly as described in this chapter.
14. Remove the balancer shaft as described in this chapter.
15. Remove the front cam chain guide (**Figure 142**).
16. Remove the upper (**Figure 143**) and lower (**Figure 144**) primary chain guides.
17. Remove the crankshaft and balancer shaft bearing inserts from the upper and lower crankcase halves. See **Figure 145**. Mark the backsides of the inserts so they can be reinstalled into the same positions.

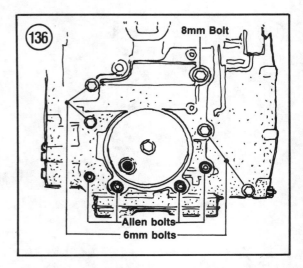

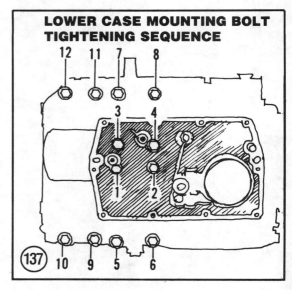

LOWER CASE MOUNTING BOLT TIGHTENING SEQUENCE

Inspection

1. Thoroughly clean the inside and outside of both crankcase halves with cleaning solvent. Dry with compressed air. Make sure there is no solvent residue left in the cases as it will contaminate the engine oil.
2. Make sure all oil passages are clean; blow them out with compressed air.
3. Check the crankcases for cracks or other damage. Inspect the mating surfaces of both halves. They must be free of gouges, burrs or any damage that could cause an oil leak.
4. Inspect the crankshaft and balancer shaft bearing inserts as described in this chapter.

Assembly

1. Before installation of all parts, coat all parts with assembly oil or engine oil.
2. Install the crankshaft and balancer shaft bearing inserts in both the upper and lower crankcase halves (**Figure 145**). If reusing old bearings, make sure that they are installed in the same location. Refer to marks made in *Disassembly*, step 17. Make sure they are locked in place (**Figure 146**).

3. Install the cam chain and primary chain tensioners.

4. Install the crankshaft/clutch housing/primary chain assembly as described in this chapter.

5. Install the balancer shaft as described in this chapter. Make sure the balancer shaft-to-crankshaft timing marks are aligned. See *Balancer Shaft Removal/Installation*.

6. Install the shift drum, shift forks and transmission assemblies as described in Chapter Seven.

> *CAUTION*
> *When installing the transmission shaft assemblies, make sure the dowel pins (A, **Figure 147**) and both 1/2 circlips (B, **Figure 147**) are in place in the upper crankcase before installing the transmission assemblies. See Chapter Seven.*

7. Make sure the case half sealing surfaces are perfectly clean and dry.

8. Install the 2 locating dowel pins. See **Figure 139** and **Figure 140**.

9. Install the front cam chain locking pin (**Figure 141**). Make sure the chain guide is positioned correctly and that the pin does not protrude above the crankcase mating surface.

10. Apply a light coat of gasket sealer to the sealing surfaces of both halves. Cover only flat surfaces, not curved bearing surfaces. Make the coating as thin as possible. Do not apply sealant close the edge of the bearing inserts (**Figure 148**) as it would restrict oil flow and cause damage.

> *NOTE*
> *Use Gasgacinch Gasket Sealer, Three Bond or equivalent. A black colored silicone sealant (RTV) works well and blends with the black crankcases.*

11. In the upper crankcase, position the shift drum into NEUTRAL. The shift forks should be located in the approximate positions shown in **Figure 149**.

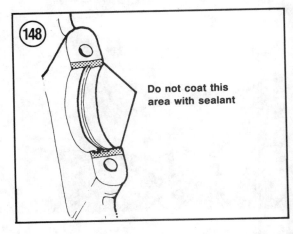

Do not coat this area with sealant

NOTE
When the transmission is in neutral, the gear positioning lever will be engaged with the shift drum cam detent. See Figure 150.

12. Position the lower crankcase onto the upper crankcase. Set the front portion down first and lower the rear while making sure the shift forks engage properly into the transmission assemblies.

13. Lower the crankcase completely.

CAUTION
Do not install any crankcase bolts until the sealing surface around the entire crankcase perimeter has seated completely.

14. Before installing the bolts, slowly spin the transmission shafts and shift the transmission through all 6 gears. This is done to check that the shift forks are properly engaged.

15. Install the breather pipe so that it fits into the passage in the upper crankcase (**Figure 138**).

16. Apply oil to the threads of all lower crankcase bolts and install them.

17. Tighten the 8 mm bolts in two stages in the torque sequence shown in **Figure 137**. Tighten to the following specifications:
    a. Stage 1: 14 N•m (10 ft.-lb.).
    b. Stage 2: 27 N•m (20 ft.-lb.).

18. Tighten the 6 mm bolts to 12 N•m (9 ft.-lb.).

19. Turn the crankcase assembly over and install all upper crankcase bolts only finger-tight (**Figure 136**). Tighten the bolts in the following sequence and to the following specifications:
    a. 8 mm bolts: 27 N•m. (10 ft.-lb.).
    b. Allen bolts: 12 N•m (9 ft.-lb.).
    c. 6 mm bolts: 12 N•m (9 ft.-lb.).

20. Install the oil pan.

21. Reverse Step 1 and Step 2 and install all engine assemblies that were removed.

22. Install the engine as described in this chapter.

CRANKSHAFT AND CONNECTING RODS

Removal/Installation

1. Split the crankcase as described in this chapter.

2. Remove the transmission countershaft (**Figure 151**).

3. Lift the clutch housing (A, **Figure 152**) and remove the mainshaft (B, **Figure 152**).

4. Remove the washer (**Figure 153**) and spacer (**Figure 154**) from the clutch housing.

5. Remove the clutch housing, primary chain and crankshaft as an assembly. See **Figure 155**.

6. Slip the primary chain off of the clutch housing sprocket and separate the crankshaft/clutch housing assembly. See **Figure 156**.

7. If it is necessary to remove the bearing inserts, refer to *Crankcase Disassembly* in this chapter.

8. Installation is the reverse of these steps. Note the following.

9. When installing the transmission shaft assemblies, make sure the dowel pins (A, **Figure 147**) and both 1/2 circlips (B, **Figure 147**) are in place in the upper crankcase before installing the transmission assemblies.

10. When installing the crankshaft, align the match mark on the crankshaft drive gear with the match mark on the balancer shaft drive gear. See **Figure 157**.

11. If removed, install the primary (A, **Figure 158**) and camshaft (B, **Figure 158**) drive chains over the crankshaft.

Crankshaft Inspection

1. Clean crankshaft thoroughly with solvent. Clean oil holes with rifle cleaning brushes; flush thoroughly and dry with compressed air. Lightly oil all oil journal surfaces immediately to prevent rust.

2. Inspect each journal (**Figure 159**) for scratches, ridges, scoring, nicks, etc.

3. If the surface on all journals is satisfactory, measure the journals with a micrometer and check out-of-roundness, taper and wear on the journals. Check against measurements given in **Table 1**.

4. Inspect the primary (A, **Figure 160**) and cam (B, **Figure 160**) chain drive sprockets. If they are worn or damaged, the crankshaft will have to be replaced.

5. Inspect the both drive chains (**Figure 161**). Stretch each chain tight and measure a 20 link length (**Figure 162**). If the length from the 1st pin to the 21st pin exceeds the limit in **Table 1**, install a new chain.

Clutch Housing Inspection

1. Lift the oil pump drive gear (**Figure 163**) off of the clutch housing.

2. Inspect the oil pump drive gear pin (**Figure 164**) for wear or looseness. Also check the gear teeth for wear, flaking or cracks. Replace the gear if necessary.

3. Inspect the pin hole in the clutch housing (**Figure 165**) for enlargement or cracks. Replace the clutch housing if necessary.

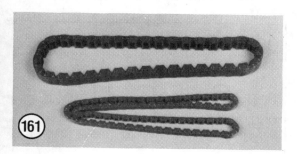

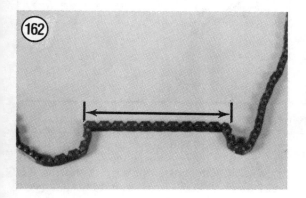

4. Check the slots in the clutch housing (**Figure 166**) for cracks, nicks or galling where they come in contact with the clutch friction disc tabs. If severe damage is evident, the housing must be replaced.

5. Slide the spacer into the clutch housing bushing and check for excessive wear (**Figure 167**). Replace the housing or bushing if necessary.

6. Install the oil pump drive gear onto the clutch housing by reversing Step 1.

Crankshaft Main Bearing Clearance Measurement

1. Check the inside and outside surfaces of the bearing inserts for wear, bluish tint (burned), flaking abrasion and scoring. If the bearings are good, they may be reused. If any insert is questionable, replace the entire set.

2. Clean the bearing surfaces of the crankshaft and the main bearing inserts.

3. Measure the main bearing clearance by performing the following steps.

4. Set the upper crankcase upside down on the workbench on wood blocks.

5. Install the existing main beaing inserts into the upper crankcase.

6. Install the crankshaft into the upper crankcase.

7. Place a piece of Plastigage over each main bearing journal parallel to the crankshaft.

CAUTION
Do not rotate crankshaft while Plastigage is in place.

8. Install the existing bearing inserts into the lower crankcase.

9. Install the lower crankcase over the upper crankcase. Install and tighten the lower crankcase 8 mm bolts as described under *Crankcase Assembly* in this chapter.

10. Remove the 8 mm bolts in the reverse order of installation.

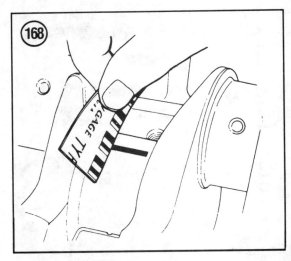

11. Carefully remove the lower crankcase and measure width of flattened Plastigage according to the manufacturer's instructions (**Figure 168**). Measure at both ends of the strip. A difference of 0.025 mm (0.001 in.) or more indicates a tapered crankpin. Confirm with a micrometer. Remove the Plastigage strips from all bearing journals.

12. New bearing clearance should be 0.020-0.044 mm (0.0008-0.017 in.) with a service limit of 0.08 mm (0.0031 in.). Remove the Plastigage strips from all bearing journals.

13. If the bearing clearance is greater than specified, use the following steps for new bearing selection.

14. If the bearing clearance is between 0.044 mm (0.017 in.) and 0.08 mm (0.003 in.), replace the bearing inserts with factory inserts painted blue and recheck the bearing clearance. Always replace all 8 inserts at the same time. The clearance may exceed 0.044 mm (0.017 in.) slightly but it must not be less than the minimum clearance of 0.020 mm (0.0008 in.) or bearing seizure will occur.

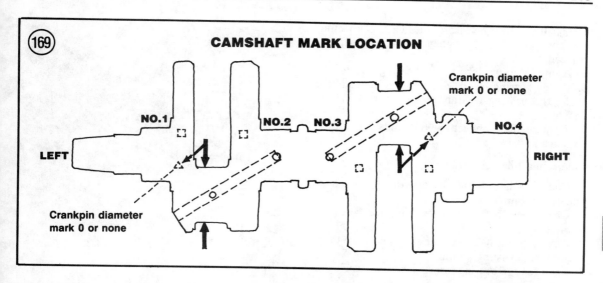

CAMSHAFT MARK LOCATION

Crankpin diameter mark 0 or none

NO.1   NO.2   NO.3   NO.4

LEFT   RIGHT

Crankpin diameter mark 0 or none

5

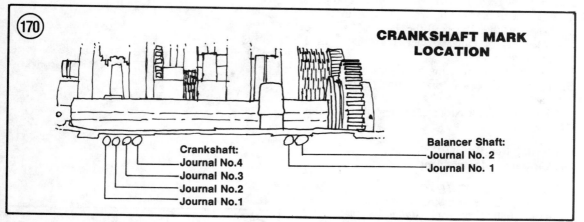

CRANKSHAFT MARK LOCATION

Crankshaft:
Journal No.4
Journal No.3
Journal No.2
Journal No.1

Balancer Shaft:
Journal No. 2
Journal No. 1

15. If the bearing clearance exceeds the service limit, measure the crankshaft journal OD with a micrometer. See **Table 1** for specifications. If any journal exceeds the wear limit, replace the crankshaft.

16. If the crankshaft has been replaced, determine new bearing inserts as follows:

a. Purchase a new crankshaft. Then cross-reference the main journal crankshaft diameter markings (**Figure 169**) with the upper crankcase half marks (**Figure 170**). Record these marks and take them to a Kawasaki dealer for new crankshaft main bearing inserts.

b. Recheck the clearance with the new inserts and crankshaft. The clearance should be less than the service limit and as close to the standard as possible, but not less than the standard.

17. Clean and oil the main bearing journals and insert faces.

Connecting Rod
Removal/Installation

1. Before disassembly, mark the rods and caps with a "1" and "2" starting from the left-hand side.

2. Remove the connecting rod cap nuts (**Figure 171**) and separate the rods from the crankshaft. Keep each cap with its original rod, with the weight mark on the end of the cap matching the mark on the rod (B, **Figure 172**).

CAUTION
Keep each bearing insert in its original place in the crankcase, rod or rod cap. If you are going to assemble the engine with the original inserts, they must be installed exactly as removed in order to prevent rapid wear.

3. Install by reversing these removal steps, noting the following procedures.

4. Install the bearing inserts into each connecting rod and cap. Make sure they are locked in place correctly.

5. Apply assembly lube to the bearing inserts.

6. If new bearing inserts are going to be installed, check the bearing clearance as described in this chapter.

7. Tighten the connecting rod nuts to torque specifications in **Table 2**.

Connecting Rod Inspection

1. Check each rod for obvious damage such as cracks and burns.

2. Check the piston pin bushing for wear or scoring.

3. Take the rods to a machine shop and have them checked for twisting and bending.

4. Examine the bearing inserts for wear, scoring or burning. They are reusable if in good condition. Make a note of the bearing size (if any) stamped on the back of the insert if the bearing is to be discarded; a previous owner may have used undersize bearings.

5. Remove the connecting rod bearing bolts and check them for cracks or twisting. Replace any bolts as required.

6. Check bearing clearance as described in this chapter.

**Connecting Rod Bearing
and Clearance Measurement**

> *CAUTION*
> *If the old bearings are to be reused, be sure that they are installed in their exact original locations.*

1. Wipe bearing inserts and crankpins clean. Install bearing inserts in rod and cap.

2. Place a piece of Plastigage on one crankpin parallel to the crankshaft.

3. Install rod and cap. Tighten nuts to torque specifications in **Table 2**.

> *CAUTION*
> *Do not rotate crankshaft while Plastigage is in place.*

4. Remove rod cap.

5. Measure width of flattened Plastigage according to the manufacturer's instructions (**Figure 173**). Measure at both ends of the strip. A difference of 0.025 mm (0.001 in.) or more indicates a tapered crankpin; the crankshaft must be replaced. Confirm with a micrometer measurement of the journal OD.

6. If the crankpin taper is within tolerance, measure the bearing clearance with the same strip

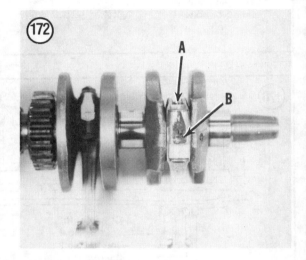

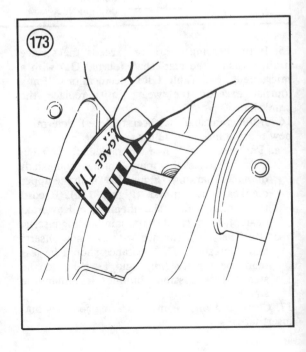

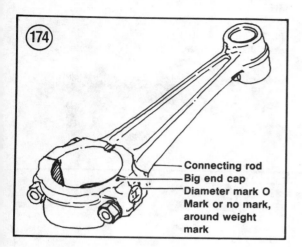

Connecting rod
Big end cap
Diameter mark O
Mark or no mark,
around weight
mark

a. Purchase a new crankshaft. Then cross-reference the crankpin journal diameter markings (**Figure 169**) with the connecting rod mark (**Figure 174**). The connecting rod will be marked with a 0 around the weight mark or there will be no 0 around the weight mark. Record these marks and take them to a Kawasaki dealer for new bearing inserts.

b. Recheck the clearance with the new inserts and crankshaft. The clearance should be less than the service limit and as close to the standard as possible, but not less than the standard.

13. Clean and oil the main bearing journals and insert faces.

14. After new bearings have been installed, recheck clearance with Plastigage. If the clearance is out of specifications, either the connecting rod or the crankshaft is worn beyond the service limit. Refer the engine to a dealer or qualified specialist.

BALANCER SHAFT

Removal/Installation

1. Split the crankcase as described in this chapter.
2. Lift the balancer shaft out of the engine (**Figure 175**).
3. If it is necessary to remove the bearing inserts, refer to *Crankcase Disassembly* in this chapter.
4. Installation is the reverse of these steps, noting the following.
5. Apply assembly lube to the balancer shaft bearing inserts before installing the shaft.
6. When installing the balancer shaft, align the match mark on the crankshaft drive gear with the match mark on the balancer shaft drive gear. See **Figure 176**.

Balancer Shaft Inspection

1. Clean balancer shaft thoroughly with solvent. Clean oil holes with rifle cleaning brushes; flush thoroughly and dry with compressed air. Lightly oil all oil journal surfaces immediately to prevent rust.
2. Inspect each journal (**Figure 177**) for scratches, ridges, scoring, nicks, etc.
3. If the surface on all journals is satisfactory, measure the journals with a micrometer and check out-of-roundness, taper and wear on the journals. Check against measurements given in **Table 1**.

Balancer Shaft Bearing Clearance Measurement

1. Check the inside and outside surfaces of the bearing inserts for wear, bluish tint (burned), flaking, abrasion and scoring. If the bearings are

of Plastigage. Correct bearing clearance is specified in **Table 1**. Remove Plastigage strips.

7. If the bearing clearance is greater than specified, use the following steps for new bearing selection.

8. New bearing clearance should be 0.036-0.066 mm (0.0014-0.0025 in.) with a service limit of 0.10 mm (0.0039 in.). Remove the Plastigage strips from all bearing journals.

9. If the bearing clearance is greater than specified, use the following steps for new bearing selection.

10. If the bearing clearance is between 0.066 mm (0.0025 in.) and 0.10 mm (0.0039 in.), replace the bearing inserts with factory inserts painted blue and recheck the bearing clearance. Always replace all 4 inserts at the same time. The clearance may exceed 0.066 mm (0.0025 in.) slightly but it must not be less than the minimum clearance of 0.036 mm (0.0014 in.) or bearing seizure will occur.

11. If the bearing clearance exceeds the service limit, measure the crankshaft journal OD with a micrometer. See **Table 1** for specifications. If any journal exceeds the wear limit, replace the crankshaft.

12. If the crankshaft has been replaced, determine new bearing inserts as follows:

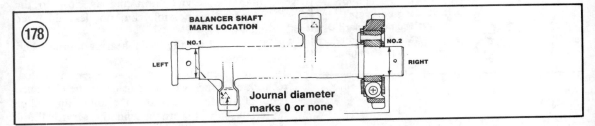

BALANCER SHAFT MARK LOCATION

NO.1

LEFT

NO.2

RIGHT

Journal diameter marks 0 or none

good, they may be reused. If any insert is questionable, replace the entire set.

2. Clean the bearing surfaces of the balancer shaft and the bearing inserts.

3. Measure the balancer shaft bearing clearance by performing the following steps.

4. Set the upper crankcase upside down on the workbench on wood blocks.

5. Install the existing balancer shaft inserts into the upper crankcase.

6. Install the balancer shaft into the upper crankcase.

7. Place a piece of Plastigage over each main bearing journal parallel to the balancer shaft.

CAUTION
Do not rotate balancer shaft while Plastigage is in place.

8. Install the existing bearing inserts into the lower crankcase.

9. Install the lower crankcase over the upper crankcase. Install and tighten the lower crankcase 8 mm bolts as described under *Crankcase Assembly* in this chapter.

10. Remove the 8 mm bolts in the reverse order of installation.

11. Carefully remove the lower crankcase and measure width of flattened Plastigage according to the manufacturer's instructions (**Figure 173**). Measure at both ends of the strip. A difference of 0.025 mm (0.001 in.) or more indicates a tapered journal. Confirm with a micrometer. Remove the Plastigage strips from all bearing journals.

12. New bearing clearance should be 0.020-0.044 mm (0.0008-0.017 in.) with a service limit of 0.08 mm (0.003 in.). Remove the Plastigage strips from all bearing journals.

13. If the bearing clearance is greater than specified, use the following steps for new bearing selection.

14. If the bearing clearance is between 0.044 mm (0.017 in.) and 0.08 mm (0.003 in.), replace the bearing inserts with factory inserts painted blue and recheck the bearing clearance. Always replace all 4 inserts at the same time. The clearance may exceed 0.044 mm (0.017 in.) slightly, but it must not be less than the minimum clearance of 0.020 mm (0.0008 in.) or bearing seizure will occur.

15. If the bearing clearance exceeds the service limit, measure the balancer shaft journal OD with a micrometer. See **Table 1** for specifications. If any journal exceeds the wear limit, replace the balancer shaft.

16. If the balancer shaft has been replaced, determine new bearing inserts as follows:

   a. Purchase a new balancer shaft. Then cross-reference the journal balancer shaft diameter markings (**Figure 178**) with the upper crankcase half marks (**Figure 170**). Record these marks and take them to a Kawasaki dealer for new balancer shaft bearing inserts.

   b. Recheck the clearance with the new inserts and balancer shaft. The clearance should be less than the service limit and as close to the standard as possible, but not less than the standard.

17. Clean and oil the bearing journals and insert races.

Table 1 ENGINE SPECIFICATIONS (1985-ON EN450)

	Standard mm (in.)	Wear limit mm (in.)
Cam lobe height	35.44 (1.3952)	
Camshaft bearing clearance	0.030-0.071	0.16
	(0.0011-0.0027)	(0.006)
Camshaft journal diameter	24.950-24.970	24.92
	(0.9822-0.9831)	(0.9811)
Camshaft bearing inside diameter	25.000-25.021	25.08
(cylinder head-to-bearing cap)	(0.9842-0.9851)	(0.9874)
Camshaft runout		0.1 (0.0039)
Camshaft chain (20 link)	127-127.4	128.9
Primary chain	(5.0-5.016)	(5.075)
20-link length	190.50-190.97	193.4
	(7.50-7.52)	(7.61)
Cam chain		
20-link length	155.5-155.9	159
	(6.12-6.14)	6.26
Rocker arm inside diameter	12.500-12.518	12.55
	(0.4921-0.4928)	(0.4941)
Rocker arm shaft outer diameter	12.466-12.484	12.44
	(0.4907-0.4915)	(0.4897)
Cylinder		
Taper (max.)		0.05 (0.002)
Out-of-round		0.01 (0.0004)
Cylinder head warpage		0.05 (0.002)
Cylinder diameter	72.494-72.506	72.6
	(2.8540-2.8545)	(2.8582)
Piston diameter		72.29 (2.8461)
Piston-to-cylinder clearance	0.044-0.071	
	(0.0017-0.0027)	
Piston ring groove clearance		
Top	0.03-0.07	0.17
	(0.0012-0.0027)	(0.0067)
Second	0.02-0.06	0.16
	(0.0007-0.0024)	(0.0063)
Piston ring groove width		
Top	1.02-1.04	1.12
	(0.0401-0.0409)	(0.0441)
Second	1.01-1.03	1.12
	(0.0397-0.0405)	(0.0441)
Oil	2.51-2.53	2.6
	(0.0988-0.0996)	(0.1023)
Piston ring thickness		
Top and second	0.97-0.99	0.9
	(0.0382-0.0389)	(0.0354)
Piston ring end gap		
Top and second	0.2-0.35	0.7
	(0.0078-0.0138)	(0.0275)
Oil	0.2-0.7	1.0
	(0.0078-0.0275)	(0.3937)
Valve head thickness		
Intake		0.25 (0.0098)
Exhaust		0.7 (0.0276)

(continued)

Table 1 ENGINE SPECIFICATIONS (1985-ON EN450) (continued)

	Standard mm (in.)	Wear limit mm (in.)
Valve stem diameter		
Intake	5.475-5.490 (0.2155-0.2161)	5.46 (0.2149)
Valve stem runout		0.05 (0.0894)
Valve guide inside diameter	5.500-5.512 (0.2165-0.2170)	5.58 (0.2197)
Valve spring free length		
Inner	36.3 (1.429)	35 (1.378)
Outer	40.4 (1.590)	39 (1.535)
Connecting rod side clearance	0.13-0.33 (0.0051-0.0129)	0.50 (0.0197)
Connecting rod bearing clearance	0.036-0.066 (0.0014-0.0025)	0.10 (0.0039)
Crankpin wear limit		37.97 (1.4948)
Crankshaft runout		0.05 (0.0019)
Crankshaft journal clearance	0.020-0.044 (0.0008-0.0017)	0.08 (0.0031)
Crankshaft main journal diameter		35.96 (1.4157)
Crankshaft thrust clearance	0.05-0.25 (0.0019-0.0098)	0.40 (0.0157)
Balancer shaft bearing clearance	0.020-0.040 (0.0008-0.0017)	0.08 (0.0031)
Balancer shaft journal diameter		27.96 (1.1007)
Oil pump		
Inner rotor clearance		0.20 (0.0078)
Pump body clearance		0.30 (0.0118)
Outer rotor diameter		40.45 (1.5925)
Body inside diameter		40.80 (1.6062)
Rotor end clearance		0.12 (0.0047)

Table 2 ENGINE TIGHTENING TORQUES (1985-ON EN450)

	N•m	ft.-lb.
Rocker arm shafts	39	29
Rocker arm bearing caps	12	9
Cylinder head cover bolts	9.8	7.2
Cylinder head bolts		
6 mm	9.8	7.2
10 mm	39	29
Camshaft cap bolts	12	104 in.-lb.
Camshaft chain tensioner bolts	8.8	78 in.-lb.
Cam sprocket bolts	15	11
Oil line banjo bolts		
At cylinder head	12	9
At crankcase	20	14.5
Connecting rod nuts	36	27
Rotor bolt	69	51
Crankcase bolts		
6 mm	12	9
8 mm	27	20
Allen bolts	12	9
Engine mount bolts		
Long bolts	39	20
Short bolts	24	17.5
Oil pan bolts	12	8.5

NOTE: If you own an EN500 model, first check the Supplement at the back of this book for any specific service information.

CHAPTER SIX

CLUTCH AND PRIMARY CHAIN

6

This chapter provides complete service procedures for the clutch and primary chain. **Table 1** (end of chapter) lists clutch wear limits.

CLUTCH AND PRIMARY CHAIN (1974-1983)

Removal/Installation

Refer to **Figure 1** (1974-1977 and 1977-1978 Deluxe A models) or **Figure 2** (1978-1983) for this procedure.

1. Drain the engine oil as described in Chapter Three.
2. Remove the ignition advance unit. See Chapter Nine.
3. Remove the right-hand footpeg assembly.
4. Remove the kickstarter pedal.
5. Remove the clutch cover screws. Then tap the cover with a rubber mallet to free it, then remove it from the engine.

> *CAUTION*
> *Do not pry the cover from the engine. If any damage occurs to either sealing surface, an oil leak will result.*

6. Remove the pressure plate bolts, washers and springs. See **Figure 3**.
7. Remove the pressure plate (**Figure 4**).

8. Remove the pressure plate lifter (**Figure 5**).
9. Using a magnet, remove the ball from inside the mainshaft.
10. Remove the steel rings, steel discs and friction discs (**Figure 6**).
11. Remove the snap ring and any shims from the transmission shaft.
12. Remove the clutch hub (**Figure 7**) and thrust washer.
13. Remove the snap ring from the primary drive sprocket.
14. Remove the clutch housing, primary chain and primary sprocket as an assembly (**Figure 8**).
15. Pull out the clutch pushrod from the left side of the engine (**Figure 9**).
16. Inspect the clutch components as described in this chapter.
17. Installation is the reverse of these steps, noting the following.
18. Replace all worn or deformed snap rings.
19. Coat all clutch parts with new engine oil.
20. Make sure the punch mark on the clutch hub aligns with the raised dot on the pressure plate (**Figure 10**).
21. Refill the engine oil as described in Chapter Three.
22. Adjust the clutch as described in Chapter Three.

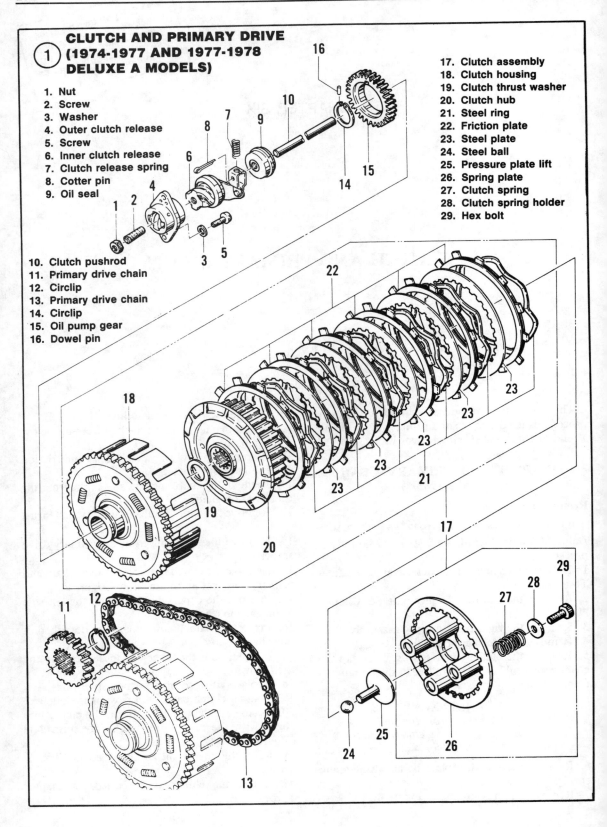

CLUTCH AND PRIMARY DRIVE
(1) **(1974-1977 AND 1977-1978 DELUXE A MODELS)**

1. Nut
2. Screw
3. Washer
4. Outer clutch release
5. Screw
6. Inner clutch release
7. Clutch release spring
8. Cotter pin
9. Oil seal
10. Clutch pushrod
11. Primary drive chain
12. Circlip
13. Primary drive chain
14. Circlip
15. Oil pump gear
16. Dowel pin

17. Clutch assembly
18. Clutch housing
19. Clutch thrust washer
20. Clutch hub
21. Steel ring
22. Friction plate
23. Steel plate
24. Steel ball
25. Pressure plate lift
26. Spring plate
27. Clutch spring
28. Clutch spring holder
29. Hex bolt

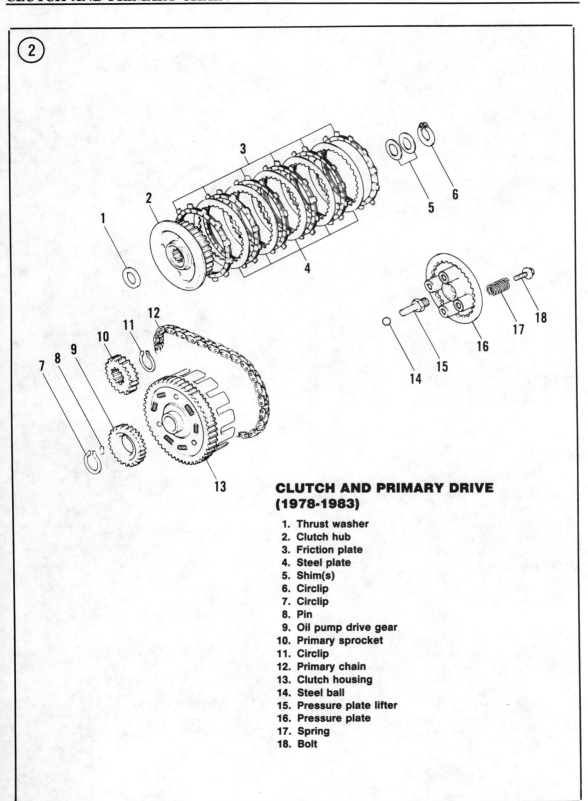

②

CLUTCH AND PRIMARY DRIVE (1978-1983)

1. Thrust washer
2. Clutch hub
3. Friction plate
4. Steel plate
5. Shim(s)
6. Circlip
7. Circlip
8. Pin
9. Oil pump drive gear
10. Primary sprocket
11. Circlip
12. Primary chain
13. Clutch housing
14. Steel ball
15. Pressure plate lifter
16. Pressure plate
17. Spring
18. Bolt

6

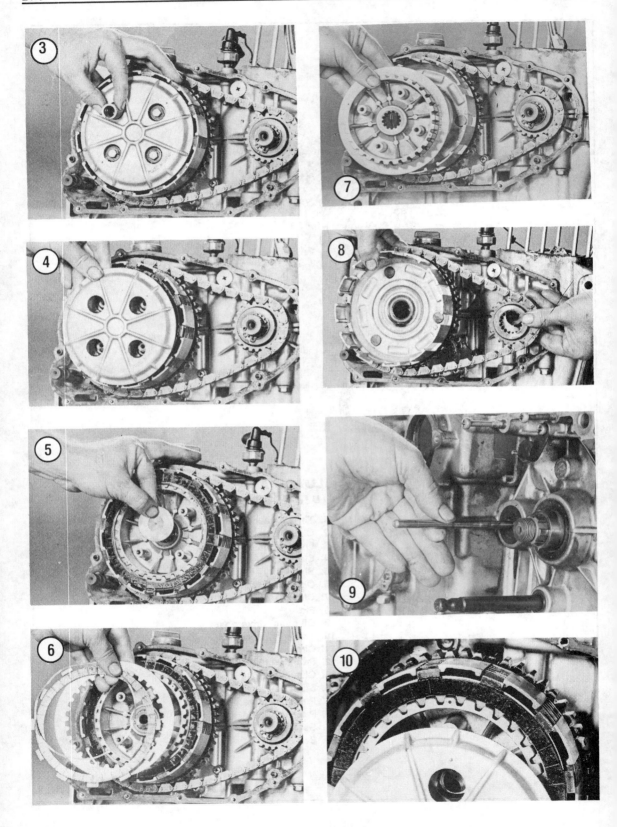

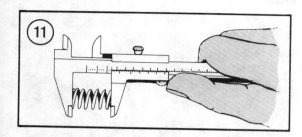

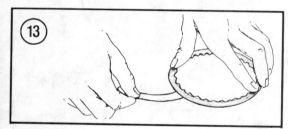

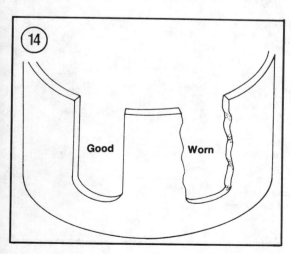

Good   Worn

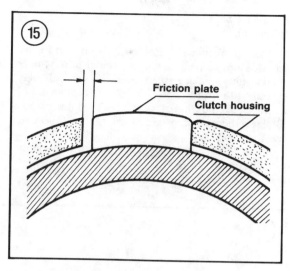

Friction plate

Clutch housing

Inspection

1. Clean all clutch parts in a petroleum-based solvent and dry thoroughly with compressed air.

2. Measure the free length of each clutch spring as shown in **Figure 11**. Replace any springs that are too short (**Table 1**).

3. Measure the thickness of each friction disc at several places around the disc as shown in **Figure 12**. See **Table 1** for specifications. Replace all friction discs if any one is found too thin. Do not replace only 1 or 2 discs.

4. Check the clutch metal plates for warpage as shown in **Figure 13**. If any plate is warped more than specified (**Table 1**), replace the entire set of plates. Do not replace only 1 or 2 plates.

5. Check the teeth on the clutch housing (**Figure 14**). Replace if necessary.

6. Inspect the clutch hub outer housing and the clutch boss assembly for cracks or galling in the grooves where the clutch friction disc tabs slide. They must be smooth for chatter-free clutch operation.

7. Inspect the shaft splines in the clutch boss assembly. If damage is only a slight amount, remove any small burrs with a fine cut file; if damage is severe, replace the assembly.

8. Inspect the long pushrod by rolling it on a flat surface, such as a piece of plate glass. Any clicking noise detected indicates that the rod is bent and should be replaced.

9. Inspect the pressure plate for signs of wear or damage; replace if necessary.

10. Measure clearance between the fingers on the clutch housing and the tangs on the friction plates (**Figure 15**). Standard clearance is listed in **Table 1**. Replace any friction disc with excessive clearance.

Primary Chain
Inspection

1. Measure primary chain wear as shown in **Figure 16**. Measure vertical play in the center of the upper chain run. Replace the chain if vertical play exceeds 20 mm (0.78 in.).

2. Measure the thickness of both chain guides. Replace them if they are worn to the following specification:

   a. *1974-1977 and 1977-1978 Deluxe A models:* 3.5 mm (0.14 in.).

   b. *1978-1983:* 2.0 mm (0.079 in.).

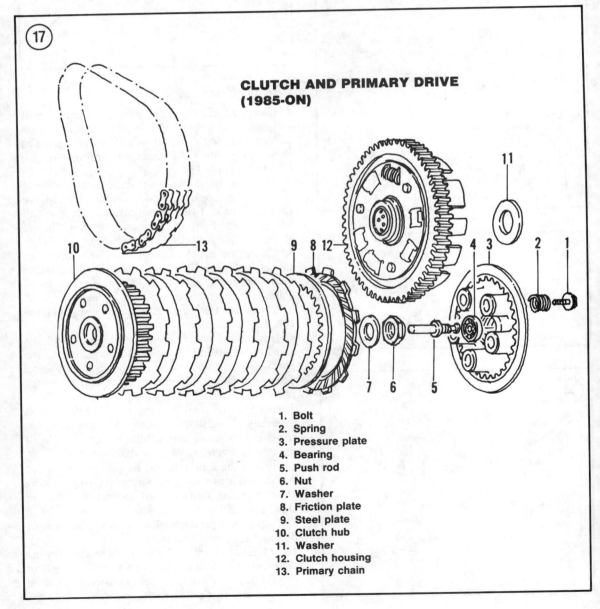

CLUTCH AND PRIMARY DRIVE (1985-ON)

1. Bolt
2. Spring
3. Pressure plate
4. Bearing
5. Push rod
6. Nut
7. Washer
8. Friction plate
9. Steel plate
10. Clutch hub
11. Washer
12. Clutch housing
13. Primary chain

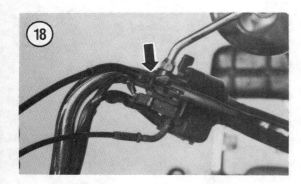

3. Apply Loctite 242 (blue) to the chain guide retaining screws when installing them.

CLUTCH (1985-ON)

Removal

Refer to **Figure 17** for this procedure.

1. Place the bike on the centerstand.
2. Drain the engine oil as described in Chapter Three.
3. Loosen and slide the cover away from the clutch lever adjustment nut at the handlebar and slacken the clutch cable (**Figure 18**).
4. Remove the following from the right-hand side.
   a. Right footpeg (**Figure 19**) rear mounting bolt.
   b. Rear brake switch assembly mounting bolt.
   c. Allow the brake switch assembly to hang down.
5. Remove the bolts securing the clutch cover in place and remove it. See **Figure 20**.
6. Loosen the 5 pressure plate screws in a crisscross pattern. Then remove the screws and springs (**Figure 21**).
7. Remove the pressure plate (**Figure 22**).
8. Remove a friction disc (**Figure 23**) and a clutch plate (**Figure 24**). Continue until all plates are removed. Stack discs and plates in order.

6

NOTE
To keep the clutch housing from turning when removing the clutch hub nut in step 9, use the "Grabbit" special tool available from Joe Bolger Products Inc., Summer Street, Barre, MA 01005. See Figure 25.

9. Straighten out the locking tab on the clutch nut and remove the clutch nut (**Figure 26**).

10. Remove the clutch boss (**Figure 27**) and thrust washer (**Figure 28**).

11. The clutch housing and primary chain (**Figure 29**) cannot be removed until the engine is removed and the crankcase disassembled. Refer to *Crankshaft Removal/Installation* in Chapter Five.

12. Inspect the clutch components as described in this chapter.

13. Installation is the reverse of these steps, noting the following.

14. Because the clutch nut is a self-locking nut, Kawasaki recommends replacing the nut every time it is removed. Install a new clutch nut (**Figure 26**). Tighten the nut to 130 N•m (98 ft.-lb.).

NOTE
Use the same tool as during removal to prevent the clutch boss from turning when tightening the clutch nut.

15. Install the friction plates so that the grooves on the side of the plate facing to the right-hand side run in a counterclockwise direction.

16. Tighten the clutch spring bolts to 9.3 N•m (82 in.-lb.).

17. Refill the engine oil as described in Chapter Three.

18. Adjust the clutch as described in Chapter Three.

19. Check the rear brake light adjustment as described in Chapter Three.

Inspection

1. Clean all clutch parts in a petroleum-based solvent such as kerosene, and thoroughly dry with compressed air.

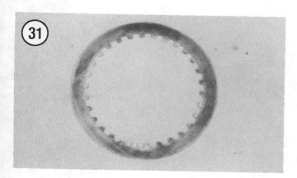

2. Measure the free length of each clutch spring as shown in **Figure 11**. Replace any springs (**Figure 30**) that are too short (**Table 1**).

3. Measure the thickness of each friction disc at several places around the disc as shown in **Figure 12**. See **Table 1** for specifications. Replace all friction discs if any one is found too thin. Do not replace only 1 or 2 discs.

4. Check the clutch metal plates (**Figure 31**) for warpage as shown in **Figure 13**. If any plate is warped more than specified (**Table 1**), replace the entire set of plates. Do not replace only 1 or 2 plates.

5. Inspect the clutch boss assembly (**Figure 32**) for cracks or galling in the grooves where the clutch friction disc tabs slide. They must be smooth for chatter-free clutch operation.

6. Inspect the shaft splines in the clutch boss assembly. If damage is only a slight amount, remove any small burrs with a fine cut file; if damage is severe, replace the assembly.

7. Inspect the the clutch release bearing (A, **Figure 33**) and pushrod (**Figure 34**) for wear or damage. Rotate the bearing race and check for excessive play or roughness. Replace if necessary.

8. Inspect the pressure plate (B, **Figure 33**) for signs of wear or damage; replace if necessary.

Primary Chain
Removal/Installation

Refer to Chapter Five. Refer to *Crankshaft Removal/Installation*.

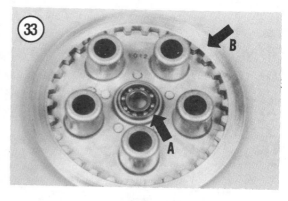

Table 1 CLUTCH WEAR LIMITS

	mm	in.
Clutch spring free length		
1974-1977	32.3	1.271
1978-1983	See footnote	See footnote
1985-on	32.2	1.267
Friction plate thickness		
1974-1977	2.5	0.098
1978-1983	2.7	0.106
1985-on	2.75	0.108
Clutch plate warpage		
1974-1977		
Friction	0.30	0.012
Steel	0.40	0.016
1978-1981 KZ400	0.40	0.016
1980-1983 KZ440	0.30	0.012
1985-on	0.30	0.012
Friction plate tangs clutch housing finger clearance		
1974-1977	0.60	0.023
1978-1983	0.70	0.027
1985-on	See footnote	See footnote

* Not specified by Kawasaki.

NOTE: If you own an EN500 model, first check the Supplement at the back of this book for any specific service information.

CHAPTER SEVEN

TRANSMISSION

This chapter describes complete transmission service procedures. **Tables 1-3** (end of chapter) list transmission wear limits.

SHIFT MECHANISM
(1974-1983)

Refer to **Figure 1** (1974-1977 and 1977-1978 Deluxe A models) or **Figure 2** (1978-1983) for this procedure.

Removal/Installation

1. Remove the sprocket or pulley cover.
2. Remove the clutch and primary chain assembly as described in Chapter Six.
3. Remove the screws (**Figure 3**) securing the shift shaft retaining plate and remove it.
4. Move the shift mechanism arm(s) from the shift drum.
5. Slide the shifter linkage and shaft out from the engine. See **Figure 4** (1974-1977 and 1977-1978 Deluxe A models) or **Figure 2**, items 1, 4 and 7 (1978-1983).
6. Installation is the reverse of these steps. Make sure to guide the shaft carefully through the crankcase to prevent damage to the shifter shaft oil seal.

Inspection

1. Measure the length of the shaft pawl spring as shown in **Figure 5**. Replace the spring if its length exceeds 31 mm (1.22 in.) for 1974-1977 and 1977-1978 Deluxe A models and 19 mm (0.75 in.) for 1978-1983.
2. Check all other parts for obvious wear or damage. Replace any which are doubtful.
3. Be sure the return spring pin is not loose. If it is, remove it, clean it and its threaded hole. Then apply Loctite 242 (blue) to the spring pin threads and install it.

SHIFT MECHANISM
(1985-ON)

Refer to **Figure 6** for this procedure.

Removal/Installation

1. Remove the engine pulley. See Chapter Twelve.
2. Drain the engine oil as described in Chapter Three.
3. Remove the circlip (**Figure 7**) and slide the shift lever off of the shift lever shaft.
4. Disconnect the neutral switch electrical connector (**Figure 8**).
5. Remove the drive shaft plug plate (A, **Figure 9**).

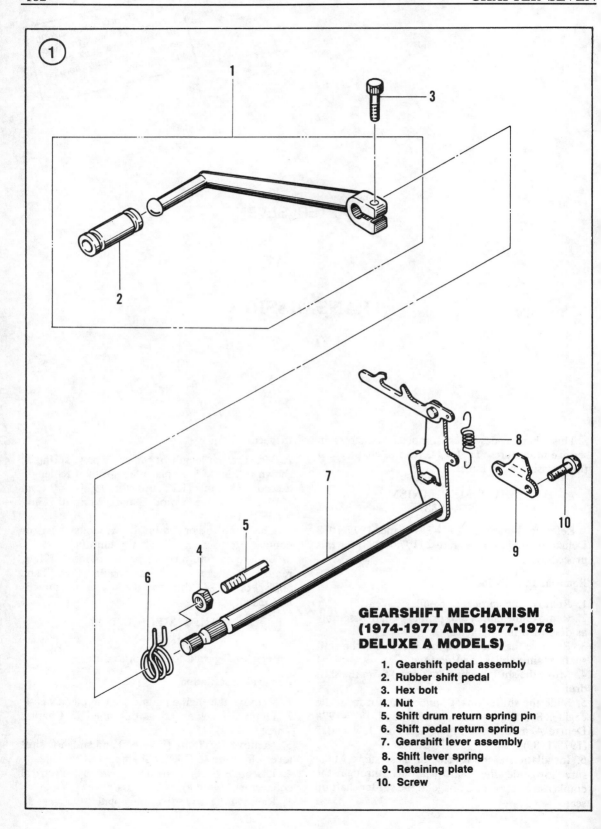

**GEARSHIFT MECHANISM
(1974-1977 AND 1977-1978
DELUXE A MODELS)**

1. Gearshift pedal assembly
2. Rubber shift pedal
3. Hex bolt
4. Nut
5. Shift drum return spring pin
6. Shift pedal return spring
7. Gearshift lever assembly
8. Shift lever spring
9. Retaining plate
10. Screw

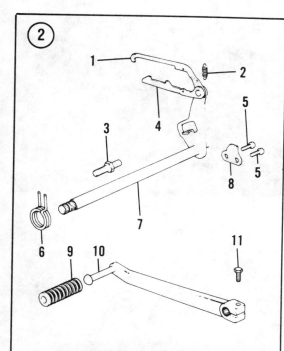

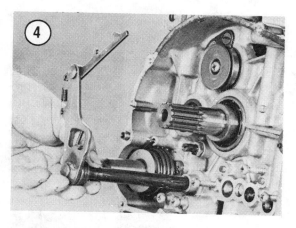

GEARSHIFT MECHANISM
(1978-1983)

1. Overshift limiter
2. Pawl spring
3. Return spring pin
4. Shift mechanism arm
5. Screw
6. Return spring
7. Shift shaft
8. Shift mechanism stop
9. Pedal rubber
10. Shift pedal
11. Bolt

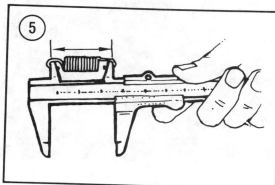

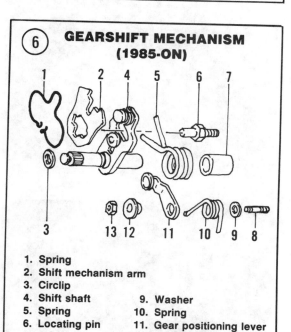

GEARSHIFT MECHANISM
(1985-ON)

1. Spring
2. Shift mechanism arm
3. Circlip
4. Shift shaft
5. Spring
6. Locating pin
7. Spacer
8. Stud
9. Washer
10. Spring
11. Gear positioning lever
12. Washer
13. Nut

7

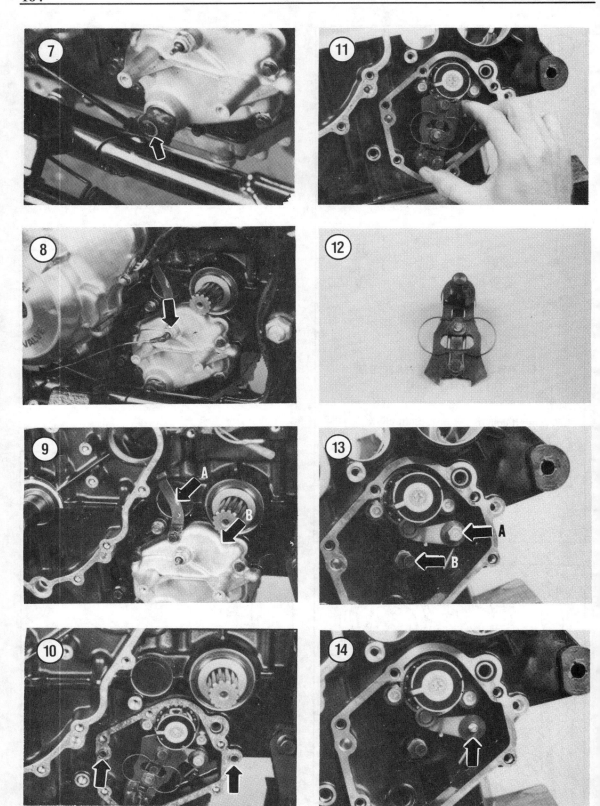

6. Remove the bolts securing the shift shaft cover and remove the cover (B, **Figure 9**).

7. Remove the 2 shift shaft cover dowel pins (**Figure 10**) and gasket.

8. Disengage the shift mechanism arm from its position on the shift drum cam by pulling the mechanism arm down (**Figure 11**). Then pull the shift shaft out of the engine together with its arm, spring, shaft return spring and spacer. See **Figure 12**.

9. Remove the gear positioning lever assembly in the following order:

    a. Bolt (A, **Figure 13**).
    b. Washer (**Figure 14**).
    c. Gear positioning lever (**Figure 15**).
    d. Spring (**Figure 16**).
    e. Washer (**Figure 17**).

10. Inspect the shift mechanism assembly as described in this chapter.

11. To install, reverse these steps. Note the following.

12. The gear positioning lever spacer must be installed so that the spacer's small diameter faces toward the crankcase.

13. Align the center of the shift mechanism spring (**Figure 16**) with the pin in the crankcase (B, **Figure 13**) when installing the shift mechanism.

14. Apply a high temperature brake grease to the shift shaft cover seal lips.

15. Refill the engine oil as described in Chapter Three.

16. Make sure the shift linkage rod is at a 90° angle as shown in **Figure 18**. If not, loosen the linkage rod locknuts and adjust the rod as necessary.

Inspection

1. Check the shift shaft for bending or spline damage (**Figure 12**). If the shaft is bent, it may be

7

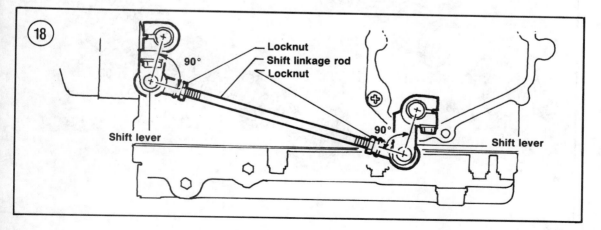

Locknut
Shift linkage rod
Locknut
90°
90°
Shift lever
Shift lever

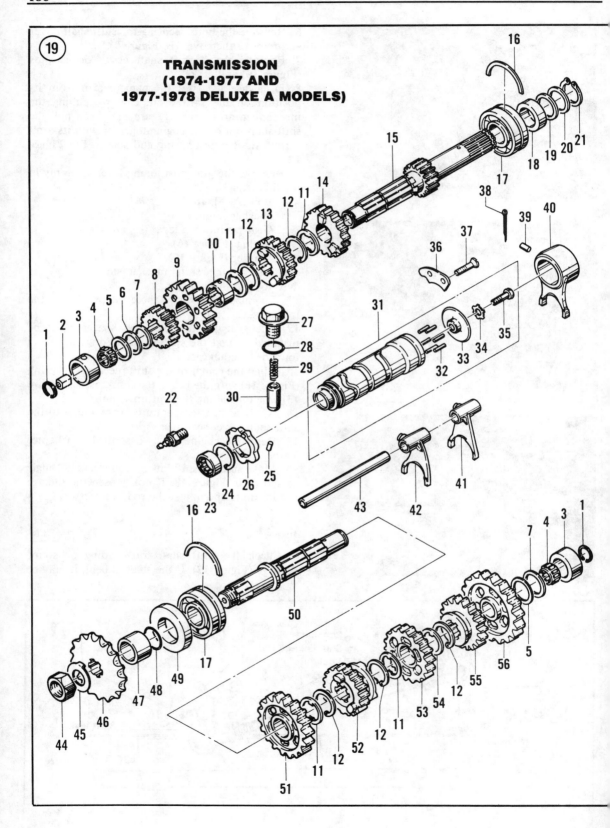

**TRANSMISSION
(1974-1977 AND
1977-1978 DELUXE A MODELS)**

1. Circlip
2. Drive shaft bushing
3. Output and drive shaft bushing
4. Needle bearing
5. Thrust washer
6. Thrust washer
7. Thrust washer
8. Drive shaft 2nd gear
9. Drive shaft top gear
10. Drive shaft top gear bushing
11. Lockwasher
12. Circlip
13. Drive shaft 3rd gear
14. Drive shaft 4th gear bushing
15. Drive shaft
16. Positioning ring
17. Ball bearing
18. Collar
19. Thrust washer
20. Thrust washer
21. Circlip
22. Neutral indicator switch
23. Needle bearing
24. Circlip
25. Dowel pin
26. Change drum operating disc
27. Neutral positioning bolt
28. O-ring
29. Spring
30. Neutral postioning pin
31. Gearshift drum assembly
32. Gearshift drum pin
33. Gearshift drum pin plate
34. Lockwasher
35. Pan head screw
36. Shift drum positioning plate
37. Countersunk head screw
38. Cotter pin
39. Dowel pin
40. 4th and top shift fork
41. Low shift fork
42. 2nd and 3rd shift fork
43. Shift rod
44. Nut
45. Lockwasher
46. Engine sprocket
47. Engine sprocket collar
48. O-ring
49. Oil seal
50. Output shaft
51. 2nd gear output shaft
52. Top gear output shaft
53. 3rd gear output shaft
54. Lockwasher
55. Output shaft 4th gear
56. Output shaft low gear

straightened by a machine shop. If the splines are damaged, the shaft must be replaced.

2. Check the springs for weakness or damage.

3. Check the shift mechanism arm (**Figure 12**) for distortion or damage.

4. Inspect the shift drum cam and neutral holder for wear or damage.

5. Inspect the gear positioning lever for wear, breakage or distortion.

6. Replace any worn or damaged parts.

5-SPEED TRANSMISSION (1974-1977 AND 1977-1978 DELUXE A MODELS)

Removal/Installation

Refer to **Figure 19** for this procedure.

1. Disassemble the engine crankcase as described in Chapter Four.

2. Lift the mainshaft and countershaft from the upper crankcase (**Figure 20**).

3. Remove the shift cam retainer plate (**Figure 21**). Then pull out the shift fork guide rail and its associated shift forks (**Figure 22**).

CAUTION
The shift forks are slightly different.
Figure 23 *shows proper assembly. Keep these parts assembled to prevent the forks from becoming interchanged.*

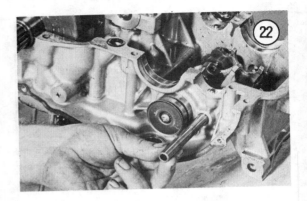

4. Remove the cotter pin and guide pin from the remaining shift fork.

5. Pull out the shift cam as far as it will go (**Figure 24**).

6. Remove the snap ring retaining the shift cam operating plate.

7. Remove the shift cam from the engine.

8. Installation is the reverse of these steps, noting the following.

9. **Figure 25** illustrates all gears and bearings assembled correctly.

10. Be sure that the countershaft oil seal is installed so that its spring is facing inward. Also be sure that both bearings engage their locating pins and that both bearing positioning rings are correct (**Figure 26**).

11. Reassemble the crankcase assembly as described in Chapter Four.

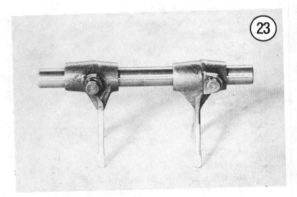

Transmission Shaft
Disassembly/Reassembly

Transmission shaft disassembly on these models requires special tools. It is recommended that transmission shafts be serviced by a Kawasaki dealer.

Inspection

1. Clean all parts in cleaning solvent and dry thoroughly.

2. Inspect the gears visually for cracks, chips, broken teeth and burnt teeth. Check the lugs (**Figure 27**) on ends of gears to make sure they are not rounded off. If lugs are rounded off, check the shift forks as described later in this chapter. More than likely, one or more of the shift forks is bent.

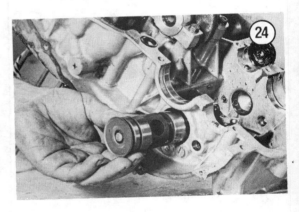

NOTE
Defective gears should be replaced, and it is a good idea to replace the mating gear even though it may not show as much wear or damage. Remember that accelerated wear to new parts is normally caused by contact from worn parts.

3. Inspect all free wheeling gear bearing surfaces for wear, discoloration and galling. Inspect the mating shaft bearing surface also. If there is any metal flaking or visible damage, replace both parts.

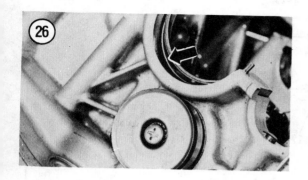

4. Inspect the mainshaft and countershaft splines for wear or discoloration. Check the mating gear internal splines also. If no visible damage is apparent, slide each gear on its respective shaft and work the gear back and forth to make sure gear operates smoothly.

5. Replace any washers that show wear.

6. Discard the circlips and replace them during assembly.

7. Measure the clearance between each shift fork and the groove on its mating gear (**Figure 28**). Replace the fork and/or gear if clearance exceeds 0.55 mm (0.022 in.).

8. Measure the width of each gear shift fork groove. Replace any gear if its groove is worn to greater than 5.25 mm (0.206 in.).

9. Measure the thickness of each shift fork finger at the points where it engages the groove in its mating gear. Replace the shift fork if it is worn to less than 4.7 mm (0.185 in.).

10. Measure the width of each groove in the shift drum. Replace the cam if any groove is worn to wider than 8.25 mm (0.325 in.).

11. Measure the thickness of each shift fork guide pin. Fourth and fifth gear guide pins must be replaced if they are worn to 7.85 mm (0.309 in.). Remaining shift forks must be replaced if their guide pins are worn to 7.93 mm (0.312 in.) or less.

12. Measure backlash between each pair of gears as shown in **Figure 29**. Hold one gear stationary, then move the mating gear with the dial indicator touching. Replace both gears if backlash exceeds 0.3 mm (0.012 in.).

13. Measure clearance between each free-spinning gear and its shaft. Replace any gear if clearance exceeds 0.16 mm (0.0063 in.).

14. Check transmission bearings by cleaning them thoroughly with solvent, then oiling them lightly. Spin each bearing by hand and check for rough or noisy operation. Replace any bearing if necessary.

5- AND 6-SPEED TRANSMISSION (1978-1983, EXCEPT 1978 DELUXE A)

Removal and installation of the transmission components and shift drum are identical on both 5- and 6-speed transmissions. Disassembly and assembly of the transmission shafts differ and are covered separately in the following procedures.

Refer to **Figure 30** (5-speed) or **Figure 31** (6-speed).

7

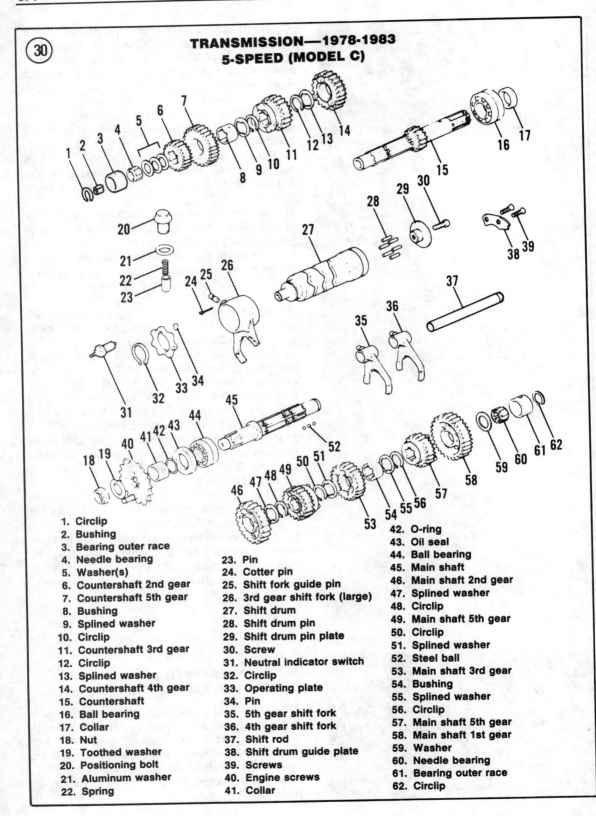

TRANSMISSION—1978-1983
5-SPEED (MODEL C)

1. Circlip
2. Bushing
3. Bearing outer race
4. Needle bearing
5. Washer(s)
6. Countershaft 2nd gear
7. Countershaft 5th gear
8. Bushing
9. Splined washer
10. Circlip
11. Countershaft 3rd gear
12. Circlip
13. Splined washer
14. Countershaft 4th gear
15. Countershaft
16. Ball bearing
17. Collar
18. Nut
19. Toothed washer
20. Positioning bolt
21. Aluminum washer
22. Spring

23. Pin
24. Cotter pin
25. Shift fork guide pin
26. 3rd gear shift fork (large)
27. Shift drum
28. Shift drum pin
29. Shift drum pin plate
30. Screw
31. Neutral indicator switch
32. Circlip
33. Operating plate
34. Pin
35. 5th gear shift fork
36. 4th gear shift fork
37. Shift rod
38. Shift drum guide plate
39. Screws
40. Engine screws
41. Collar

42. O-ring
43. Oil seal
44. Ball bearing
45. Main shaft
46. Main shaft 2nd gear
47. Splined washer
48. Circlip
49. Main shaft 5th gear
50. Circlip
51. Splined washer
52. Steel ball
53. Main shaft 3rd gear
54. Bushing
55. Splined washer
56. Circlip
57. Main shaft 5th gear
58. Main shaft 1st gear
59. Washer
60. Needle bearing
61. Bearing outer race
62. Circlip

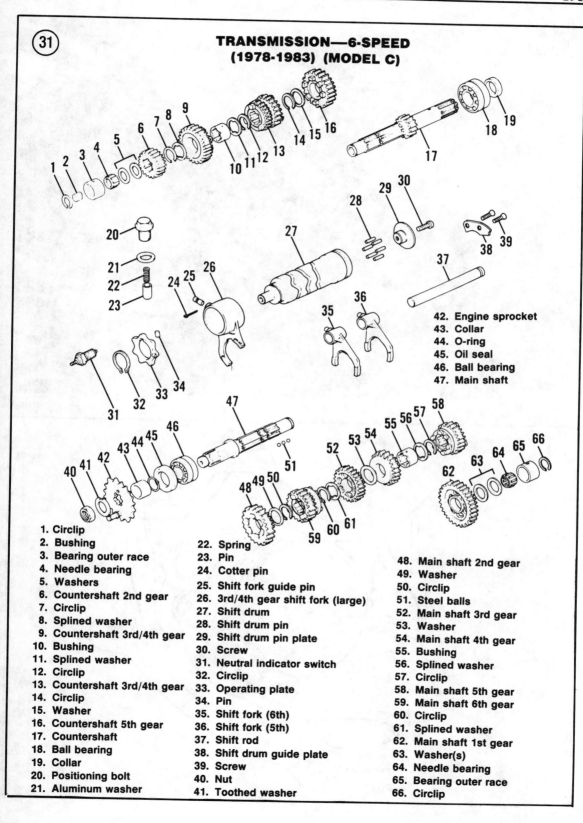

(31)

TRANSMISSION—6-SPEED
(1978-1983) (MODEL C)

1. Circlip
2. Bushing
3. Bearing outer race
4. Needle bearing
5. Washers
6. Countershaft 2nd gear
7. Circlip
8. Splined washer
9. Countershaft 3rd/4th gear
10. Bushing
11. Splined washer
12. Circlip
13. Countershaft 3rd/4th gear
14. Circlip
15. Washer
16. Countershaft 5th gear
17. Countershaft
18. Ball bearing
19. Collar
20. Positioning bolt
21. Aluminum washer
22. Spring
23. Pin
24. Cotter pin
25. Shift fork guide pin
26. 3rd/4th gear shift fork (large)
27. Shift drum
28. Shift drum pin
29. Shift drum pin plate
30. Screw
31. Neutral indicator switch
32. Circlip
33. Operating plate
34. Pin
35. Shift fork (6th)
36. Shift fork (5th)
37. Shift rod
38. Shift drum guide plate
39. Screw
40. Nut
41. Toothed washer
42. Engine sprocket
43. Collar
44. O-ring
45. Oil seal
46. Ball bearing
47. Main shaft
48. Main shaft 2nd gear
49. Washer
50. Circlip
51. Steel balls
52. Main shaft 3rd gear
53. Washer
54. Main shaft 4th gear
55. Bushing
56. Splined washer
57. Circlip
58. Main shaft 5th gear
59. Main shaft 6th gear
60. Circlip
61. Splined washer
62. Main shaft 1st gear
63. Washer(s)
64. Needle bearing
65. Bearing outer race
66. Circlip

7

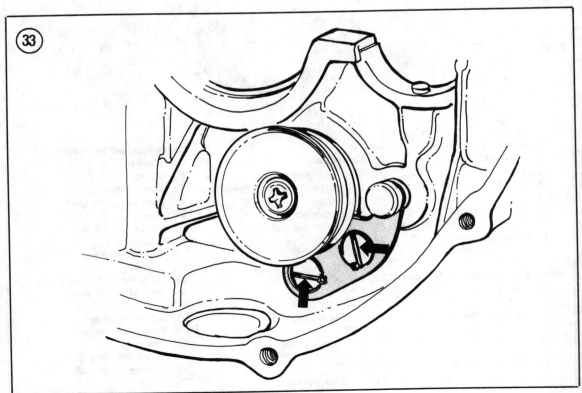

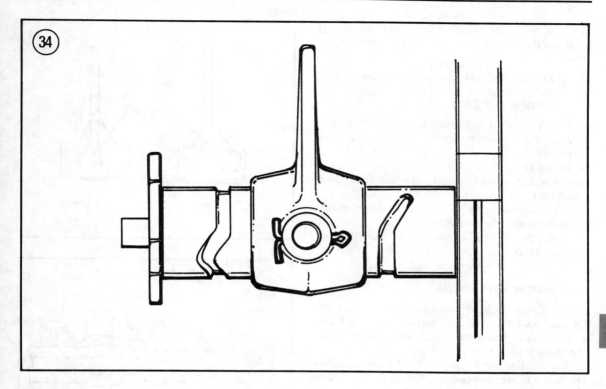

Removal

Refer to **Figure 30** and **Figure 31**.

1. Disassemble the crankcase halves as described in Chapter Four.

2. Lift the mainshaft and countershaft assemblies from the crankcase (**Figure 32**).

3. Remove the shift drum positioning bolt (20), washer, spring and pin (23).

4. Remove the 2 screws (**Figure 33**) securing the shift drum guide plate.

5. Withdraw the shift rod while removing both shift forks.

6. Remove the circlip (32) securing the operating plate (33) and remove it.

7. Remove the operating plate pin (34).

8. Remove the cotter pin (24) securing the large shift fork (26) and remove the guide pin (25).

9. Hold onto the large shift fork and withdraw the shift fork drum.

Installation

1. Coat all surfaces of the shift drum, shift forks and shift shaft with new engine oil.

2. Partially install the shift drum into the crankcase. Position the large shift drum with the guide pin housing facing toward the crankshaft and slide the shift drum in the remaining way until it seats.

3. Install the operating plate pin into the shift drum and install the operating plate with the projection facing toward the neutral switch. Install the circlip.

4. Install the large shift fork so that the guide pin will fit into the middle of the 3 grooves in the shift drum.

5. Install the guide pin (25) into the large shift fork and install a new cotter pin (**Figure 34**).

NOTE
Always install a new cotter pin; never install a used one.

6. *6-speed:* Insert the shift rod (37, **Figure 31**) partially into the crankcase. Correctly position the 5th and 6th gear shift forks with their guide pins located in the shift drum. Slide the shift rod through both forks until it completely seats.

NOTE
These 2 shift forks are identical so there is no problem of intermixing their positions.

7. *5-speed:* Insert the shift rod (37, **Figure 30**) partially into the crankcase. Correctly position the 4th gear shift fork (guide pin on the right-hand side of the fork hub) and insert the rod through the 5th gear shift fork (guide pin on the left-hand side of

the fork hub). See **Figure 35**. Be sure to correctly position their guide pins into the shift drum.

NOTE
*These 2 shift forks are slightly different and must be installed in their original positions. See **Figure 35**.*

8. Install the shift fork guide plate and stake both screws with a centerpunch to prevent them from working loose.

9. Install the shift drum positioning pin, spring, a new washer and bolt. Tighten the bolt to 35 N•m (25 ft.-lb.).

10. Install the mainshaft and countershaft assemblies into the crankcase.

11. Reassemble the crankcase as described in Chapter Four.

Transmission Service Notes

1. A divided container such as an egg carton can be used to help maintain correct alignment and positioning of the parts as they are removed from the transmission shafts.

2. The circlips are a tight fit on the transmission shafts. It is recommended to replace all circlips during reassembly.

3. When removing and installing circlips, they have a tendency to turn sideways and make removal and installation difficult. To ease replacement open the circlips with a pair of circlip pliers while at the same time holding the back of the circlip with a pair of needlenose pliers.

Countershaft Disassembly/Assembly (6-Speed)

Refer to **Figure 31** for this procedure.

1. Slide off the bearing outer race (3).

2. Remove the circlip (1) and slide off the needle bearing (4), washers (5) and second gear (6).

3. Remove the circlip (7). Then remove the splined washer (8), sixth gear (9), bushing (10) and splined washer (11).

4. Remove the circlip (12) and slide off third/fourth gear combination (13).

5. Remove the circlip (14) and washer (15) and slide off fifth gear (16).

6. If necessary, remove the ball bearing (18) and collar (19). Removal requires the use of a bearing puller.

7. Assemble by reversing these disassembly steps. Refer to **Figure 36** for correct positioning of gears. Make sure that all circlips are correctly seated in the countershaft grooves. See **Figure 37**.

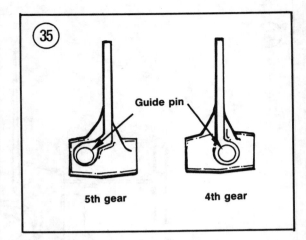

5th gear   4th gear

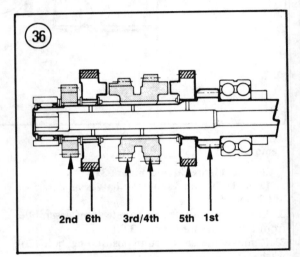

2nd   6th   3rd/4th   5th   1st

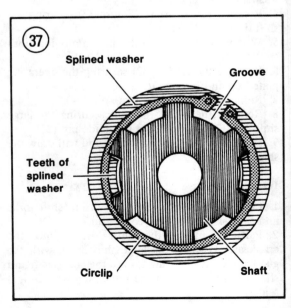

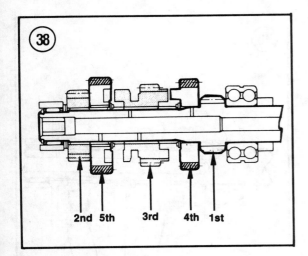

2nd 5th   3rd   4th 1st

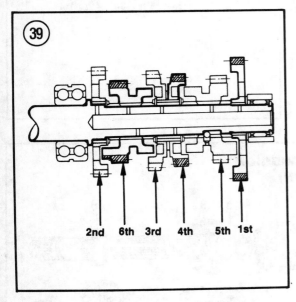

2nd 6th 3rd   4th   5th 1st

NOTE
*Install all splined washers and circlips
as indicated in* **Figure 37**.

**Mainshaft Disassembly/Assembly
(6-speed)**

Refer to **Figure 31** for this procedure.
1. Slide off the bearing outer race (65).
2. Remove the circlip (66) and slide off the needle bearing (64), washers (63) and first gear (62).
3. Remove fifth gear (58). Fifth gear has 3 steel balls located between the gear and the shaft. This is used for NEUTRAL location when shifting from first gear. To remove the gear spin the shaft in a vertical position holding onto 3rd gear. Pull fifth gear up and off the shaft.

NOTE
*Perform this procedure over and close
down to a workbench with some shop
cloths spread over it. This lessens the
chance of losing the balls when the gear
comes off.*

4. Remove the circlip (57) and slide off the splined washer (56), fourth gear (54), washer (53), third gear (52), bushing (55) and the splined washer (61).
5. Remove the circlip (60) and slide off sixth gear (59).
6. Remove the circlip (50) and washer (49) and slide off second gear (48).
7. If necessary, remove the ball bearing (46) with a bearing puller.
8. Assemble by reversing these disassembly steps. Refer to **Figure 38** for correct placement of gears. Make sure that all circlips are seated correctly in the mainshaft grooves.

NOTE
*Install all splined washers and circlips
as indicated in* **Figure 37**.

9. When installing third/fourth gear bushing (55) align the bushing oil holes with the holes in the mainshaft.
10. When installing the 3 balls into the 5th gear, *do not use grease* to hold them in place. They must be able to move freely during normal operation of the transmission.

**Countershaft Disassembly/Assembly
(5-speed)**

Refer to **Figure 30** for this procedure.
1. Slide off the bearing outer race (3).
2. Remove the circlip (1) and slide off the needle bearing (4), washer (5), second gear (6), bushing (8) and the splined washer (9).
3. Remove the circlip (10) and slide off third gear (11).
4. Remove the circlip (12) and the splined washer (13).
5. Slide off fourth gear (14).
6. If necessary, remove the ball bearing (16) and collar (17). Removal requires the use of a bearing puller.
7. Assemble by reversing these disassembly steps. Refer to **Figure 39** for the correct positioning of gears. Make sure that all circlips are correctly seated in the countershaft grooves.

NOTE
*Install splined washers and circlips as
indicated in* **Figure 37**.

7

Mainshaft Disassembly/Assembly
(5-speed)

Refer to **Figure 30** for this procedure.

1. Slide off the bearing outer race (61).

2. Remove the circlip (62) and slide off the needle bearing (60), washer (59) and first gear (58).

3. Remove fourth gear (57). Fourth gear has 3 steel balls located between the gear and the shaft. This is used for NEUTRAL location when shifting from first gear. To remove the gear, spin the shaft in a vertical position, holding onto third gear. Pull the fourth gear up and off the shaft.

NOTE
Perform this procedure over and close down to a workbench with some shop cloths spread over it. This will lessen the chance of losing the balls when the gear comes off.

4. Remove the circlip (56), splined washer (55), third gear (53), bushing (54) and the splined washer (51).

5. Remove the circlip (50) and slide off fifth gear (49).

6. Remove the circlip (48), splined washer (47) and second gear (46).

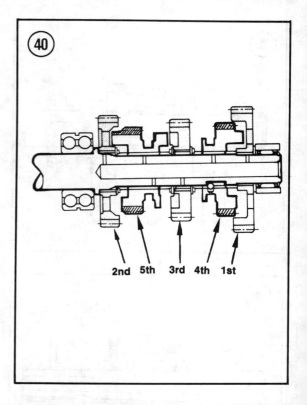

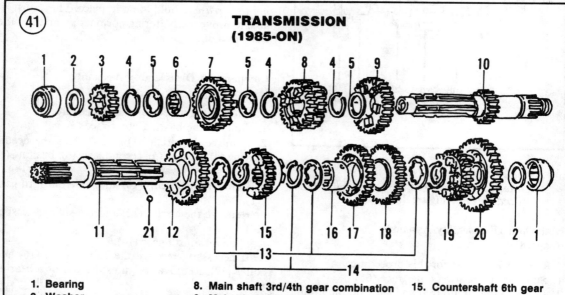

TRANSMISSION
(1985-ON)

1. Bearing	8. Main shaft 3rd/4th gear combination
2. Washer	9. Main shaft 5th gear
3. Main shaft 2nd gear	10. Main shaft/1st gear
4. Circlip	11. Countershaft
5. Washer	12. Countershaft 2nd gear
6. Bearing	13. Washer
7. Main shaft 6th gear	14. Circlip

15. Countershaft 6th gear
16. Bearing
17. Countershaft 4th gear
18. Countershaft 3rd gear
19. Countershaft 5th gear
20. Countershaft 1st gear

7. Remove the ball bearing if necessary. Removal requires the use of a bearing puller.

8. Assemble by reversing these disassembly steps. Refer to **Figure 40** for correct placement of gears. Make sure all circlips are seated correctly in the mainshaft grooves.

NOTE
*Refer to **Figure 37** for correct installation of splined washers and circlips.*

9. When installing the third gear bushing (54) align the bushing oil holes with the holes in the mainshaft.

10. When installing the 3 steel balls into fourth gear, *do not use grease* to hold them in place. They must be able to move freely during transmission operation.

Inspection

1. Clean all parts in cleaning solvent and dry thoroughly.

2. Inspect the gears visually for cracks, chips, broken teeth and burnt teeth. Check the lugs (**Figure 27**) on ends of gears to make sure they are not rounded off. If lugs are rounded off check the shift forks as described later in this chapter. More than likely, one or more of the shift forks is bent.

NOTE
Defective gears should be replaced. It is a good idea to replace the mating gear even though it may not show as much wear or damage. Remember that accelerated wear to new parts is normally caused by contact from worn parts.

3. Inspect all free wheeling gear bearing surfaces for wear, discoloration and galling. Inspect the mating shaft bearing surface also. If there is any metal flaking or visible damage, replace both parts.

4. Inspect the mainshaft and countershaft splines for wear or discoloration. Check the mating gear internal splines also. If no visible damage is apparent, install each sliding gear on its respective shaft and work the gear back and forth to make sure gear operates smoothly.

5. Check all circlips and washers. Replace any circlips that may have been damaged during operation or removal as well as any washers that show wear.

6. If some of the transmission components were damaged, make sure to remove the shift drum and shift forks as described later in this section and inspect all components carefully.

TRANSMISSION (1985-ON)

Removal/Installation

Refer to **Figure 41** for this procedure.

1. Split the crankcase as described in this chapter.

2. Remove the transmission countershaft (**Figure 42**).

3. Lift the clutch housing (A, **Figure 43**) and remove the mainshaft (B, **Figure 43**) from the clutch housing. Set the clutch housing back into the crankcase.

4. Remove the washer (**Figure 44**) and spacer (**Figure 45**) from the clutch housing.

5. Install by reversing these steps. Note the following:

    a. Before installing any components, coat all bearing surfaces with assembly oil.

    b. Install the spacer (**Figure 45**) and washer (**Figure 44**) into the clutch housing.

    c. When installing the transmission shaft assemblies, make sure the dowel pins (A, **Figure 46**) and both 1/2 circlips (B, **Figure 46**) are in place in the upper crankcase before installing the transmission assemblies.

> *CAUTION*
> *If the mainshaft and countershaft bearings do not engage the dowel pins and 1/2 circlips correctly, there will be no clearance between the crankcase and the outer bearing races.*

    d. Assemble the crankcase as described in Chapter Five.

Transmission
Service Notes

1. A divided container such as an egg carton (**Figure 47**) can be used to help maintain correct alignment and positioning of the parts as they are removed from the transmission shafts.

2. The circlips are a tight fit on the transmission shafts. It is recommended to replace all circlips during reassembly.

3. When removing and installing circlips, they have a tendency to turn sideways and make removal and installation difficult. To ease replacement, open the circlips with a pair of circlip pliers while at the same time holding the back of the circlip with a pair of needlenose pliers as shown in **Figure 48**.

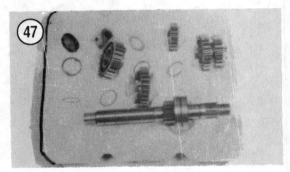

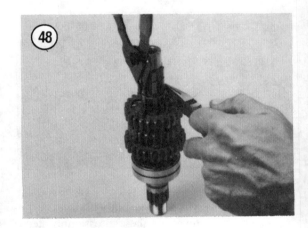

Mainshaft Disassembly/Assembly

Refer to **Figure 41** for the following procedure.

1. Remove the seal (**Figure 49**) and bearing (**Figure 50**).

2. Remove the washer (**Figure 51**) and slide off second gear (**Figure 52**).

3. Remove the circlip and washer (**Figure 53**).

4. Slide off sixth gear (**Figure 54**).

5. Remove the washer and circlip (**Figure 55**) and slide off the fourth/third gear combination (**Figure 56**).

6. Remove the circlip and washer (**Figure 57**) and slide off fifth gear (**Figure 58**).

7. If necessary, remove the mainshaft bearing (**Figure 59**) with a bearing puller.

8. Inspect the mainshaft assembly as described in this chapter.

9. Assemble by reversing these disassembly steps. Note the following.

10. Install the splined washers and circlips as shown in **Figure 60**.

11. Align the sixth gear bushing oil hole with the hole in the mainshaft (**Figure 61**).

12. Refer to **Figure 62** for correct placement of the gears.

13. Make sure each gear engages properly to the adjoining gear where applicable.

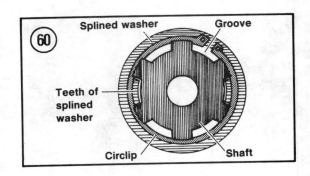

Countershaft Disassembly/Assembly

Refer to **Figure 41** for the following procedure.

1. Slide the needle bearing (**Figure 63**) off the countershaft.

2. Remove the washer (**Figure 64**) and slide off 1st gear (**Figure 65**).

3. Remove 5th gear (**Figure 66**) as follows. The 5th gear (**Figure 67**) has 3 steel balls located between the gear and the shaft. These are used for NEUTRAL location when shifting from 1st gear. To remove the gear, spin the shaft in a vertical position while holding onto 3rd gear. Pull 5th gear up and off the shaft.

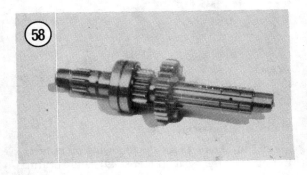

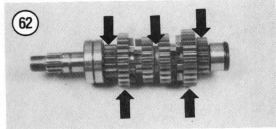

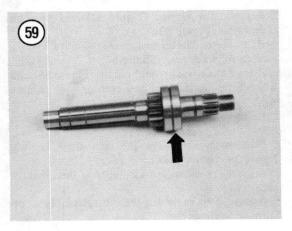

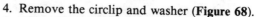

4. Remove the circlip and washer (**Figure 68**).

5. Slide off 3rd (**Figure 69**).

6. Slide off 4th gear (**Figure 70**) and its bushing (**Figure 71**).

7. Remove the washer and circlip (**Figure 72**) and slide off 6th gear (**Figure 73**).

8. Remove the circlip and washer (**Figure 74**) and slide off 2nd gear (**Figure 75**).

9. Remove the oil seal (A, **Figure 76**).

10. If necessary, remove the bearing (B, **Figure 76**) with a bearing puller.

11. Inspect the countershaft assembly as described in this chapter.

7

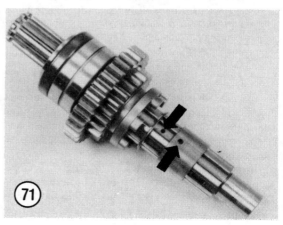

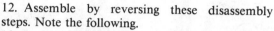

12. Assemble by reversing these disassembly steps. Note the following.

13. Install the splined washers and circlips as shown in **Figure 60**.

14. Align the 4th gear bushing oil hole with the hole in the mainshaft (**Figure 71**).

15. When installing the 3 balls (**Figure 67**) into the 5th gear, *do not use grease* to hold them in place. The balls must be able to move freely during normal transmission operation.

16. Refer to **Figure 77** for correct placement of the gears.

17. Make sure each gear engages properly to the adjoining gear where applicable.

Inspection

1. Clean all parts in cleaning solvent and dry thoroughly.

2. Inspect the gears visually for cracks, chips, broken teeth and burnt teeth. Check the lugs (**Figure 78**) on ends of gears to make sure they are not rounded off. If lugs are rounded off, check the shift forks as described later in this chapter. More than likely one or more of the shift forks is bent.

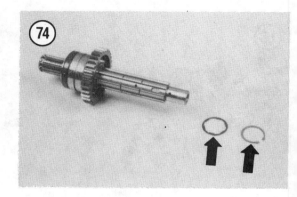

> *NOTE*
> *Defective gears should be replaced. It is a good idea to replace the mating gear even though it may not show as much wear or damage. Remember that accelerated wear to new parts is normally caused by contact from worn parts.*

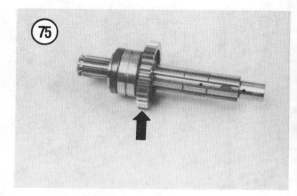

3. Inspect all free wheeling gear bearing surfaces for wear, discoloration and galling. Inspect the mating shaft bearing surface also. If there is any metal flaking or visible damage, replace both parts. See **Figure 79**.

4. Inspect the mainshaft and countershaft shaft splines for wear or discoloration. Check the mating gear internal splines also. If no visible damage is apparent, install each sliding gear on its respective

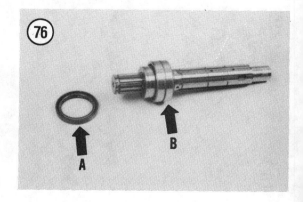

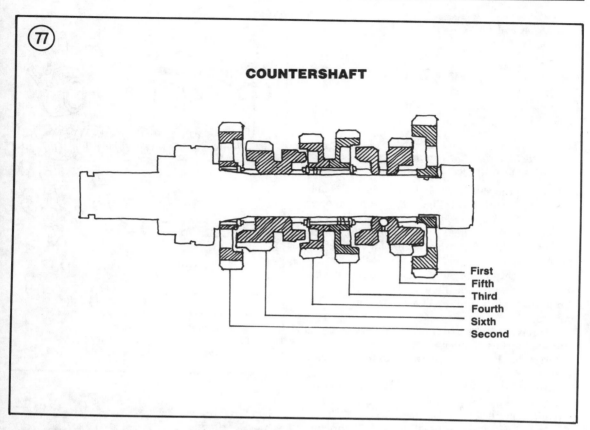

COUNTERSHAFT

First
Fifth
Third
Fourth
Sixth
Second

7

shaft and work the gear back and forth to make sure gear operates smoothly.

5. Replace any washers that show wear.

6. Discard the circlips and replace them during assembly.

7. Inspect the needle bearings and their housings (**Figure 80**) for wear or damage. Replace if necessary.

8. Check the countershaft slot (**Figure 81**) where the 5th gear ball bearings engage. If the slot is worn or damaged, the countershaft must be replaced.

Shift Drum and Forks
Removal/Installation

Refer to **Figure 82**.
1. Remove the mainshaft and countershaft as described in this chapter.
2. Remove the shift drum mounting bolts (A, **Figure 83**).

NOTE
Label the shift forks so that they can be reinstalled in their original positions.

3. Remove the shift fork shaft (B, **Figure 83**) and remove the 2 shift forks (**Figure 84**) from the lower crankcase. See **Figure 85**.
4. Remove the cotter pin (**Figure 86**). Then remove the third/fourth gear shift fork guide pin (**Figure 87**).
5. Pull the shift drum out partway and remove the 3rd/4th gear shift fork (**Figure 88**).
6. Pull the shift drum (**Figure 89**) out of the crankcase.
7. Inspect the shift drum and fork assembly as described in this chapter.
8. Insert the shift drum partway into the crankcase (**Figure 89**).
9. Install the 3rd/4th gear shift fork onto the shift drum so that the long end faces toward the neutral switch (**Figure 88**).
10. Push the shift drum in all the way (**Figure 90**).
11. Apply Loctite 242 (blue) to the shift drum mounting bolts and tighten them securely. See A, **Figure 83**.
12. Align the guide pin hole in the shift fork with the middle shift drum groove. Then install the guide pin (**Figure 87**) and secure it with a new cotter pin. Bend the cotter pin over to lock it. See **Figure 91**.

NOTE
When bending the cotter pin over spread the cotter pin so that the long end faces inward.

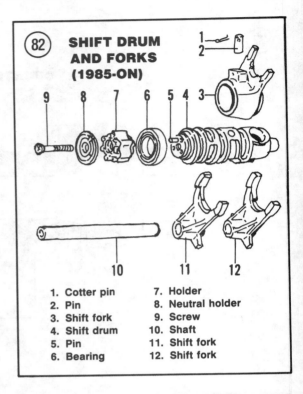

82 **SHIFT DRUM AND FORKS (1985-ON)**

1. Cotter pin	7. Holder
2. Pin	8. Neutral holder
3. Shift fork	9. Screw
4. Shift drum	10. Shaft
5. Pin	11. Shift fork
6. Bearing	12. Shift fork

83

81

84

13. Place the shift forks into the upper crankcase so that the long end of each fork faces toward the external shift mechanism. See **Figure 84**.

14. Slide the shift shaft through the crankcase and engage both shift forks.

Shift Drum Disassembly

1. Remove the screw (**Figure 92**) from the end of the shift drum. Then remove the following parts:
   a. Neutral holder (**Figure 93**).
   b. Shift drum cam (**Figure 94**).
   c. Ball bearing (**Figure 95**).
   d. Dowel pin (**Figure 96**).

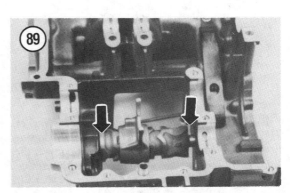

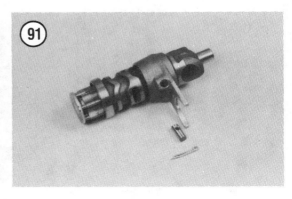

2. Inspect the shift drum as described in this section.

3. Install the dowel pin (**Figure 97**) into the largest hole in the end of the shift drum.

4. Install the ball bearing (**Figure 95**).

5. Align the groove in the end of the shift drum cam (**Figure 98**) with the dowel pin (**Figure 96**) and install the cam.

6. The shift drum cam has 6 points, of which 1 point is higher than the other 5 (**Figure 99**). Align the highest point with the back of the neutral holder and install the neutral holder (**Figure 93**).

> *NOTE*
> *If the neutral holder is installed incorrectly, the neutral indicator light will not light when the transmission is in NEUTRAL.*

7. Apply Loctite 242 (blue) to the screw and install it into the shift drum. Tighten the screw securely.

Inspection

1. Inspect each shift fork for signs of wear or cracking. See **Figure 100** and **Figure 101**. Examine the shift forks at the points where they contact the slider gear. This surface should be smooth with no signs of wear or damage. Make sure the forks slide smoothly on the shaft (**Figure 102**) or shift drum (**Figure 91**). Make sure the shaft is not bent. This

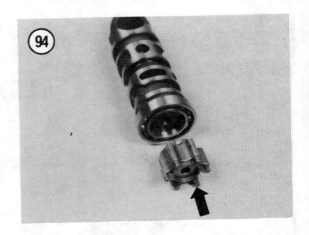

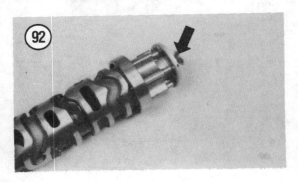

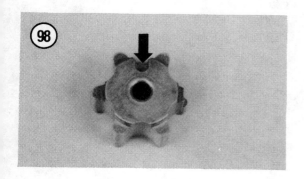

can be checked by removing the shift forks from the shaft and rolling the shaft (**Figure 103**) on a piece of plate glass. Any clicking noise detected indicates that the shaft is bent.

2. Measure the thickness of each shift fork finger. Compare to the specificatons in **Table 3**. Replace a shift fork if the finger thickness is too thin.

3. Check grooves in the shift drum (**Figure 104**) for wear or roughness. Measure the grooves with a vernier caliper. Replace the shift drum if any groove is too wide (**Table 3**).

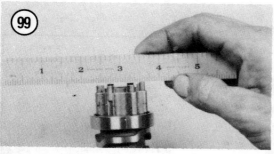

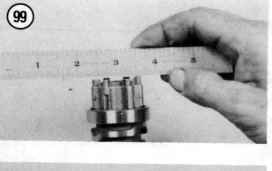

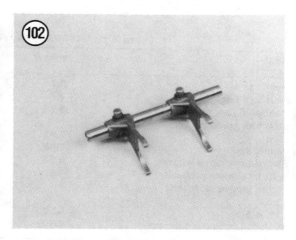

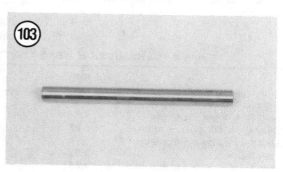

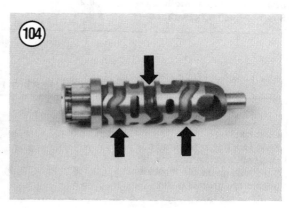

7

4. Measure the shift fork guide pin diameters with a micrometer. Replace the shift fork if the guide pin diameter is too small (**Table 3**).

5. Check the shift drum bearing. Make sure it operates smoothly with no signs of wear or damage.

6. Inspect the neutral holder (**Figure 105**) for wear, damage or roughness. Replace if necessary.

Table 1 TRANSMISSION WEAR LIMITS (1974-1977)

	mm	in.
Gear backlash	0.3	0.012
Shift fork finger thickness	4.7	0.185
Gear shift fork groove width	5.25	0.206
Shift fork guide pin diameter		
3rd	7.93	0.3122
4th & 5th	7.85	0.3090
Shift drum groove width	8.25	0.3248
Shift fork guide pin/shift		
drum groove clearance		
3rd	0.30	0.0118
4th & 5th	0.38	0.0149
Shaft-to-bushing clearance	0.16	0.0063

Table 2 TRANSMISSION WEAR LIMITS (1978-1981 KZ400 AND ALL KZ440)

	mm	in.
Gear backlash	0.3	0.012
Shift fork finger thickness	4.7	0.185
Gear shift fork groove width	5.25	0.206
Shift fork guide pin diameter		
5th & 6th	7.93	0.3122
1st & 4th and 2nd & 3rd	7.85	0.3090
Shift drum groove width	8.25	0.3248
Shaft-to-bushing clearance	0.16	0.0063

Table 3 TRANSMISSION WEAR LIMITS (1985-ON)

	mm	in.
Gear backlash	0.24	0.009
Shift fork finger thickness	4.8	0.189
Gear shift fork groove width	5.3	0.208
Shift fork guide pin diameter	7.8	0.307
Shift drum groove width	8.3	0.3267

NOTE: If you own an EN500 model, first check the Supplement at the back of this book for any specific service information.

CHAPTER EIGHT

FUEL AND EMISSION CONTROL SYSTEMS

8

This chapter describes complete procedures for servicing the fuel and emission control systems.

CARBURETOR

Removal/Installation

1. Park the motorcycle on the centerstand.
2. Remove both side covers.
3. Remove the fuel tank.
4. Loosen all front and rear carburetor boot clamps (**Figure 1**).
5. Remove the carburetor-to-air filter rubber boots.
6. Label and disconnect all hoses at the carburetor (**Figure 2**).
7. Slide the carburetors downward and to the right to disconnect them from the intake boots.
8. Disconnect the throttle cable from the carburetor brackets and remove the carburetor assembly.
9. Installation is the reverse of these steps. Adjust the throttle cable as described in Chapter Three.

Disassembly/Assembly
(1974-1977 and 1977-1978
Deluxe A Models)

Refer to **Figure 3** for this procedure.
1. Remove the cap (**Figure 4**).

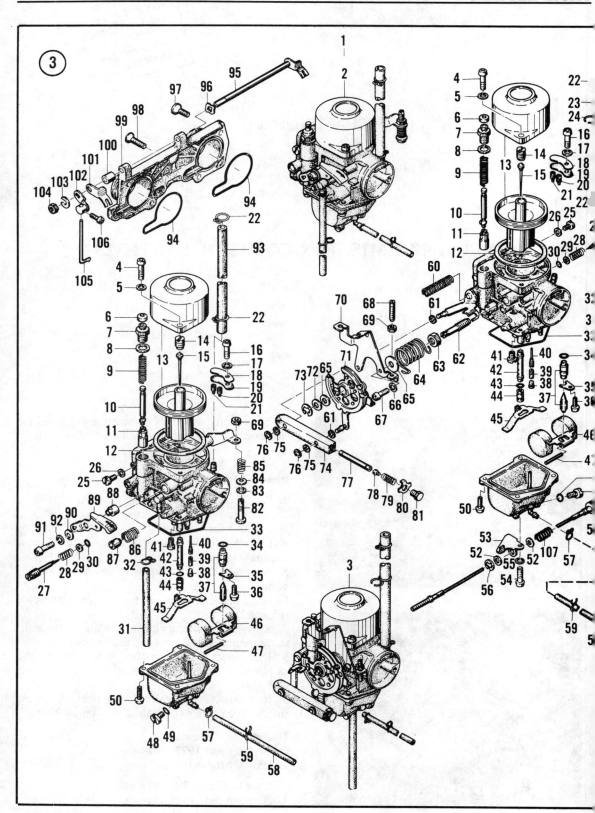

CARBURETOR
(1974-1977 AND 1977-1978 DELUXE A MODELS)

Carburetor assembly	55. Washer
Carburetor	56. Snap ring
Carburetor	57. Clamp
Screw	58. Tube
Washer	59. Clamp
Cap	60. Spring
Cap	61. Washer
Washer	62. Balance screw
Spring	63. Nut
Shaft	64. Spring
Plunger	65. Washer
Gasket	66. Washer
Piston and carburetor cap	67. Screw
Holder	68. Screw
Jet needle	69. Nut
Screw	70. Holder
Washer	71. Pulley
Plate	72. Washer
Gasket	73. Snap ring
Air jet	74. Link
Air jet	75. Washer
Clamp	76. Snap ring
Tube	77. Rod
Clamp	78. Plug
Screw	79. Spring
Washer	80. Washer
Pilot screw	81. Bolt
Spring	82. Screw
Washer	83. Washer
Pilot screw O-ring	84. Washer
Tube	85. Spring
Clamp	86. Spring
O-ring	87. Contact
O-ring	88. Collar
Plate	89. Lever
Screw	90. Washer
Float valve	91. Screw
Cap	92. Washer
Pilot jet	93. Tube
Slow jet	94. O-ring
Starter jet	95. Shaft
Needle jet	96. Washer
O-ring	97. Screw
Main jet	98. Screw
Plate	99. Plate
Float	100. Collar
Float pin	101. Lever
Screw	102. Lever
O-ring	103. Washer
Screw	104. Nut
Throttle stop screw	105. Rod
Washer	106. Screw
Plate	107. Spring
Screw	

2. Remove the piston assembly (**Figure 5**) and its gasket.

3. Remove the jet cover plate and its gasket (**Figure 6**).

4. Remove both air jets (**Figure 7**).

5. Remove the float bowl (**Figure 8**).

6. Remove the jet keeper (**Figure 9**).

7. Note how the float is installed, then pull out the pivot pin and remove the float (**Figure 10**).

8

8. Remove the float needle (**Figure 11**).

9. Remove the float needle seat retainer, then use pliers with taped jaws to pull out the float valve seat (**Figure 12**).

10. Using pliers with taped jaws, pull out the main jet (**Figure 13**).

11. Remove the needle jet (**Figure 14**).

12. Remove the starter jet (**Figure 15**).

13. Remove the pilot passage plug (**Figure 16**).

14. Remove the pilot jet (**Figure 17**). Then remove the slow jet, which is visible after the pilot jet is removed.

15. If it is necessary to remove the jet needle, take out the retaining screw that is inside the piston bore (**Figure 18**).

16. Repeat for the opposite carburetor.

17. Separation of the carburetors is not required for cleaning.

18. Clean and inspect the carburetors as described in this chapter.

19. Installation is the reverse of these steps, noting the following.

20. Install new gaskets during reassembly.

21. Check the fuel level. See *Fuel Level Measurement* in this chapter.

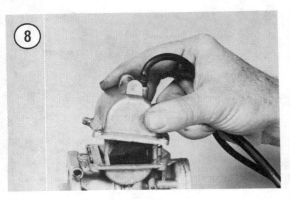

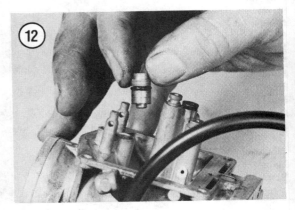

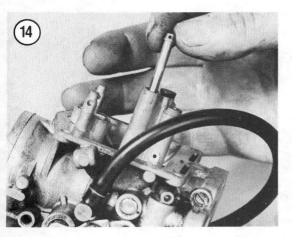

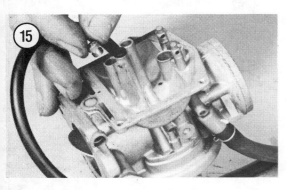

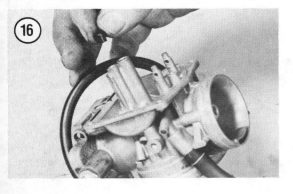

Disassembly/Assembly
(1978-1981 KZ400)

Refer to **Figure 19** (1978-1981 KZ400).

1. Remove the screws securing the upper chamber cover (39) and remove it.

2. Remove the idle adjust screw bracket (6) and return spring (17).

3. Remove the vacuum piston (45) and diaphragm (44).

4. Remove the circlip (41), jet needle holder (42) and jet needle (43).

5. Remove the idle limiter (54). See A, **Figure 20**.

6. Remove the pilot screw (53), spring (52), washer (51) and O-ring (50). See B, **Figure 20**.

7. Remove the float bowl (73) and O-ring (72).

8. Remove the primary main jet (60). See A, **Figure 21**.

9. Remove the main jet bleed pipe (59).

10. Remove the secondary main jet (65). See B, **Figure 21**.

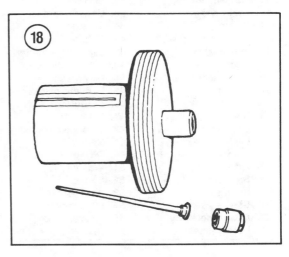

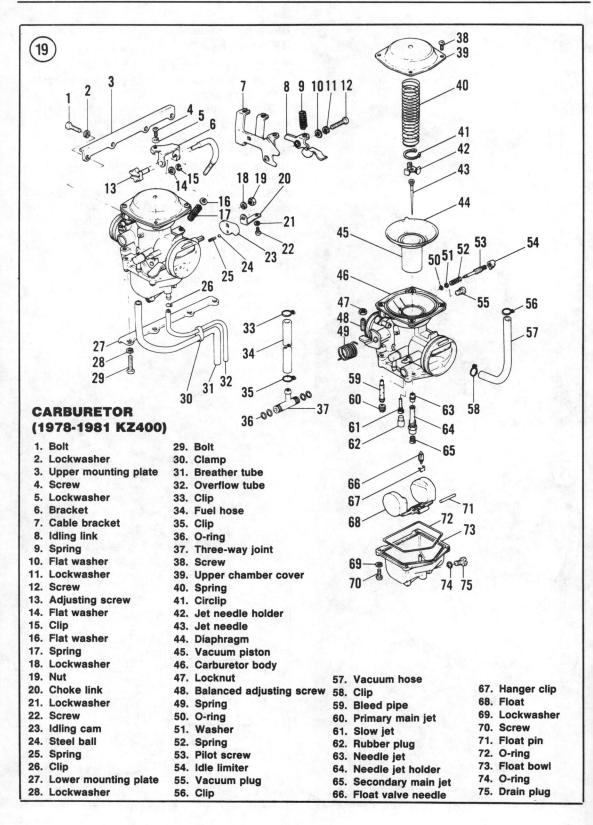

**CARBURETOR
(1978-1981 KZ400)**

1. Bolt
2. Lockwasher
3. Upper mounting plate
4. Screw
5. Lockwasher
6. Bracket
7. Cable bracket
8. Idling link
9. Spring
10. Flat washer
11. Lockwasher
12. Screw
13. Adjusting screw
14. Flat washer
15. Clip
16. Flat washer
17. Spring
18. Lockwasher
19. Nut
20. Choke link
21. Lockwasher
22. Screw
23. Idling cam
24. Steel ball
25. Spring
26. Clip
27. Lower mounting plate
28. Lockwasher
29. Bolt
30. Clamp
31. Breather tube
32. Overflow tube
33. Clip
34. Fuel hose
35. Clip
36. O-ring
37. Three-way joint
38. Screw
39. Upper chamber cover
40. Spring
41. Circlip
42. Jet needle holder
43. Jet needle
44. Diaphragm
45. Vacuum piston
46. Carburetor body
47. Locknut
48. Balanced adjusting screw
49. Spring
50. O-ring
51. Washer
52. Spring
53. Pilot screw
54. Idle limiter
55. Vacuum plug
56. Clip
57. Vacuum hose
58. Clip
59. Bleed pipe
60. Primary main jet
61. Slow jet
62. Rubber plug
63. Needle jet
64. Needle jet holder
65. Secondary main jet
66. Float valve needle
67. Hanger clip
68. Float
69. Lockwasher
70. Screw
71. Float pin
72. O-ring
73. Float bowl
74. O-ring
75. Drain plug

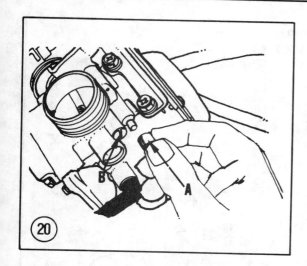

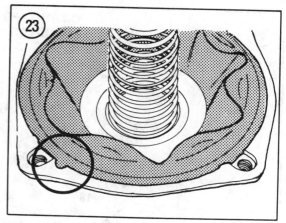

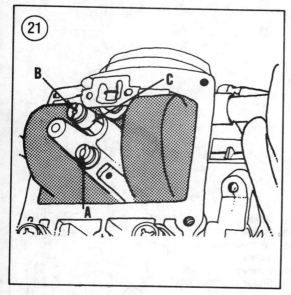

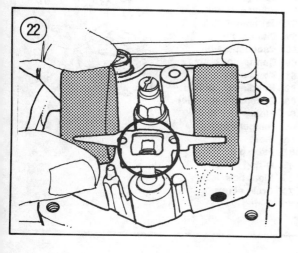

8

11. Remove the needle jet holder (64). See C, **Figure 21**.

12. Push out the float pin (71) and remove the float (68).

NOTE
Be sure to catch the float valve needle (66) and its hanger clip (67). See **Figure 22**.

13. Remove the rubber plug (62) and slow jet (61).
14. Repeat for the opposite carburetor.
15. Separation of the carburetors is not required for cleaning.
16. Clean and inspect the carburetors as described in this chapter.
17. Reassembly is the reverse of these steps, noting the following.
18. Install new gaskets during reassembly.
19. Make sure to align the tab on the diaphragm with the notch on the upper chamber cover (**Figure 23**). Fit the sealing lip of the diaphragm into the groove in the upper chamber cover.
20. When installing the upper chamber cover, push up on the piston just enough so that there is no crease on the diaphragm lip. Install the upper chamber cover and 3 screws. Attach the idle adjust bracket and the remaining screw.
21. Check the fuel level. See *Fuel Level Measurement* in this chapter.

Disassembly/Reassembly (1980-1983 KZ440)

Refer to **Figure 24** for this procedure.
1. Remove the screws securing the upper chamber cover (54) and remove it and the spring (55).
2. Remove the vacuum piston (59) and diaphragm (58).
3. Remove the screw (56) and remove the jet needle (57).

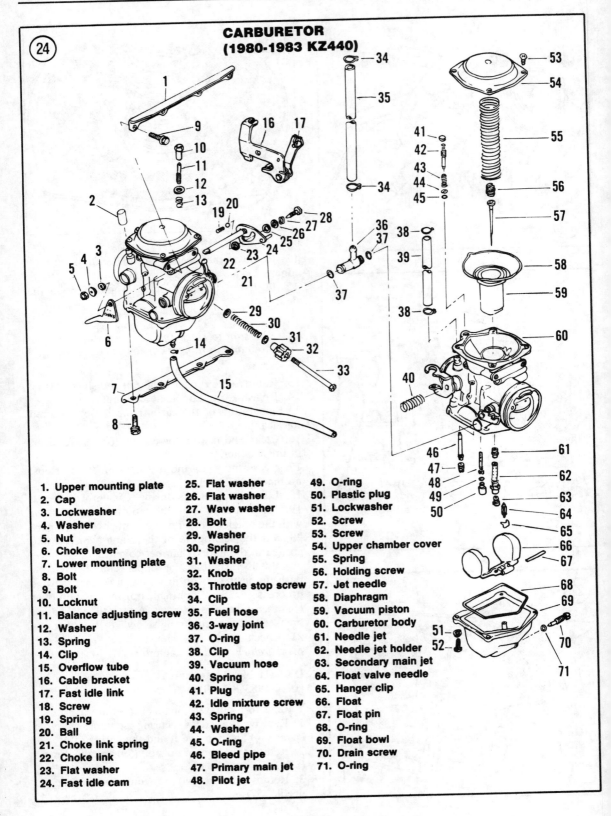

CARBURETOR
(1980-1983 KZ440)

1. Upper mounting plate
2. Cap
3. Lockwasher
4. Washer
5. Nut
6. Choke lever
7. Lower mounting plate
8. Bolt
9. Bolt
10. Locknut
11. Balance adjusting screw
12. Washer
13. Spring
14. Clip
15. Overflow tube
16. Cable bracket
17. Fast idle link
18. Screw
19. Spring
20. Ball
21. Choke link spring
22. Choke link
23. Flat washer
24. Fast idle cam
25. Flat washer
26. Flat washer
27. Wave washer
28. Bolt
29. Washer
30. Spring
31. Washer
32. Knob
33. Throttle stop screw
34. Clip
35. Fuel hose
36. 3-way joint
37. O-ring
38. Clip
39. Vacuum hose
40. Spring
41. Plug
42. Idle mixture screw
43. Spring
44. Washer
45. O-ring
46. Bleed pipe
47. Primary main jet
48. Pilot jet
49. O-ring
50. Plastic plug
51. Lockwasher
52. Screw
53. Screw
54. Upper chamber cover
55. Spring
56. Holding screw
57. Jet needle
58. Diaphragm
59. Vacuum piston
60. Carburetor body
61. Needle jet
62. Needle jet holder
63. Secondary main jet
64. Float valve needle
65. Hanger clip
66. Float
67. Float pin
68. O-ring
69. Float bowl
70. Drain screw
71. O-ring

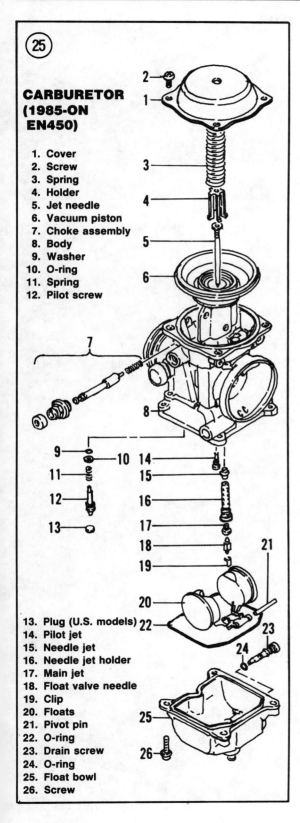

㉕

CARBURETOR
(1985-ON
EN450)

1. Cover
2. Screw
3. Spring
4. Holder
5. Jet needle
6. Vacuum piston
7. Choke assembly
8. Body
9. Washer
10. O-ring
11. Spring
12. Pilot screw

13. Plug (U.S. models)
14. Pilot jet
15. Needle jet
16. Needle jet holder
17. Main jet
18. Float valve needle
19. Clip
20. Floats
21. Pivot pin
22. O-ring
23. Drain screw
24. O-ring
25. Float bowl
26. Screw

4A. *All models except U.S.:* Carefully screw in the mixture screw until it *lightly* seats. Count and record the number of turns so it can be installed in the same position during assembly. Then remove the idle mixture screw (42), spring (43), washer (44) and O-ring (45).

4B. *U.S. models:* The idle mixture is sealed at the factory. Remove it as described in *Idle Mixture Screw Removal/Installation* in this chapter.

5. Remove the float bowl (69) and O-ring (68).

6. Remove the primary main jet (47). See A, **Figure 21**.

7. Remove the main jet bleed pipe (46).

8. Remove the secondary main jet (63). See B, **Figure 21**.

9. Remove the needle jet holder (62). See C, **Figure 21**.

10. Push out the float pin (67) and remove the float (66).

> *NOTE*
> *Be sure to catch the float valve needle (64) and its hanger clip (65). See* **Figure 22**.

11. Remove the rubber plug (50) and pilot jet (48).

12. Repeat for the opposite carburetor.

13. Separation of the carburetors is not required for cleaning.

14. Clean and inspect the carburetors as described in this chapter.

15. Reassembly is the reverse of these steps, noting the following.

16. Install new gaskets during reassembly.

17. Make sure to align the tab on the diaphragm with the notch on the upper chamber cover (**Figure 23**). Fit the sealing lip of the diaphragm into the groove in the upper chamber cover.

18. When installing the upper chamber cover, push up on the piston just enough so that there is no crease on the diaphragm lip. Install the upper chamber cover screws.

19. Check the fuel level. See *Fuel Level Measurement* in this chapter.

**Disassembly/Reassembly
(1985-on EN450)**

Refer to **Figure 25** for this procedure.

1. Remove the upper chamber cover (**Figure 26**).

2. Remove the spring and spring seat (**Figure 27**).

3. Remove the diaphragm (**Figure 28**) and jet needle (**Figure 29**).

4. Remove the float bowl (**Figure 30**) and gasket.

5. Remove the float pin (**Figure 31**) and float (**Figure 32**).

8

NOTE
Be sure to catch the float valve needle
*and its hanger clip (**Figure 32**).*

6. Remove the pilot jet (**Figure 33**).

7. Remove the main jet (**Figure 34**).

8. Remove the needle jet holder (**Figure 35**).

9. Remove the needle jet (**Figure 36**).

10A. *All models except U.S.:* Carefully screw in the mixture screw until it *lightly* seats. Count and record the number of turns so it can be installed in the same position during assembly. Then remove the idle mixture screw (**Figure 37**), spring, washer and O-ring.

10B. *U.S. models:* The idle mixture screw is sealed at the factory. If necessary, remove it as described under *Idle Mixture Screw Removal/Installation* in this chapter.

11. Repeat for the opposite carburetor.

12. Separation of the carburetors is not required for cleaning.

13. Clean and inspect the carburetors as described in this chapter.

14. Reassembly is the reverse of these steps, noting the following.

15. Install new O-rings during reassembly.

16. Install the needle jet so that the small diameter end goes in first.

17. When installing the upper chamber cover, push up on the piston just enough so that there is no crease on the diaphragm lip. Install the upper chamber cover and screws.

18. Check the fuel level. See *Fuel Level Measurement* in this chapter.

Idle Mixture Screw Removal/Installation (1980-on U.S. Models)

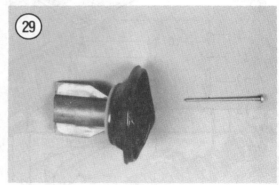

The idle mixture screw is sealed at the factory. When disassembling the carburetors for overhaul, the bonding agent and cover must be removed for access to the screw, O-ring and spring.

1. Carefully scrape out the bonding agent from the recess in the carburetor body.
2. Punch and pry out the plug with a small screwdriver or awl.
3. Carefully screw in the idle mixture screw (**Figure 37**) until it seats *lightly*. Count and record the number of turns so it can be installed in the *same* position during assembly.
4. Remove the mixture screw, O-ring and spring from the carburetor body.
5. Repeat for the other carburetor. Make sure to keep each carburetor's parts separate.
6. Inspect the O-ring and the end of the mixture screw; replace if damaged or worn.

8

7. Install the mixture screws in the same position as noted during removal (Step 3).

8. Install new plugs. Secure the plugs with a small amount of non-hardening bonding agent.

CAUTION
Apply only a small amount of bonding agent. Too much may close off the air passage.

Cleaning and Inspection

1. Clean all parts in carburetor cleaning solution. Dry parts with compressed air. Clean jets and other delicate parts with compressed air after the float bowl has been removed.

2. Inspect the vacuum piston and diaphragm (**Figure 29**) (on models so equipped) for cracks, deterioration or other damage. Check the sides of the piston (**Figure 18**) for excessive wear. Install the piston into the carburetor body and move it up and down in the bore. The piston valve should move smoothly with no binding or excessive play.

3. Inspect the float valve needle (**Figure 32**) and seat for steps, uneven wear or other damage. Install the needle and check for smooth operation.

4. Make sure all openings in the carburetor and jets are clear.

5. Inspect the jet needle taper for excessive wear or damage.

6. Inspect the float for deterioration or damage. Submerge the float in a container of water and check for bubbles indicating a leak.

7. Make sure the throttle wheel/shaft moves smoothly and returns the throttle to the closed position.

8. Replace all gaskets and O-rings during reassembly.

CARBURETOR ADJUSTMENT

Fuel Level Measurement

Carburetors leave the factory with float levels properly adjusted. Rough riding, a worn needle valve or bent float arm can cause the float level to change. To adjust the float level on these carburetors, perform the following.

WARNING
Some gasoline will drain from the carburetors during this procedure. Work in a well-ventilated area, at least 50 feet from any open flame. Do not smoke. Wipe up spills immediately.

1974-1983

1. Turn the fuel valve to the OFF position.

2. Remove the float bowl drain plug. Then install the fuel level gauge midway between the side float

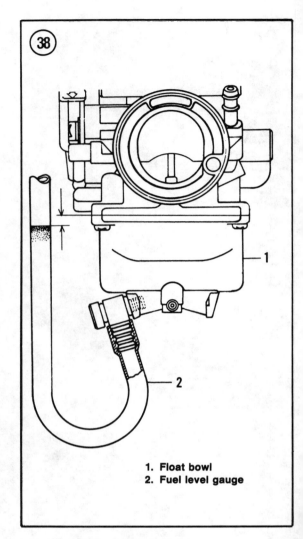

1. Float bowl
2. Fuel level gauge

bowl screws. If no gauge is available, one can be fabricated from a length of clean plastic tubing and a fitting which screws into the drain plug hole. See **Figure 38**.

3. Turn the fuel valve to the ON position.

4. Hold the fuel level gauge against the carburetor body (**Figure 38**). The fuel level should be as follows:

    a. *1974-1977 and 1977-1978 Deluxe A models:* 1.5-3.5 mm (0.059-0.137 in.).

    b. *1978-1983:* Below the bottom surface of the carburetor body.

5. If adjustment is required, turn the fuel valve to the OFF position. Remove the carburetor float and bend its tang (**Figure 39**) as required to raise or lower the fuel level. On some models, it is necessary to remove the carburetor for the float bowl removal.

6. Remove the fuel level gauge when the level is correct.

1985-on

1. Remove the carburetors as described in this chapter.

2. Mount the carburetors on a fabricated wooden stand or blocks so that they are in a perfectly vertical position.

3. Remove the fuel tank and place it on wood blocks higher than the carburetors. Then connect a length

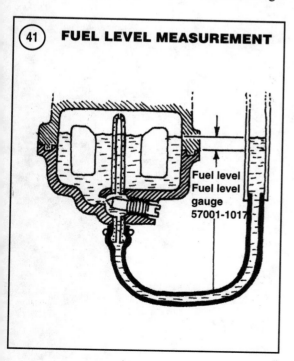

(41) FUEL LEVEL MEASUREMENT

Fuel level
Fuel level
gauge
57001-1017

of fuel hole, 6 mm in diameter and approximately 300 mm long, to the fuel tank and carburetor.

4. Connect a length of hose to the float bowl as shown in **Figure 40**. Connect a fuel level gauge (part No. 57001-1017) to the opposite end of the carburetor so that the "0" line on the gauge is several millimeters higher than the carburetor's bottom edge (**Figure 40**).

5. Turn the fuel valve to PRI. Then turn the carburetor drain plug a few turns.

6. Wait until the fuel in the gauge settles. Then slowly lower the gauge until the "" line is even with the bottom edge of the carburetor body (**Figure 40**). The fuel level should be 0.5 ± 0.004 in.) above the edge of the carburetor body.

7. Turn the fuel valve to the ON position.

8. If adjustment is required, remove the carburetor float and bend its tang (**Figure 39**) as required to raise or lower the fuel level.

9. Remove the fuel level gauge when the level is correct.

EMISSION CONTROL (1985-ON CALIFORNIA MODELS)

All 1985-on models sold in California are equipped with an evaporative emission control system to meet the CARB regulations in effect at the time of the model's manufacture. When the engine is running, fuel vapors are routed into the engine for burning; when the engine is stopped, fuel vapors are routed into a canister.

Inspection/Replacement

Maintenance to the evaporative emission control system consists of periodic inspection of the hoses for proper routing and a check of the canister mounting brackets.

When removal or replacement of an emission part is required, refer to **Figure 41**.

> *WARNING*
> *Because the evaporative emission control system stores fuel vapors, make sure the work area is free of all flames or sparks before working on the emission system.*

1. Whenever servicing the evaporative system, make sure the ignition switch is in the OFF position.

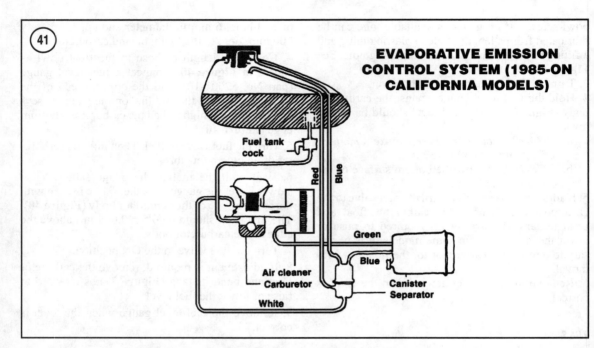

2. Make sure all hoses are attached as indicated in **Figure 41** and that they are not damaged or pinched.

3. When removing the separator, it is important not to turn the separator upside down or sideways. Doing so will allow gasoline to flow into the canister.

4. Replace any worn or damaged parts immediately.

5. The canister is capable of working through the motorcycle's life without maintenance, provided that it is not damaged or contaminated.

NOTE: If you own an EN500 model, first check the Supplement at the back of this book for any specific service information.

CHAPTER NINE

ELECTRICAL SYSTEMS

This chapter describes service procedures for the electrical system. **Tables 1-4** at the end of the chapter list electrical specifications.

CHARGING SYSTEM
(1974-1983)

All models are equipped with 3-phase alternators, solid-state rectifiers and electromechanical voltage regulators. If charging system problems are suspected, as in the case of dim lights or a chronically undercharged battery, the following checks should isolate the problem. Before beginning any charging system test, be sure that the battery is in good condition and that it is at or near full charge (see Chapter Three).

Alternator Output Test
(1974-1977 and 1977-1978
Deluxe A Models)

1. Remove the left-hand side cover and the headlight unit.
2. Disconnect the 6-pole connector from the left-hand side and the 9-pole connector in the headlight housing.
3. Disconnect the white wire from the rectifier at the battery positive lead.
4. Connect the positive terminal of a 0-20 DC voltmeter to the white wire which was removed.

Connect the negative voltmeter terminal to a good ground (**Figure 1**).
5. Remove the right-hand side cover.

CAUTION
In the next step, do not allow green and brown leads to touch anything. Also, do not leave them connected for any longer than is required to make this test.

6. Disconnect the green and brown leads from the voltage regulator. Temporarily connect these leads together.
7. Start the engine and run it at idling speed (1,100-1,300 rpm). Do *not* run it at a faster speed.
8. Observe voltmeter. If it indicates 14 volts or greater, the alternator is okay. If output voltage is less than specified, either the alternator or the rectifier is defective.
9. Stop the engine. Refer to **Figure 2**. Connect a one ohm, 200-watt variable resistor, such as a commercial carbon pile, between the white wire and ground. Do not disconnect the voltmeter.
10. Start the engine, then gradually increase its speed to 5,000 rpm. Adjust resistor at the same time engine speed is increasing so that output voltage is maintained at 14.5 volts.
11. Stop the engine. Do not change the setting determined in Step 10.

9

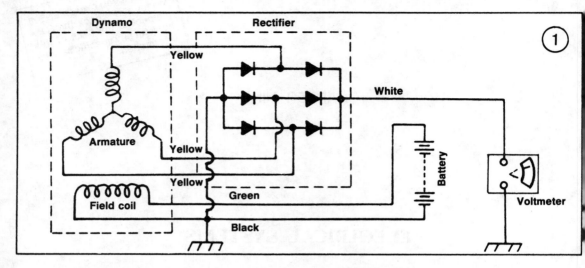

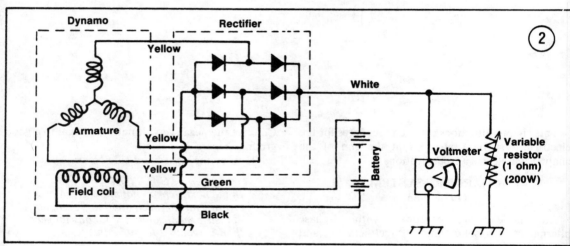

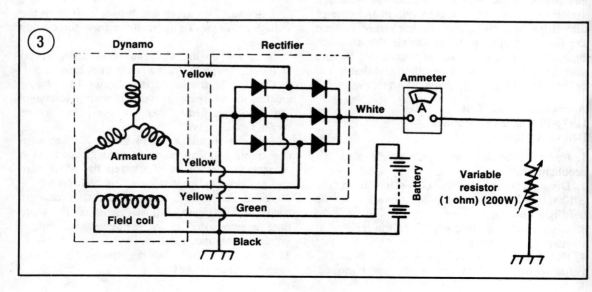

12. Referring to **Figure 3**, connect the positive terminal of a 0-20 DC ammeter to the white wire which goes to the rectifier and the negative terminal to the carbon pile.

13. Start the engine, then run it at 5,000 rpm. If the ammeter does not indicate 13 amperes or more, the alternator or rectifier is defective.

Alternator Checks
(1974-1977 and 1977-1978
Deluxe A Models)

If the charging system failed the *Alternator Output Test*, Steps 1 through 13, the following checks should isolate any problem with the alternator.

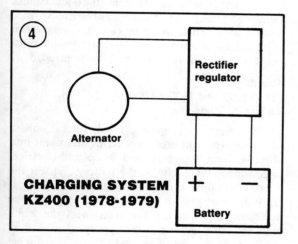

CHARGING SYSTEM KZ400 (1978-1979)

1. Disconnect the left-hand electrical connector below the voltage regulator.

2. Measure resisance between each pair of yellow wires from the alternator. Resistance should be 0.4-0.6 ohms for each pair. Replace stator if any pair differs from this value.

3. Using the highest ohmmeter range, measure insulation resistance between any yellow lead and ground. Insulation resistance must be essentially infinite. Replace stator if ohmmeter indicates any continuity.

4. Reconnect all connectors.

Alternator Rotor Testing
(1974-1977 and 1977-1978
Deluxe A Models)

1. Measure resistance between green and black leads at the alternator electrical connector. Resistance should be approximately 5 ohms. Replace field coil if specifications are incorrect.

2. Using the highest ohmmeter range, measure insulation resistance between green or black lead and ground. Replace field coil if insulaton resistance is not infinite.

Initial Inspection
(1978-1983)

Refer to **Figure 4** (1978-1979 KZ400) or **Figure 5** (1980-1981 KZ400 and all KZ440).

1. Before making this test, start the bike and let it reach normal operating temperature.

2. Turn the engine off.

9

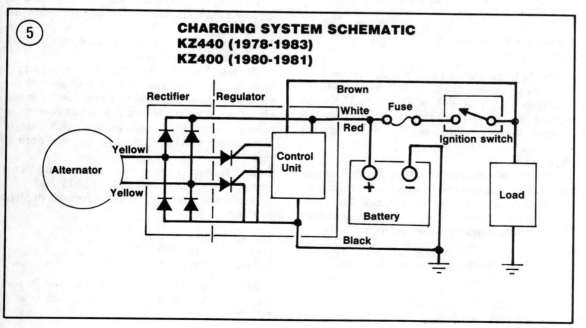

**CHARGING SYSTEM SCHEMATIC
KZ440 (1978-1983)
KZ400 (1980-1981)**

3. Remove the left-hand side cover and raise the seat.

4. Connect a 0-20 DC voltmeter to the battery as shown in **Figure 6**.

5. Start the engine and run at 4,000 rpm. Observe the voltage.

6. The voltage should be at or near battery voltage at idle and it should increase with engine speed, up to about 15 volts. If the reading is much higher, the regulator/rectifier is defective and should be replaced. If the reading is less than specified or does not increase with rpm, check the alternator and regulator/rectifier.

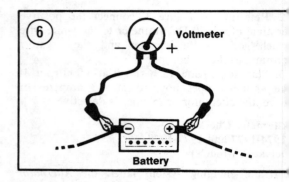

Alternator Output Test
(1978-1983)

Refer to **Figure 4** (1978-1979 KZ400) or **Figure 5** (1980-1981 KZ400 and all KZ440).

1. Before making this test, start the bike and let it reach normal operating temperature.

2. Turn the engine off.

3. Remove the engine sprocket cover.

4. Disconnect the 2 yellow electrical leads coming from the alternator.

5. Set a voltmeter to the 250 volt AC range and connect the meter leads to the yellow alternator leads.

6. Start the engine and run at 4,000 rpm.

7. The voltage reading should be about 75 volts. If the output voltage is less than specified, the alternator is defective and must be replaced.

Alternator Stator Test
(1978-1983)

Use an ohmmeter, set at R×1, and measure the resistance between the 2 yellow leads from the alternator. See **Figure 4** or **Figure 5**. The value should be 0.26-0.38 ohms. If the resistance is greater than specified or no meter reading (infinity), the stator has an open and must be replaced.

Change the ohmmeter setting to the hightest range and measure the resistance between each yellow lead and the chassis (ground). The meter should read infinity; it it doesn't, this indicates a short and the stator must be replaced.

NOTE
If the stator winding resistance is within the specified range, but the voltage output is incorrect, the rotor has probably lost some of its magnetism and must be replaced.

Alternator Rotor Testing
(1978-1983)

The rotor is permanently magnetized and canno' be tested except by replacement with a roto' known to be good. A rotor can lose magnetism from old age or a sharp blow. If defective, the roto' must be replaced. It cannot be remagnetized.

Rectifier
(1974-1977 and 1977-1978
Deluxe A Models)

The rectifier (**Figure 7**) converts 3-phase alternating current produced by the alternator into direct current, which is used to operate electrical accessories and to charge the battery. To test the rectifier, perform the following.

1. With the engine not running, remove the left-hand side cover. Then disconnect the white wire from the rectifier at the battery.

2. Remove the right-hand side cover. Disconnec' the left-hand white electrical connector below the voltage regulator.

3. Measure and record the resistance between each yellow lead and white lead.

4. Reverse the ohmmeter leads, then repeat Step 3. Each pair of measurements must be high with the ohmmeter connected one way and low when the ohmmeter leads are reversed. It is not possible to specify exact meter readings, but each pair of measurements should differ by a factor of not less than 10.

5. Repeat Steps 3 and 4, but make measurements between each yellow lead and the black lead.

6. Replace the rectifier if it fails any check of Steps 3, 4 or 5.

Voltage Regulator Tests
(1974-1977 and 1977-1978
Deluxe A Models)

Before making any voltage regulator test, be sure that the battery is in good condition and is at or near full charge.

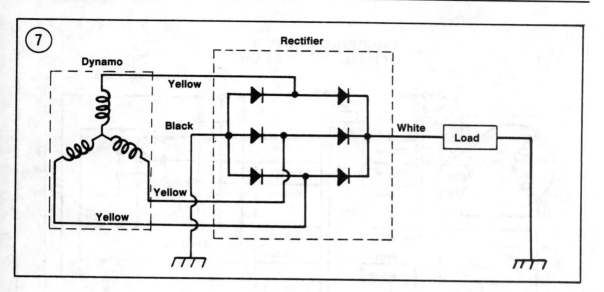

1. Remove the left side cover and the headlight unit.
2. Remove the 6-pole connector from the left-hand side of the motorcycle and the 9-pole connector from the headlight housing.
3. Connect an accurate 0-20 DC voltmeter across the battery terminals (**Figure 6**).
4. Start the engine and run it at 1,600 rpm. Voltmeter should indicate 14.0-15.0 volts.
5. Gradually increase the engine speed to 4,000 rpm. Voltmeter should again indicate 14.0-15.0 volts. Do not allow engine speed to decrease until the second measurement is made.
6. If the readings are incorrect, remove the voltage regulator cover and clean the contacts with emery cloth. Reinstall the cover and retest. If the readings are still incorrect, replace the voltage regulator.

**Voltage Regulator Test
(1978-1983)**

1. Remove the right-hand side cover. Turn the ignition switch to the OFF position.
2. Disconnect the electrical connector containing 3 wires—2 yellow and 1 black.

> *CAUTION*
> *Do not short-circuit the voltage regulator when connecting the test leads or it will be damaged.*

3. Use an ohmmeter set at R×1, and measure the resistance between each yellow lead and the black one. Attach the ohmmeter positive (+) lead to the yellow leads and the ohmmeter negative – lead to the black lead. The value should be less than 20 ohms.

4. Reset the ohmmeter at R×K ohms. Attach the positive (+) lead to the black lead and the negative (-) lead to the yellow leads. Their value should be more than 100 ohms.
5. If any 2 leads are too high or too low in both directions the voltage regulator/rectifier must be replaced.

**Voltage Regulator Performance Test
(1978-1983)**

Connect a voltmeter to the battery terminals. Start the engine and let it idle; increase engine speed until the voltage going to the battery reaches 14.0-15.0 volts. At this point, the voltage regulator must divert the current to ground. If this does not happen, the voltage regulator/rectifier must be replaced.

**CHARGING SYSTEM
(1985-ON)**

Before beginning any charging system tests, be sure that the battery is in good condition and that it is at or near full charge.

**Regulator/Rectifier
Output Voltage Check**

Refer to **Figure 8**.
1. Start the bike and allow to warm to normal operating temperature.
2. Turn the engine off and remove the seat.
3. Pull the white/red connector out of its holder to gain access to it (**Figure 8**).

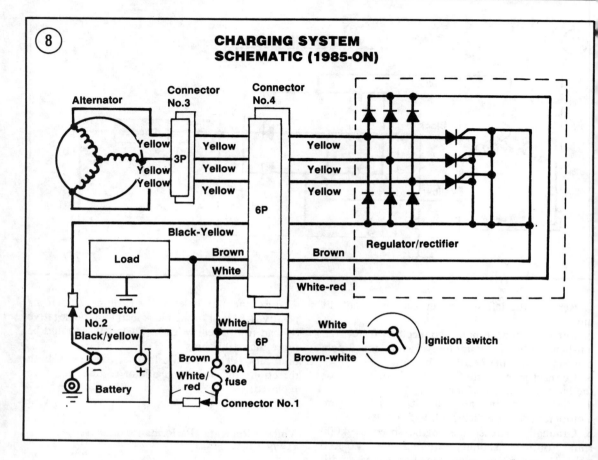

CHARGING SYSTEM SCHEMATIC (1985-ON)

(8)

Alternator

Connector No.3

Connector No.4

Yellow — 3P — Yellow — Yellow
Yellow — Yellow — Yellow
Yellow — Yellow — Yellow

6P

Regulator/rectifier

Black-Yellow

Load — Brown — Brown
White

White-red

Connector No.2
Black/yellow

White — 6P — White — Ignition switch
Brown — Brown-white

Battery — + —
Brown
White/red — 30A fuse
Connector No.1

CAUTION
The white/red connector is connected directly to the battery positive terminal. When attaching the voltmeter lead to the white/red connector, make sure the lead does not touch any part of the chassis.

4. Set a voltmeter to the 25 volt DC range. Attach the red voltmeter lead to the white/red connector and the black lead to the black/yellow connector.

NOTE
To turn the headlight off on U.S. models when performing Step 4, disconnect the black/yellow lead in the headlight housing.

5. Start the engine and and allow to idle. Record the voltage readings at various rpm speeds and with the headlight turned alternately to the ON and OFF positions. The readings should be approximately 12 volts at low rpm and increase to, but not exceed, 15 volts at higher rpms.
6. Turn off the engine and interpret results as follows:

a. If the voltage is correct as tested in Step 4, the charging system is working correctly.
b. If the voltage did not rise as the engine speed was increased in Step 4, the regulator/rectifier is defective or the alternator output is insufficient.
c. If the voltage exceeded 15 volts in Step 4, the regulator/rectifier is damaged or the regulator/rectifier leads are loose or disconnected.

Alternator Checks

1. Turn the ignition switch to the OFF position and remove the seat.
2. Remove the air filter assembly.
3. Disconnect connector 3 from the alternator. See **Figure 8**.
4. Connect the positive terminal of an AC voltmeter to one yellow lead and the negative voltmeter lead to the mating yellow wire.
5. Start the engine and run it at 4,000 rpm.
6. Observe the voltmeter. If it indicates approximately 60 volts, the alternator is operating

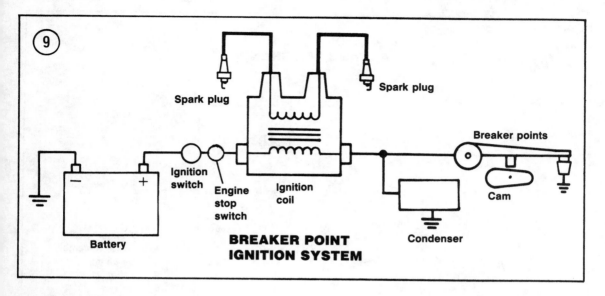

⑨

Spark plug

Spark plug

Breaker points

Ignition switch

Engine stop switch

Ignition coil

Cam

Battery

Condenser

**BREAKER POINT
IGNITION SYSTEM**

correctly and the regulator/rectifier is damaged. If the reading is much lower than 60 volts, the alternator is defective.

7. Turn the engine off.

8. Repeat Steps 4-7 for each of the 3 yellow wires.

Stator Test

Use an ohmmeter, set at R×1, and measure the resistance between the 2 yellow leads from the alternator (**Figure 8**). The value should be about 0.3-0.6 ohms. If the resistance is greater than specified or no meter reading (infinity), the stator has an open and must be replaced.

Change the ohmmeter setting to the hightest range and measure the resistance between each yellow lead and the chassis (ground). The meter should read infinity; if it doesn't, this indicates a short and the stator must be replaced.

NOTE
If the stator winding resistance is within the specified range, but the voltage output is incorrect, the rotor has probably lost some of its magnetism and must be replaced.

Voltage Rectifier Tests

Before making any voltage regulator test, be sure that the battery is in good condition and is at or near full charge.

1. Remove the seat.

2. Disconnect connector 4. See **Figure 8**. It has 6 wires—1 white/red, 1 brown, 1 black/yellow and 3 yellow.

3. Measure and record resistance between each white/red and yellow lead.

4. Reverse ohmmeter leads, then Repeat Step 3. Each pair of measurements must be high with the ohmmeter connected one way and low when the ohmmeter leads are connected the other way. It is not possible to specify exact meter readings, but each pair of measurements should differ by a factor of not less than 10.

5. Repeat Steps 3 and 4, but make measurements between each yellow lead and the black/yellow lead.

6. Replace the rectifier if it fails any check of Steps 3, 4 or 5.

BREAKER POINT IGNITION

Figure 9 is a functional diagram of a typical KZ400 breaker point ignition system. A single set of points and a coil with a double-ended secondary winding fire both spark plugs simultaneously.

Troubleshooting is covered in Chapter Two.

Service

Two major service items are required on battery ignition models: breaker point service and ignition timing. Both are important for proper engine operation and reliability. Refer to Chapter Three for complete service.

**Ignition Advance Unit
Removal/Installation**

Refer to **Figure 10**.

1. Remove the breaker point cover.

2. Remove the breaker plate, breaker points and condenser as an assembly. See **Figure 11**.

3. Remove the smaller bolt from the end of the crankshaft.

9

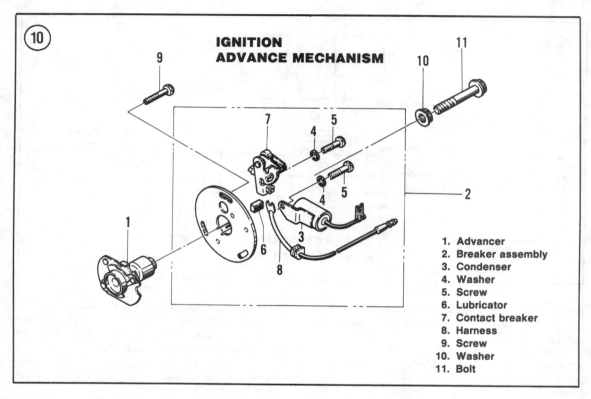

⑩

**IGNITION
ADVANCE MECHANISM**

1. Advancer
2. Breaker assembly
3. Condenser
4. Washer
5. Screw
6. Lubricator
7. Contact breaker
8. Harness
9. Screw
10. Washer
11. Bolt

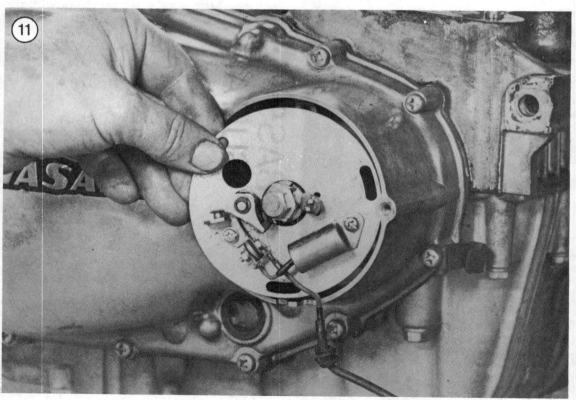

⑪

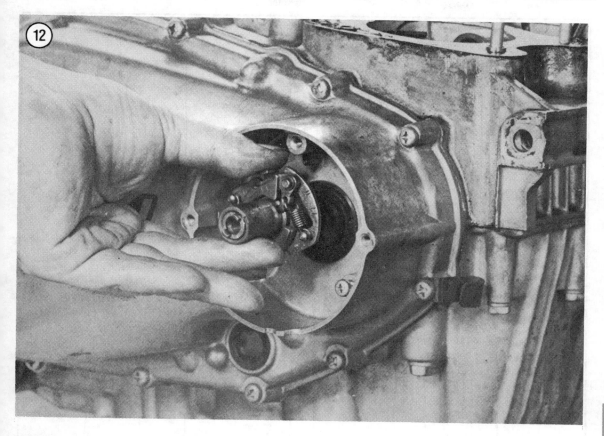

4. Pull the advance mechanism from the crankshaft (**Figure 12**).

5. Check all parts for wear or binding. Be sure that neither spring is broken.

6. If disassembled, when installing the cam be sure to align the mark on the cam with the notch on the advance unit.

7. Install the timing advancer onto the crankshaft—be sure to align the notch on the back of the advancer with the pin on the end of the crankshaft. Tighten the retaining bolt to 23-27 N•m (16.5-19.5 ft.-lb.).

8. After installing the advance mechanism, it is necessary to apply a small quantity of distributor cam lubricant to the breaker cam. Check and adjust the ignition timing. See Chapter Three.

Inspection

1. Inspect the flyweights and springs for wear or damage. Check also that the springs are not stretched or distorted.

2. Check the flyweight pivots on the plate for wear or looseness. Replace if necessary.

Ignition Coil
Removal/Installation

1. Remove the fuel tank.

2. Disconnect the spark plug leads by grasping the spark plugs leads as near to the plug as possible and pulling them off the plugs.

3. Disconnect the primary leads to the ignition coil.

4. Remove the coil mounting bolts and the coils and brackets. Note any ground leads that are attached with the bracket bolts.

5. Install by reversing these steps.

Ignition Coil Testing

1. Measure coil primary resistance, using an ohmmeter, between both coil primary terminals (**Figure 13**). See **Tables 1-3** for specifications.

2. Measure coil secondary resistance between both spark plug caps (**Figure 14**). See **Tables 1-3** for specifications.

3. Replace the coil if it did not meet the resistance values in Steps 2 or 3. If the coil exhibits visible damage, it should be replaced.

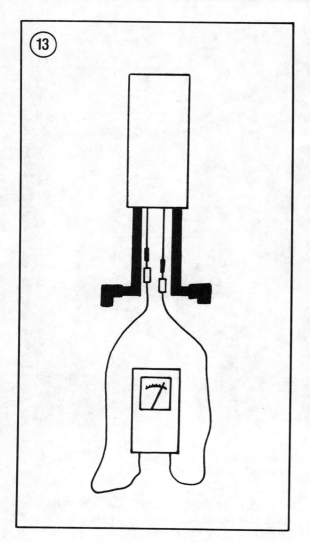

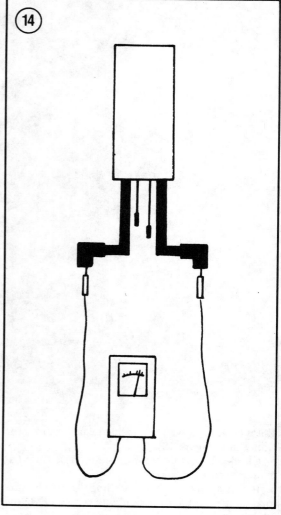

TRANSISTORIZED IGNITION
(1981-1983)

The ignition system consists of 2 spark plugs, one ignition coil, an IC igniter unit and a timing pickup unit. See **Figure 15**.

Troubleshooting is covered in Chapter Two.

Ignition Coil
Removal/Installation

The ignition coil is under the fuel tank and the IC igniter is mounted next to it (**Figure 16**).
1. Remove the fuel tank.
2. Disconnect the spark plug leads by grasping the leads as near to the plugs as possible and pulling them off the plugs.
3. Disconnect the primary leads to the ignition coil.

4. Remove the coil mounting bolts and the coils and brackets. Note any ground leads that are attached by the bracket bolts.
5. Install by reversing these steps.

Ignition Coil Testing

1. Using an ohmmeter, measure coil primary resistance between both coil primary terminals (**Figure 13**). See **Table 2** and **Table 3** for specifications.
2. Measure coil secondary resistance between both spark plug caps (**Figure 14**). See **Table 2** and **Table 3** for specifications.
3. Replace the coil if it did not meet the resistance values in Steps 2 or 3. If the coil exhibits visible damage, it should be replaced.

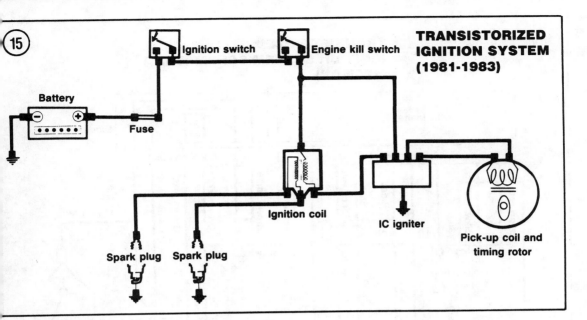

TRANSISTORIZED IGNITION SYSTEM (1981-1983)

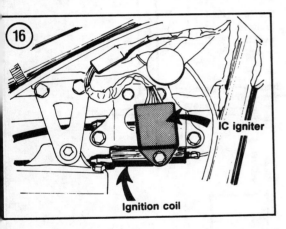

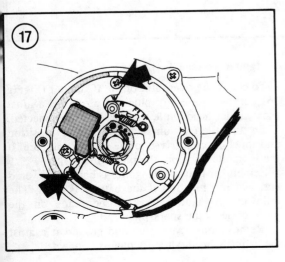

Pick-up Coil
Removal/Installation

The pickup coil is under the timing cover on the right-hand side of the engine.
1. Remove the fuel tank and disconnect the 2-pole pickup coil/IC igniter connector.
2. Remove the 2 timing plate screws and the plate with the pickup coil (**Figure 17**).
3. Install by reversing these steps.

Pickup Coil Inspection

1. Remove the fuel tank.
2. Disconnect the 2-pole pickup coil/IC igniter connector.
3. With an ohmmeter set at $R \times 100$, measure the resistance between the pickup coil leads. The resistance should be about 360-540 ohms.
4. Set the ohmmeter at its highest scale and check the resistance between either lead and the chassis ground. The reading should be infinite.
5. If the pickup coil fails either of these tests, check the wiring to the coil. Replace the coil if the wiring is okay.

Timing Advancer
Removal/Installation

1. Remove the timing cover.
2. Remove the pickup coil assembly as described in this chapter.
3. Remove the smaller bolt from the end of the crankshaft.

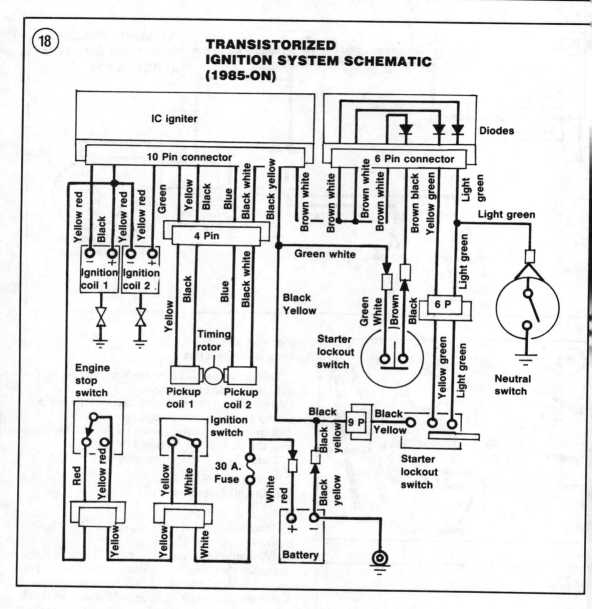

(18) **TRANSISTORIZED IGNITION SYSTEM SCHEMATIC (1985-ON)**

4. Pull the timing advancer mechanism from the crankshaft (**Figure 12**).

5. Check all parts for wear or binding. Be sure that neither spring is broken.

6. When installing the cam, be sure to align the mark on the cam with the notch on the advance unit.

7. Install the timing advancer onto the crankshaft—be sure to align the notch on the back of the advancer with the pin on the end of the crankshaft. Tighten the retaining bolt to 25 N•m (18 ft.-lb.).

8. Check the ignition timing. See Chapter Three.

IC Igniter Voltage Test

To check the operation of the IC igniter (**Figure 16**), remove one spark plug and ground it against the cylinder head while the plug lead is connected. Then turn the ignition switch to the ON position and touch a screwdriver to the pickup coil core. If the IC igniter is good, the plug will spark.

Remember that the IC igniter is battery-powered and will not function if the battery is dead. The following IC igniter test can be made on the motorcycle to the spark plug lead.

1. Remove one spark plug and ground it against the cylinder head while its plug is connected.

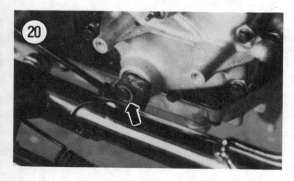

2. Disconnect the 2-pole connector from the pickup coil.

3. Turn the ignition coil to the ON position. Connect a positive (+) 12-volt source to the black lead and a negative (-) 12-volt source to the blue lead. As the voltage is connected, the plug should spark.

4. If the IC igniter fails these tests, install a new one. If the IC igniter passes these tests, but you still have an ignition problem, have a Kawasaki dealer perform an IC igniter resistance test.

Ignition System Wiring Test

A DC voltmeter is required to perform this test.
1. Remove the fuel tank.
2. Locate the IC igniter under the main frame tube. Make sure the 2 IC igniter lead connectors are clean and properly connected.
3. Turn the ignition switch to the ON position and test as follows.
4. Set the voltmeter to the 25V DC scale. Connect the positive test lead to the yellow/red or yellow/blue IC igniter wire. Connect the negative test lead to ground. The voltmeter should read 12 volts.
5. Set the voltmeter to the 10V DC scale. Connect the positive test lead to the IC igniter blue wire. Connect the negative test lead to ground. The voltmeter should read 0.8-3.0 volts.

6. Connect the positive test lead to the IC igniter black wire. Connect the negative test lead to ground. The voltmeter should read 0.5-1.0 volts.
7. Turn the ignition switch to the OFF position. If the test results in Steps 4-6 were incorrect, there is a wiring problem in the ignition system. This could be a short to ground, a broken wire or possibly a dirty connector. Refer to the ignition system wiring diagram in **Figure 15** and the wiring diagrams at the end of the book to aid in locating the wiring problem. Repair or replace any part as necessary.

TRANSISTORIZED IGNITION (1985-ON)

The ignition system consists of 2 ignition coils, an IC igniter unit and 2 timing pickup units. See **Figure 18**.

Troubleshooting is covered in Chapter Two.

Ignition Coil
Removal/Installation

1. Remove the fuel tank.
2. Disconnect the spark plug leads by grasping the leads as near to the plugs as possible and pulling them off the plugs.
3. Disconnect the primary leads to the ignition coil.
4. Remove the coil mounting bolts and the coils and brackets. Note any ground leads that are attached with the bracket bolts.
5. Install by reversing these steps.

Pick-up Coil
Removal/Installation

The pickup coil is located inside the alternator cover.
1. Raise the seat and disconnect the battery negative lead.
2. Remove the left-hand footpeg and the gearshift lever.
3. Remove the engine pulley cover.
4. Remove the circlip and washer (**Figure 19**) from the front gearshift pivot shaft. Then remove the circlip from the shift lever shaft (**Figure 20**).
5. Disconnect the alternator connectors.
6. Place an oil pan underneath the alternator cover.
7. Remove the alternator cover bolts and remove the cover (**Figure 21**). Note the path of the wire harness as it must be routed through the same path during installation.
8. Remove the screws securing the pickup coils and remove the coils. See **Figure 22**.
9. Install by reversing these steps, noting the following.

9

10. Install a new alternator cover gasket and the 2 dowel pins. See **Figure 23**.

11. Apply silicone sealant, such as RTV, underneath the rubber wiring grommet in the cover.

12. Make sure the gearshift pivot shaft (**Figure 24**) is installed through the cover before installing it.

Pickup Coil Inspection

1. Remove the fuel tank.

2. Disconnect the 2-pole pickup coil/IC igniter connector.

3. With an ohmmeter set at $R \times 100$, measure the resistance between the pickup coil leads. The resistance should be about 400-490 ohms.

4. Set the ohmmeter at its highest scale and check the resistance between either lead and the chassis ground. The reading should be infinite.

5. If the pickup coil fails either of these tests, check the wiring to the coil. Replace the coil if the wiring is okay.

IC Igniter
Removal/Installation

The IC igniter (**Figure 25**) is installed underneath the seat. To replace it, remove the attaching bolts and disconnect the electrical connector. Reverse to install.

IC Igniter Test

The IC igniter on these models should only be tested with a Kawasaki tester. Refer service to a Kawasaki dealer.

Diode Testing

The diode is located by raising the seat. It is next to the rear fender and its connector has 6 wires. See **Figure 18** for wire color codes. Unplug the connector and remove the diode. With an

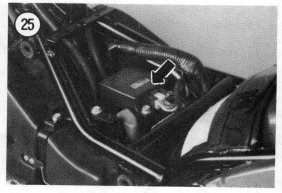

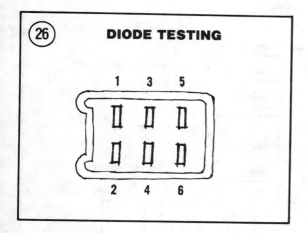

DIODE TESTING

1 3 5

2 4 6

ohmmeter set at R×1, measure the resistance across each set of terminals (**Figure 26**). Switch the leads and recheck the resistance. The resistance should be low in one direction and read more than 10 times as high when the leads are switched. If the diode tested incorrectly, replace it.

Rectifier/Regulator
Removal/Installation

The rectifier/regulator assembly (**Figure 27**) is installed on the upper frame tube on the right-hand side.

1. Turn the ignition switch to the OFF position.
2. Remove the fuel tank.
3. Remove the radiator cap/reservoir tank covers.
4. Disconnect the electrical connector at the rectifier/regulator.
5. Remove the rectifier/regulator mounting bolts and remove the unit.
6. Reverse these steps to install.

ELECTRIC STARTER

The starter circuit includes the starter button, starter relay, battery and starter motor. **Figure 28** (1974-1983) and **Figure 29** (1985-on) illustrate typical starter circuits.

Removal/Installation

Refer to Chapter Four (1974-1983) or Chapter Five (1985-on).

9

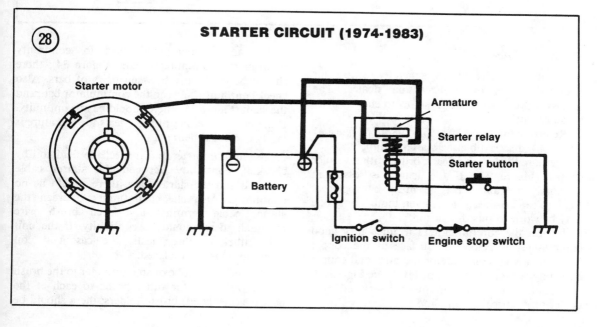

STARTER CIRCUIT (1974-1983)

Starter motor

Armature

Starter relay

Starter button

Battery

Ignition switch   Engine stop switch

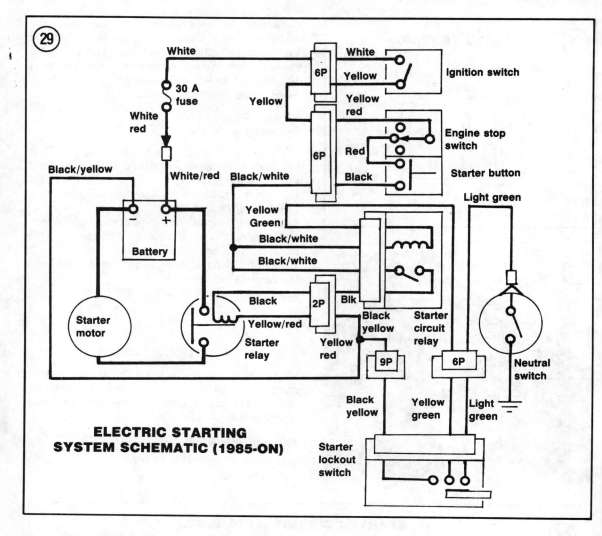

**ELECTRIC STARTING
SYSTEM SCHEMATIC (1985-ON)**

Disassembly/Reassembly

Starter motor repair is generally a job for electrical shops or a Kawasaki dealer. The following procedure describes how to check starter brush condition.

1. Referring to **Figure 30** (1974-1983) or **Figure 31** (1985-on), disassemble the starter motor.

2. Measure the length of each brush with a vernier caliper (**Figure 32**). If the length is less than specified in **Tables 1-4**, it must be replaced. Replace the brushes as a set even though only one may be worn to this dimension.

3. Inspect the commutator. The mica in a good commutator is below the surface of the copper bars. On a worn commutator the mica and copper bars may be worn to the same level. See **Figure 33**. If necessary, have the commutator serviced by a dealer or electrical repair shop.

4. Use an ohmmeter and check for continuity between the commutator bars (**Figure 34**); there should be continuity between pairs of bars. Also check continuity between the commutator bars and the shaft (**Figure 35**); there should be no continuity. If the unit fails either of these tests the armature is faulty and must be replaced.

5. Use an ohmmeter and inspect the field coil by checking continuity between the starter cable terminal and the starter case; there should be no continuity. Also check continuity between the starter cable terminal and each brush wire terminal; there should be continuity. If the unit fails either of these tests, the case/field coil assembly must be replaced.

6. Connect one probe of an ohmmeter to the brush holder plate and the other probe to each of the positive (insulated) brush holders; there should be

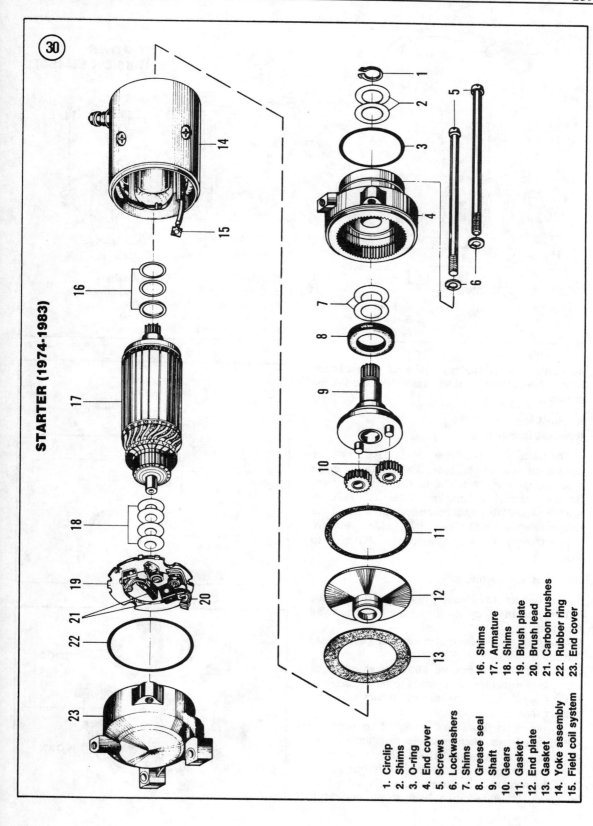

STARTER (1974-1983)

1. Circlip
2. Shims
3. O-ring
4. End cover
5. Screws
6. Lockwashers
7. Shims
8. Grease seal
9. Shaft
10. Gears
11. Gasket
12. End plate
13. Gasket
14. Yoke assembly
15. Field coil system
16. Shims
17. Armature
18. Shims
19. Brush plate
20. Brush lead
21. Carbon brushes
22. Rubber ring
23. End cover

9

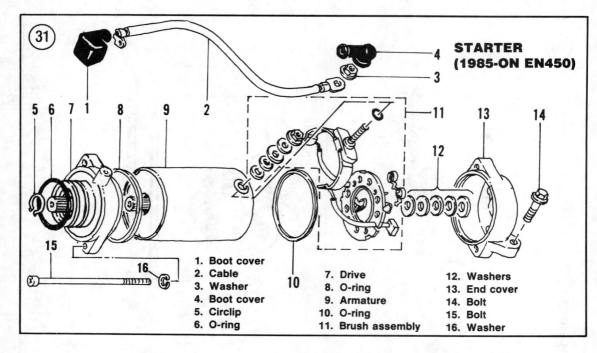

**STARTER
(1985-ON EN450)**

1. Boot cover
2. Cable
3. Washer
4. Boot cover
5. Circlip
6. O-ring
7. Drive
8. O-ring
9. Armature
10. O-ring
11. Brush assembly
12. Washers
13. End cover
14. Bolt
15. Bolt
16. Washer

no continuity. If the unit fails at either brush holder, the brush holder assembly should be replaced.

Starter Relay
Removal/Installation

The starter relay (A, **Figure 36**) is installed on the right-hand side of the bike. To replace it, make sure the ignition switch is in the OFF position. Remove the right-hand air filter on 1985-on models. Then label and disconnect the wires at the starter relay and pull it out of its holder. Remove any attaching screws, if necessary. Reverse to install.

Starter Relay Testing

1. Disconnect the starter motor lead and the battery positive cable from the starter relay terminal.
2. Connect an ohmmeter across the relay terminals.
3. Press the starter button. The relay should click and the ohmmeter should indicate zero resistance. If the relay clicks, but the meter indicates any value greater than zero, replace the relay.
4. If the relay does not click, disconnect the remaining wires, then measure resistance across the relay coil terminals. If the resistance is not close to zero resistance, the relay is defective.
5. If the resistance is close to zero, the relay may be good but inoperative because no current is

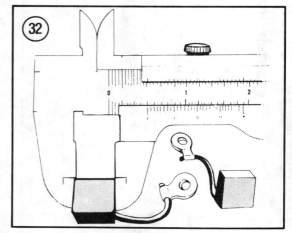

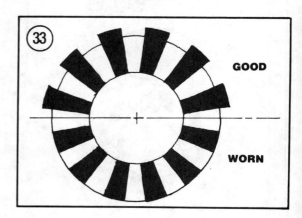

GOOD

WORN

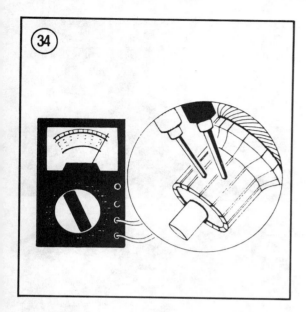

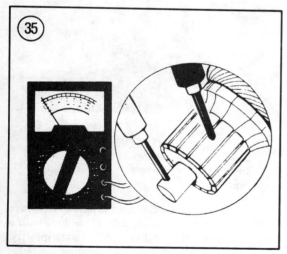

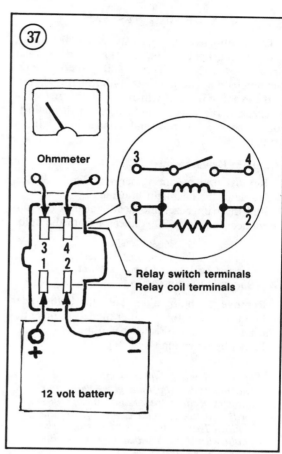

9

reaching it. Connect the positive voltmeter lead to the black wire and the negative voltmeter lead to the black/yellow wire, then press the starter switch. If the meter indicates battery voltage, the relay is defective. If there is no voltage reading, the switch or wiring is defective.

Starter Circuit Relay Testing (1985-on)

All 1985 models have a starter circuit relay in the starting circuit. The starter circuit relay (B, **Figure 36**) is located beside the starter relay.

1. Disconnect the wires at the starter circuit relay and remove it.

2. Connect an ohmmeter and a 12-volt battery to the starter circuit relay as shown in **Figure 37**. Interpret results as follows:

   a. When the battery is connected, the ohmmeter should read zero resistance.

   b. When the battery is disconnected, the ohmmeter should read infinite resistance.

3. If the test results in Step 2 were incorrect, replace the starter circuit relay.

LIGHTING SYSTEM

The lighting system consists of the headlight, taillight/brakelight combination, directional signals, warning lights and speedometer, tachometer and cooling system illumination lights. In the event of trouble with any light, the first thing to check is the affected bulb itself. If the bulb is good, check all wiring and connections with a testlight.

Headlight Replacement

1. Remove the mounting screws (**Figure 38**) on each side of the headlight housing.
2. Pull the trim bezel and headlight unit out and disconnect the electrical connector from the bulb.

> *WARNING*
> *If the headlight has just burned out or turned off it will be hot. Do **not** touch the bulb until it cools off.*

3. Remove the bulb cover. Turn the bulb holder and remove the bulb. On other models remove the clips and remove the sealed beam unit.
4. Install by reversing these steps.

> *CAUTION*
> *On models with quartz-halogen bulbs, do not touch the bulb glass with your fingers because traces of oil on the bulb will drastically reduce the life of the bulb. Clean any traces of oil from the bulb with a cloth moistened in alcohol or lacquer thinner.*

5. Adjust the headlight as described in this chapter.

Headlight Adjustment

Adjust the headlight horizontally and vertically according to the Department of Motor Vehicles regulations in your area. To adjust, proceed as follows:

a. Horizontal adjustment—Turn the screw clockwise to move the beam to the left and counterclockwise to move the beam to the right. See B, **Figure 38** and A, **Figure 39** (typical).

b. Vertical adjustment—Loosen the headlight mounting nuts or bolts (B, **Figure 39**) and turn the headlight shell up or down to adjust the beam. On some models, it will be necessary to remove the headlight unit and loosen the nuts on the inside of the headlight housing.

Taillight Replacement

All models are equipped with 2 double-filament bulbs in the taillight/brake light assembly for safety purposes.

> *CAUTION*
> *During this procedure, do **not** overtighten the screws or the lens may crack.*

Remove the screws securing the lens and remove it. Wash the inside and outside of the lens with a mild detergent. Rinse thoroughly and wipe dry. Wipe off the reflective base surrounding the bulbs with a soft cloth. Replace the bulbs and install the lens. Do not overtighten the screws or the lens may crack.

Directional Signal Light Replacement

Remove the two screws securing the lens. Remove the lens. Wash the inside and outside of the lens with a mild detergent. Replace the bulb. Install the lens; do not overtighten the screws or the lens will crack.

Instrument Panel Illumination Bulb Replacement

1. Disconnect the speedometer or tachometer cables.

HORN SWITCH

Position	Wire color	
	BK/W	BK/Y
Push	•———————•	
Off		

SWITCHES (1974-1977 AND 1977-1978 DELUXE A MODEL)

IGNITION SWITCH

Switch position	Wire color			
	W	BR	BL	R
Off				
On	•———•		•———•	
Park	•———•			

HORN/PASSING SWITCH

Switch position	Wire color			
	BK	*	R/BK	BR
Off				
On	•———•		•———•	
Switch	Horn		Passing	

*Ground

DIMMER SWITCH

Switch position	Wire color		
	R/BK	BL	R/Y
Low	•———•		
High		•———•	

HEADLIGHT SWITCH (EUROPEAN)

Switch position	Wire color		
	BR	BL	R
Po	•———————•		
On	•———•		
Off			

2. Remove the bolts securing the speedometer/tachometer brace and pull it away from the steering head.

3. Remove the outside cover (as necessary) to gain access to the blown bulb.

4. Remove the bulb from the connector and install a new one.

5. Installation is the reverse of these steps.

SWITCHES

Switches can be tested for continuity with an ohmmeter, as described in Chapter One, or with a test light at the switch connector plug by operating the switch in each of its operating positions and comparing results with the switch operation. For example, **Figure 40** shows a continuity diagram for a typical horn button switch. It shows which terminals should show continuity when the horn button is in a given position.

When the horn button is pushed, there should be continuity between terminals BK/W and BK/Y. This is indicated by the line on the continuity diagram. An ohmmeter connected between these 2 terminals should indicate little or no resistance and a test lamp should light. When the horn button is free, there should be no continuity between the same terminals.

If a switch doesn't perform properly, replace it. Refer to the following figures when testing the switches:

  a. **Figure 41**: 1974-1977 and 1977-1978 Deluxe A models.

  b. **Figure 42**: 1978-1981 KZ400.

  c. **Figure 43**: 1980-1983 KZ440.

  d. **Figure 44**: 1985-on EN450.

When testing switches, note the following:

  a. First check the fuse.

  b. Check the battery as described in Chapter Three and bring the battery to the correct state of charge, if required.

  c. When separating 2 connectors, pull on the connector housings and not the wires.

  d. After locating a defective circuit, check the connectors to make sure they are clean and properly connected. Check all wires going into a connector housing to make sure each wire is properly positioned and that the wire end is not loose.

  e. To properly connect connectors, push them together until they click into place.

  f. When replacing handlebar switch assemblies, make sure the cables are routed correctly so that they are not crimped when the handlebar is turned from side to side.

9

SWITCHES (1978-1981 KZ400)

IGNITION SWITCH

Switch position	Wire color			
	W	BR	R/BL	R
On	●—●		●—●	
Off				
Lock				
Park	●—			—

HORN/PASSING SWITCH

Switch position	Wire color			
	BK	*	R/BK	BR
Off				
On	●—●		●—●	
Switch	Horn		Passing	

*Ground

DIMMER SWITCH

Switch position	Wire color		
	R/BK	BL	R/Y
High	●—●		
Low		●—●	

HEADLIGHT SWITCH (EUROPEAN)

Switch position	Wire color		
	BR	BR/W	BL/W
Off			
Running lights	●—●		
On	●—		—●

HORN

Removal/Installation

1. Disconnect the horn electrical connector.
2. Remove the bolts securing the horn.
3. Installation is the reverse of these steps.

Testing

1. Disconnect horn wires from harness.
2. Connect horn wires to 12-volt battery. If it is good, it will sound.

FUSES

Whenever a fuse blows, find out the reason for the failure before replacing the fuse. Usually, the trouble is a short circuit in the wiring. This may be caused by worn-through insulation or a disconnected wire shorting to ground.

> *CAUTION*
> *Never substitute aluminum foil or wire for a fuse. Never use a higher amperage fuse than specified. An overload could result in fire and complete loss of the bike.*

Refer to your model's wiring diagram at the end of this book for fuse ratings.

SWITCHES (1980-1983 KZ440)

IGNITION SWITCH

Switch position	Wire color			
	W	BR	R/BL	R
On	●—●		●—●	
Off				
Lock				
Park	●—			—●

DIMMER SWITCH

Switch position	Wire color		
	R/BK	BL	R/Y
High	●—●		
Low		●—●	

HEADLIGHT SWITCH (EUROPEAN)

Switch position	Wire color		
	BR	BR/W	BL/W
Off			
Running lights	●—●		
On	●—●		

(44)   **SWITCHES (1985-ON EN450)**

HEADLIGHT SWITCH

Switch position	Wire color			
	R/W	R/BL	BL	BL/Y
Off				
Running lights	●——————●			
On	●——————●		●——————●	

DIMMER SWITCH (U.S. & CANADA)

Switch position	Wire color			
	BL/Y	BL/O	R/Y	R/BK
High	●——————●		●——————●	
Low	●——————●		●——————●	

IGNITION SWITCH

Switch position	Wire color				
	BR/W	W	Y	BL	R
Off, lock					
On	●——●——●——●——●				
Park		●——————●			

DIMMER SWITCH (EUROPEAN)

Switch position	Wire color		
	R/BK	BL/Y	R/Y
High		●——————●	
Low	●——————●		

Table 1 ELECTRICAL SPECIFICATIONS
(1974-1977 AND 1977-1978 DELUXE A MODELS)

Charging system output test	
Idle speed	1,100-1,300 rpm
Voltage	14 volts or more
Armature resistance test	
Yellow leads	0.4-0.6 ohms
Field coil test	
Green and black leads	3.8-5.8 ohms
Ignition coil	
Primary resistance	3.2-4.8
Secondary resistance	10.4-15.6 K ohms
Starter motor	
Brush wear limit	6 mm (0.236 in.)

9

Table 2 ELECTRICAL SPECIFICATIONS (1978-1981 KZ400)

Charging system	
Voltage test	14.5 volts @ 4,000 rpm
Alternator output test	75 volts AC @ 4,000 rpm
Resistance check	0.26-0.38 ohms
Ignition system	
Ignition coil	
1978-1980	
Primary	3.2-4.8 ohms
Secondary	10.4-15.6 K ohms
1981	
Primary	1.8-2.8 ohms
Secondary	10.4-15.6 ohms
Pickup coil resistance	
1981	360-540 ohms
Starter motor	
Brush wear limit	6mm (0.236 in.)

Table 3 ELECTRICAL SPECIFICATIONS (1980-1983 KZ440)

Charging system	
Regulator/rectifier output	
voltage	12-15 volts
Alternator output test	75 volts AC @ 4,000 rpm
Resistance check	0.26-0.38 ohms
Ignition system	
Ignition coil	
1980	
Primary	3.2-4.8 ohms
Secondary	10.4-15.6 K ohms
1981-1983	
Primary	1.8-2.8 ohms
Secondary	10.4-15.6 ohms
Pickup coil resistance	
1981-1983	360-540 ohms
Starter motor	
Brush wear limit	6 mm (0.236 in.)

Table 4 ELECTRICAL SPECIFICATIONS (1985-ON)

Charging system	
Regulator/rectifier output	
voltage	12-15 volts
Alternator output test	60 volts AC @ 4,000 rpm
Resistance check	0.3-0.6 ohms
Ignition system	
Ignition coil	
Primary	2.1-3.2 ohms
Secondary	10-16 K ohms
Pickup coil resistance	400-490 ohms
Starter motor	
Brush wear limit	6.5 mm (0.256 in.)

NOTE: If you own an EN500 model, first check the Supplement at the back of this book for any specific service information.

CHAPTER TEN

COOLING SYSTEM

The pressurized cooling system consists of the radiator, water pump, radiator cap, thermostat, electric cooling fan and a coolant reservoir tank. **Figure 1** shows the main cooling system components.

It is important to keep the coolant level to the FULL mark on the coolant reservoir tank (**Figure 2**). Always add coolant to the reservoir tank rather than to the radiator.

CAUTION
*Drain and flush the cooling system at least every 2 years. Refill with a mixture of ethylene glycol antifreeze (formulated for aluminum engines) and purified water. Do not reuse the old coolant as it deteriorates with use. Do **not** operate the cooling system with only purified water (even in climates where antifreeze protection is not required). This is important because the engine is all aluminum; it will not rust but it will oxidize internally and have to be replaced. Refer to **Coolant Change** in Chapter Three.*

This chapter describes repair and replacement of cooling system components. **Table 1** at the end of the chapter lists all of the cooling system specifications. For routine maintenance of the system, refer to Chapter Three.

WARNING
Do not remove the radiator cap when the engine is hot. The coolant is very hot and and is under pressure. Severe scalding could result if the coolant comes in contact with your skin.

WARNING
The radiator fan and fan switch are connected to the battery. Whenever the engine is warm or hot, the fan may start even with the ignition switch in the OFF position. Never work around the fan or touch the fan until the engine is completely cool.

The cooling system must be cooled before removing any component of the system.

COOLING SYSTEM INSPECTION

1. If a substantial coolant loss is noted, the head gasket may be blown. In extreme cases sufficient coolant will leak into a cylinder(s) when the bike is left standing for several hours so the engine cannot be turned over with the starter. White smoke (steam) might also be observed at the muffler(s) when the engine is running. Coolant may also find its way into the oil. To check, observe the oil level indicator on the clutch cover (**Figure 3**). If the oil looks like a "green chocolate malt" there is coolant

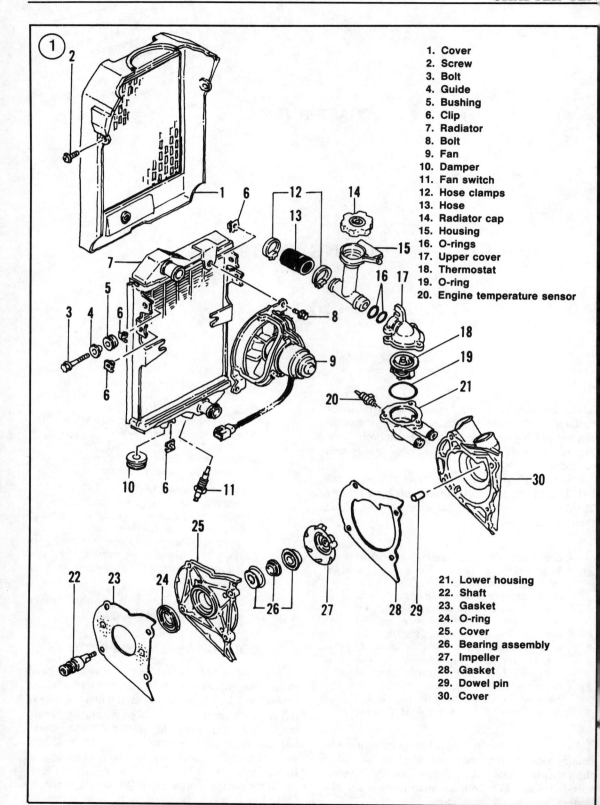

1. Cover
2. Screw
3. Bolt
4. Guide
5. Bushing
6. Clip
7. Radiator
8. Bolt
9. Fan
10. Damper
11. Fan switch
12. Hose clamps
13. Hose
14. Radiator cap
15. Housing
16. O-rings
17. Upper cover
18. Thermostat
19. O-ring
20. Engine temperature sensor

21. Lower housing
22. Shaft
23. Gasket
24. O-ring
25. Cover
26. Bearing assembly
27. Impeller
28. Gasket
29. Dowel pin
30. Cover

in the oil system. If so, correct the problem immediately.

> *CAUTION*
> *After the problem is corrected, drain and thoroughly flush out the engine oil system to eliminate all coolant residue. Refill with fresh engine oil; refer to* ***Chapter Three****.*

2. Check the radiator for clogged or damaged fins. If more than 15 percent of the radiator fin area is damaged, repair or replace the radiator.

3. Check all coolant hoses for cracks or damage. Replace all questionable parts. Make sure the hose clamps are tight, but not so tight that they cut the hoses.

4. Pressure test the cooling system as described in Chapter Three.

RADIATOR AND FAN

> *WARNING*
> *The radiator fan and fan switch are connected to the battery. Whenever the engine is warm or hot, the fan may start even with the ignition switch in the OFF position. Never work around the fan or touch the fan until the engine is completely cool.*

Removal/Installation

The radiator and fan are removed as an assembly.

1. Place the bike on the centerstand.
2. Drain the cooling system as described in Chapter Three.
3. Disconnect the fan switch lead (**Figure 4**) and the fan motor connector (**Figure 5**).
4. Remove the radiator grille (**Figure 6**) from the front of the radiator.
5. Remove the left-hand front side cover.

6. Loosen the clamping screws on the upper and lower (**Figure 7**) radiator hose bands. Move the bands back onto the hoses and off of the necks of the radiator.

7. Remove the radiator mounting bolts (**Figure 8**). Disconnect the fan switch ground lead from the left-hand side (**Figure 9**).

8. Lower the radiator and remove it and the fan assembly.

9. Replace the radiator hoses if deterioration or damage is noted. See A, **Figure 10**.

10. Installation is the reverse of these steps. Note the following.

11. Make sure the fan switch ground lead is attached as shown in **Figure 9**.

12. Refill the coolant as described in Chapter Three.

Inspection

1. Flush off the exterior of the radiator with a garden hose on low pressure. Spray both the front and the back to remove all road dirt and bugs. Carefully use a whisk broom or stiff paint brush to remove any stubborn dirt.

> *CAUTION*
> *Do not press too hard or the cooling fins and tubes may be damaged causing a leak.*

2. Carefully straighten out any bent cooling fins (**Figure 11**) with a broad-tipped screwdriver.

3. Check for cracks or leakage (usually a moss-green colored residue) at the filler neck, the inlet and outlet hose fittings and the upper and lower tank seams.

Cooling Fan
Removal/Installation

1. Remove the radiator as described in this chapter.

2. Remove the bolts (B, **Figure 10**) securing the fan shroud and fan assembly and remove the assembly.

3. Installation is the reverse of these steps.

4. Refill the cooling system with the recommended type and quantity of coolant. See Chapter Three.

THERMOSTAT

Removal/Installation

1. Remove the seat and the left-hand front side cover.

2. Remove the fuel tank.

3. Disconnect the water temperature sensor lead (A, **Figure 12**) at the thermostat housing.

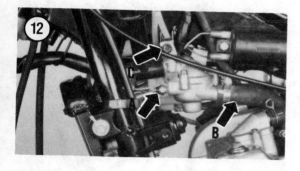

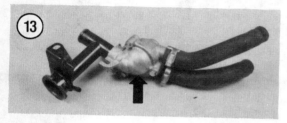

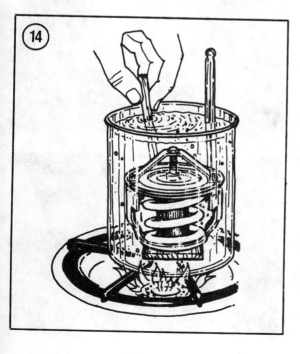

4. Drain the cooling system as described in Chapter Three.

5. Loosen the clamping screws on the 2 radiator hoses at the thermostat (B, **Figure 12**). Slide the clamps off of the thermostat neck.

6. Loosen the thermostat housing clamp bolt (C, **Figure 12**).

7. Loosen and remove the thermostat mounting bolt.

8. Pull the thermostat out of the water pipe and remove it.

9. Remove the thermostat housing cover (**Figure 13**) and remove the thermostat.

10. Install by reversing these steps, noting the following.

11. Replace the thermostat-to-water pipe O-rings if they are starting to deteriorate or are brittle.

12. Refill the cooling system with the recommended type and quantity of coolant. Refer to Chapter Three.

Inspection

Test the thermostat to ensure proper operation. The thermostat should be replaced if it remains open at normal room temperature or stays closed after the specified temperature has been reached during the test procedure.

Place the thermostat on a small piece of wood in a pan of water (**Figure 14**). Place a cooking thermometer with a heat range higher than the test temperature in the pan of water. Gradually heat the water and continue to gently stir the water until it reaches 157.1-162.5° F (69.5-72.5° C). At this temperature the thermostat should open.

NOTE
Valve operation is sometimes sluggish; it usually takes 3-5 minutes for the valve to operate properly.

If the valve fails to open, the thermostat should be replaced (it cannot be serviced). Be sure to replace it with one of the same temperature rating.

WATER PUMP

Removal/Installation

1. Drain the engine oil as described in Chapter Three.

2. Drain the cooling system as described in Chapter Three.

3. Shift the transmission into first gear.

4. Remove the right-hand footpeg assembly mounting bolts. Pull the footpeg assembly away from the frame and allow it to hang down.

10

5. Loosen the clamp on the water pump cover radiator hose (**Figure 7**). Then twist the hose and slide if off the cover neck.

6. With the water pipe attached to the water pump cover, cover bolts and cover (**Figure 15**).

7. Apply the rear brake.

NOTE
*The impeller must be turned **clockwise** for removal.*

8. Turn the impeller nut clockwise and remove the impeller (**Figure 16**).

9. Pull the water pump housing from the crankcase (**Figure 17**).

10. Installation is the reverse of these steps, noting the following.

NOTE
*The impeller must be turned **counterclockwise** for installation.*

11. Turn the impeller shaft nut counterclockwise to tighten it. Tighten to 9.8 N•m (87 in.-lb.).

12. Install the 2 water pump housing dowel pins (A, **Figure 18**) and a new gasket (B, **Figure 18**).

13. Install new O-rings on the water pipe.

14. Refill the cooling system with the recommended type and quantity of coolant. Refer to Chapter Three.

Inspection

1. Inspect the impeller (**Figure 19**) for corrosion or damaged blades. Replace the impeller if necessary.

2. Inspect the rubber seal on the backside of the impeller (**Figure 20**). Replace it if worn or damaged by prying it out of the impeller. Clean the seal area with solvent and allow to thoroughly dry. Apply clean coolant to the new seal and install it by hand.

3. Inspect the water pump oil seal (**Figure 21**) and the mechanical seal (**Figure 22**) for wear or damage. If necessary, remove the water pump seal with a hook or screwdriver. The removal of the mechanical seal requires the use of Kawasaki driver (57001-1139). Install the new seals as follows:

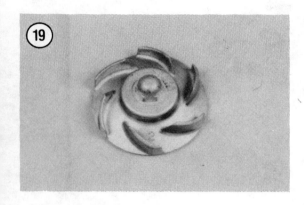

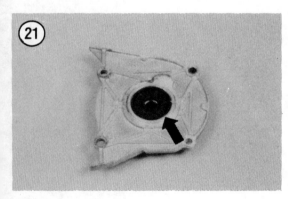

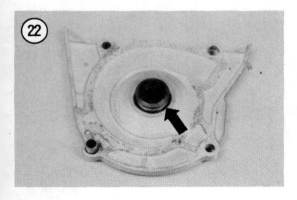

a. *Water pump oil seal:* Install the new seal by driving it into the water pump with a socket of the appropriate size placed on the outside of the seal. Install the seal until it is flush with the housing.

b. *Mechanical seal:* Install the new seal by driving it into the water pump housing until the seal flange touches the housing surface.

HOSES

Hoses deteriorate with age and should be replaced periodicaly or whenever they show signs of cracking or leakage. To be safe, replace the hoses every 2 years. The spray of hot coolant from a cracked hose can injure the rider and passenger. Loss of coolant can also cause the engine to overheat, causing damage.

Whenever any component of the cooling system is removed, inspect the hoses(s) and determine if replacement is necessary.

THERMOSTATIC FAN SWITCH AND WATER TEMPERATURE SENSOR

Removal/Installation

1. Drain the cooling system as described in Chapter Three.

2A. *Thermostatic fan switch:* Perform the following:

a. Disconnect the connector at the switch (**Figure 23**).

b. Unscrew the switch from the bottom of the radiator and remove it.

NOTE
Do not use a liquid gasket on the fan switch threads during installation.

c. Install the switch and tighten to 7.4 N•m (65 in.-lb.).

2B. *Water temperature sensor:* Perform the following:

a. Remove the thermostat as described in this chapter.

b. Unscrew the sensor (**Figure 24**) from the thermostat housing.

c. Apply a liquid gasket to the sensor threads before installation.

d. Tighten the sensor to 7.8 N•m (69 in.-lb.).

e. Install the thermostat as described in this chapter.

3. Refill the cooling system with the recommended type and quantity of coolant. See Chapter Three.

10

Table 1 COOLING SYSTEM SPECIFICATIONS (1985-ON)

Capacity	1.4 L (1.5 qt.)
Coolant type	Antifreeze suited for aluminum engines
Mix ratio	57% purified water/43% coolant
Radiator cap pressure	0.75-1.05 kg/cm² (11-15 psi)
Thermostat	
Opening temperature	157.1-162.5 F° (69.5-72.5° C)
Valve opening lift	Not less than 8 mm (0.315 in.)
	@ 203° F (95° C)

NOTE: If you own an EN500 model, first check the Supplement at the back of this book for any specific service information.

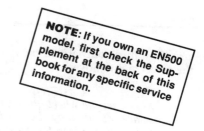

CHAPTER ELEVEN

FRONT SUSPENSION AND STEERING

This chapter discusses service operations on suspension components, steering, wheels and related items. **Table 1** lists front suspension wear limits. **Tables 1-5** are at the end of the chapter.

FRONT WHEEL

Removal/Installation

1. Support the motorcycle so that the front wheel is clear of the ground.

2. Remove the front axle cotter pin (if so equipped). Loosen the front axle nut (**Figure 1**).

3. Remove the axle clamp pinch nuts (**Figure 2**) or loosen the pinch bolt (**Figure 3**).

4. On models with front drum brake, loosen the brake cable at the handlebar. Then disconnect the brake cable at the brake lever (A, **Figure 4**). Also disconnect the torque link (B, **Figure 4**).

5. Disconnect the speedometer cable at at the front hub (**Figure 5**).

6. Remove the axle nut.

7. Push the axle out with a drift or screwdriver and remove it.

8A. *Drum brake:* Pull the wheel forward and remove the brake drum from the front wheel assembly. Remove the wheel.

8B. *Disc brake:* Pull the wheel forward to disengage the brake disc from the caliper. Then

11

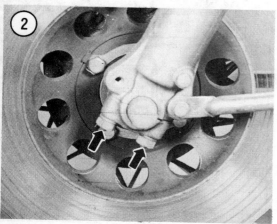

turn the caliper outward to provide clearance for the wheel and remove it.

CAUTION
Do not set the wheel down on the disc surface as it may be scratched or warped. Either lean the wheel against a wall or place it on a couple of wood blocks.

NOTE
Insert a piece of wood in the caliper in place of the disc. This way, if the brake lever is inadvertently squeezed, the piston will not be forced out of the cylinder. If this does happen, the caliper might have to be disassembled to reseat the piston and the system will have to be bled. By using the wood, bleeding the brake is not necessary when installing the wheel.

9. When servicing the wheel assembly, install the spacer, speedometer drive gear, washer and nut on the axle to prevent their loss.

10. Installation is the reverse of these steps, noting the following.

11. Tighten the axle nut to specifications in **Tables 2-5.**

12. Make sure that the speedometer gear housing does not move as the axle nut is tightened.

13. Install a new cotter pin, if so equipped.

14. Install the axle clamp so that the arrow (if so stamped) faces forward.

15. On models with drum brakes, adjust the front brake as described in Chapter Three.

16. On models with disc brakes, *carefully* insert the disc between the pads when installing the wheel.

17. Apply the front brake and compress the front forks several times to make sure the axle is installed correctly without binding the forks. Then tighten the axle pinch nuts to specifications (**Tables 2-5**).

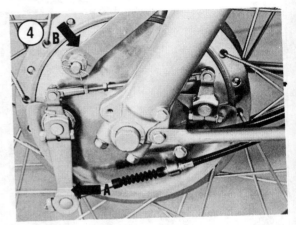

Inspection

1. Remove any corrosion on the front axle with a piece of fine emery cloth.

2. Measure the runout of the wheel rim with a dial indicator as shown in **Figure 6**. If runout exceeds 0.8 mm (0.03 in.), check the wheel bearings. If the wheel bearings are okay on aluminum wheels, the stock aluminum wheel cannot be serviced, but must be replaced. On spoked wheels, refer to *Wheels* in this chapter for information on spoke tightening and wheel truing.

3. Check the rims for cracks or damage as described under *Rims* in this chapter.

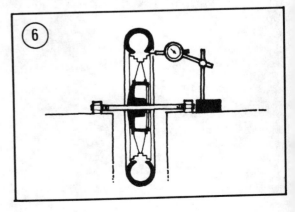

⑦

FRONT HUB (KZ400B AND KZ400C)

1. Cotter pin
2. Axle nut
3. Washer
4. Cam lever
5. Nut
6. Pin
7. Return spring
8. Cotter pin
9. Washer
10. Dust seal
11. Brake panel
12. Camshaft
13. Shoe spring
14. Brake shoe
15. Speedometer gear
16. Grease seal
17. Ball bearing
18. Distance collar
19. Front hub
20. Ball bearing
21. Grease seal
22. Bolt
23. Bolt
24. Joint
25. Locknut
26. Connecting rod
27. Joint
28. Indicator
29. Washer
30. Washer
31. Speedometer pinion
32. Bushing
33. Cap
34. Front axle

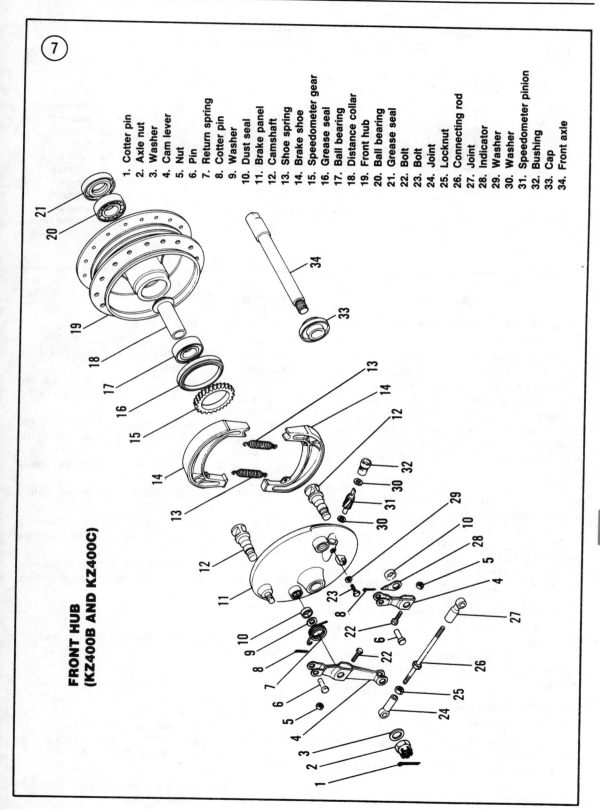

11

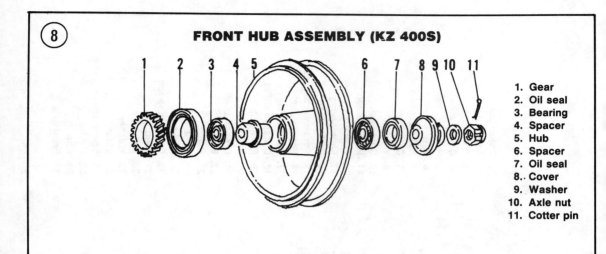

FRONT HUB ASSEMBLY (KZ 400S)

1. Gear
2. Oil seal
3. Bearing
4. Spacer
5. Hub
6. Spacer
7. Oil seal
8. Cover
9. Washer
10. Axle nut
11. Cotter pin

FRONT HUB

Disassembly/Inspection/Reassembly (Drum Brake Models)

Refer to **Figure 7** (KZ400B and KZ400C) or **Figure 8** (KZ400S) for this procedure.

1. Remove the cap and grease seal.
2. Using a long drift and hammer, drive out the bearing on the cap side by tapping evenly around its outer race. The spacer will come out.
3. Insert a long drift into the hub from the hub side, then remove the opposite bearing through the cap side.
4. If necessary, remove the speedometer gear with a gear puller. Then remove the grease seal.
5. Installation is the reverse of these steps, noting the following.
6. Pack bearings thoroughly with grease before assembling the front hub.
7. Tap bearings into place carefully using a suitable size socket placed on the outer bearing race.
8. Install new grease seals. Drive them in squarely using a large diameter socket on the outer portion of the seal.
9. After installing the speedometer gear, punch 2-4 points alongside the gear and drum to lock the gear in place.

Disassembly/Inspection/Reassembly (Disc Brake Models)

Refer to the following illustrations when performing this procedure:

   a. **Figure 9**: (1974-1977 and 1977-1978 Deluxe A models).
   b. **Figure 10**: (1978-1980 KZ400).
   c. **Figure 11**: (1981 KZ400 and 1980-1981 KZ440).
   d. **Figure 12**: (1982-1983 KZ440).
   e. **Figure 13**: (1985-on EN450).

1. Remove the cap, grease seal and snap ring (if so equipped).
2. Using a long drift and hammer, drive out the bearing on the disc side by tapping evenly around its outer race.
3. Pry out the grease seal, then tap out the remaining bearing. The spacer will come out at the same time.
4. Installation is the reverse of these steps, noting the following.
5. Pack bearing thoroughly with grease before assembling the front hub.
6. Tap bearings into place carefully using a suitable size socket placed on the outer bearing race.
7. Install new grease seals. Drive them in squarely using a large diameter socket on the outer portion of the seal (**Figure 14**).

Inspection

1. Clean bearings thoroughly in solvent and dry with compressed air.

> *WARNING*
> *Do not spin the bearing with the air jet while drying. Instead hold the inner race with your hand. Because the air jet can spin the bearing race at higher speeds than it was designed for, the bearing may disintegrate and possibly cause severe eye injuries.*

2. Clean the inside and outside of the hub with solvent. Dry with compressed air.

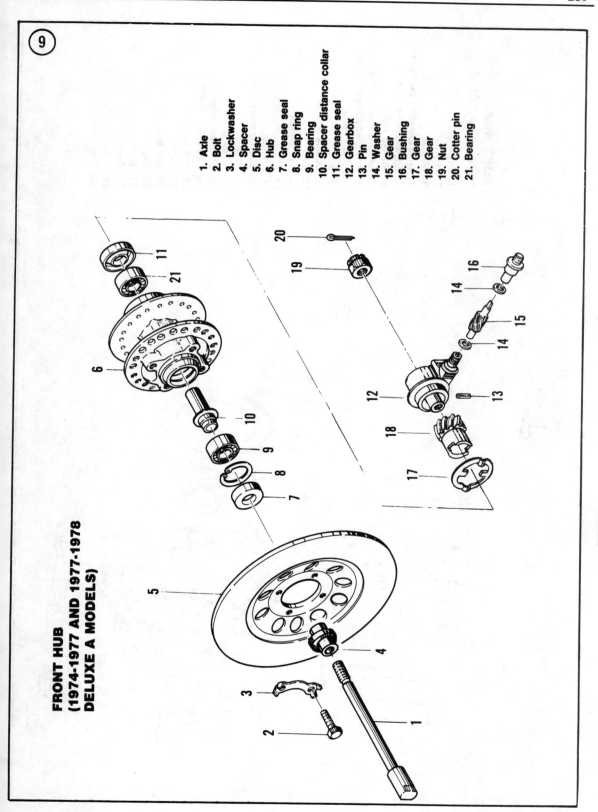

⑨

FRONT HUB
(1974-1977 AND 1977-1978
DELUXE A MODELS)

1. Axle
2. Bolt
3. Lockwasher
4. Spacer
5. Disc
6. Hub
7. Grease seal
8. Snap ring
9. Bearing
10. Spacer distance collar
11. Grease seal
12. Gearbox
13. Pin
14. Washer
15. Gear
16. Bushing
17. Gear
18. Gear
19. Nut
20. Cotter pin
21. Bearing

11

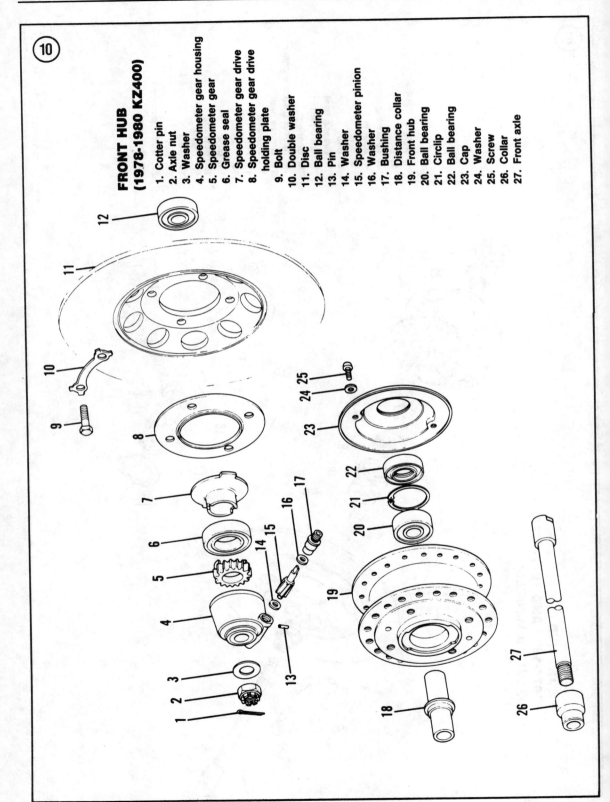

FRONT HUB (1978-1980 KZ400)

1. Cotter pin
2. Axle nut
3. Washer
4. Speedometer gear housing
5. Speedometer gear
6. Grease seal
7. Speedometer gear drive
8. Speedometer gear drive holding plate
9. Bolt
10. Double washer
11. Disc
12. Ball bearing
13. Pin
14. Washer
15. Speedometer pinion
16. Washer
17. Bushing
18. Distance collar
19. Front hub
20. Ball bearing
21. Circlip
22. Ball bearing
23. Cap
24. Washer
25. Screw
26. Collar
27. Front axle

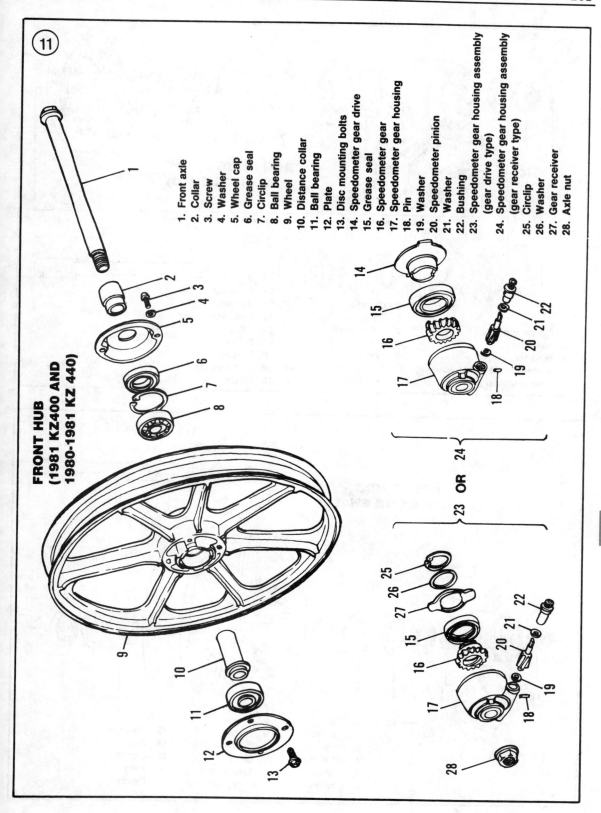

**FRONT HUB
(1981 KZ400 AND
1980-1981 KZ 440)**

1. Front axle
2. Collar
3. Screw
4. Washer
5. Wheel cap
6. Grease seal
7. Circlip
8. Ball bearing
9. Wheel
10. Distance collar
11. Ball bearing
12. Plate
13. Disc mounting bolts
14. Speedometer gear drive
15. Grease seal
16. Speedometer gear
17. Speedometer gear housing
18. Pin
19. Washer
20. Speedometer gear pinion
21. Washer
22. Bushing
23. Speedometer gear housing assembly
    (gear drive type)
24. Speedometer gear housing assembly
    (gear receiver type)
25. Circlip
26. Washer
27. Gear receiver
28. Axle nut

11

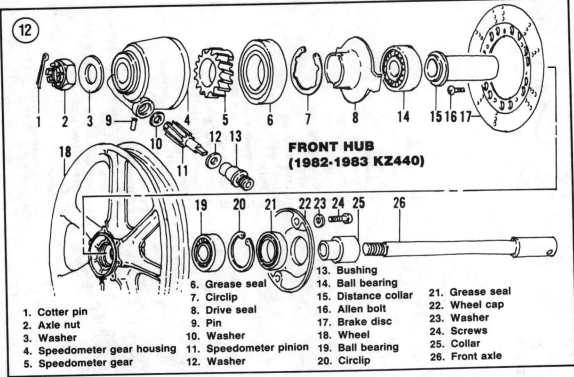

**FRONT HUB
(1982-1983 KZ440)**

1. Cotter pin
2. Axle nut
3. Washer
4. Speedometer gear housing
5. Speedometer gear
6. Grease seal
7. Circlip
8. Drive seal
9. Pin
10. Washer
11. Speedometer pinion
12. Washer
13. Bushing
14. Ball bearing
15. Distance collar
16. Allen bolt
17. Brake disc
18. Wheel
19. Ball bearing
20. Circlip
21. Grease seal
22. Wheel cap
23. Washer
24. Screws
25. Collar
26. Front axle

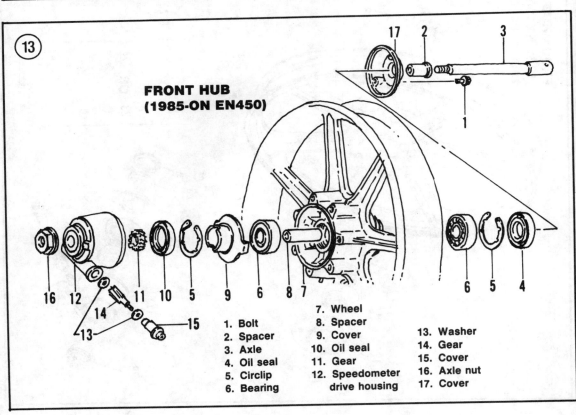

**FRONT HUB
(1985-ON EN450)**

1. Bolt
2. Spacer
3. Axle
4. Oil seal
5. Circlip
6. Bearing
7. Wheel
8. Spacer
9. Cover
10. Oil seal
11. Gear
12. Speedometer
   drive housing
13. Washer
14. Gear
15. Cover
16. Axle nut
17. Cover

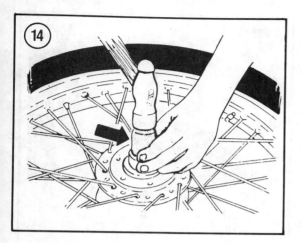

3. Turn each bearing by hand (**Figure 15**), making sure it turns smoothly. Check balls for evidence of wear, pitting or excessive heat (bluish tint). Replace bearings if necessary; always replace as a complete set.

WHEEL BALANCE

An unbalanced wheel results in unsafe riding conditions. Depending on the degree of unbalance and the speed of the motorcycle, the rider may experience anything from a mild vibration to a violent shimmy and loss of control.

On the stock aluminum wheels, weights are attached to the rim (**Figure 16**). On spoke wheels, weights are clamped to the spokes (**Figure 17**). Weights for both aluminum and spoke wheels can be purchased from most motorcycle dealers or motorcycle supply stores.

> *NOTE*
> *On models so equipped, be sure to balance the wheel with the brake disc attached as it also affects the balance.*

Before attempting to balance the wheels, check to be sure that the wheel bearings are in good condition and properly lubricated. The wheel must rotate freely.

1. Remove the wheel as described in this chapter or in Chapter Twelve.
2. Mount the wheel on a fixture such as the one in **Figure 18** so it can rotate freely.
3. Give the wheel a spin and let it coast to a stop. Mark the tire at the lowest point.

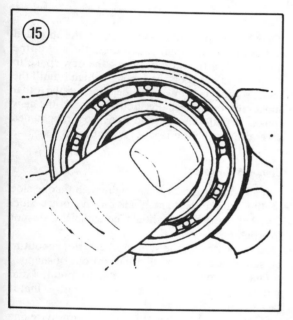

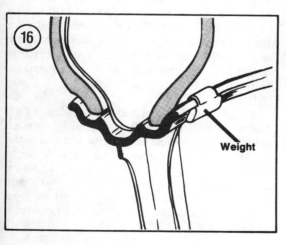

Weight

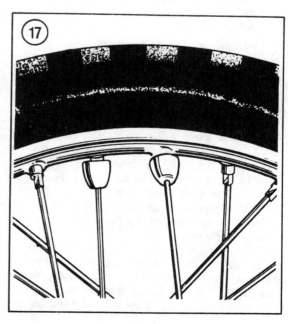

11

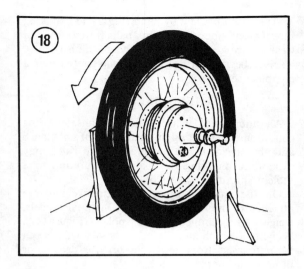

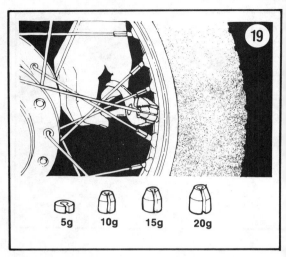

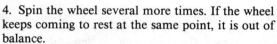

5g   10g   15g   20g

4. Spin the wheel several more times. If the wheel keeps coming to rest at the same point, it is out of balance.

5. Tape a test weight to the upper (or light) side of the wheel.

6. Experiment with different weights until the wheel, when spun, comes to rest at a different position each time.

7. Remove the test weight and install the correct size weight. See **Figure 16** or **Figure 19**.

> *NOTE*
> *When installing crimp-type weights to aluminum rims, it may be necessary to let some air out of the tire. After installing the weight, refill the tire to the correct air pressure as described in Chapter Three.*

Spoke Inspection and Replacement

Spokes loosen with use and should be checked periodically. The "tuning fork" method for checking spoke tightness is simple and works well. Tap the center of each spoke with a spoke wrench or the shank of a screwdriver and listen for a tone. A tightened spoke will emit a clear, ringing tone and a loose spoke will sound flat or dull. All the spokes in a correctly tightened wheel will emit tones of similar pitch. The tension of the spokes does not determine wheel balance.

Bent, stripped or broken spokes should be replaced, as soon as they are detected, as they can destroy an expensive hub.

Unscrew the nipple from the spoke and depress the nipple into the rim far enough to free the end of the spoke; take care not to push the nipple all the way in. Remove the damaged spoke from the hub and use it to match a new spoke of identical length.

If necessary, trim the new spoke at the threaded end to match the original and dress the end of the thread with a thread die. Install the new spoke in the hub and screw on the nipple; tighten it until the spoke's tone is similar to the tone of the other spokes in the wheel. Periodically check the new spoke; it will stretch and must be retightened several times before it takes a final seat.

Spoke Adjustment

If all spokes appear loose, tighten all on one side of the hub, then tighten all on the other side. One-half to one turn should be sufficient; do not overtighten.

After tightening the spokes, check rim runout to be sure you haven't pulled the rim out of shape.

One way to check rim runout is to mount a dial indicator on the front fork or swing arm, so that it bears against the rim.

If you don't have a dial indicator, improvise one as shown in **Figure 6**. Position a bolt until it rests just clear of the rim. Rotate the rim and note whether the clearance increases or decreases. Mark the tire with chalk or light crayon at areas that produce significantly large or small clearances. Clearance must not change by more than 0.5 mm (0.019 in.).

To pull the rim out, tighten spokes which terminate on the same side of the hub and loosen spokes which terminate on the opposite side of the hub (**Figure 20**). In most cases, only a slight amount of adjustment is necessary to true a rim. After adjustment, rotate the rim and make sure another area has not been pulled out of true. Continue adjustment and checking until runout is less than 0.5 mm (0.019 in.).

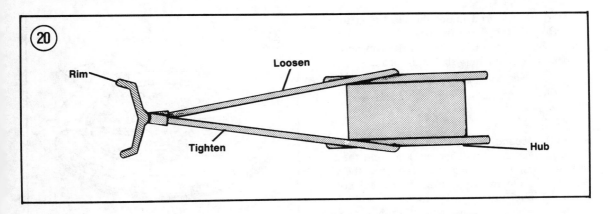

Rim Replacement

If the rim should become bent or damaged, it should be replaced immediately. A bent or dented wheel is very dangerous to the handling of the bike.

If the spokes are not bent or damaged also, they may be reused. This procedure describes how to replace the rim without removing the spokes.

1. Remove the tire as described in this chapter.
2. Securely fasten the spokes together with wire, string or tape at each point where they cross.
3. Place the replacement rim on top of the old rim and align the nipple holes of both rims. This is to make sure the replacement rim is the correct one. When the rims are aligned correctly, mark one spoke and its corresponding nipple hole on the new rim.
4. Remove the nipples from the spokes using a spoke wrench. If they are coated with dirt or rust, clean them in solvent and allow to dry. Then check the nipples for signs of cracking or other damage. Spoke nipples in this condition can strip when the wheel is later trued. Replace all nipples as necessary.
5. Lift the hub and spokes out of the old rim, making sure not to knock the spokes out of alignment.
6. Position the hub and spokes into the new rim, making sure to align the marks made in Step 3. Then insert the spokes into the rim until they are all in place.
7. Place a drop of oil onto the threaded end of each spoke and install the nipples. Thread the nipples halfway onto the spokes, or before they make contact with the rim.
8. Lift the wheel and stand it up on the workbench. Check the hub to make sure it is centered in the rim. If not, reposition it by hand.
9. With the hub centered in the rim, thread the nipples until they just seat against the rim. True the wheel as described in this chapter.

Seating Spokes

When spokes loosen or when installing new spokes, the head of the spoke should be checked for proper seating in the hub. If it is not seated correctly, it can loosen further and may cause severe damage to the hub. If one or more spokes require reseating, hit the head of the spoke with a punch. True the wheel as described in this chapter.

NOTE
To prevent the punch from damaging the chrome on the spoke head, apply strips of tape to the end of the punch before using it.

TIRE CHANGING

The wheels used on all models can easily be damaged during tire removal. Special care must be taken with tire irons when changing a tire to avoid scratches and gouges to the outer rim surface. Insert scraps of leather between the tire iron and the rim to protect the rim from damage.

The stock cast wheels are designed for use with either tubeless or tube-type tires. The spoked wheels are designed for tube-type tires only. Tire removal and installation are basically the same for tube and tubeless tires; where differences occur they are noted. Tire repair is different and is covered in separate procedures.

When removing a tubeless tire, take care not to damage the tire beads, inner liner of the tire or the wheel rim flange. Use tire levers or flat handled tire irons with rounded ends.

Removal

1. Remove the valve core to deflate the tire.
2. Press the entire bead on both sides of the tire into the center of the rim.
3. Lubricate the beads with soapy water.

11

4. Insert the tire iron under the bead next to the valve (**Figure 21**). Force the bead on the opposite side of the tire into the center of the rim and pry the bead over the rim with the tire iron.

> *NOTE*
> *Insert scraps of leather between the tire irons and the rim to protect the rim from damage.*

5. Insert a second tire iron next to the first to hold the bead over the rim. Then work around the tire with the first tool prying the bead over the rim (**Figure 22**). On tube-type tires, be careful not to pinch the inner tube with the tools.

6. On tube-type tires, use your thumb and push the valve from its hole in the rim to the inside of the tire. Carefully pull the tube out of the tire and lay it aside.

> *NOTE*
> *Step 7 is required only if it is necessary to completely remove the tire from the rim, such as for tire replacement or tubeless tire repair.*

7. Turn the wheel over. Insert a tire tool between the second bead and the same side of the rim that the first bead was pried over (**Figure 23**). Force the bead on the opposite side from the tool into the center of the rim. Pry the second bead off the rim, working around the wheel with 2 tire irons as with the first.

8. On tubeless tires, inspect the rubber O-ring where the valve stem seats against the inner surface of the wheel. Replace it if it's starting to deteriorate or has lost its resiliency. This is a common location of air loss.

Installation

1. Carefully inspect the tire for any damage, especially on the inside.

2. A new tire may have balancing rubbers inside. These are not patches and should not be disturbed. A colored spot near the bead indicates a lighter point on the tire. This spot should be placed next to the valve stem (**Figure 24**). In addition, most tires have directional arrows labeled on the side of the tire that indicate which direction the tire should rotate. Make sure to install the tire accordingly.

3. On tube-type tires, inflate the tube just enough to round it out. Too much air will make installation difficult. Place the tube inside the tire.

4. Lubricate both beads of the tire with soapy water.

5. Place the backside of the tire into the center of the rim. On tube-type tires, insert the valve stem

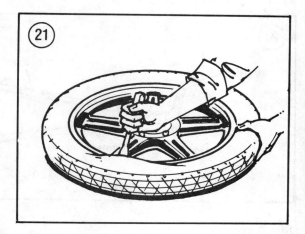

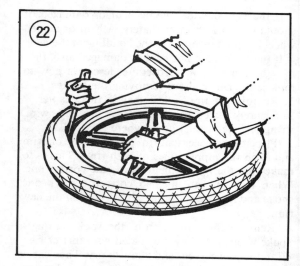

through the stem hole in the wheel. The lower bead should go into the center of the rim and the upper bead outside. Work around the tire in both directions (**Figure 25**). Use a tire iron for the last few inches of bead (**Figure 26**).

6. Press the upper bead into the rim opposite the valve (**Figure 27**). Pry the bead into the rim on both sides of the initial point with a tire tool, working around the rim to the valve.

7. On tube-type tires, wiggle the valve to be sure the tube is not trapped under the bead. Set the valve stem squarely in its hole before screwing on the valve nut to hold it against the rim.

8. Check the bead on both sides of the tire for an even fit around the rim.

9. On tube-type tires, inflate the tire slowly to seat the beads in the rim. It may be necessary to bounce the tire to complete the seating.

10. On tubeless tires place an inflatable band around the circumference of the tire. Slowly inflate the band until the tire beads are pressed against the rim. Inflate the tire enough to seat it, deflate the band and remove it.

> *WARNING*
> *Never exceed 56 psi (4.0 k/cm²) inflation pressure as the tire could burst, causing severe injury. Never stand directly over the tire while inflating it.*

11. Inflate the tire to the required pressure as described in Chapter Three. Tighten the valve stem locks and screw on the cover cap.

12. Balance the wheel assembly as described in this chapter.

TIRE REPAIRS

Tubeless-type tires

Patching a tubeless tire on the road is very difficult. If both beads are still in place against the rim, a can of pressurized tire sealant may inflate the tire and seal the hole. The beads must be against the wheel for this method to work. Another solution is to carry a spare inner tube that could be temporarily installed and inflated. This will enable you to get to a service station where the tire can be correctly repaired. Be sure that the tube is designed for use with a tubeless tire.

The motorcycle tire industry recommends that the tubeless tire be patched from the inside. Therefore, do not patch the tire with an external type plug. If you find an external patch on a tire, it is recommended that it be patch-reinforced from the inside.

11

Due to the variations of material supplied with different tubeless tire repair kits, follow the instructions and recommendations supplied with the repair kit.

Tube-type tires

Every rider will eventually experience trouble with a tire or tube. Repairs and replacement are fairly simple and every rider should know the techniques.

Patching a motorcycle tube is only a temporary fix. A motorcycle tire flexes too much and the patch could rub off. However, a patched tube should get you far enough to buy a new tube.

Due to the variations of material supplied with different tubeless tire repair kits, follow the instructions and recommendations supplied with the repair kit.

STEERING HEAD

Removal/Disassembly

1. Support the bike on the centerstand.
2. Remove the front wheel.
3. Remove the fuel tank.

4. On disc brake models, remove the brake caliper assembly. See Chapter Thirteen.
5. On disc brake models, remove the master cylinder. See Chapter Thirteen.
6. Remove the front fender.
7. Remove the front fork as described in this chapter.
8. Disconnect the cable at the tachometer.
9. Disconnect the leads at the front brake light switch.
10. Remove the headlight assembly from its housing.

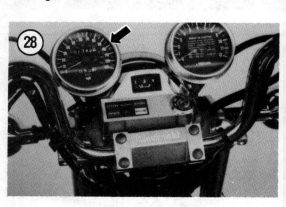

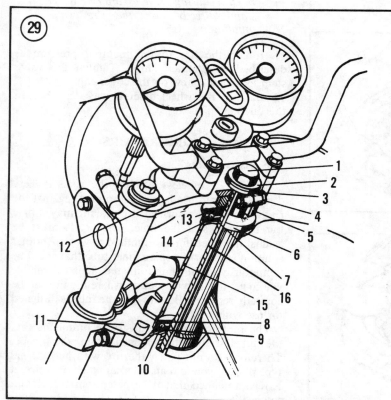

STEERING STEM (1974-1983)

1. Stem head bolt
2. Washer
3. Washer
4. Stem head clamp bolt
5. Steering stem locknut
6. Steeering stem cap
7. Steel balls
8. Lower outer race
9. Lower inner race
10. Steel balls
11. Stem base
12. Stem head
13. Upper inner race
14. Upper outer race
15. Frame head pipe
16. Steering stem

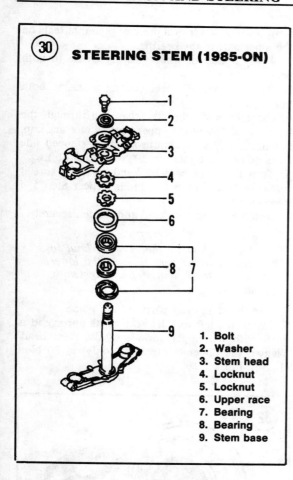

30 **STEERING STEM (1985-ON)**

1. Bolt
2. Washer
3. Stem head
4. Locknut
5. Locknut
6. Upper race
7. Bearing
8. Bearing
9. Stem base

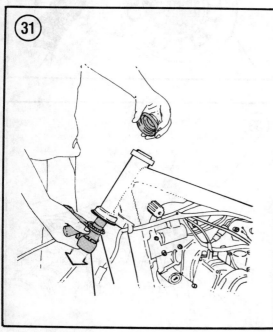

31

NOTE
When performing Step 11, the standard wires are color coded so reconnecting them should not be a problem. However, if the wiring has been changed, it will be easier to tag the mating wires before disconnecting them.

11. Disconnect the wire harness plugs inside the headlight housing. Remove the headlight housing assembly.

12. Remove the instrument cluster (**Figure 28**) from the steering stem head.

13A. *1974-1983:* Referring to **Figure 29**, perform the following:
   a. Remove the stem head bolt (1).
   b. Remove the stem head clamp bolt (4).
   c. Remove the washers (2 and 3).

13B. *1985-on:* Referring to **Figure 30**, remove the steering stem head bolt and washer.

14. Tap the bottom of the steering stem head lightly with a plastic mallet until the fork covers and turn signals lamps can be removed.

15. Continue tapping the bottom of the stem head until it is free of the steering stem and remove it (**Figure 31**).

16A. *1974-1983:* Perform the following:
   a. Push the stem base upward, then remove the locknut (5, **Figure 29**).

NOTE
As the steering stem is removed, a number of steel balls may fall out. Be prepared to catch them.

NOTE
Keep the upper and lower balls separate. There are a total of nineteen 1/4 in. balls each in the upper and lower races.

   b. Remove the steering stem and stem base as a unit. Remove all balls which still adhere.
   c. Remove the steering stem cap (6), upper inner race (13) and the upper balls (7).

16B. *1985-on:* Perform the following:
   a. Remove the 2 steering stem nuts.
   b. Remove the steering stem cap.
   c. Pull the steering stem out of the frame.
   d. Remove the upper bearing from the frame tube.
   e. If necessary, remove the lower bearing from the steering stem with a bearing puller.

11

Assembly/Installation (1974-1983)

Refer to **Figure 29**.

Installation is the reverse of Steps 1-16, noting the following.

1. Perform the following:
   a. Apply a coat of wheel bearing grease to the lower bearing race cone on the steering stem and fit 19 ball bearings around it.
   b. Apply a coat of wheel bearing grease to the upper bearing race cone and fit 19 ball bearings around it (**Figure 32**).

2. Carefully slide the stem base up through the frame neck (**Figure 33**). Install the upper bearing race and cap. Install the steering stem locknut and tighten initially to 27-30 N•m (19.5-22 ft.-lb.).

3. Tap the stem head partway into place.

4. Install the left fork leg so that its upper end is flush with the upper surface of the stem head. Tigthen the upper clamp bolts (only) to specifications in **Tables 2-4**.

5. Repeat Step 5 for the right fork leg.

6. Tap the stem head until it is fully in place.

7. Install washers (2 and 3). The thicker, or wave washer, goes on top. Install the stem head bolt (1). Do not tighten at this point.

8. Install the stem head clamp bolt (4). Do not tighten at this point.

9. Tighten the stem base clamp bolts to specifications (**Tables 2-4**).

10. Tighten or loosen the steering stem locknut (5) until the entire front end assembly continues moving under its own momentum when it is pushed lightly to either side, and no play can be felt when the lower ends of the forks are pushed forward and backward.

11. Tighten the steering stem head bolt to the specifications in **Tables 2-4**.

12. Tighten the stem head clamp bolt to the specifications in **Tables 2-4**.

13. Loosen the lower clamp bolts to allow the front fork tubes to reseat themselves. Then tighten to 20-30 N•m (14-22 ft.-lb.).

14. Recheck the steering adjustment. Repeat if necessary.

15. Bleed the brake system as described in Chapter Thirteen.

Installation (1985-on)

Refer to **Figure 30**.

Installation is the reverse of Steps 1-16, noting the following.

1. If the lower bearing was removed from the stem base, install it by driving it into position with a stem bearing driver or a piece of pipe that seats on the inner part of the bearing.

2. Apply a coat of wheel bearing grease to both bearings.

3. Apply a coat of wheel bearing grease to both bearing races.

4. Carefully slide the stem base up through the frame neck. Install the upper bearing race and cap. Install the stepped locknut so that the stepped side faces down and tighten to 39 N•m (29 ft.-lb.).

5. Turn the stem base by hand to make sure it turns freely and does not bind. Repeat Step 5 if necessary.

6. Install the upper locknut and tighten securely.

NOTE
When tightening the upper locknut in Step 7, make sure to hold the lower locknut to prevent it from tightening further.

7. Tap the stem head partway into place.

8. Install the left fork leg so that its upper end is flush with the upper surface of the stem head. Tighten the upper clamp bolts (only) to 20 N•m (14.5 ft.-lb.).

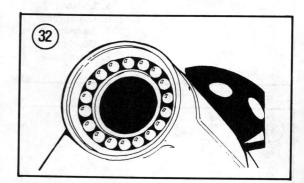

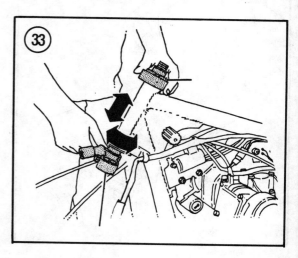

9. Repeat Step 9 for the right fork leg.

10. Tap the stem head until it is fully in place.

11. Install the washer and stem head bolt. Tighten the bolt to 42 N•m (31 ft.-lb.).

12. Tighten the stem base clamp bolts to 25 N•m (18 ft.-lb.).

13. Recheck the steering adjustment. Repeat if necessary.

14. Bleed the brake system as described in Chapter Thirteen.

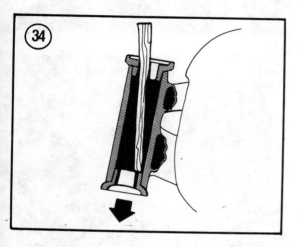

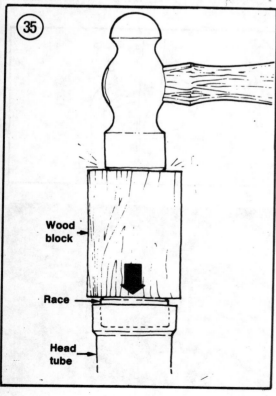

Inspection

1. Clean the bearing races in the steering head and all bearings with solvent.

2. Check for broken welds on the frame around the steering head. If any are found, have them repaired by a competent frame shop or welding service familiar with motorcycle frame repair.

3A. *1974-1983:* Check the balls for pitting, scratches, or discoloration indicating wear or corrosion. Replace them in sets if any are bad.

3B. *1985-on:* Check the bearings for pitting, scratches or discoloration indicating wear or corrosion. Replace them in sets if any are bad.

4. Check the upper and lower races in the steering head for pitting, galling and corrosion. If any of these conditions exist, replace the races as described in this chapter.

5. Check steering stem for cracks and check its race for damage or wear. Replace if necessary.

Bearing Race Replacement

The headset and steering stem bearing races are pressed into place. Because they are easily bent, do not remove them unless they are worn and require replacement. Take old races to the dealer to ensure exact replacement.

To remove a headset race, insert a hardwood stick into the head tube and carefully tap the race out from the inside (**Figure 34**). Tap all around the race so that neither the race nor the head tube is bent. To install a race, fit it into the end of the head tube. Tap it slowly and squarely with a block of wood (**Figure 35**).

FRONT FORK

Removal/Installation

1. Place the motorcycle on the centerstand.

2. Remove the front wheel as described in this chapter.

3. One brake disc models, remove the brake caliper as described in Chapter Thirteen.

> *NOTE*
> *Insert a piece of wood in the caliper in place of the disc. That way, if the brake lever is inadvertently squeezed, the piston will not be forced out of the caliper. If this happens, the caliper might have to be disassembled to reseat the piston. By using the wood, bleeding the brake is not necessary when installing the wheel.*

4. Remove the fork cap top cover, if so equipped.

11

5. On models with air forks, remove the air valve cap and depress the valve (A, **Figure 36**) to release fork air pressure. Repeat on opposite fork.

6. Loosen the pinch bolts (B, **Figure 36**) on the upper fork bridge bolts.

> *NOTE*
> *Step 7 describes how to loosen the fork cap while the forks are still held in the triple clamps.*

> *WARNING*
> *The fork caps are held under spring pressure. Take precautions to prevent the caps from flying into your face during removal. Furthermore, if the fork tubes are bent, the fork caps will be under considerable pressure; have them removed by a Kawasaki dealer.*

7A. *Models with screw-on fork cap:* Loosen the fork cap (**Figure 37**) and remove it.

7B. *Models with circlip held caps:* The fork cap and spring are held in position by a circlip (**Figure 38**). To remove the circlip, it is necessary to have an assistant depress the fork cap using a suitable size drift. Then pry the circlip out of its groove in the fork with a small screwdriver. When the circlip is removed, release tension from the fork cap and remove it together with the fork spring.

8. Loosen the lower fork bridge bolts. See **Figure 39**.

9. Remove the fork tube. It may be necessary to slightly rotate the tube while removing it.

10. Repeat for the opposite side.

11. Install by reversing these removal steps, noting the following.

12A. *Models with screw on fork caps:* Apply a coat of light machine oil to the fork cap threads and install them securely.

12B. *Models with circlip held caps:* Install the fork spring and fork cap. Have an assistant compress the fork cap and install a new circlip (**Figure 38**). Make sure the circlip seats fully in the groove in the fork tube before releasing the fork cap.

13. On disc brake models, if it is necessary, bleed the brake caliper. See Chapter Thirteen.

**Disassembly/Assembly
(1974-1977 and 1977-1978
Deluxe A Models)**

Refer to **Figure 40** for this procedure.

1. The fork cap was loosened during removal. Remove the fork cap.

2. Remove the fork spring (18, **Figure 40**).

3. Remove the fork from the vise, pour the oil out and discard it. Pump the fork several times by hand to expel most of the remaining oil.

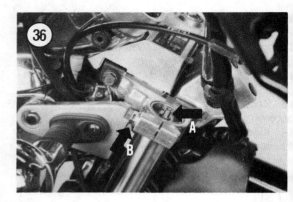

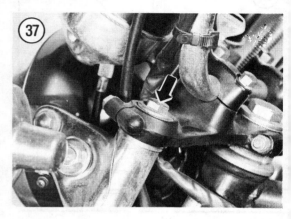

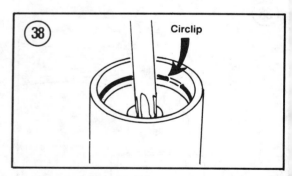

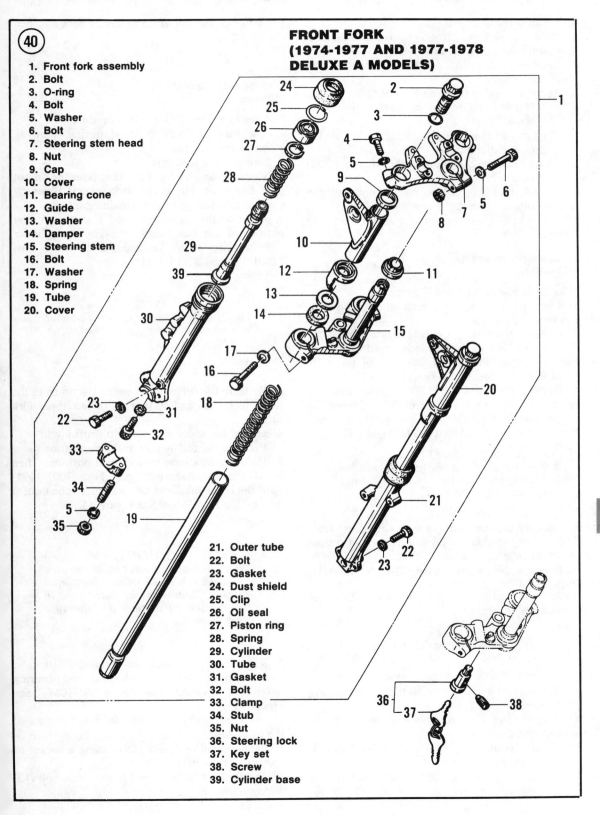

40

**FRONT FORK
(1974-1977 AND 1977-1978
DELUXE A MODELS)**

1. Front fork assembly
2. Bolt
3. O-ring
4. Bolt
5. Washer
6. Bolt
7. Steering stem head
8. Nut
9. Cap
10. Cover
11. Bearing cone
12. Guide
13. Washer
14. Damper
15. Steering stem
16. Bolt
17. Washer
18. Spring
19. Tube
20. Cover

21. Outer tube
22. Bolt
23. Gasket
24. Dust shield
25. Clip
26. Oil seal
27. Piston ring
28. Spring
29. Cylinder
30. Tube
31. Gasket
32. Bolt
33. Clamp
34. Stub
35. Nut
36. Steering lock
37. Key set
38. Screw
39. Cylinder base

11

4. Remove the dust seal (24).
5. Hold the cylinder (29) and remove the bolt (32).
6. Pull the fork tubes apart.
7. Remove the cylinder (29) and spring (28) together.
8. Remove the clip (25) and oil seal (26).
9. Installation is the reverse of these steps, noting the following.
10. Tap the oil seal (26) into place, using a socket of appropriate diameter.
11. Apply Loctite 242 (blue) to the Allen bolt (32) during reassembly.
12. Install the spring (18) so that the end with the tighter coils is upward.
13. Pour in the correct amount of fork oil. See Chapter Three.

Disassembly/Assembly
(1978-1983)

Refer to **Figure 41** for this procedure.
1. The fork cap was loosened during removal. Remove the fork cap.
2. Remove the fork spring (26, **Figure 41**).
3. Remove the fork from the vise, pour the oil out and discard it. Pump the fork several times by hand to expel most of the remaining oil.
4. Remove the Allen bolt (13) and gasket from the bottom of the outer tube (9 or 34). Prevent the cylinder (6) from turning with Kawasaki tools (part Nos. 57001-183 and 57001-1-11) (**Figure 42**).

NOTE
The Allen bolt may be removed without holding the cylinder if an impact driver is used.

5. Pull the fork tubes apart.
6. Remove the dust seal (1) from the outer tube.
7. Remove the cylinder (6) and its spring (7) from the inner tube.
8. Remove the cylinder base (8) from the outer tube.
9. Remove the retainer (2) from the outer tube and remove the oil seal (3).

NOTE
It may be necessary to slightly heat the area around the seal on the outer tube before removal.

10. Installation is the reverse of these steps, noting the following.
11. Tap the oil seal (3) into place, using a socket of appropriate diameter.
12. Apply Loctite 242 (blue) to the Allen bolt (13) during reassembly.
13. Install the spring (26) so that the end with the tighter coils is upward.

14. Pour in the correct amount of fork oil. See Chapter Three.

Disassembly/Reassembly
(1985-on)

Refer to **Figure 43** for this procedure.
1. The fork cap was loosened during removal. Remove the fork cap.
2. Remove the fork spring.
3. Remove the fork from the vise, pour the oil out and discard it. Pump the fork several times by hand to expel most of the remaining oil.
4. Remove the Allen bolt and gasket from the bottom of the outer tube. Prevent the cylinder from turning with Kawasaki tools (part Nos. 57001-183 and 57001-1-11).

NOTE
The Allen bolt may be removed without holding the cylinder if an impact driver is used.

5. Remove the rubber boot out of the notch in the lower fork tube and slide it off of the upper fork tube.
6. Clamp the slider in a vise with soft jaws.
7. Remove the retainer from the outer tube.
8. Hold the fork tube in a vertical position. Then install the Kawasaki tool (part No. 57001-1091) onto the inner tube and tap the outer tube until it falls off the inner tube. See **Figure 44**.

CAUTION
Do not tap on the outer tube when the fork assembly is placed in a horizontal position. Removing the outer tube in this position will damage the inner tube guide bushing.

9. Remove the oil seal, washer and outer tube guide bushing with the oil seal and bearing remover (Kawasaki tool no. 57001-1058). See **Figure 45**.
10. Remove the cylinder base from the bottom of the outer tube.
11. Tap the oil seal into place, using a socket of appropriate diameter.
12. Apply Loctite 242 (blue) to the Allen bolt (13) during reassembly.

(41)

1. Dust seal
2. Retainer
3. Oil seal
4. Spacer
5. Piston ring
6. Piston and cylinder unit
7. Spring
8. Cylinder base
9. Outer tube
10. Gasket

11. Drain screw
12. Gasket
13. Allen bolt
14. Cap
15. Retaining ring
16. Top plug
17. O-ring
18. Bolt

19. Lockwasher
20. Fork cover
21. Stem base cover
22. Damper ring
23. Rubber damper
24. Lockwasher
25. Bolt
26. Spring
27. Inner tube

28. Stem head
29. Bolt
30. Nut
31. Lockwasher
32. Steering stem
33. Stem base
34. Outer tube
35. Stud
36. Axle clamp
37. Lockwasher
38. Nut

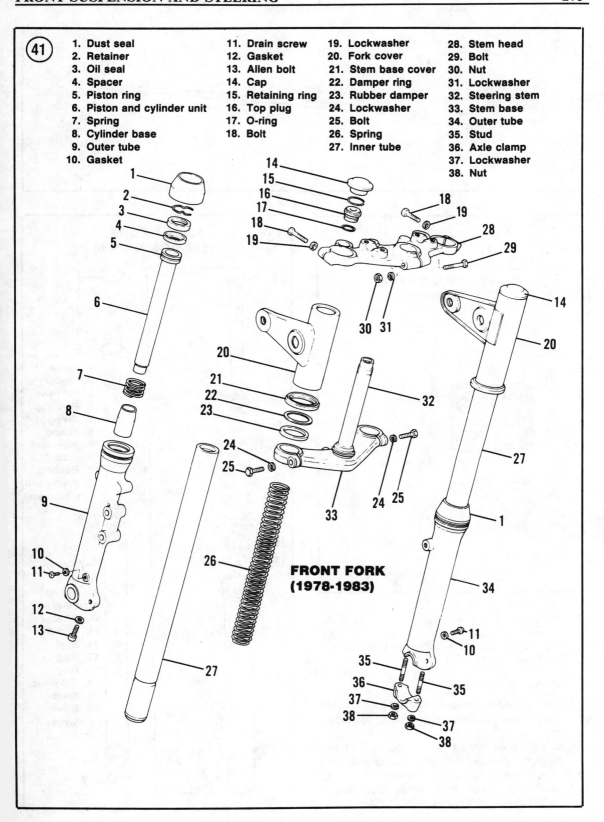

**FRONT FORK
(1978-1983)**

11

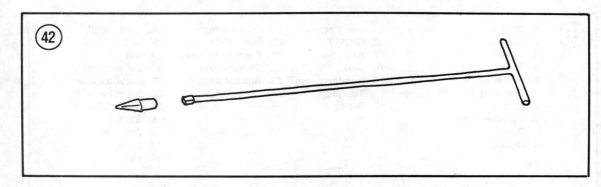

(42)

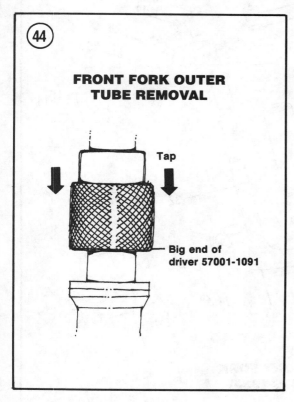

(44)

FRONT FORK OUTER TUBE REMOVAL

Tap

Big end of
driver 57001-1091

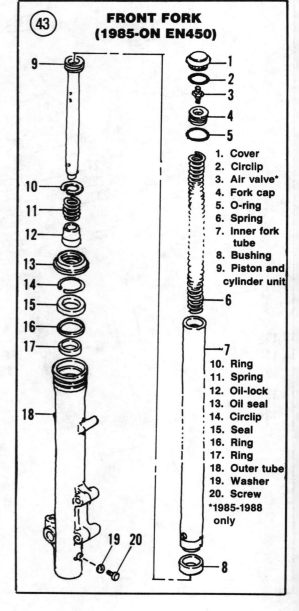

(43)

FRONT FORK
(1985-ON EN450)

1. Cover
2. Circlip
3. Air valve*
4. Fork cap
5. O-ring
6. Spring
7. Inner fork
   tube
8. Bushing
9. Piston and
   cylinder unit

10. Ring
11. Spring
12. Oil-lock
13. Oil seal
14. Circlip
15. Seal
16. Ring
17. Ring
18. Outer tube
19. Washer
20. Screw
*1985-1988
only

13. Install the spring so that the end with the tighter coils is upward.

14. Pour in the correct amount of fork oil. See Chapter Three.

Inspection

1. Check the upper fork tube exterior for scratches and straightness. If bent or scratched, it should be replaced.

2. Check the lower fork tube for dents or exterior damage that may cause the upper fork tube to hang up during riding. Replace if necessary.

3. Measure the front fork spring free length. Replace the spring if it is too short (**Table 1**).

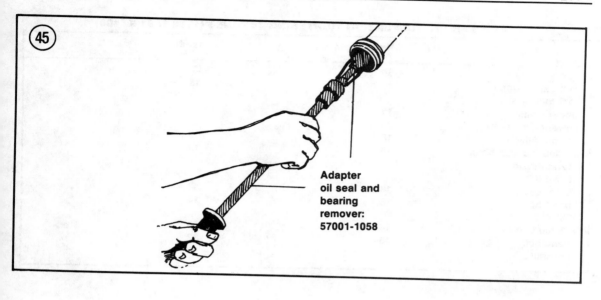

Adapter oil seal and bearing remover: 57001-1058

Table 1 FRONT SUSPENSION WEAR LIMITS

	mm	in.
Steering stem ball bearing specification*	—	1/4 O.D.
Fork spring free length		
1974-1977 KZ400	465	18.30
1978-1980 KZ400	475	18.70
1981 KZ400	510	20.07
1980-1981 KZ440A, D	510	20.07
1980-1981 KZ440B, C	475	18.70
1982-1983 KZ440	511	20.11
1985-on EN450	433	17.04

* Quantity: 19 top and 19 bottom.

11

Table 2 FRONT SUSPENSION TIGHTENING TORQUES
(1974-1977 AND 1977-1978 DELUXE A MODELS)

	N·m	ft.-lb.
Front axle nut	70-90	51-65
Front axle clamp nuts	16-22	11.5-16
Front fork		
Cap bolts	25-30	18-22
Upper clamp bolts	16-22	11.5-16
Lower clamp bolts	20-30	14.5-22
Steering stem		
Clamp bolt	16-22	11.5-16
Head bolt	55	40
Handlebar bolts	16-22	11.5-16

Table 3 FRONT SUSPENSION TIGHTENING TORQUES (1978-1981 KZ400)

	N•m	ft.-lb.
Front axle nut	80	18
Front axle clamp nuts	18	13
Front fork		
Upper clamp bolts	18	13
Lower clamp bolts	30	22
Bottom Allen bolt	18	13
Handlebar clamp bolts	18	13
Steering stem		
1978-1980		
Clamp bolt	18	13
Head bolt	18	13
1981		
Clamp bolt	18	13
Head bolt	45	33
Locknut	30	22

Table 4 FRONT SUSPENSION TIGHTENING TORQUES (1980-1983 KZ440)

	N•m	ft.-lb.
Front axle nut	65	47
Front axle clamp nuts	20	14.5
Front fork		
Upper clamp bolts	20	14.5
Lower clamp bolts	30	22
Bottom Allen bolt	18	13
Handlebar clamp bolts	21	15
Steering stem		
Clamp bolt	20	14.5
Head bolt	55	40
Locknut	30	22

Table 5 FRONT SUSPENSION TIGHTENING TORQUES (1985-ON EN450)

	N•m	ft.-lb.
Front axle nut	88	65
Front fork		
Upper clamp bolts	20	14.5
Lower clamp bolts	25	18
Bottom Allen bolt	20	14.5
Handlebar clamp bolts	19	13.5
Steering stem head bolt	42	31
Steering stem locknut	39	29

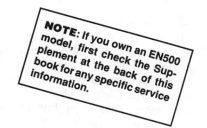
NOTE: If you own an EN500 model, first check the Supplement at the back of this book for any specific service information.

CHAPTER TWELVE

REAR SUSPENSION

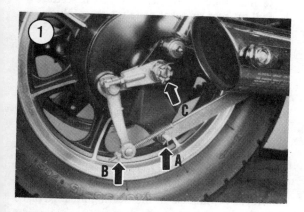

This chapter includes repair and replacement procedures for the rear wheel, drive chain, drive belt and rear suspension components.

Tables 1-7 are at the end of the chapter.

REAR WHEEL

Removal/Installation

1. Support the bike so that the rear wheel clears the ground.
2. Disconnect the torque link (A, **Figure 1**) at the rear brake. Then remove the rear brake adjuster nut (B, **Figure 1**).
3. Loosen the drive chain or drive belt adjusting locknuts and adjuster bolts (**Figure 2**).
4. Remove the cotter pin, rear axle nut and washer (C, **Figure 1**).
5. Slide the axle out of the wheel and allow the wheel to drop to the ground.
6. Remove the axle spacer.
7. Lift the drive chain or drive belt off of the sprocket and remove the rear wheel.
8. If the wheel is going to be off for any length of time, or if it is to be taken to a shop for repair, install the chain adjusters and axle spacers on the axle along with the axle nut to prevent losing any parts.

12

9. Install by reversing these removal steps, noting the following.
10. Adjust the drive chain or drive belt as described in Chapter Three.
11. Tighten the torque link nut securely. Secure the nut with a new cotter pin.
12. Tighten the axle nut to specifications in **Tables 4-7**. Secure the nut with a new cotter pin.
13. Adjust the rear brake as described in Chapter Three.
14. Spin the wheel several times to make sure it rotates freely and that the brakes work properly.

Inspection

Measure the axial and radial runout of the wheel with a dial indicator as shown in **Figure 3**. The maximum allowable axial runout is 0.5 mm (0.019 in.) and the radial runout is 0.8 mm (0.031 in). If the runout exceeds this dimension, check the wheel bearings. Some of this condition can be corrected on spoke wheels as described in Chapter Eleven. If the wheel bearings are in good condition on cast wheels and no other cause can be found, the wheel will have to be replaced as it cannot be serviced. Inspect the wheel for signs of cracks, fractures, dents or bends.

> *WARNING*
> *Do not try to repair any damage to cast wheels as it will result in an unsafe riding condition.*

REAR HUB

Bearing removal usually destroys the bearings. Check the bearings for wear while they are still installed in the hub. Replace any questionable bearings.

Disassembly/Inspection/ Reassembly (1974-1977 and 1977-1978 Deluxe A Models)

Refer to **Figure 4** for this procedure.
1. Using a long drift, drive out the bearing (2, **Figure 4**) by tapping evenly around its outer race. Remove the spacer (3).
2. Drive out the opposite bearing (5) in the same manner.
3. Clean the hub thoroughly in solvent and check for cracks or damage in the bearing area. Replace the hub if necessary.
4. Blow any dirt or foreign matter out of the hub before installing the bearings.
5. Pack non-sealed bearings with grease before installation. Sealed bearings do not require packing.

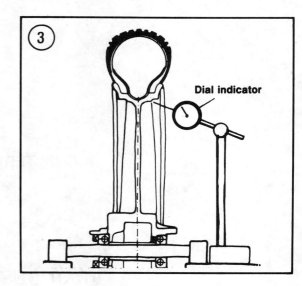

6. Tap the bearing (5) into position with a socket placed on the outer bearing race (**Figure 5**). Then install the spacer (3) and install the opposite bearing (2).

Disassembly/Inspection/ Reassembly (1978-on)

Refer to **Figure 6** (typical) for this procedure.
1. Pull the rear sprocket/coupling assembly or rear pulley/coupling assembly from the hub. See 3 and 8, **Figure 6**.
2. Remove the rubber damper (10).
3. Remove the circlip (24).
4. Insert a long drift punch from the right-hand side and remove the left-hand bearing (21). Tap evenly around the inner race so that the bearing will not get cocked in its bore during removal.
5. Remove the distance collar (11).
6. Turn the wheel over and repeat Step 4 to drive out the right-hand bearing (23).
7. Clean the hub thoroughly in solvent and check for cracks or damage in the bearing area. Replace the hub if necessary.
8. Blow any dirt or foreign matter out of the hub before installing the bearings.
9. Pack non-sealed bearings with grease before installation. Sealed bearings do not require packing.

> *NOTE*
> *Install the right-hand bearing (23) with the flush side facing outward.*

10. Tap the bearing (23) into position with a socket placed on the outer bearing race (**Figure 5**). Then install the distance collar (11) and install the opposite bearing (21).

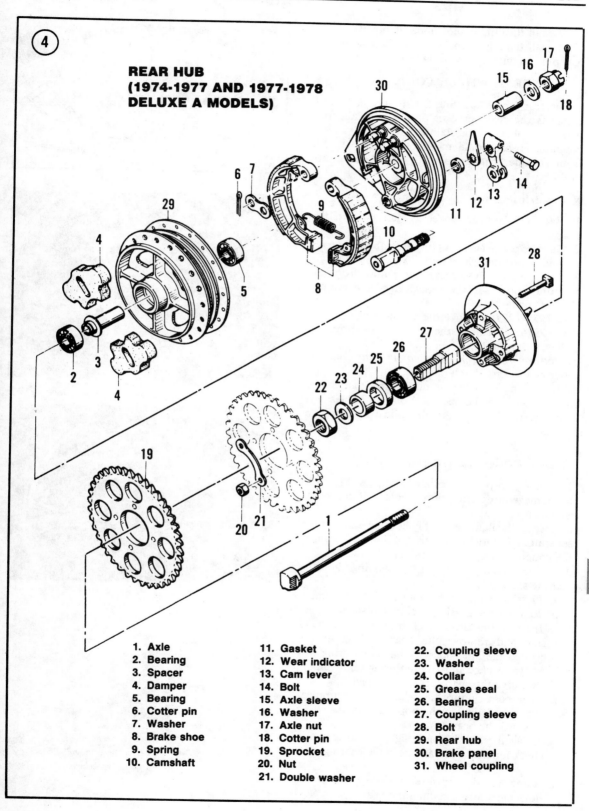

④

**REAR HUB
(1974-1977 AND 1977-1978
DELUXE A MODELS)**

1. Axle
2. Bearing
3. Spacer
4. Damper
5. Bearing
6. Cotter pin
7. Washer
8. Brake shoe
9. Spring
10. Camshaft

11. Gasket
12. Wear indicator
13. Cam lever
14. Bolt
15. Axle sleeve
16. Washer
17. Axle nut
18. Cotter pin
19. Sprocket
20. Nut
21. Double washer

22. Coupling sleeve
23. Washer
24. Collar
25. Grease seal
26. Bearing
27. Coupling sleeve
28. Bolt
29. Rear hub
30. Brake panel
31. Wheel coupling

11. Install the circlip and rubber damper.
12. Install the rear sprocket/coupling assembly or rear pulley/coupling assembly into the hub.

REAR WHEEL COUPLING

The rear wheel coupling (31, **Figure 4**, typical) connects the rear sprocket or pulley to the rear wheel. Rubber shock dampers installed in the coupling absorb some of the shock that results from torque changes during acceleration or braking.

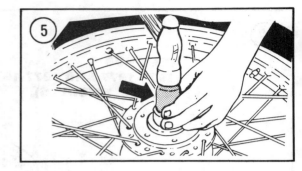

Removal/Installation

1. Remove the rear wheel as described in this chapter.
2. Pull the rear wheel coupling assembly (**Figure 7**) up and out of the wheel hub.
3. To remove the sprocket or pulley from the assembly, pry back the lockwashers and remove the nuts or bolts.
4A. *1974-1983:* Remove the sprocket.
4B. *1985-on:* Remove the cover and remove the pulley.
5. Perform *Inspection/Disassembly/Reassembly* as described in this chapter.
6. Install the sprocket or pulley and tighten the nuts or bolts to the specifications in **Tables 4-7**. Bend up the lockwasher tab against each nut to lock it.

Inspection/Disassembly/Reassembly

1. Visually inspect the rubber dampers (**Figure 8**) for damage or deterioration. Replace, if necessary, as a complete set.
2. Inspect the flange assembly housing and damper separators (**Figure 9**) for cracks or damage. Replace the coupling housing if necessary.
3. If necessary, replace the coupling housing bearing(s) as follows:

   a. Pry the seal from the housing, if so equipped.
   b. Remove the bearing circlip(s), if so equipped.
   c. Insert a long drift punch from the right-hand side and remove the bearing. Tap evenly around the inner race so that the bearing will not get cocked in its bore during removal.
   d. Remove the spacer, if so equipped.
   e. If necessary, turn the wheel over and repeat Sub-step c to drive out the opposite bearing.
   f. Discard the bearings.
   g. Clean the housing thoroughly in solvent and check for cracks or damage in the bearing area.

   h. Blow any dirt or foreign matter out of the housing before installing the bearings.

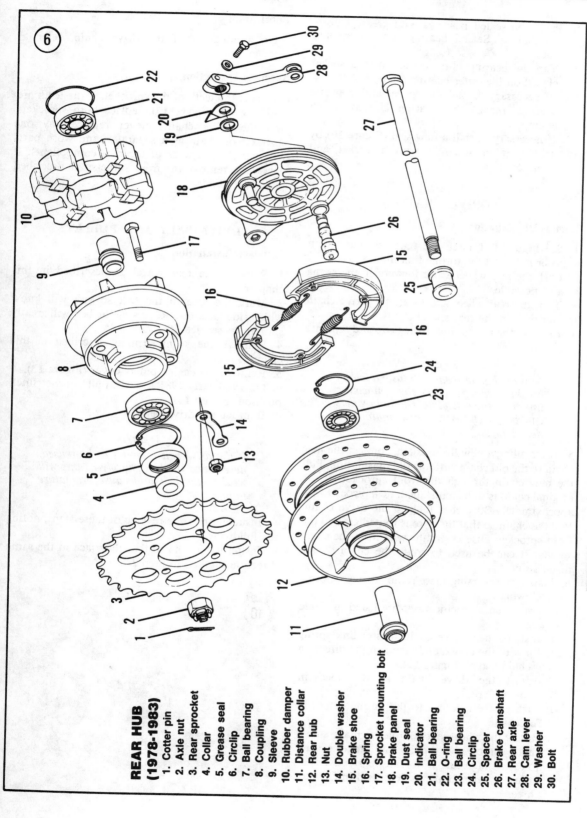

**REAR HUB
(1978-1983)**
1. Cotter pin
2. Axle nut
3. Rear sprocket
4. Collar
5. Grease seal
6. Circlip
7. Ball bearing
8. Coupling
9. Sleeve
10. Rubber damper
11. Distance collar
12. Rear hub
13. Nut
14. Double washer
15. Brake shoe
16. Spring
17. Sprocket mounting bolt
18. Brake panel
19. Dust seal
20. Indicator
21. Ball bearing
22. O-ring
23. Ball bearing
24. Circlip
25. Spacer
26. Brake camshaft
27. Rear axle
28. Cam lever
29. Washer
30. Bolt

12

i. Pack non-sealed bearings with grease before installation. Sealed bearings do not require packing.

j. Tap the bearing into position with a socket placed on the outer bearing race.

k. If necessary, install the spacer and opposite bearing. Install the bearing circlips, if so equipped.

l. If necessary, install a new seal (**Figure 10**) by driving it in squarely with a socket and hammer.

DRIVE CHAIN

Removal/Installation

1. See **Figure 1**. Loosen the rear axle nut, chain adjuster nuts and the torque link nut.
2. Push the rear wheel as far forward in the swing arm as possible.
3. Turn the rear wheel and locate the drive chain master link on the rear sprocket.
4. Remove the master link spring clip and separate the chain.

> *NOTE*
> *It may be necessary to use a chain breaking tool to press the connecting link from the side plate. Chain breakers can be purchased at most motorcycle dealerships.*

5. If installing a new drive chain, connect the new chain to the old chain with the old master link. Pull the new chain through the front sprocket. If the original chain is to be reinstalled, tie a piece of wire approximately 30 inches long to the drive chain. Pull the chain so that the wire is routed around the front sprocket. Disconnect the wire from the chain so that it can be used to route the chain during installation.
6. Install by reversing these removal steps, noting the following:

   a. Drive chain specifications are listed in **Table 2**.

   b. Install a new drive chain master link spring clip with the closed end facing in the direction of chain travel (**Figure 11**).

   c. Adjust the drive chain as described in Chapter Three.

   d. Tighten the axle nut to the torque values in **Tables 4-6**.

   e. Rotate the wheel several times to make sure it rotates smoothly. Apply the brake several times to make sure it operates correctly.

   f. Adjust the rear brake as described in Chapter Three.

Lubrication

For lubrication of the drive chain, refer to Chapter Three.

Sprocket Inspection

Inspect the teeth of the sprocket. If the teeth are visibly worn (**Figure 12**), replace both sprockets and the drive chain. Never replace any one sprocket or chain as a separate item; worn parts will cause rapid wear of the new components. If necessary, remove the front sprocket as described in Chapter Four.

DRIVE BELT AND PULLEYS

Removal/Installation

1. Remove the rear wheel as described in this chapter.
2. Mark the side of the belt so you will know which side faces out. Reversing the belt will greatly shorten its service life.
4. Remove the swing arm as described in this chapter.
5. Remove the engine pulley cover (**Figure 13**).
6. On 1980-early 1981 models, pull out the clutch pushrod (**Figure 14**).
7. Remove the drive belt.

> *CAUTION*
> *If the drive belt is going to be reused, never bend the belt sharply as this will weaken the belt and cause premature failure.*

8. Installation is the reverse of these steps, noting the following.
9. Install used belts so that they face in the same direction marked in Step 2.

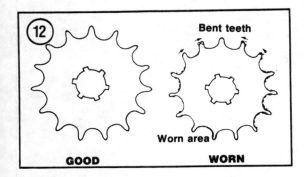

1. Master link
2. Clip opening

Bent teeth

Worn area

GOOD · WORN

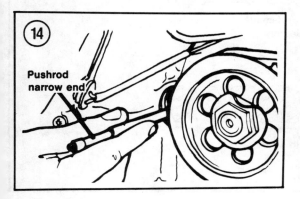

Pushrod narrow end

10. Install new belts with the marked edge facing inward, toward the rear wheel.

11. On 1980-early 1981 models, install the clutch pushrod with the narrow end pointing out.

12. Adjust the drive belt tension and alignment initially and after 500 miles, then according to the maintenance schedule in Chapter Three.

Front Pulley
Removal/Installation

1. Remove the engine pulley cover (**Figure 13**).

2. Loosen the rear axle as described under *Rear Wheel Removal/Installation*.

3. Push the rear wheel as far forward as it will go.

4. Remove the pulley holding plate bolts and remove the holding plate (A, **Figure 15**).

5. Remove the pulley (B, **Figure 15**).

6. Install by reversing these steps. Note the following.

7. Align the holding plate so that it locks the pulley when installed.

Inspection

1. Inspect the drive belt for wear or damage. Replace any belt that appears questionable (**Figure 16**). Also inspect the belt to see if the nylon facing of the belt teeth is worn through so that the underlying urethane compound is showing through at any point. If so, the belt must be replaced.

> *CAUTION*
> *When handling a drive belt, never bend the belt sharply as this will weaken the belt and cause premature failure.*

2. Whenever the drive belt is replaced, inspect the pulleys also.

12

⑯

DRIVE BELT INSPECTION

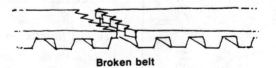

Broken belt

Missing teeth

Cracked teeth

Severe wear or
cracks on belt face

Belt wear or damage
on one side only

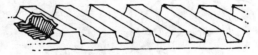

Tooth wear

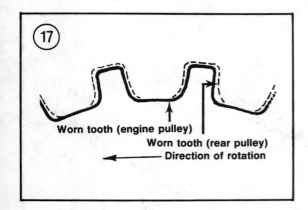

Worn tooth (engine pulley)
Worn tooth (rear pulley)
Direction of rotation

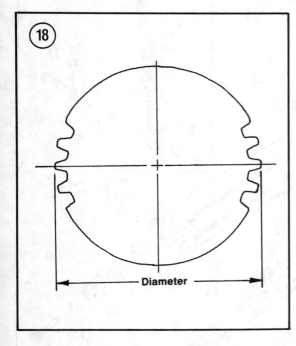

Diameter

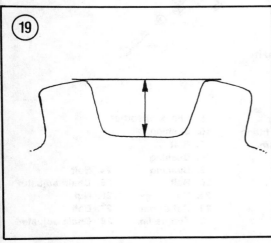

Pulley Inspection

1. Check the front and rear pulley for worn teeth as shown in **Figure 17**.
2. *Front pulley measurement:* On all models except 1985-on, measure the maximum diameter across the pulley teeth (**Figure 18**). Replace the pulley if it is worn smaller than the limits in **Table 3**. On 1985-on models, measure the pulley tooth height as shown in **Figure 19**. Replace the pulley if the tooth height is too short (**Table 3**).
3. *Rear pulley measurement:* Measure the maximum diameter across the pulley teeth (**Figure 18**). Replace the pulley if it is worn smaller than the limits in **Table 3**.

WHEEL BALANCING

For complete information refer to *Wheel Balancing* in Chapter Eleven.

TIRE CHANGING

Refer to Chapter Eleven.

REAR SWING ARM

Removal/Installation

Refer to **Figure 20**, **Figure 21** or **Figure 22** for this procedure.
1. Carefully remove the brake light switch spring from the tab on the brake pedal.
2. Remove the mufflers.
3. Remove the rear wheel as described in this chapter.
4. Remove both chain adjusters from the swing arm.
5. Remove both shock absorbers.
6. Remove the pivot shaft nut (**Figure 23**). Then remove the pivot shaft.
7. Pull the swing arm away from the motorcycle. The bearing caps may fall as the swing arm is removed.
8. Remove the drive chain or drive belt, if necessary.
9. Installation is the reverse of these steps, noting the following.
10. After installing the swing arm, use a grease gun to force grease into the fitting until it comes out at both sides.
11. Make sure to install the bearing caps on both sides of the swing arm before installation.
12. Tighten the pivot shaft nut to specifications (**Tables 4-7**).
13. Adjust the drive chain or belt and rear brake as described in Chapter Three.

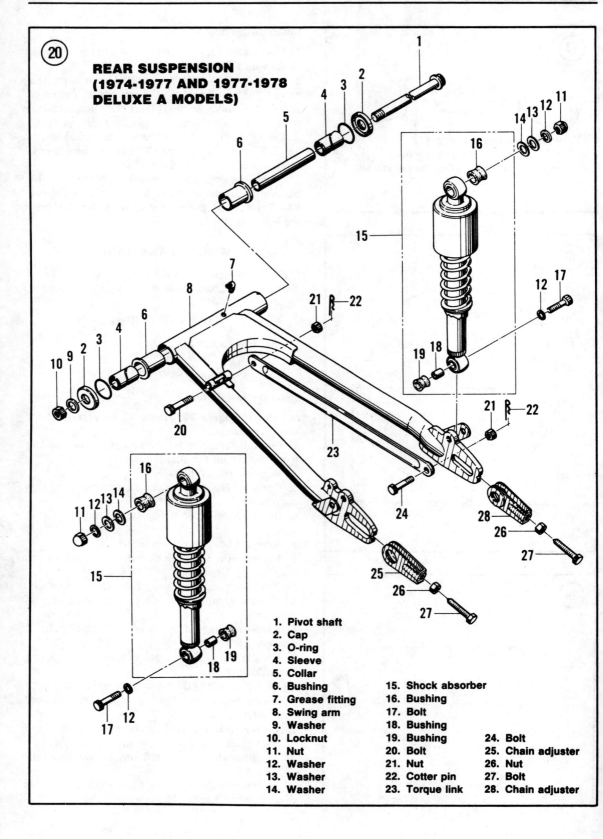

REAR SUSPENSION
(1974-1977 AND 1977-1978
DELUXE A MODELS)

1. Pivot shaft
2. Cap
3. O-ring
4. Sleeve
5. Collar
6. Bushing
7. Grease fitting
8. Swing arm
9. Washer
10. Locknut
11. Nut
12. Washer
13. Washer
14. Washer
15. Shock absorber
16. Bushing
17. Bolt
18. Bushing
19. Bushing
20. Bolt
21. Nut
22. Cotter pin
23. Torque link
24. Bolt
25. Chain adjuster
26. Nut
27. Bolt
28. Chain adjuster

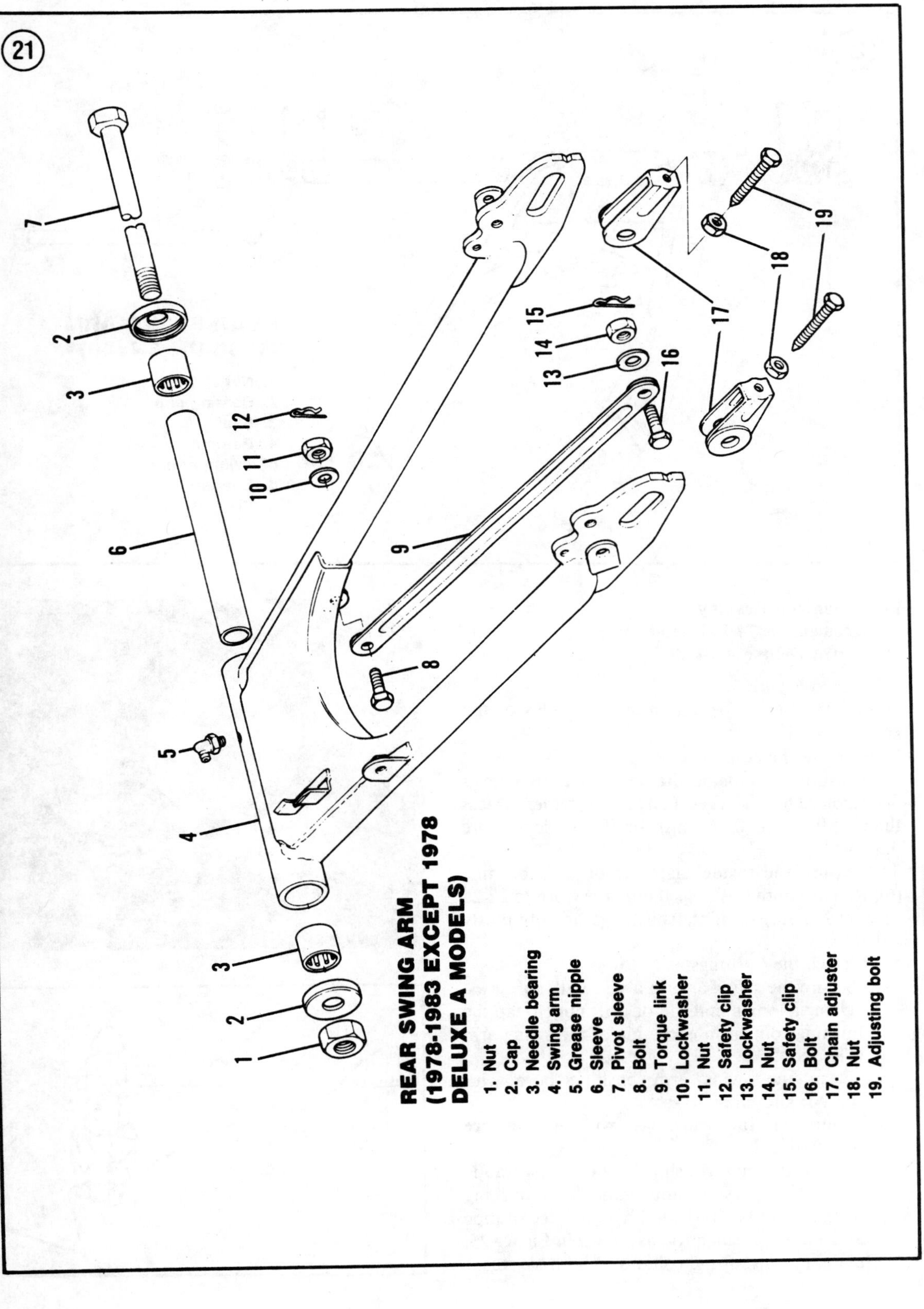

㉑

REAR SWING ARM
(1978-1983 EXCEPT 1978
DELUXE A MODELS)

1. Nut
2. Cap
3. Needle bearing
4. Swing arm
5. Grease nipple
6. Sleeve
7. Pivot sleeve
8. Bolt
9. Torque link
10. Lockwasher
11. Nut
12. Safety clip
13. Lockwasher
14. Nut
15. Safety clip
16. Bolt
17. Chain adjuster
18. Nut
19. Adjusting bolt

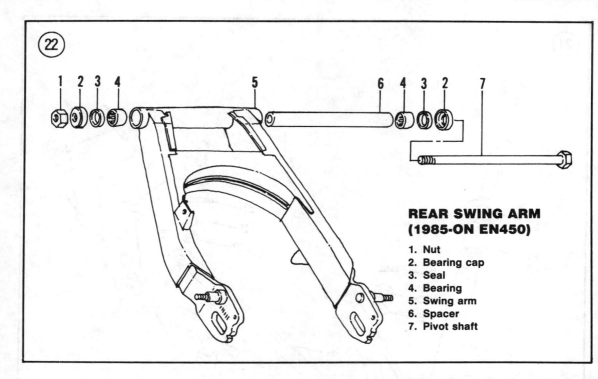

**REAR SWING ARM
(1985-ON EN450)**

1. Nut
2. Bearing cap
3. Seal
4. Bearing
5. Swing arm
6. Spacer
7. Pivot shaft

**Inspection and Bushing
Replacement (1974-1977 and
1977-1978 Deluxe A Model)**

Refer to **Figure 20**.

1. Pull the sleeve (4) out from both sides of the swing arm.

2. Remove the collar (5).

3. Measure the outside diameter of both sleeves (4). Replace both sleeves if any measurement is less than 21.95 mm (0.864 in.), or if the sleeves are damaged.

4. Measure the inside diameter of each bushing (6). Replace both bushings if either is worn to 22.26 mm (0.876 in.) or if the bushings are obviously defective.

5. Replace the bushings as follows:

  a. Secure the swing arm in a vise with soft jaws.

  b. Using a long metal rod or drift punch, tap the bushings out from each side of the swing arm (**Figure 24**).

  c. Clean the swing arm bushing bore with solvent and allow to dry.

  d. Lubricate the bushings with oil before installation.

  e. Install the new bushings with a hydraulic press. If a press is not available, a bushing installer can be fabricated with a piece of pipe and a long threaded rod as shown in **Figure 25**.

6. Grease and install the collar and both sleeves.

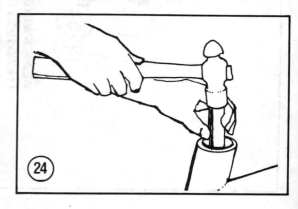

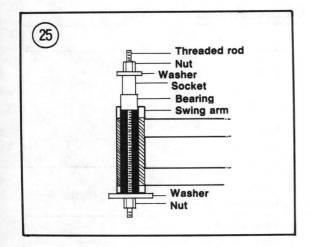

Threaded rod
Nut
Washer
Socket
Bearing
Swing arm

Washer
Nut

Inspection and Bearing Replacement (1978-on)

Refer to **Figure 21** or **Figure 22**.

1. The roller bearings wear very slowly and the wear is difficult to measure. Turn the bearings by hand. Make sure they rotate smoothly. Check the rollers for evidence of wear, pitting or color change indicating heat from lack of lubrication. In severe instances the needles will fall out of the bearing cage.

2. Replace the bearings as follows:

   a. Using a long metal rod or drift punch, tap one of the bearings out of the swing arm (**Figure 24**).

   b. Remove the center sleeve and remove the opposite bearing.

   c. Clean the swing arm bearing bore with solvent and allow to dry.

   d. Lubricate the bushings with oil before installation.

   e. Using a new bearings and a hydraulic press, install the first bearing. Install the center sleeve. Install the rest of the bearings. If a press is not available, a bearing installer can be fabricated with a piece of pipe and a long threaded rod as shown in **Figure 25**.

   CAUTION
   Never reinstall a needle bearing that has been removed. During removal it is damaged and is no longer true to alignment. If installed it will damage the sleeve and create an unsafe riding condition.

   f. Apply a coat of molybdenum disulfide grease to the inner needle bearing surfaces.

SHOCK ABSORBERS

The rear shocks are spring controlled and hydraulically damped. Spring preload can be adjusted on all models. Refer to Chapter Three.

Removal/Installation

This procedure is easier if the rear shocks are removed and installed one at a time. The remaining unit will support the rear of the bike and maintain the correct relationship between the top and bottom mounts. If both shock absorbers must be removed at the same time, cut a piece of metal a few inches longer than the shock absorber and drill two holes in the metal the same distance apart as the bolt holes in a shock absorber. Install the steel support after one shock absorber is removed. This will allow the bike to be easily moved around until the shock absorbers are reinstalled or replaced.

1. Place the bike on the centerstand.

2. Remove the upper and lower bolts or nuts (**Figure 26**).

3. Pull the shock off.

4. Install by reversing these removal steps. Torque the upper and lower bolts to the specifications listed in **Tables 4-7**.

Inspection

1. Check the rubber bushings. Replace them if they are worn, cracked, hardened or defective.

2. Compress each shock absorber fully. Resistance to compression should increase as you try to compress the unit faster. Likewise, resistance to extension should increase as you try to extend the unit faster. Replace both units if either does not perform as specified or if there is a noticeable difference in action between them.

3. Check each unit for oil leakage. Replace both units if either of them leaks.

Table 1 REAR SUSPENSION WEAR LIMITS (KZ400 AND KZ440)

	mm	ft.-lb.
Rim runout	2	0.078
Axle runout	0.7	0.027
Swing arm (1974-1977)		
Sleeve diameter	21.95	0.864
Bushing inside diameter	22.26	0.876
Pivot shaft runout	0.14	0.005
Swing arm (1978-1981 KZ400; KZ440)		
Sleeve diameter	21.96	0.864

Table 2 DRIVE CHAIN SPECIFICATIONS

Model	Number of links
KZ400	100
KZ440	
1980, A	104
1980-1982, B and C	100
1982-1983, H	102

Table 3 PULLEY DIAMETER WEAR LIMITS

	mm	in.
KZ440		
1980, D		
Front	95	3.740
Rear	264.0	10.393
1981-1983, D		
Front	103.85	4.088
Rear	286.25	11.269
EN450		
Front pulley tooth height	6.3	0.248
Rear pulley diameter	299.63	11.796

Table 4 REAR SUSPENSION TIGHTENING TORQUES
(1974-1977 AND 1977-1978 DELUXE A MODELS)

	N·m	ft.-lb.
Rear axle nut	100-140	72-101
Torque link nuts	26-35	19-25
Rear sprocket nuts	35-43	25-31
Shock absorber		
Bolts and cap nuts	26-35	19-25
Swing arm pivot shaft nut	60-100	43-72

Table 5 REAR SUSPENSION TIGHTENING TORQUES (1978-1981 KZ400)

	N·m	ft.-lb.
Rear axle nut	120	87
Rear shock absorber	30	22
Rear sprocket nuts	40	29
Swing arm pivot shaft nut	80	58

Table 6 REAR SUSPENSION TIGHTENING TORQUES (1980-1983 KZ440)

	N·m	ft.-lb.
Rear axle nut	75	54
Rear shock absorber	33	24
Rear sprocket/pulley nuts	33	24
Swing arm pivot shaft nut	90	65

Table 7 REAR SUSPENSION TIGHTENING TORQUES (1985-ON EN450)

	N·m	ft.-lb.
Rear axle nut	125	94
Rear shock absorber	See foot note	See foot note
Rear pulley nuts	88	65
Swing arm pivot shaft nut	88	65

* Not specified; see torque chart in Chapter One.

12

NOTE: If you own an EN500 model, first check the Supplement at the back of this book for any specific service information.

CHAPTER THIRTEEN

BRAKES

This chapter describes repair and replacement procedures for all brake components.

Refer to **Tables 1-4** for brake wear limits. **Tables 1-8** are found at the end of the chapter.

FRONT DISC BRAKES

The front disc brake is actuated by hydraulic fluid controlled by the hand lever on the right-hand side of the handlebar. As the brake pads wear, the brake fluid level drops in the master cylinder reservoir and automatically adjusts for pad wear. However, brake lever free play must be maintained. Refer to *Front Brake Lever Adjustment* in Chapter Three.

When working on a hydraulic brake system, it is necessary that the work area and all tools be absolutely clean. Any tiny particles of foreign matter or grit on the caliper assembly or the master cylinder can damage the components. Also, sharp tools must not be used inside the caliper or on the caliper piston. If there is any doubt about your ability to correctly and safely carry out major service on the brake components take the job to a Kawasaki dealer or brake specialist.

When adding brake fluid use only a type clearly marked DOT 3 and use it from a sealed container. Brake fluid will draw moisture which greatly reduces its ability to perform correctly, so it is a good idea to purchase brake fluid in small containers and discard what is not used.

Whenever *any* component has been removed from the brake system the system is considered "opened" and must be bled to remove air bubbles. Also, if the brake feels "spongy," this usually means there are air bubbles in the system and it must be bled. For safe brake operation, refer to *Bleeding the System* in this chapter for complete details.

> #### CAUTION
> *Disc brake components rarely require disassembly, so do not disassemble unless absolutely necessary. Do not use solvents of any kind on the brake system's internal components. Solvents will cause the seals to swell and distort. When disassembling and cleaning brake components, except brake pads, use new brake fluid.*

FRONT BRAKE PAD REPLACEMENT

There is no recommended mileage interval for changing the friction pads on the disc brakes. Pad wear depends greatly on riding habits and conditions. The pads should be checked for wear at specified intervals. See Chapter Three.

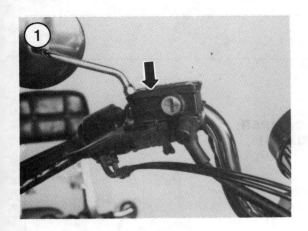

Service Notes

Observe the following service notes before replacing brake pads.

1. Brake pads should be replaced only as a set.
2. Disconnecting the hydraulic brake hose is not required for brake pad replacement. Disconnect the hose only if caliper removal is required.
3. When new pads are installed in the caliper, the master cylinder brake fluid level will rise as the caliper piston is repositioned. Clean the top of the master cylinder of all dirt and foreign matter. Remove the cap (**Figure 1**) and diaphragm. Then slowly push the caliper piston into the caliper. Constantly check the reservoir to make sure brake fluid does not overflow. Remove fluid, if necessary, before it overflows. The pistons should move freely. If they don't, and there is evidence of it sticking in the cylinder, the caliper should be removed and serviced as described under *Caliper Rebuilding* in this chapter.
4. Push the caliper piston in to allow room for the new pads.
5. Refill the master cylinder reservoir, if necessary, to maintain the correct fluid level. Install the diaphragm and top cap.

> *WARNING*
> *Use brake fluid clearly marked DOT 3 from a sealed container. Other types may vaporize and cause brake failure. Always use the same brand name; do not intermix brake fluids. Many brands are not compatible.*

> *WARNING*
> *Do not ride the motorcycle until you are sure the brake is operating correctly. If necessary, bleed the brake as described under* **Bleeding the System** *in this chapter.*

Pad Replacement
(1974-1979 Model D)

Refer to **Figure 2** for this procedure.
1. Remove the front wheel.
2. Remove the screw (19), lockwasher (18), plate (17) and pad (16).
3. Operate the brake hand lever several times to force out the pad (15).
4. Remove the cap (2) from the bleeder valve (3). Open valve slightly.
5. With the valve open, push in the piston (11) fully. Close the bleeder valve (3) and install the cap (2).

> *CAUTION*
> *Spilled brake fluid will damage painted surfaces. Wipe up any spills immediately.*

6. Align the projection on the new brake pad (15) with that on the shim (14).
7. Insert the pad and shim into the brake caliper (6).
8. Install the new brake pad (16) and plate (17). Apply a thread-locking cement to the screw (19).
9. Refill the brake fluid, if necessary, and replace the top cap. See *Service Notes*.

> *WARNING*
> *Use only brake fluid marked DOT 3 on its container. Use only fluid from a sealed container. Never reuse old brake fluid.*

10. Operate the hand lever to take up brake pad clearance, then recheck the fluid level. Replenish it if necessary.

Pad Replacement
(1974-1979 Model B)

Refer to **Figure 3** for this model.
1. Remove the 2 caliper mounting bolts, lockwashers and washers (**Figure 4**).
2. Push pad B (15) toward the piston then remove it from the caliper opening.
3. Slide pad A (14) toward the piston and remove it.
4. Slide the shim off of each pad. The anti-rattle spring will come out at the same time.
5. Clean the pad recess and the end of the piston with a soft brush. Do not use solvent, wire brush or any hard tool which would damage the cylinder or piston.
6. Lightly coat the end of the piston and the backs of the new pads, *not* the friction material, with disc brake lubricant.

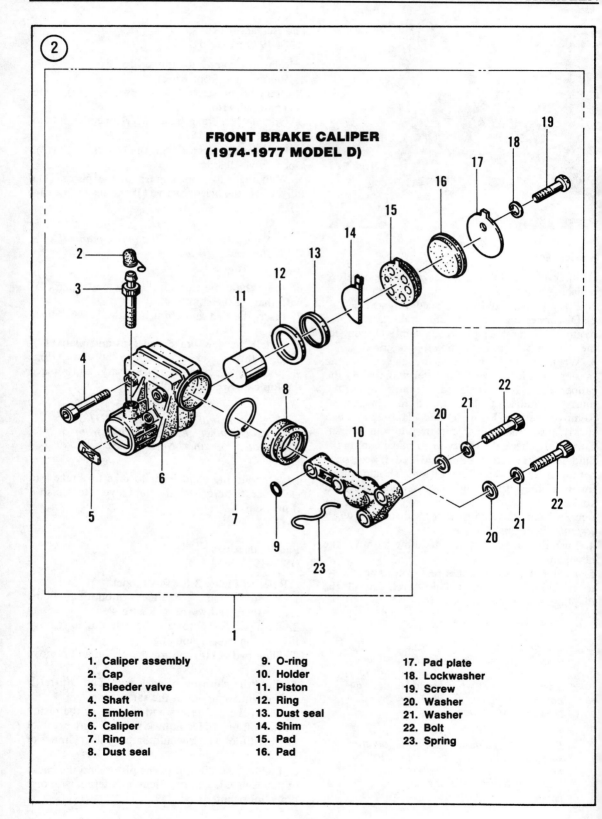

②

**FRONT BRAKE CALIPER
(1974-1977 MODEL D)**

1. Caliper assembly
2. Cap
3. Bleeder valve
4. Shaft
5. Emblem
6. Caliper
7. Ring
8. Dust seal

9. O-ring
10. Holder
11. Piston
12. Ring
13. Dust seal
14. Shim
15. Pad
16. Pad

17. Pad plate
18. Lockwasher
19. Screw
20. Washer
21. Washer
22. Bolt
23. Spring

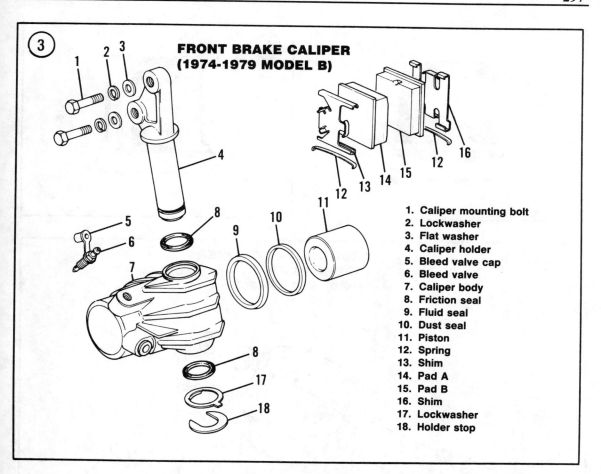

③ **FRONT BRAKE CALIPER (1974-1979 MODEL B)**

1. Caliper mounting bolt
2. Lockwasher
3. Flat washer
4. Caliper holder
5. Bleed valve cap
6. Bleed valve
7. Caliper body
8. Friction seal
9. Fluid seal
10. Dust seal
11. Piston
12. Spring
13. Shim
14. Pad A
15. Pad B
16. Shim
17. Lockwasher
18. Holder stop

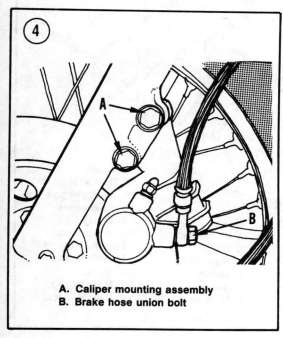

A. Caliper mounting assembly
B. Brake hose union bolt

7. Brake pads A and B and their respective shims have a long and short side. Place the anti-rattle spring into the long side of the shim and slide both the shim and spring onto the respective pad. Make sure to install the long side of the shim (and spring) onto the long side of the pad. For correct positioning, refer to **Figure 5** (pad A) or **Figure 6** (pad B).

NOTE
Pad A is the thicker of the two and pad B has a notch that indicates the usable pad thickness.

8. Install pad A on the piston side of the caliper.
9. Install pad B in the caliper.
10. Carefully install the caliper assembly onto the disc and install the caliper mounting bolts, flat washers and lockwashers. Tighten the bolts to 40 N•m (29 ft.-lb.).

13

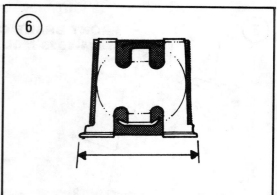

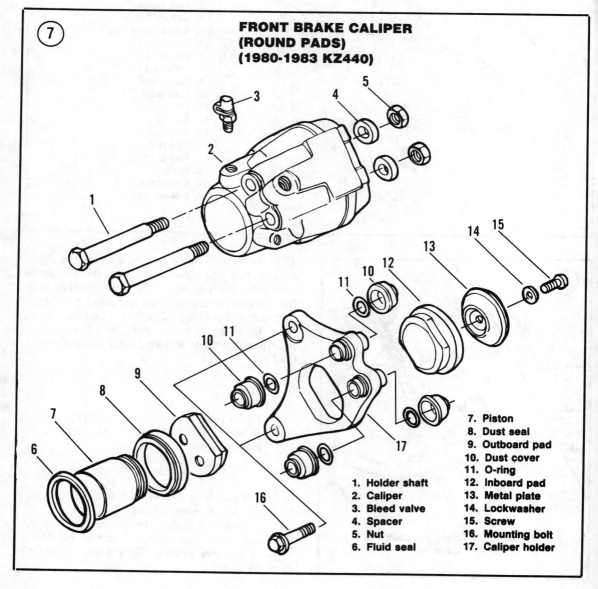

**FRONT BRAKE CALIPER
(ROUND PADS)
(1980-1983 KZ440)**

1. Holder shaft
2. Caliper
3. Bleed valve
4. Spacer
5. Nut
6. Fluid seal
7. Piston
8. Dust seal
9. Outboard pad
10. Dust cover
11. O-ring
12. Inboard pad
13. Metal plate
14. Lockwasher
15. Screw
16. Mounting bolt
17. Caliper holder

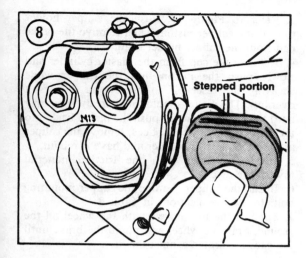

Stepped portion

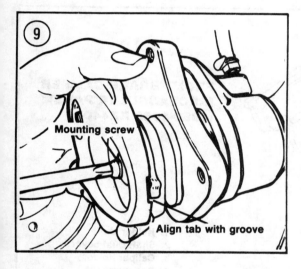

Mounting screw

Align tab with groove

2. Remove the screw, lockwasher and plate securing the inboard pad (12).

3. Remove the inboard pad (12).

4. Slide the caliper holder toward the bleed valve and remove the outboard pad (9).

NOTE
If the pad won't come out, squeeze the brake lever a few times until the piston pushes the pad out.

5. Remove the cap from the master cylinder and slowly push the piston into the caliper while checking the reservoir to make sure it doesn't overflow. The piston should move freely. You may need to use a C-clamp to push the piston back into the caliper. If the piston sticks, remove the caliper as described in this chapter and have it rebuilt.

6. Install the outboard pad against the caliper piston, with the stepped side of the pad toward the disc (**Figure 8**).

7. Install the inboard pad, aligning the tab on the pad with the groove in the caliper (**Figure 9**). Use Loctite 242 (blue) on the mounting screw threads.

8. Install the caliper. Torque the caliper mounting bolts as specified in **Table 6** or **Table 7**.

9. Support the motorcycle with the front wheel off the ground. Spin the front wheel and pump the brake lever until the pads are seated against the disc.

10. Refill the brake fluid if necessary and replace the top cap. See *Service Notes*.

WARNING
Do not ride the bike until you are sure that the brake is operating correctly with full hydraulic advantage. If necessary, bleed the brakes as described in this chapter.

Pad Replacement
(1980-1983 Rectangular Pads)

Refer to **Figure 10** for this procedure.

1. Remove the 2 caliper shaft bolts and lift the caliper off the pad holder.

2. Remove the brake pads.

3. Remove the cap from the master cylinder and slowly push the piston into the caliper while checking the reservoir to make sure it doesn't overflow. The piston should move freely. You may need to use a C-clamp to push the piston back into the caliper. If the piston sticks, remove the caliper and rebuild it as described in this chapter.

4. Make sure the brake pad guides are in place.

5. Install the pads with the friction material toward the disc.

6. Install the caliper. Torque the caliper mounting bolts to the specifications in **Table 6** or **Table 7**.

11. Block the motorcycle up so that the front wheel is off the ground. Spin the front wheel and activate the brake lever for as many times as it takes to refill the cylinder in the caliper and correctly locate the pads.

12. Refill the brake fluid, if necessary, and replace the top cap. See *Service Notes*.

WARNING
Do not ride the bike until you are sure that the brake is operating correctly with full hydraulic advantage. If necessary, bleed the brakes as described in this chapter.

Pad Replacement
(1980-1983 Round Pads)

Refer to **Figure 7** for this procedure.

1. Remove the 2 caliper mounting bolts and lift the caliper off of the brake disc.

13

7. Support the motorcycle with the wheel off the ground. Spin the wheel and pump the brake until the pads are seated against the disc.

8. Refill the brake fluid, if necessary, and replace the top cap. See *Service Notes*.

WARNING
Do not ride the motorcycle until you are sure the brakes are working correctly.

Pad Replacement
(1985-on)

Refer to **Figure 11**.

1. Remove the 2 caliper bolts and lift the caliper off the pad holder (A, **Figure 12**).

2. Remove the brake pad next to the caliper piston.

3. Refer to **Figure 13**. Push the caliper holder toward the caliper piston. Then remove the brake pad from the caliper holder shaft.

4. Remove the cap from the master cylinder and slowly push the piston into the caliper while checking the reservoir to make sure it doesn't overflow. The piston should move freely. You may need to use a C-clamp to push the piston back into the caliper. If the piston sticks, remove the caliper as described in this chapter and have it rebuilt.

5. Install the pads with the friction material toward the disc.

6. Install the caliper. Torque the caliper mounting bolts to the specifications in **Table 8**.

7. Support the motorcycle with the wheel off the ground. Spin the wheel and pump the brake until the pads are seated against the disc.

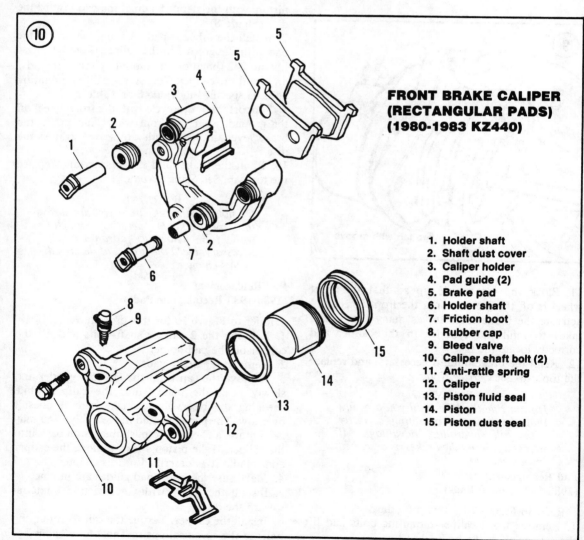

**FRONT BRAKE CALIPER
(RECTANGULAR PADS)
(1980-1983 KZ440)**

1. Holder shaft
2. Shaft dust cover
3. Caliper holder
4. Pad guide (2)
5. Brake pad
6. Holder shaft
7. Friction boot
8. Rubber cap
9. Bleed valve
10. Caliper shaft bolt (2)
11. Anti-rattle spring
12. Caliper
13. Piston fluid seal
14. Piston
15. Piston dust seal

8. Refill the brake fluid, if necessary, and replace the top cap. See *Service Notes*.

> *WARNING*
> *Do not ride the motorcycle until you are sure the brakes are working correctly.*

FRONT CALIPER

Removal/Installation

1. Drain the master cylinder as follows:
   a. Attach a hose to the brake caliper bleed screw (B, **Figure 12**).
   b. Place the end of the hose in a clean container (**Figure 14**).

c. Open the bleed screw (B, **Figure 12**) and operate the brake lever to drain all brake fluid from the master cylinder reservoir.
d. Close the bleed screw and disconnect the hose.
e. Discard the brake fluid.

2. Remove the front wheel as described in Chapter Eleven.

3. Remove the union bolt and copper sealing washers attaching the brake hose to the caliper. Cap the end of the brake hose and tie it up to the fender. Be sure to cap or tape the ends to prevent the entry of moisture and dirt.

4. Remove the bolt(s) securing the caliper assembly to the lower fork leg and remove it. See A, **Figure 12**, typical.

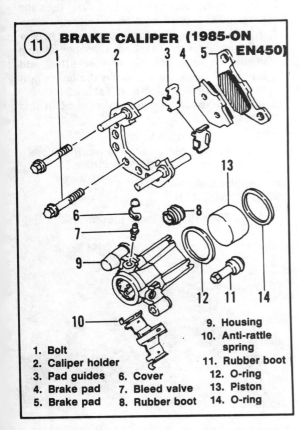

BRAKE CALIPER (1985-ON EN450)

1. Bolt
2. Caliper holder
3. Pad guides
4. Brake pad
5. Brake pad
6. Cover
7. Bleed valve
8. Rubber boot
9. Housing
10. Anti-rattle spring
11. Rubber boot
12. O-ring
13. Piston
14. O-ring

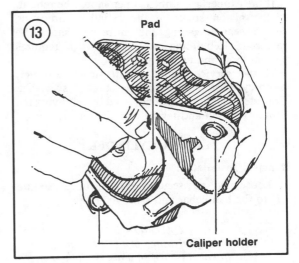

Pad

Caliper holder

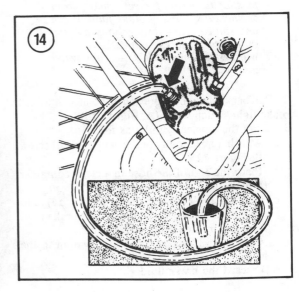

13

5. Installation is the reverse of these steps, noting the following:

    a. Torque the caliper attaching bolts to specifications in **Tables 5-8**.

    b. Install the brake hose using new copper washers.

    c. Tighten the brake hose union bolt to specifications in **Tables 5-8**.

    d. Bleed the brakes as described in this chapter.

WARNING
Do not ride the motorcycle until you are sure that the brakes are operating properly.

Caliper Rebuilding

If the caliper leaks, the caliper should be rebuilt. If the piston sticks in the cylinder, indicating severe wear or galling, the entire unit should be replaced. Rebuilding a leaky caliper requires special tools and experience.

Caliper service should be entrusted to a dealer, motorcycle repair shop or brake specialist. Considerable money can be saved by removing the caliper yourself and taking it in for repair.

MASTER CYLINDER

Removal/Installation

1. Loosen the nut securing the mirror (A, **Figure 15**) to the handlebar and remove it.

CAUTION
Cover the fuel tank, front fender and instrument cluster with a heavy cloth or plastic tarp to protect them from accidental spilling of brake fluid. Wash any spilled brake fluid off any painted or plated surfaces immediately, as it will destroy the finish. Use soapy water and rinse completely.

2. Pull back the rubber boot and disconnect the front brake light switch wires (A, **Figure 16**).

3. Drain the master cylinder as follows:

    a. Attach a hose to the brake caliper bleed screw (B, **Figure 12**).

    b. Place the end of the hose in a clean container (**Figure 14**).

    c. Open the bleed screw (B, **Figure 12**) and operate the brake lever to drain all brake fluid from the master cylinder reservoir.

    d. Close the bleed screw and disconnect the hose.

    e. Discard the brake fluid.

4. Remove the union bolt securing the brake hose to the master cylinder (B, **Figure 16**). Remove the brake hose and both copper sealing washers. Cover the end of the hose to prevent the entry of foreign matter and moisture. Tie the hose end up to the handlebar to prevent the loss of brake fluid.

5. Remove the front brake lever, if necessary.

6. Remove the 2 clamping bolts and clamp securing the master cylinder (B, **Figure 15**) to the handlebar. Remove the master cylinder.

7. Install by reversing these removal steps, noting the following:

    a. Install the master cylinder clamp with the arrow facing upward, if so marked.

    b. Tighten the upper clamp bolt first, then the lower bolt. Tighten both bolts securely.

    c. Install the brake hose onto the master cylinder. Be sure to place a copper sealing washer on each side of the hose fitting and install the union bolt. Tighten the union bolt to the specification listed in **Tables 5-8**.

    d. Bleed the brake system as described in this chapter.

WARNING
Do not ride the motorcycle until the front brake is operating correctly.

Disassembly/Assembly
(1974-1977 Model D)

Refer to **Figure 17** for these procedures.

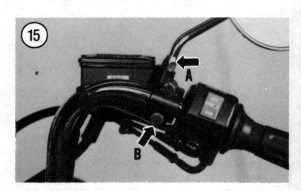

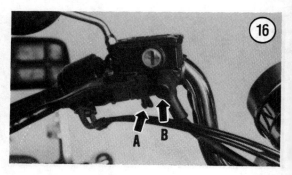

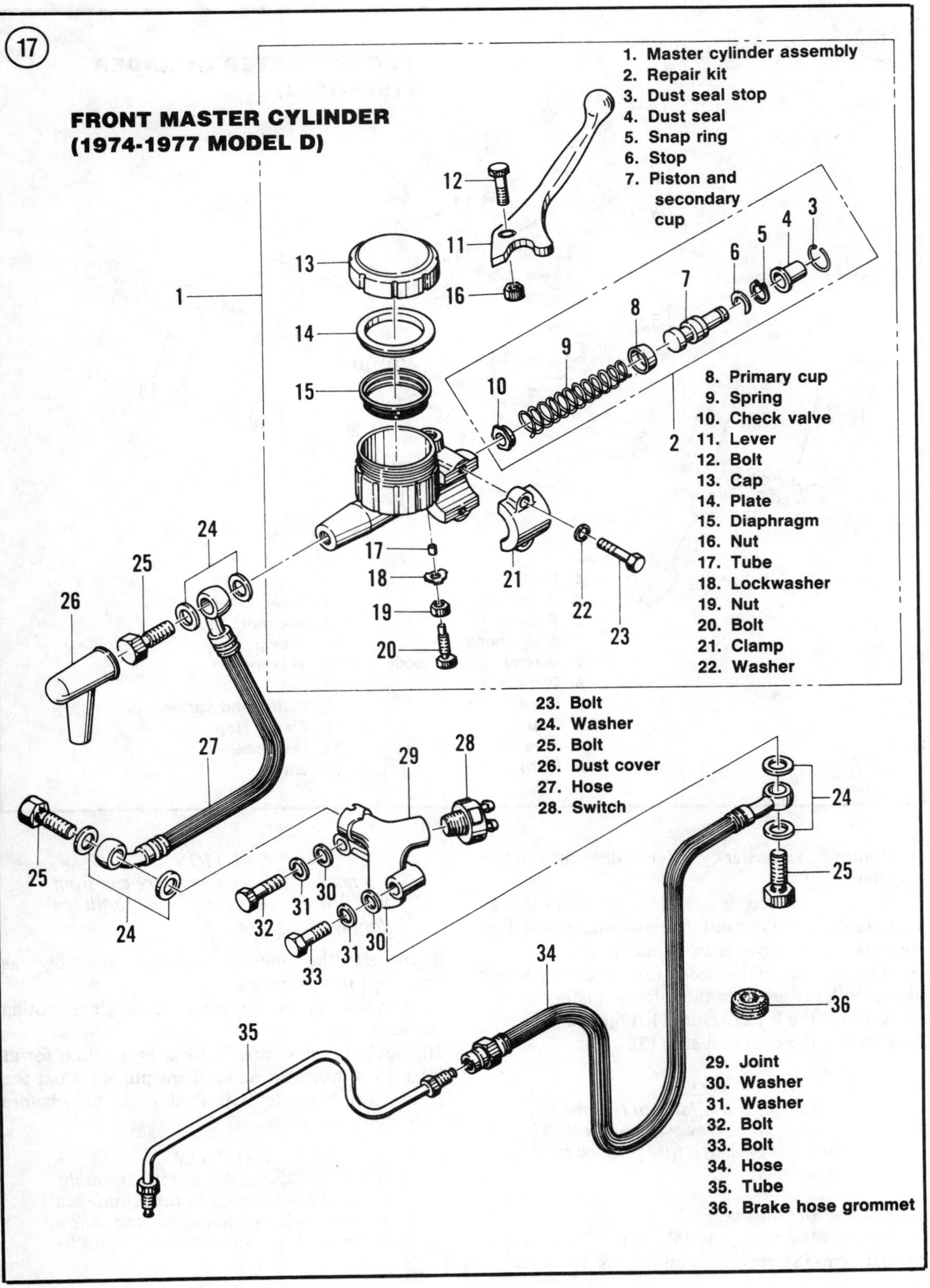

⑰

**FRONT MASTER CYLINDER
(1974-1977 MODEL D)**

1. Master cylinder assembly
2. Repair kit
3. Dust seal stop
4. Dust seal
5. Snap ring
6. Stop
7. Piston and secondary cup
8. Primary cup
9. Spring
10. Check valve
11. Lever
12. Bolt
13. Cap
14. Plate
15. Diaphragm
16. Nut
17. Tube
18. Lockwasher
19. Nut
20. Bolt
21. Clamp
22. Washer
23. Bolt
24. Washer
25. Bolt
26. Dust cover
27. Hose
28. Switch
29. Joint
30. Washer
31. Washer
32. Bolt
33. Bolt
34. Hose
35. Tube
36. Brake hose grommet

13

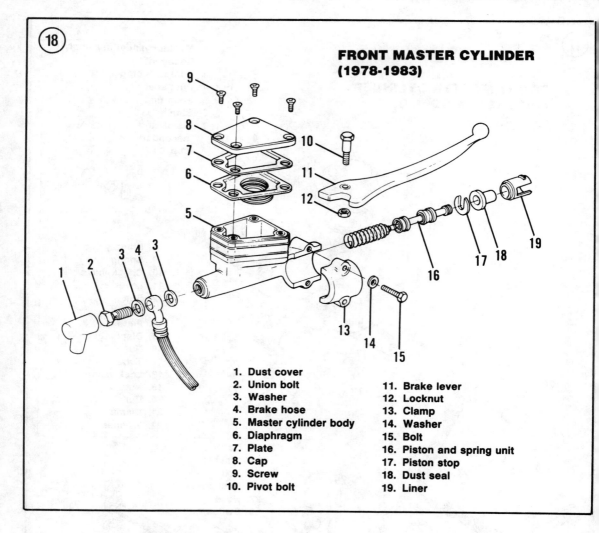

(18)

**FRONT MASTER CYLINDER
(1978-1983)**

1. Dust cover
2. Union bolt
3. Washer
4. Brake hose
5. Master cylinder body
6. Diaphragm
7. Plate
8. Cap
9. Screw
10. Pivot bolt
11. Brake lever
12. Locknut
13. Clamp
14. Washer
15. Bolt
16. Piston and spring unit
17. Piston stop
18. Dust seal
19. Liner

1. Remove the master cylinder as described in this chapter.

2. Remove the screws securing the reservoir cap and diaphragm. Pour out the remaining brake fluid and discard it. *Never* reuse brake fluid.

3. Remove the rubber boot from the area where the hand lever actuates the internal piston.

4. Remove the brake lever (11, **Figure 17**).

5. Remove the dust seal stop (3).

NOTE
A special tool is available to remove the dust seal stop. However, a piece of welding rod or heavy wire may be bent to do the job.

6. Remove the dust seal (4).

7. Remove the snap ring (5), stop (6), piston (7), primary cup (8), spring (9) and check valve (10).

CAUTION
Do not remove the secondary cup from the piston. Doing so will result in damage.

8. Inspect the master cylinder assembly as described in this chapter.

9. Assembly is the reverse of these steps, noting the following.

10. Soak the new caps in fresh brake fluid for at least 15 minutes to make them pliable. Coat the inside of the cylinder with fresh brake fluid before assembling the parts.

CAUTION
When installing the piston assembly, do not allow the cups to turn inside out as they will be damaged and allow brake fluid to leak within the cylinder bore.

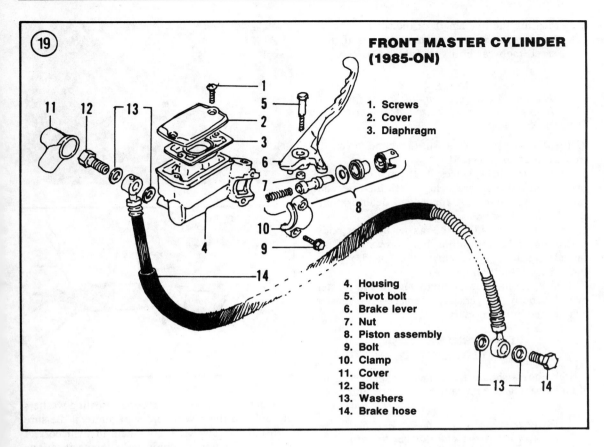

FRONT MASTER CYLINDER (1985-ON)

1. Screws
2. Cover
3. Diaphragm
4. Housing
5. Pivot bolt
6. Brake lever
7. Nut
8. Piston assembly
9. Bolt
10. Clamp
11. Cover
12. Bolt
13. Washers
14. Brake hose

Disassembly/Reassembly (1978-on)

Refer to **Figure 18** (1978-1983) or **Figure 19** (1985-on).

1. Remove the master cylinder as described in this chapter.

2. Remove the screws securing the reservoir cap and diaphragm. Pour out the remaining brake fluid and discard it. *Never* reuse brake fluid.

3. Remove the rubber boot from the area where the hand lever acuates the internal piston.

4. Remove the brake lever.

5. Use a small-bladed screwdriver to press the locking tabs on the liner and remove the liner.

6. Remove the piston assembly in the order shown in Figure 18 or **Figure 19**.

7. Inspect the master cylinder assembly as described in this chapter.

8. Assembly is the reverse of these steps. Note the following.

9. Soak the new caps in fresh brake fluid for at least 15 minutes to make them pliable. Coat the inside of the cylinder with fresh brake fluid before assembling the parts.

CAUTION
When installing the piston assembly, do not allow the cups to turn inside out as they will be damaged and allow brake fluid to leak within the cylinder bore.

10. Install the master cylinder piston assembly in the order shown in **Figure 18** or **Figure 19**. Make sure the liner is firmly seated in the groove in the cylinder.

Inspection

1. Clean all parts in fresh brake fluid. Inspect the cylinder bore and piston contact surfaces for signs of wear or damage. If either part is less than perfect, replace it.

2. Check the end of the piston for wear caused by the hand lever. Replace the entire piston assembly if any portion of it requires replacement.

3. On 1974-1983 models, use a micrometer and vernier caliper and perform the following checks:
   a. Measure the master cylinder bore.
   b. Measure the piston diameter.
   c. Measure the primary cup diameter.
   d. Measure the secondary cup diameter.

13

e. Measure the free length of the spring.

f. Replace any worn or damaged parts if they exceed the wear limits in **Tables 1-3**.

NOTE
The service specifications in Step 3 for 1985 and later models are not specified by Kawasaki.

4. Inspect the pivot hole in the hand lever. If worn, it must be replaced.

5. Make sure the passages in the bottom of the brake fluid reservoir are clear. Check the reservoir cap and diaphragm for damage and deterioration. Replace if necessary.

6. Inspect the threads in the master cylinder body where the brake hose union bolt screws in. If the threads are damaged or partially stripped, replace the master cylinder body.

7. Check the hand lever pivot lug on the master cylinder body for cracks. Replace the master cylinder body if necessary.

FRONT BRAKE HOSE REPLACEMENT

Brake hoses should be replaced whenever signs of cracking, leakage or damage are apparent.

CAUTION
Cover the front wheel, fender and fuel tank with a heavy cloth or plastic tarp to protect it from the accidental spilling of brake fluid. Wash any spilled brake fluid off of any painted or plated surface immediately, as it will destroy the finish. Use soapy water and rinse completely.

1. Drain the master cylinder as follows:

   a. Attach a hose to the brake caliper bleed screw (B, **Figure 12**).

   b. Place the end of the hose in a clean container (**Figure 14**).

   c. Open the bleed screw (B, **Figure 12**) and operate the brake lever to drain all brake fluid from the master cylinder reservoir.

   d. Close the bleed screw and disconnect the hose.

   e. Discard the brake fluid.

2. Remove the union bolt and copper sealing washers securing the brake hose to the caliper and remove it. See A, **Figure 20**.

3. Disconnect the hose from clamp on the fork (B, **Figure 20**).

4. Remove the union bolt (**Figure 16**) securing the hose to the master cylinder.

5. Remove the brake hoses.

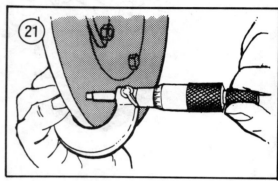

6. Install new brake hoses, copper sealing washers and bolts in the reverse order of removal. Be sure to install the new sealing washers in their correct positions. Tighten all union bolts to specifications in **Tables 5-8**.

7. Refill the master cylinder with fresh brake fluid clearly marked DOT 3. Bleed the brake as described in this chapter.

WARNING
Do not ride the motorcycle until you are sure that the brakes are operating properly.

FRONT BRAKE DISC

Removal/Installation

1. Remove the front wheel as described in this chapter.

NOTE
Place a piece of wood in the caliper in place of the disc. This way, if the brake lever is inadvertently squeezed, the piston will not be forced out of the cylinder. If this does happen, the caliper might have to be disassembled to reseat the piston and the system will have to be bled. By using the wood, bleeding the system is not necessary when installing the wheel.

2. If equipped with lockwashers, straighten the locktabs on the lockwashers.
3. Remove the bolts securing the disc to the wheel.
4. Install by reversing these removal steps. Install the bolts and tighten to specifications in **Tables 5-8**. Install new lockwashers (if so equipped) and bend over the locktabs after the bolts are tightened.

Inspection

It is not necessary to remove the disc from the wheel to inspect it. Small marks on the disc are not important, but deep radial scratches, deep enough to snag a fingernail, reduce braking effectiveness and increase brake pad wear. If these grooves are found, the disc should be resurfaced or replaced.
1. Measure the thickness around the disc at several locations with a vernier caliper or micrometer (**Figure 21**). The disc must be replaced if the thickness at any point is less than specified in **Tables 1-4**.
2. Make sure the disc bolts are tight before performing this check. Check the disc runout with a dial indicator as shown in **Figure 22**. Slowly rotate the wheel and watch the dial indicator. If the runout is 0.3 mm (0.012 in.) or greater, the disc must be replaced.
3. Clean the disc of any rust or corrosion and wipe clean with lacquer thinner. Never use an oil based solvent that may leave a oil residue on the disc.

DRUM BRAKES

Some KZ400 and KZ440 models are equipped with front drum brakes. All models are equipped with rear drum brakes.

Front Drum Brake
Disassembly/Reassembly

Refer to **Figure 23** (1974-1977 and 1977-1978 Deluxe A models) or **Figure 24** (1978-1981).
1. Remove the front wheel as described in Chapter Eleven.
2. Pull the brake assembly straight up and out of the brake drum.

> *NOTE*
> *Before performing Step 3, mark the left and right shoe. If the shoes are to be reused, they must be installed in their original positions.*

3. Protect the brake shoes with a clean shop cloth. Then pull the brake shoes (**Figure 25**) and springs up and off the guide pins and camshaft.
4. Remove the return springs and separate the shoes. If the shoes will be reused, place a clean shop rag around the linings to protect them from oil and grease.
5. If necessary, remove the camshafts as follows:
   a. Mark the position of the cam lever on the camshaft so that it may be installed at the same angle.
   b. Remove the cam levers, return spring, wear indicator, washer and gasket.
   c. Pull the camshafts out of the brake panel.
6. To remove the speedometer pinion gear, perform the following:
   a. Unscrew the speedometer pinion gear bushing.
   b. Remove the pinion gear and washers.
7. Assemble the brake by reversing the disassembly steps, noting the following.
8. Grease the camshaft and anchor posts with a light coat of molybdenum disulfide grease; avoid getting any grease on the brake plate where the linings come in contact with it.
9. When installing the brake arm onto the brake camshaft, be sure to align the punch marks on the brake lever and housing and to tighten the bolt securely.
10. Insert the brake panel assembly into the brake drum.
11. Install the front wheel as described in Chapter Eleven.
12. Adjust the front brake as described in Chapter Three.

Rear Drum Brake
Removal/Installation

Refer to **Figure 26**, **Figure 27** or **Figure 28**.
1. Remove the rear wheel as described in Chapter Twelve.

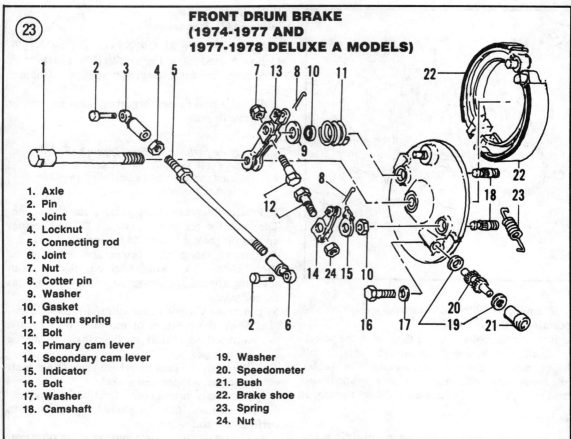

**FRONT DRUM BRAKE
(1974-1977 AND
1977-1978 DELUXE A MODELS)**

1. Axle
2. Pin
3. Joint
4. Locknut
5. Connecting rod
6. Joint
7. Nut
8. Cotter pin
9. Washer
10. Gasket
11. Return spring
12. Bolt
13. Primary cam lever
14. Secondary cam lever
15. Indicator
16. Bolt
17. Washer
18. Camshaft
19. Washer
20. Speedometer
21. Bush
22. Brake shoe
23. Spring
24. Nut

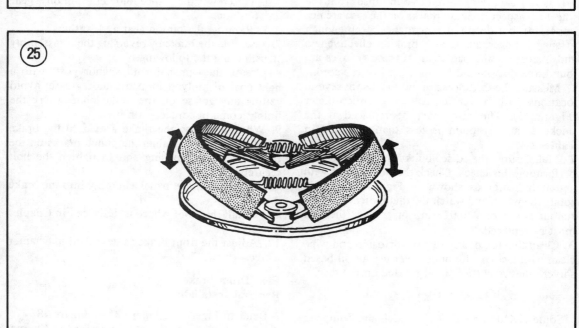

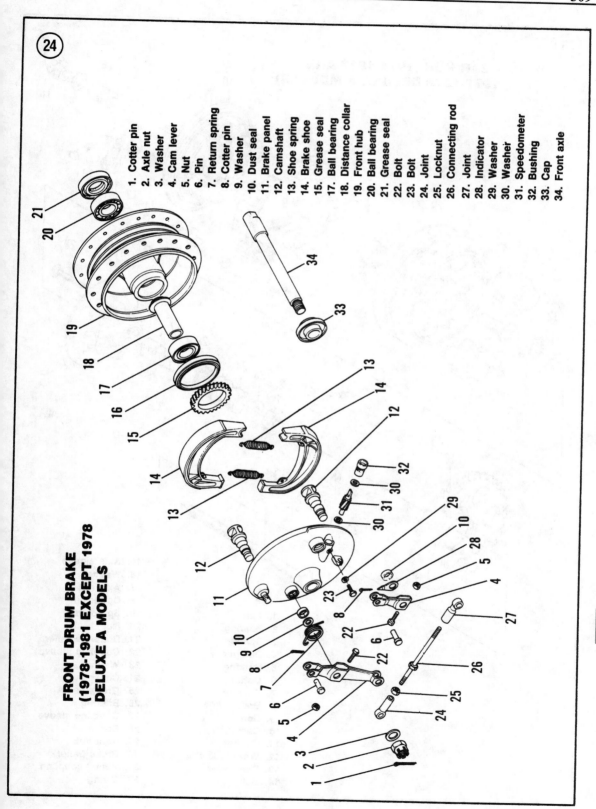

**FRONT DRUM BRAKE
(1978-1981 EXCEPT 1978
DELUXE A MODELS**

1. Cotter pin
2. Axle nut
3. Washer
4. Cam lever
5. Nut
6. Pin
7. Return spring
8. Cotter pin
9. Washer
10. Dust seal
11. Brake panel
12. Camshaft
13. Shoe spring
14. Brake shoe
15. Grease seal
17. Ball bearing
18. Distance collar
19. Front hub
20. Ball bearing
21. Grease seal
22. Bolt
23. Bolt
24. Joint
25. Locknut
26. Connecting rod
27. Joint
28. Indicator
29. Washer
30. Washer
31. Speedometer
32. Bushing
33. Cap
34. Front axle

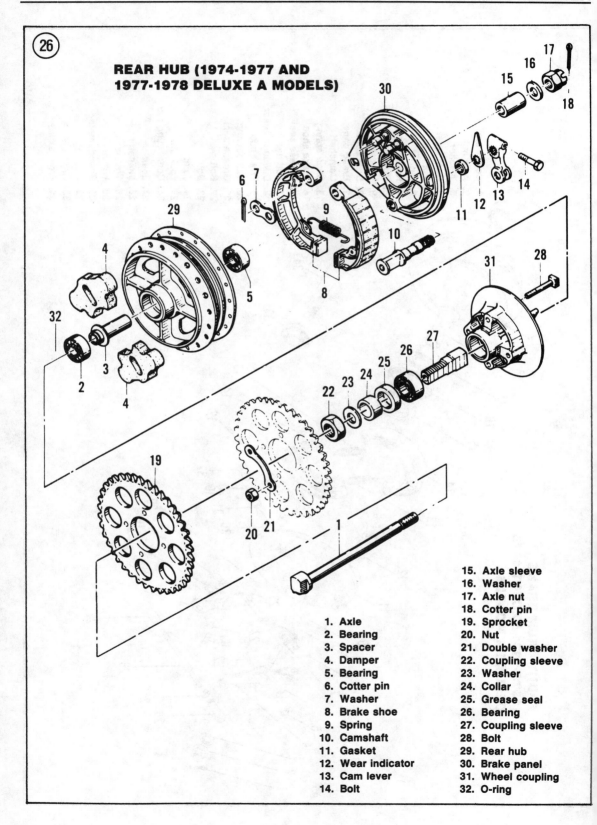

**REAR HUB (1974-1977 AND
1977-1978 DELUXE A MODELS)**

1. Axle
2. Bearing
3. Spacer
4. Damper
5. Bearing
6. Cotter pin
7. Washer
8. Brake shoe
9. Spring
10. Camshaft
11. Gasket
12. Wear indicator
13. Cam lever
14. Bolt
15. Axle sleeve
16. Washer
17. Axle nut
18. Cotter pin
19. Sprocket
20. Nut
21. Double washer
22. Coupling sleeve
23. Washer
24. Collar
25. Grease seal
26. Bearing
27. Coupling sleeve
28. Bolt
29. Rear hub
30. Brake panel
31. Wheel coupling
32. O-ring

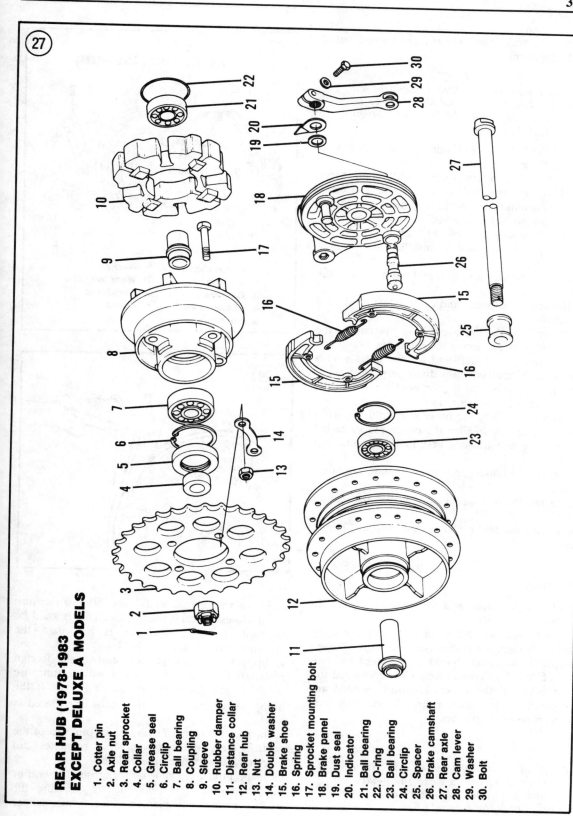

㉗

REAR HUB (1978-1983 EXCEPT DELUXE A MODELS

1. Cotter pin
2. Axle nut
3. Rear sprocket
4. Collar
5. Grease seal
6. Circlip
7. Ball bearing
8. Coupling
9. Sleeve
10. Rubber damper
11. Distance collar
12. Rear hub
13. Nut
14. Double washer
15. Brake shoe
16. Spring
17. Sprocket mounting bolt
18. Brake panel
19. Dust seal
20. Indicator
21. Ball bearing
22. O-ring
23. Ball bearing
24. Circlip
25. Spacer
26. Brake camshaft
27. Rear axle
28. Cam lever
29. Washer
30. Bolt

2. Pull the brake assembly straight up and out of the brake drum.

NOTE
Before performing Step 3, mark the left and right shoe. If the shoes are to be reused, they must be installed in their original position.

3. Pull the brake shoes (**Figure 25**) and springs up and off the guide pins and camshaft.
4. Remove the return springs and separate the shoes. If the shoes will be reused, place a clean shop rag around the linings to protect them from oil and grease while removed.
5. Mark the position of the cam lever on the camshaft so that it will be installed at the same angle.
6. Loosen the clamping bolt and remove the brake arm.
7. Remove the wear indicator, dust seal and camshaft.
8. Assemble the brake by reversing the disassembly steps, noting the following.
9. Grease the camshaft and anchor posts with a light coat of molybdenum disulfide grease; avoid getting any grease on the brake plate where the linings come in contact with it.
10. When installing the brake arm onto the brake camshaft, be sure to align the punch marks on the brake lever and housing and to tighten the bolt securely.
11. Insert the brake panel assembly into the brake drum.
12. Install the rear wheel as described in Chapter Twelve.
13. Adjust the rear brake as described in Chapter Three.

Inspection

1. Thoroughly clean and dry all parts except the linings.
2. Check the contact surface of the drum for scoring. If there are grooves deep enough to snag a fingernail, the drum should be reground and new shoes fitted. This type of wear can be avoided to a great extent if the brakes are disassembled and thoroughly cleaned after riding the motorcycle in water, mud or deep sand.

NOTE
If oil or grease is on the drum surface clean it off with a clean rag soaked in lacquer thinner—do not use any solvent that may leave an oil residue.

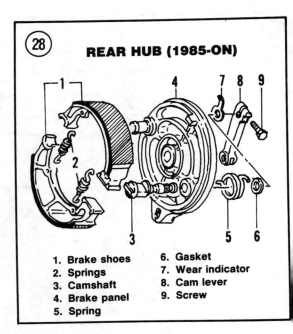

REAR HUB (1985-ON)

1. Brake shoes
2. Springs
3. Camshaft
4. Brake panel
5. Spring
6. Gasket
7. Wear indicator
8. Cam lever
9. Screw

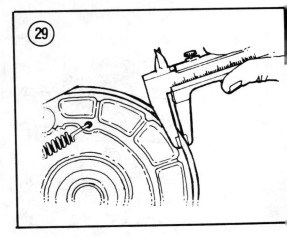

3. Use a vernier caliper (**Figure 29**) and measure the thickness of each brake shoe. They should be replaced if lining thickness is less than the minimum specified in **Tables 1-4**.
4. Inspect the linings for embedded foreign material. Dirt can be removed with a stiff wire brush. Check for traces of oil or grease. If the linings are contaminated, they must be replaced as a set.
5. Inspect the cam lobe and pivot pin area of the shaft for wear and corrosion. Minor roughness can be removed with fine emery cloth.
6. Inspect the brake shoe return springs for wear or distortion. On 1974-1983 models, measure the brake shoe spring free length with a vernier caliper.

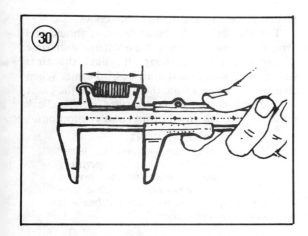

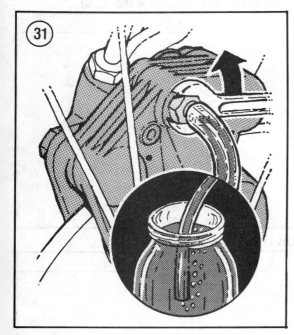

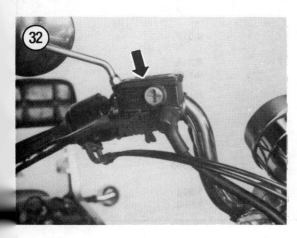

(**Figure 30**). Replace the springs if they are too long (**Tables 1-3**). If they are stretched, they will not fully retract the brake shoes from the drum, resulting in a power-robbing drag on the drums and premature wear of the linings. Replace as necessary and always replace as a pair.

NOTE
Kawasaki does not specify brake spring free length for 1985 and later models.

BLEEDING THE SYSTEM

This procedure is necessary only when the brakes feel spongy, there is a leak in the hydraulic system, a component has been replaced or the brake fluid has been replaced.

1. Flip off the dust cap from the brake bleeder valve.

2. Connect a length of clear tubing to the bleeder valve on the caliper. Place the other end of the tube into a clean container. Fill the container with enough fresh brake fluid to keep the end submerged. The tube should be long enough so that a loop can be made higher than the bleeder valve to prevent air from being drawn into the caliper during bleeding. See **Figure 31**.

CAUTION
Cover the front wheel, fender and fuel tank with a heavy cloth or plastic tarp to protect it from the accidental spilling of brake fluid. Wash any spilled brake fluid off of any painted or plated surface immediately, as it will destroy the finish. Use soapy water and rinse completely.

3. Clean the top of the master cylinder of all dirt and foreign matter. Remove the cap and diaphragm (**Figure 32**). Fill the reservoir to about 10 mm (3/8 in.) from the top. Install the diaphragm to prevent the entry of dirt and moisture.

WARNING
Use brake fluid clearly marked DOT 3 only. Others may vaporize and cause brake failure. Always use the same brand name. Do not intermix the brake fluids, as many brands are not compatible.

4. Slowly apply the brake lever several times. Hold the lever in the applied position and open the bleeder valve about 1/2 turn. Allow the lever to travel to its limit. When this limit is reached, tighten the bleeder screw. As the brake fluid enters the system, the level will drop in the master cylinder reservoir. Maintain the level at about 10 mm (3/8 in.) from the top of the reservoir to prevent air from being drawn into the system.

13

5. Continue to pump the lever and fill the reservoir until the fluid emerging from the hose is completely free of air bubbles.

> *NOTE*
> *If bleeding is difficult, it may be necessary to allow the fluid to stabilize for a few hours. Repeat the bleeding procedure when the tiny bubbles in the system settle out.*

6. Hold the lever in the applied position and tighten the bleeder valve. Remove the bleeder tube and install the bleeder valve dust cap.

7. If necessary, add fluid to correct the level in the master cylinder reservoir. It must be above the LOWER level line (**Figure 32**).

8. Install the cap and tighten the screws.

9. Test the feel of the brake lever. It should feel firm and should offer the same resistance each time it's operated. If it feels spongy, it is likely that air is still in the system and it must be bled again. When all air has been bled from the system, and the brake fluid level is correct in the reservoir, double-check for leaks and tighten all fittings and connections.

> *WARNING*
> *Before riding the motorcycle, make certain that the brake is operating correctly by operating the lever several times. Then make the test ride a slow one at first to make sure the brake is operating correctly.*

Table 1 BRAKE WEAR LIMITS (1974-1977 AND 1977-1978 DELUXE A MODELS)

	mm	in.
Master cylinder		
Inside diameter	14.08	0.554
Piston diameter	13.90	0.547
Primary/secondary cup diameter	14.50	0.571
Spring free length	48.0	1.89
Brake disc		
Runout	0.3	0.012
Thickness	6.0	0.236
Brake drum inside diameter	180.75	7.116
Brake lining thickness		
Front	2.5	0.098
Rear	2.0	0.078
Brake spring free length		
Front (KZ400S)	48.5	1.909
Rear	58	2.283

Table 2 BRAKE WEAR LIMITS (1978-1981 KZ400)

	mm	in.
Master cylinder		
Inside diameter	14.08	0.554
Piston diameter	13.90	0.547
Primary cup diameter	14.1	0.555
Secondary cup diameter	14.5	0.571
Spring free length	40.7	1.602
Brake disc		
Runout	0.3	0.012
Thickness		
1978	6.0	0.236
1979-1981	4.5	0.177
Brake drum inside diameter		
Front	180.75	7.116
Rear	160.75	6.328
Brake lining thickness (drum)		
Front	2.5	0.098
Rear	2	0.078
Brake lining thickness (disc)	1	0.0393
Brake spring free length		
Front	48.5	1.909
Rear	50	1.968

Table 3 BRAKE WEAR LIMITS (1980-1983 KZ440)

	mm	in.
Master cylinder		
Inside diameter	14.08	0.554
Piston diameter	13.90	0.547
Primary cup diameter	14.1	0.555
Secondary cup diameter	14.5	0.571
Spring free length	40.7	1.602
Brake disc		
Runout	0.3	0.012
Thickness	4.5	0.177
Brake drum inside diameter		
Front	180.75	7.116
Rear	160.75	6.328
Brake lining thickness (drum)		
Front	2.5	0.098
Rear	2	0.078
Brake lining thickness (disc)	1	0.0393
Brake spring free length		
Front	48.5	1.909
Rear	50	1.968

Table 4 BRAKE WEAR LIMITS (1985-ON EN450)

	mm	in.
Brake disc		
Runout	0.3	0.012
Thickness	4.5	0.177
Rear brake drum inside diameter		
Front	180.75	7.116
Rear brake lining thickness	2.5	0.098
Front brake lining thickness	1	0.0393
Brake spring free length	See foot note	See foot note

* Not specified by Kawasaki.

Table 5 BRAKE TIGHTENING TORQUES
(1974-1977 AND 1977-1978 DELUXE A MODELS)

	N·m	ft.-lb.
Brake disc bolts	18-20	13-14.5
Caliper mounting bolts	34-46	25-33
Brake pipe nipple	17-19	12-13.5
Master cylinder clamp	6-9	4-6.5
Union bolts	29-31	21-22
Torque link nuts	26-35	19-25

13

Table 6 BRAKE TIGHTENING TORQUES (1978-1981 KZ400)

	N·m	ft.-lb.
Brake disc bolts		
1978	40	29
1979-1981 (except KZ400G)	33	24
1981 KZ400G	23	16.5
Caliper mounting bolts	40	29
Caliper holder shaft nuts		
1979-1981 (except KZ400G)	26	19
1981 KZ400G	18	13
Union bolts	30	22
Torque link nuts	30	22

Table 7 BRAKE TIGHTENING TORQUES (1980-1983 KZ440)

	N·m	ft.-lb.
Brake disc bolts		
1981	33	24
1982-1983	23	16.5
Caliper mounting bolts		
1981	40	29
1982-1983	30	22
Caliper holder shaft nuts		
1981	26	19
- 1982-1983	18	13
Union bolts	30	22
Torque link nuts	33	24

Table 8 BRAKE TIGHTENING TORQUES (1985-ON EN450)

	N·m	ft.-lb.
Brake disc bolts	23	16.5
Brake caliper bolts	29	22
Union bolts	29	22
Torque link nuts	29	22

SUPPLEMENT

EN500 SERVICE INFORMATION

The following supplement provides procedures unique to the EN500 models. The chapter headings in this supplement correspond to those in the main body of this book. If a procedure is not included in the supplement, then refer to the information provided for the EN450 models in the main body of this book and the specifications shown within **Tables 1-17** of this supplement.

CHAPTER THREE

PERIODIC LUBRICATION, MAINTENANCE AND TUNE-UP

ROUTINE CHECKS

Tire Pressure

Table 1 lists new tire air pressure specifications for EN500 models.

PERIODIC LUBRICATION

Engine Oil and Filter Change

Table 2 lists recommended engine oil type and **Table 3** lists approximate refill capacity.

Front Fork Oil Change

Follow the procedure outlined for the EN450 while noting the following. A collar and spring seat is located below the fork cap. Refer to **Table 2** for oil specification and **Table 3** for oil quantity.

PERIODIC MAINTENANCE

Final Drive Belt Inspection/Adjustment

Belt deflection should be 1/4-1/2 in. (6-12.5 mm).

Disc Brake Fluid Level Inspection

Maintain fluid level above lower level line on outside of reservoir housing (**Figure 1**). The reservoir cap must be removed to view the upper level line.

Rear Brake Light Switch Adjustment

Refer to **Figure 2** for the following procedure. The rear brake light switch (A) is located behind the right footpeg assembly (B). To adjust, remove the

footpeg mounting bolts (C) and rotate the footpeg assembly to expose the brake light switch. Rotate the switch adjusting nut to alter the switch activation. Do not allow the switch to rotate during the adjustment procedure.

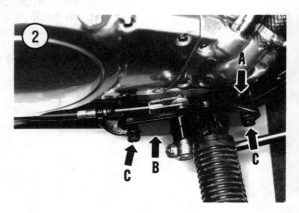

Air Filter Removal/Installation

1. Remove the right-hand side cover (**Figure 3**).
2. Remove the three screws securing the air filter cover (**Figure 4**).

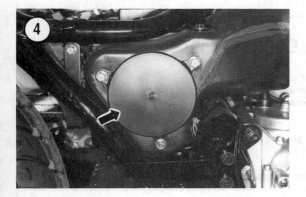

3. Remove the air filter and frame assembly (**Figure 5**).
4. Install by reversing these steps.

Air Filter Cleaning/Inspection

> *WARNING*
> *Wear suitable protective clothing and eye protection when working with solvent.*

1. Separate the air filter element from the frame.
2. Clean the element in a high flash-point solvent.
3. Dry the element by shaking or blow dry with compressed air from the inside of the element.
4. Inspect the element for tears or other damage that would allow unfiltered air to pass into the engine. Check the sponge gasket on each end of the element for tears. Replace the element if necessary.
5. Apply SE class SAE 30 oil to the element, then squeeze between a clean rag to expel all excess oil. Be careful not to tear or puncture the element.

Rear Shock Spring Adjustment

The rear shock absorbers feature adjustable spring preload. To adjust spring preload, use the spanner wrench in your motorcycle tool kit to turn both preload adjusters (**Figure 6**) to the same setting. Spring preload adjustment is rated between 1 and 5 with the lightest setting being 1 and the strongest setting being 5. The standard setting is 2.

> *WARNING*
> *Both rear shock absorbers must be set at the same preload settings for safe handling.*

Coolant Change

Table 4 lists cooling system specifications for EN500 models.

TUNE-UP

Tune-up specifications for EN500 models are shown in **Table 5**.

Tables 1-5 are on the following page.

Table 1 TIRES AND TIRE PRESSURE

Tire size	Pressure @ load	
	0-215 lb. (0-97.5 kg)	Over 215 lb. (Over 97.5 kg)
Front-100/90-19 57S	28 psi (196 kPa)	28 psi (196 kPa)
Rear-140/90-15 70S	28 psi (196 kPa)	32 psi (221 kPa)

Table 2 RECOMMENDED LUBRICANTS AND FUEL

Engine oil	Rated SE or SF
	10W-40—20° F and above*
	10W-50—20° F and above*
	20W-50—32° F and above*
Front fork oil	SAE 10W-20
Brake fluid	DOT 3
Fuel	87 pump octane (RON + MON)/2
	91 research octane (RON)
Battery	Distilled water
Cooling system	Permanent type antifreeze compounded for aluminum engines and radiator

*50 weight oil should be used when engine is operated under high ambient temperatures and heavy loads.

Table 3 OIL CAPACITIES

Engine	
Without filter change	2.8 liters (2.9 U.S. qt.)
With filter change	3.0 liters (3.2 U.S. qt.)
After overhaul	3.4 liters (3.6 U.S. qt.)
Front fork	
Oil change (approximate)	330 cc (11.1 U.S. oz.)
Dry capacity	385 cc (13.1 U.S. oz.)
Oil level with fork spring removed and fork fully compressed	128 mm (5.04 in.)

Table 4 COOLING SYSTEM SPECIFICATIONS

Capacity	1.4 liters (1.5 U.S. qt.)
Coolant ratio	50% purified water:50% coolant
Radiator cap	11-15 psi (0.75-1.05 kg/cm^2)
Thermostat	
Opening temperature	157.1-162.5° F (69.5-72.5° C)
Valve opening lift	Not less than 8 mm (5/16 in.) @ 203° F (95° C)

Table 5 TUNE-UP SPECIFICATIONS

Spark plug	
Type	
U.S. and Swiss	NGK D9EA or ND X27ES-U
All others	NGK DR8ES or ND X27ESR-U
Gap	0.6-0.7 mm (0.024-0.028 in.)
Valve clearance (cold)	
Intake	0.13-0.18 mm (0.005-0.007 in.)
Exhaust	0.18-0.23 mm (0.007-0.009 in.)
Idle speed	
California models	1,250-1,350 rpm
All others	1,150-1,250 rpm
Compression	129-213 psi (9.1-15 kg/cm^2)

CHAPTER FIVE

ENGINE (1990-ON EN500)

Complete engine specifications for EN500 models are listed in **Table 6**. **Table 7** lists engine tightening torques.

Table 6 ENGINE SPECIFICATIONS

	Standard mm (in.)	Wear limit mm (in.)
Cam lobe height	35.536-35.644 (1.399-1.403)	35.44 (1.395)
Camshaft bearing clearance	0.030-0.071 (0.0011-0.0027)	0.16 (0.006)
Camshaft journal diameter	24.950-24.970 (0.9822-0.9831)	24.92 (0.9811)
Camshaft bearing inside diameter (cylinder head-to-bearing cap)	25.000-25.021 (0.9842-0.9851)	25.08 (0.9874)
Camshaft runout	—	0.1 (0.0039)
Camshaft chain (20 link)	127-127.4 (5.0-5.016)	128.9 (5.075)
Primary chain 20-link length	190.50-190.97 (7.50-7.52)	193.4 (7.61)
Cam chain 20-link length	155.5-155.9 (6.12-6.14)	159 (6.26)
Rocker arm inside diameter	12.500-12.518 (0.4921-0.4928)	12.55 (0.4941)
Rocker arm shaft outer diameter	12.466-12.484 (0.4907-0.4915)	12.44 (0.4897)
Cylinder head warpage	—	0.05 (0.002)
Cylinder diameter	74.000-74.012 (2.9133-2.9138)	74.1 (2.917)
Piston diameter	73.942-73.957 (2.9111-2.9117)	73.79 (2.905)
Piston-to-cylinder clearance	0.043-0.070 (0.0017-0.0027)	—
Piston ring groove clearance Top	0.03-0.07 (0.0012-0.0027)	0.17 (0.0067)
Second	0.02-0.06 (0.0007-0.0024)	0.16 (0.0063)
Piston ring groove width Top	0.82-0.84 (0.0323-0.0331)	0.92 (0.0362)
Second	1.01-1.03 (0.0397-0.0405)	1.11 (0.0437)
Oil	2.01-2.03 (0.0791-0.0799)	2.11 (0.0831)

(continued)

Table 6 ENGINE SPECIFICATIONS (continued)

	Standard mm (in.)	Wear limit mm (in.)
Piston ring thickness		
Top	0.77-0.79 (0.0303-0.0311)	0.7 (0.0275)
Second	0.97-0.99 (0.0382-0.0389)	0.9 (0.0354)
Piston ring end gap		
Top and second	0.2-0.35 (0.0078-0.0138)	0.7 (0.0275)
Oil	0.2-0.7 (0.0078-0.0275)	1.0 (0.3937)
Valve head thickness		
Intake	0.5 (0.02)	0.25 (0.0098)
Exhaust	1.0 (0.04)	0.7 (0.0275)
Valve stem diameter		
Intake	5.475-5.490 (0.2155-0.2161)	5.46 (0.2149)
Exhaust	5.455-5.470 (0.2147-0.2153)	5.44 (0.2141)
Valve stem runout	—	0.05 (0.0894)
Valve guide inside diameter	5.500-5.512 (0.2165-0.2170)	5.58 (0.2197)
Valve spring free length		
Inner	36.3 (1.429)	35 (1.378)
Outer	40.4 (1.590)	39 (1.535)
Connecting rod side clearance	0.13-0.33 (0.0051-0.0129)	0.50 (0.0197)
Connecting rod bearing clearance	0.036-0.066 (0.0014-0.0025)	0.10 (0.0039)
Crankpin	—	37.97 (1.4948)
Crankshaft runout	—	0.05 (0.0019)
Crankshaft journal clearance	0.020-0.044 (0.0008-0.0017)	0.08 (0.0031)
Crankshaft main journal diameter	—	35.96 (1.4157)
Crankshaft thrust clearance	0.05-0.25 (0.0019-0.0098)	0.40 (0.0157)
Balancer shaft bearing clearance	0.020-0.044 (0.0008-0.0017)	0.08 (0.0031)
Balancer shaft journal diameter	—	27.96 (1.1007)
Oil pump		
Inner rotor clearance	—	0.20 (0.0078)
Pump body clearance	—	0.30 (0.0118)
Outer rotor diameter	—	40.45 (1.5925)
Body inside diameter	—	40.80 (1.6062)
Rotor end clearance	—	0.12 (0.0047)

Table 7 ENGINE TIGHTENING TORQUES

	N·m	ft.-lb.
Rocker arm shafts	51	38
Cylinder head cover bolts	9.8	7.2
Cylinder head bolts		
6 mm	9.8	7.2
10 mm	51	38
Camshaft cap bolts	12	104 in.-lb.
Camshaft chain tensioner bolts	8.8	78 in.-lb.
Cam sprocket bolts	15	11
Oil line banjo bolts		
At cylinder head	12	9
At crankcase	20	14.5
Connecting rod nuts	36	27
Rotor bolt	69	51
Crankcase bolts		
6 mm	12	9
8 mm	27	20
Engine mount nuts	39	20
Engine bracket	25	18
Oil pan bolts	12	8.5
Valve adjuster locknuts	25	18

CHAPTER SIX

CLUTCH AND PRIMARY CHAIN

Table 8 lists clutch wear limits for EN500 models.

Table 8 CLUTCH WEAR LIMITS

Clutch spring free length	33.1 mm (1.303 in.)
Friction plate thickness	2.75 mm (0.108 in.)
Clutch plate warpage	0.30 mm (0.012 in.)

CHAPTER SEVEN

TRANSMISSION

Table 9 lists transmission wear limits for EN500 models.

14

SHIFT MECHANISM

The distance between the front locknut and the rear locknut on the shift linkage rod should be 137.5 mm (5.4 in.). Refer to **Figure 18** on page 185.

Table 9 TRANSMISSION WEAR LIMITS

	mm	in.
Gear backlash	0.24	0.009
Shift fork finger thickness	4.8	0.189
Gear shift fork groove width	5.3	0.208
Shift fork guide pin diameter	7.8	0.307
Shift drum groove width	8.3	0.3267

CHAPTER EIGHT

FUEL AND EMISSION CONTROL SYSTEMS

Table 10 lists carburetor specifications for EN500 models.

Table 10 CARBURETOR SPECIFICATIONS

Carburetor model No.	CVK34 Keihin
Main jet	
Left carburetor	105 (U.S.)
	112 (U.K.)
Right carburetor	105 (U.S.)
	115 (U.K.)
Main air jet	100
Jet needle	
Left carburetor	N60T (U.S.)
	N60Q (U.K.)
Right carburetor	N60S (U.S.)
	N60Q (U.K.)
Pilot jet	35
Pilot air jet	150
Pilot screw	2 turns out
Starter jet	45
Fuel level above bottom edge of the carburetor body	0.5 ± 1 mm (0.02 ± 0.04 in.)
Float height	17.0 mm (0.67 in.)
Idle speed	
California models	1,250-1,350 rpm
All others	1,150-1,250 rpm

CHAPTER NINE

ELECTRICAL SYSTEMS

Table 11 lists electrical specifications for EN500 models.

NOTE
The headlight must be disconnected to turn the light off on U.S. and Canadian models.

CHARGING SYSTEM

Refer to **Figure 7** for charging system schematic on EN500 models.

TRANSISTORIZED IGNITION

Refer to **Figure 8** for ignition system schematic on EN500 models.

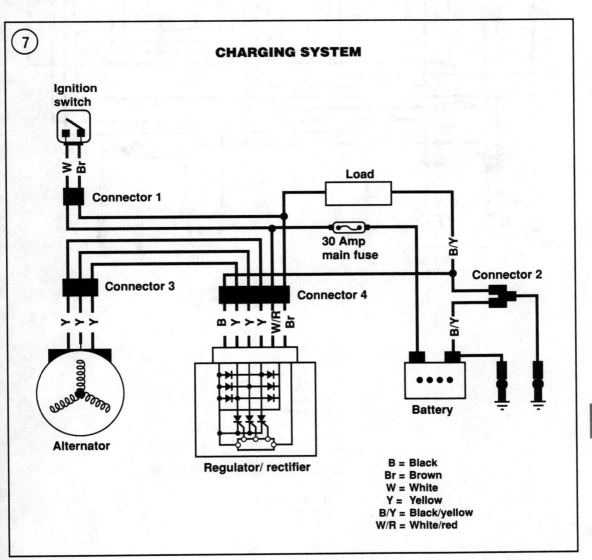

⑦ **CHARGING SYSTEM**

Ignition switch

W Br

Connector 1

Load

30 Amp main fuse

B/Y

Connector 3

Connector 4

Connector 2

Y Y Y

B Y Y Y W/R Br

B/Y

Alternator

Battery

Regulator/ rectifier

B = Black
Br = Brown
W = White
Y = Yellow
B/Y = Black/yellow
W/R = White/red

14

⑧

IGNITION SYSTEM

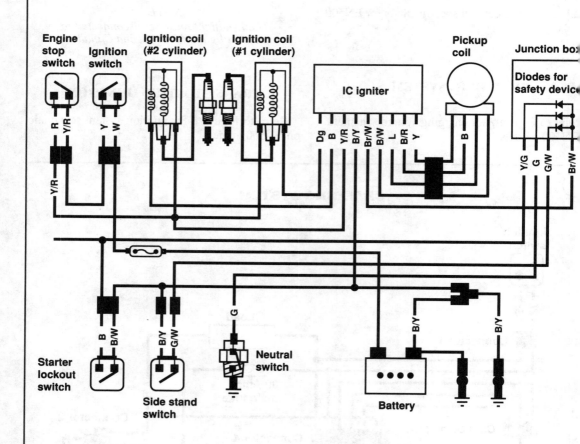

B = Black
Dg = Dark green
G = Green
L = Blue
R = Red
W = White
Y = Yellow
B/R = Black/red
B/W = Black/white
Br/W = Brown/white
B/Y = Black/yellow
G/W = Green/white
Y/G = Yellow/green
Y/R = Yellow/red

NOTE

NOTE
When connecting the ignition coil wires, connect the green and yellow/red wires to the number 1 ignition coil and the black and yellow/red wires to the number 2 ignition coil.

ELECTRIC STARTER

Refer to **Figure 9** for starter system schematic on EN500 models.

The brush plate in the starter motor houses the positive brush and the negative brush as a single unit assembly. Only one positive and one negative brush is used. The brush plate assembly must be replaced to service either brush.

The starter circuit relay is housed in the junction box. To test the starter circuit relay, refer to *Junction Box and Fuses* in this chapter.

LIGHTING SYSTEM

Headlight Replacement

1. Remove the headlight trim bezel screw on the left- and right-hand side (**Figure 10**).

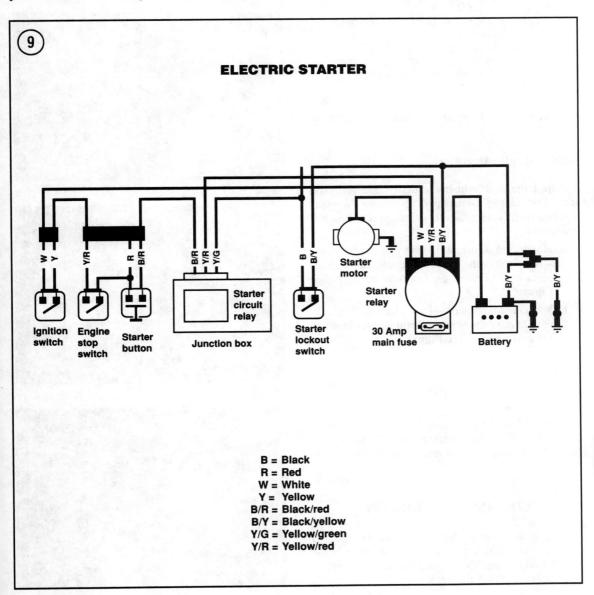

⑨

ELECTRIC STARTER

Ignition switch — Engine stop switch — Starter button — Junction box — Starter circuit relay — Starter lockout switch — Starter motor — Starter relay — 30 Amp main fuse — Battery

B = Black
R = Red
W = White
Y = Yellow
B/R = Black/red
B/Y = Black/yellow
Y/G = Yellow/green
Y/R = Yellow/red

2. Pull the trim bezel and headlight unit out and disconnect the electrical connector from the bulb.

> ### WARNING
> *If the headlight has just burned out or been turned off, it will be hot. Do **not** touch the bulb until it cools off.*

3. Remove the bulb cover. Release the spring clip retaining the bulb holder and remove the bulb.

4. Install by reversing these steps. Position the headlight so that the "TOP" mark on the lens points up.

> ### CAUTION
> *Do not touch the bulb glass with your fingers because traces of oil on the bulb will drastically reduce the life of the bulb. Clean any traces of oil from the bulb with a cloth moistened in alcohol or lacquer thinner.*

5. Adjust the headlight as described in this chapter.

Headlight Adjustment

Adjust the headlight horizontally and vertically according to the Department of Motor Vehicles regulations in your area. To adjust, proceed as follows:

a. Horizontal adjustment—Turn the screw clockwise to move the beam to the left and counterclockwise to move the beam to the right. See **Figure 11**.

b. Vertical adjustment—Turn the screw clockwise to raise the beam and counterclockwise to lower the beam. See **Figure 12**.

SWITCHES

Figure 13 shows 2 switches that differ from those used on EN450 models. Refer to *Switches* in Chapter Nine of the main body for testing procedure.

COOLING FAN CIRCUIT

A 2 wire thermostatic fan switch is used on EN500 models. The switch does not ground through the switch body as on EN450 models. Refer to **Figure 14** for circuit wiring diagram.

JUNCTION BOX AND FUSES

The junction box (**Figure 15**) is located on the top of the battery. The junction box includes fuses, diodes and relays. The diodes and relays are an integral part of the circuit board and cannot be removed and replaced as on previous models. If any of the diodes or relays are faulty, the entire junction box must be replaced. The fuses are the only items that can be removed and replaced. Refer to the wiring diagram shown in **Figure 16** for U.S. and Canadian models and to **Figure 17** for all other models.

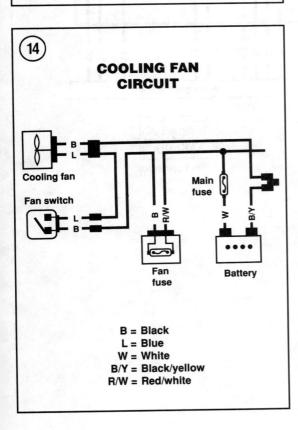

IGNITION SWITCH

Switch position	Wire color				
	Br	W	Y	Bl	R
Off, lock					
On	●——●——●			●——●	
Park		●————————●			

DIMMER SWITCH

Switch position	Wire color		
	R/B	Bl/Y	R/Y
Low		●——●	
High	●——●		

COOLING FAN CIRCUIT

Cooling fan

Fan switch

Fan fuse

Main fuse

Battery

B = Black
L = Blue
W = White
B/Y = Black/yellow
R/W = Red/white

Junction Box
Removal/Installation

1. Remove the seat.
2. Carefully remove the junction box from the rubber mount.
3. Disconnect the electrical connectors from the junction box and remove the box.
4. Install by reversing these steps.

Fuse Replacement

There are 4 fuses located in the junction box. If there is an electrical system failure, first check for a blown fuse.
1. Remove the seat.
2. Remove the fuse cover (**Figure 18**) from the junction box.
3. Use needlenose pliers and pull the fuse straight up and out of the fuse panel.
4. Install a new fuse with the same amperage rating.

NOTE
The junction box is equipped with several replacement fuses. Always carry spare fuses. Whenever a fuse blows, find out the reason for the failure before replacing the fuse. Usually, the trouble is a short circuit in the wiring. Check by testing the circuit that the fuse protects. A blown fuse may be caused by a worn-through insulation or a disconnected wire shorting to ground.

CAUTION
Never substitute aluminum foil or wire for a fuse. Never use a higher amperage fuse than specified. An overload could cause a fire, resulting in complete loss of the bike.

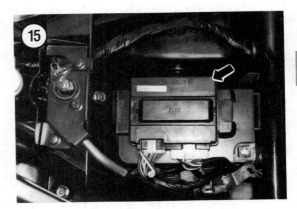

14

JUNCTION BOX
(U.S. AND CANADA)

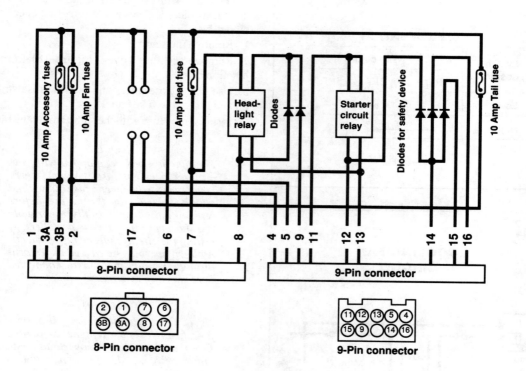

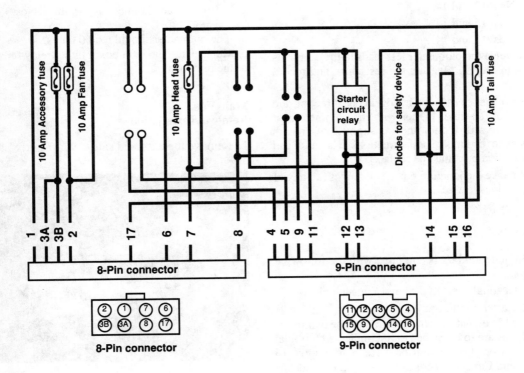

**JUNCTION BOX
(OTHER THAN U.S. AND CANADA)**

Diode Circuit Test

The ohmmeter test leads are to be placed on the indicated terminal numbers on the junction box. Refer to **Figure 16** (U.S. and Canada models) or **Figure 17** (all other models).

1. Remove the junction box from the top of the battery.

2. Connect the ohmmeter test leads to each of the following junction box terminals. Measure the resistance and record it.

   a. Nos. 13 and 8 (U.S. and Canada only).

   b. Nos. 13 and 9 (U.S. and Canada only).

   c. Nos. 12 and 14.

   d. Nos. 15 and 14.

   e. Nos. 16 and 14.

3. Reverse the ohmmeter test leads to the terminals made in Step 2. Measure the resistance and record it.

4. The resistance should be low in one direction and more than 10 times higher with the ohmmeter test leads reversed. If the diode(s) shows low or high resistance readings in both directions, it is faulty and the junction box must be replaced.

5. Replace the junction box if the diodes fail any of the previous tests.

Relay Test

The junction box is equipped with the following relays:

   a. Headlight relay (U.S. and Canada only).

   b. Starter circuit relay.

The 12 volt battery connections and the ohmmeter test leads are to be placed on the indicated terminal numbers on the junction box. Refer to **Figure 16** (U.S. and Canada) or **Figure 17** (all other models).

Battery disconnected

1. Remove the junction box from the top of the battery.

2. Connect an ohmmeter to the following terminals:

   a. Headlight relay (U.S. and Canada): Nos. 7 and 8, then Nos. 7 and 13.

   b. Starter relay: Nos. 11 and 13, then Nos. 12 and 13.

3. The ohmmeter should read infinity for all tests.

4. Replace the junction box if either relay fails any of the previous tests.

Battery connected

1. Remove the junction box from the top of the battery.

2. To test the headlight relay (U.S. and Canada), perform the following:

   a. Connect a 12-volt battery to terminals Nos. 9 and 13.

   b. Connect an ohmmeter to terminals Nos. 7 and 8.

3. The ohmmeter should read 0 ohms.

4. To test the starter relay, perform the following:

   a. Connect a 12-volt battery to terminals Nos. 11 and 12.

   b. Connect an ohmmeter to terminals Nos. 11 and 13.

5. The ohmmeter should read 0 ohms.

6. Replace the junction box if either relay fails any of the previous tests.

Main Fuse
Removal/Installation

1. Remove the left-hand side cover (**Figure 19**).

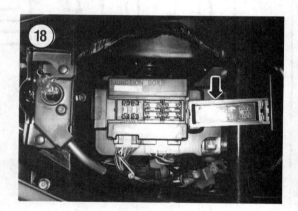

2. Remove the fuse cover (**Figure 20**).

3. Use needlenose pliers and pull the fuse (**Figure 21**) straight out of the starter relay.

4. Install a new fuse with the same amperage rating.

NOTE
The junction box is equipped with a replacement fuse. Refer to the previous ***Fuse Replacement*** *procedure. Always carry a spare fuse. Whenever a fuse blows find out the reason for the failure before replacing the fuse. Usually, the trouble is a faulty component or a short circuit in the wiring. Isolate components and wiring until the failure is found.*

CAUTION
Use a tool specific for circuit testing. Never substitute aluminum foil or wire for a fuse. Never use a higher amperage fuse than specified. An overload could cause a fire, resulting in complete loss of the bike.

5. Install by reversing these steps.

Table 11 ELECTRICAL SPECIFICATIONS

Charging system	
Regulator/rectifier output voltage	12-15 volts
Alternator output test	60 volts AC @ 4,000 rpm
Resistance check	0.3-0.6 ohms
Ignition system	
Ignition coil	
Primary	2.2-3.5 ohms
Secondary	10-16 K ohms
Pickup coil resistance	400-490 ohms
Starter motor	
Brush wear limit	8.5 mm (0.335 in.)

CHAPTER TEN

COOLING SYSTEM

Table 4 lists cooling system specifications for EN500 models.

14

CHAPTER ELEVEN

FRONT SUSPENSION
AND STEERING

Table 12 lists front suspension wear limits for EN500 models. **Table 13** lists front suspension tightening torques.

FRONT FORKS

Follow the procedure outlined in the main body and refer to **Figure 43** on page 276 and note the following.

1. Air valve (component 3) is not used.

2. A collar and spring seat is located below the fork cap.

3. Install the front fork with the inner fork tube flush with the top surface of the stem head.

Table 12 FRONT SUSPENSION WEAR LIMIT

Fork spring free length	365 mm (14.37 in.)

Table 13 FRONT SUSPENSION TIGHTENING TORQUES

	N·m	ft.-lb.
Front axle nut	88	65
Front axle clamp nut	16	11.5
Front fork		
Upper clamp bolts	20	14.5
Lower clamp bolts	25	18
Bottom Allen bolt	20	14.5
Oil drain bolt	7.4	65 in.-lb.
Handlebar clamp bolts	23	16.5
Steering stem head bolt	42	31
Steering stem locknut	4.9	43 in.-lb.

CHAPTER TWELVE

REAR SUSPENSION

Table 14 lists pulley wear limits for EN500 models. **Table 15** lists rear suspension tightening torques.

Table 14 PULLEY WEAR LIMITS

	mm	in.
Front pulley tooth height	6.1	0.240
Rear pulley tooth height	6.3	0.248

Table 15 REAR SUSPENSION TIGHTENING TORQUES

	N·m	ft.-lb.
Rear axle nut	125	94
Rear shock absorber	25	18
Rear pulley nuts	69	51
Swing arm pivot shaft nut	88	65

CHAPTER THIRTEEN

BRAKES

Table 16 lists brake wear limits for EN500 models. **Table 17** lists brake tightening torques.

MASTER CYLINDER

Disassembly/Reassembly

A round reservoir front master cylinder is used. Refer to **Figure 22**.
1. Remove the master cylinder as outlined in the main body.
2. Remove the screws securing the reservoir cap and diaphragm. Pour out the remaining brake fluid and discard it. *Never* reuse brake fluid.
3. Remove the brake lever.
4. Remove the dust cover from the area where the hand lever actuates the internal piston.
5. Remove the retaining clip and withdraw the piston assembly.
6. Inspect the master cylinder assembly as described in the main body.

7. Assembly is the reverse of these steps. Note the following.
8. Soak the new cups in fresh brake fluid for at least 15 minutes to make them pliable. Coat the inside of the cylinder with fresh brake fluid before assembling the parts.

> *CAUTION*
> *When installing the piston assembly, do not allow the cups to turn inside out as they will be damaged and allow brake fluid to leak within the cylinder bore.*

9. Install the master cylinder piston assembly in the order shown in **Figure 22**. Make sure the retaining clip is seated in its groove and the dust cover seats against the clip.
10. Install the master cylinder as outlined in the main body.
11. Bleed the master cylinder and front brake system as outlined in the main body of the book.

Figure 22 and Tables 16-17 are on the following pages.

14

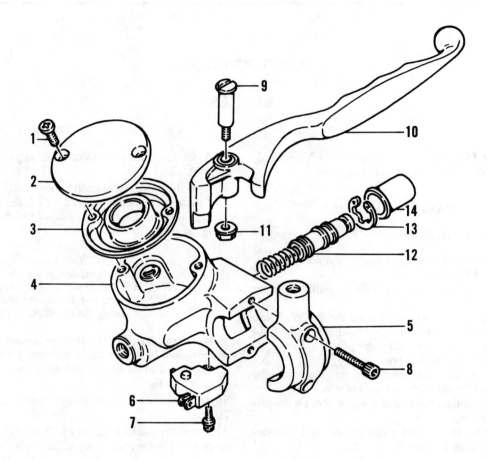

FRONT MASTER CYLINDER

1. Screw
2. Cover
3. Diaphragm
4. Reservoir and housing
5. Clamp
6. Brake switch
7. Screw
8. Allen screw
9. Pivot bolt
10. Lever
11. Nut
12. Piston assembly
13. Retaining clip
14. Dust cover

Table 16 BRAKE WEAR LIMITS

	mm	in.
Brake disc		
Runout	0.3	0.012
Thickness	4.5	0.177
Rear brake drum inside diameter	180.75	7.116
Rear brake shoe lining thickness	2.0	0.079
Front brake pad lining thickness	1.0	0.0393

Table 17 BRAKE TIGHTENING TORQUES

	N·m	ft.-lb.
Brake disc bolts	23	16.5
Brake caliper bolts	39	29
Union bolts	25	18
Torque link nuts	29	22

14

INDEX

15

WIRING DIAGRAMS

1974-1977 KZ400S AND A — U.S.
1978 KZ400A — U.S.

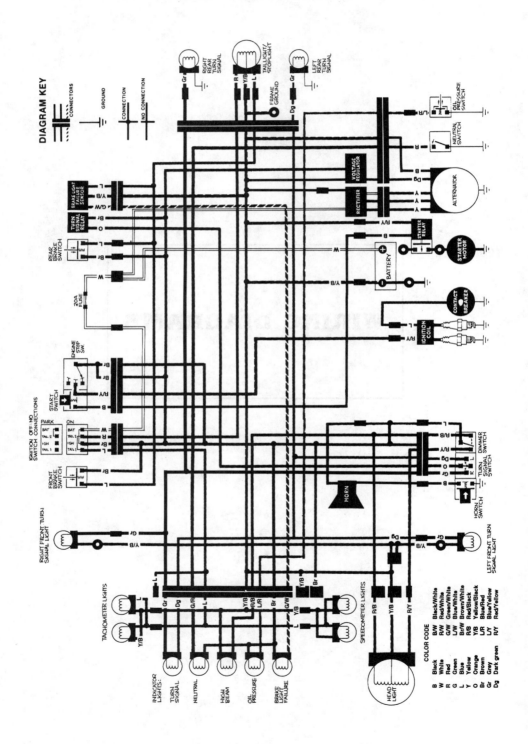

1978-1979 KZ400B — U.S. AND CANADA

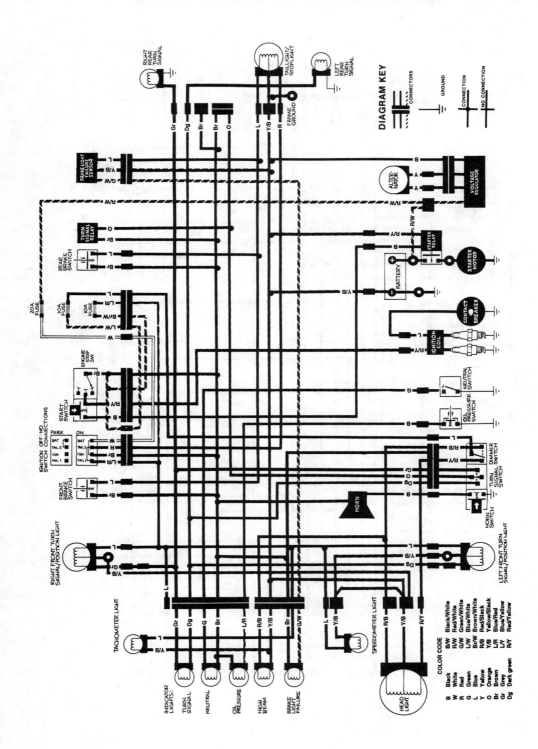

1978-1979 KZ400B — EUROPE

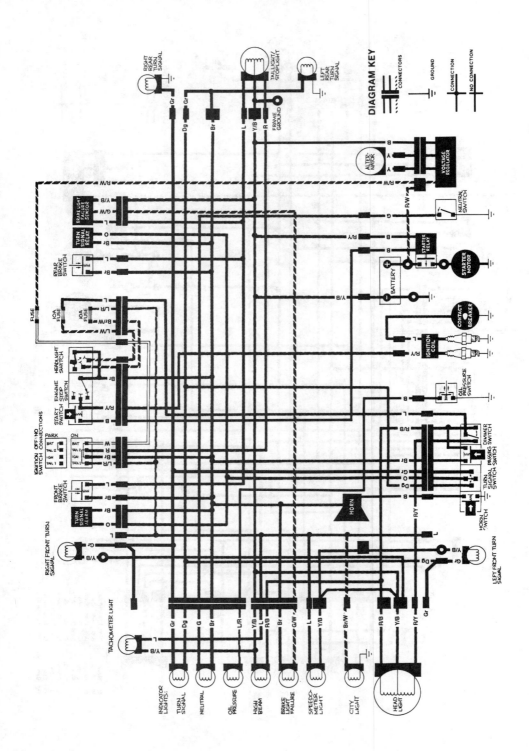

1978 KZ400C — U.S.

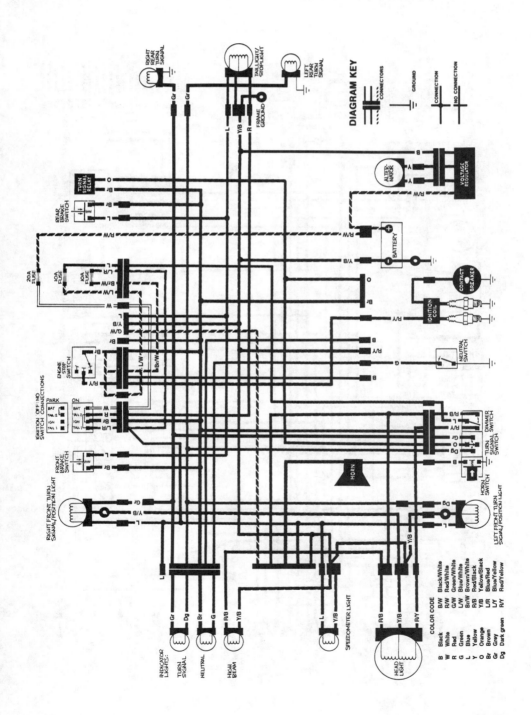

1979 KZ400H (LTD)
1980 KZ440A AND D — U.S. AND CANADA

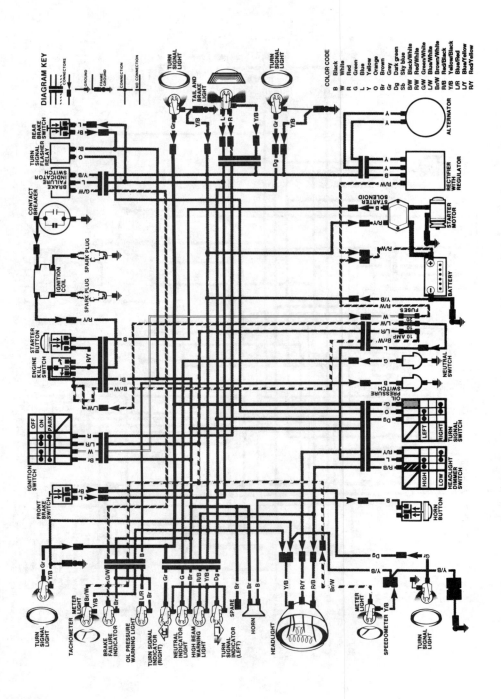

1980 KZ400B — U.S. AND CANADA

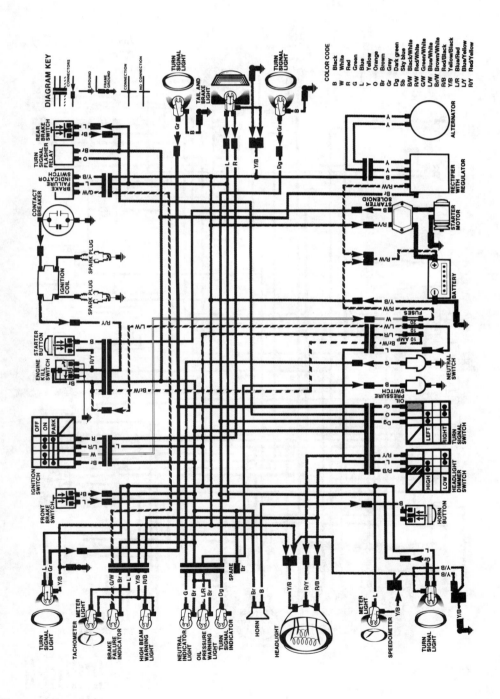

1980 KZ400 B3 AND G2

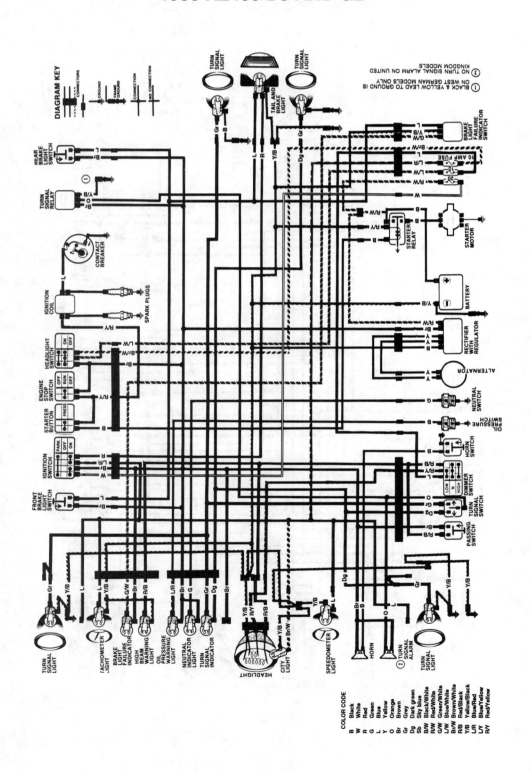

1980 Z440C — EUROPE

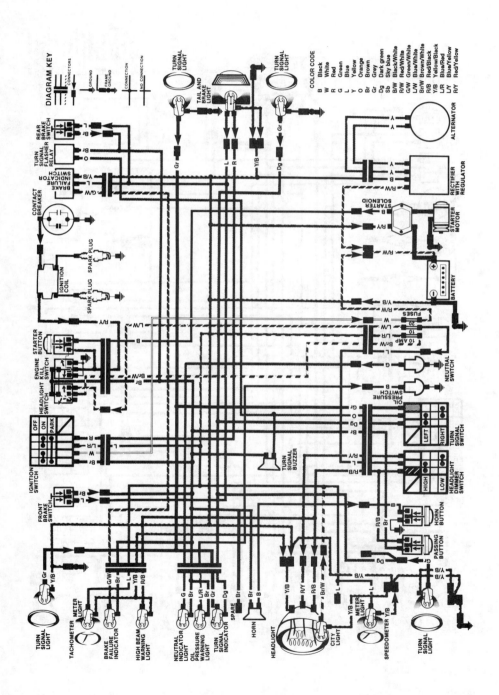

1980 Z440A — EUROPE

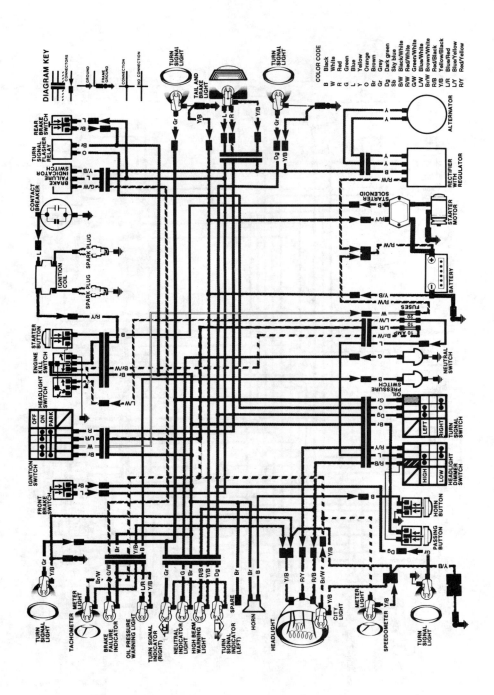

1981 KZ400 G3

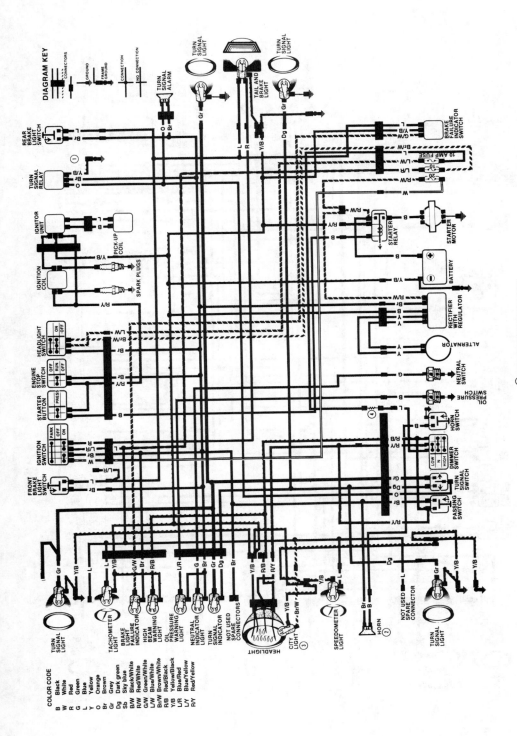

1981 KZ400H3

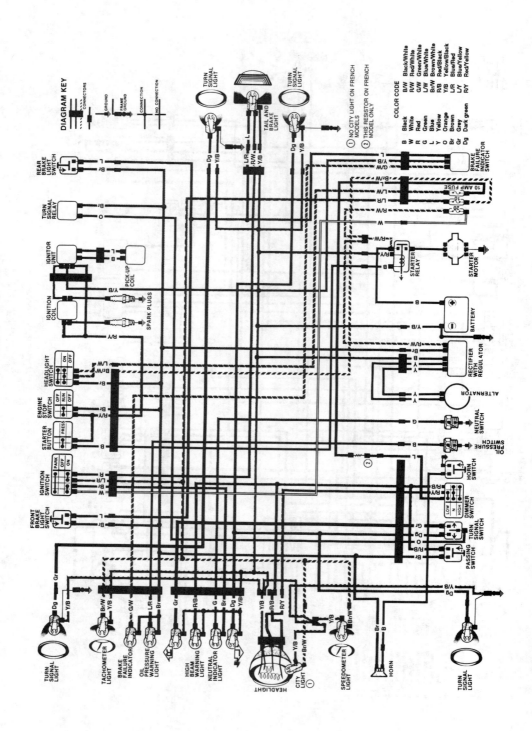

1981 KZ440A AND D — U.S. AND CANADA

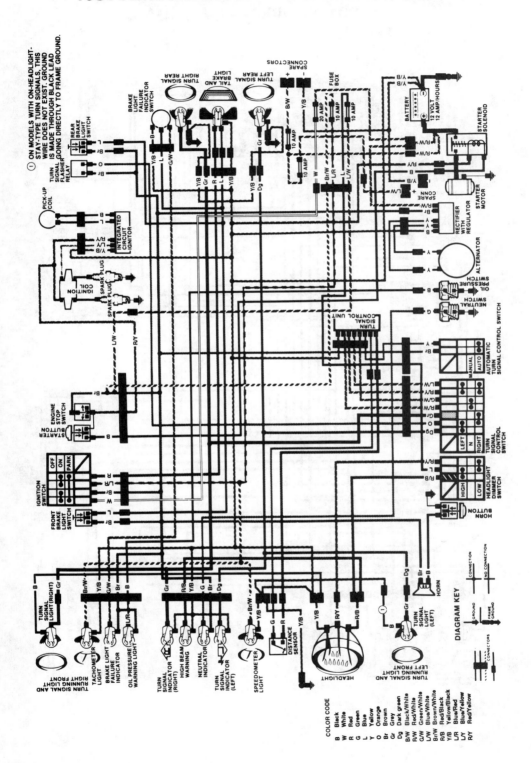

1981 KZ440B — U.S. AND CANADA
1981 KZ440C — CANADA

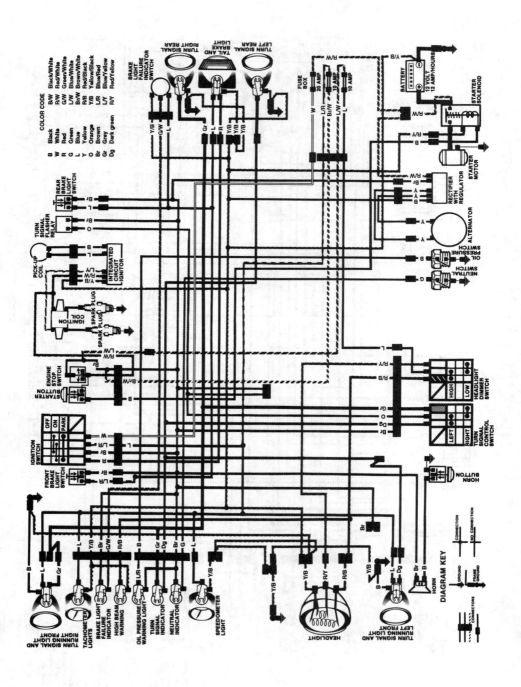

1981 Z440C — EUROPE

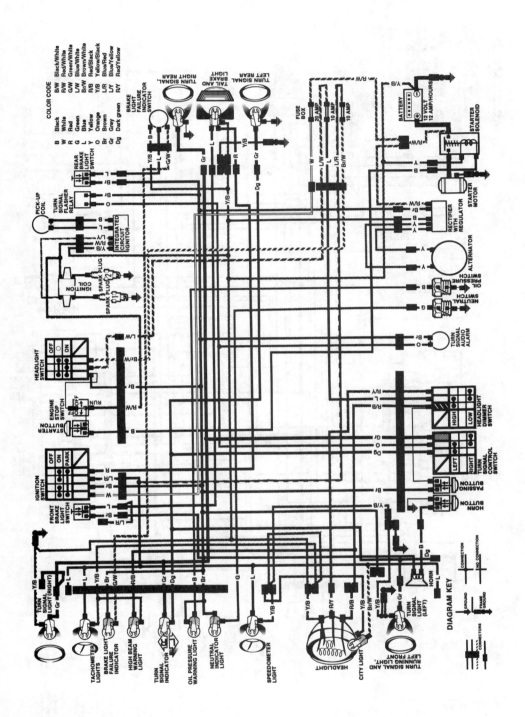

1981-1983 Z440A AND D — EUROPE

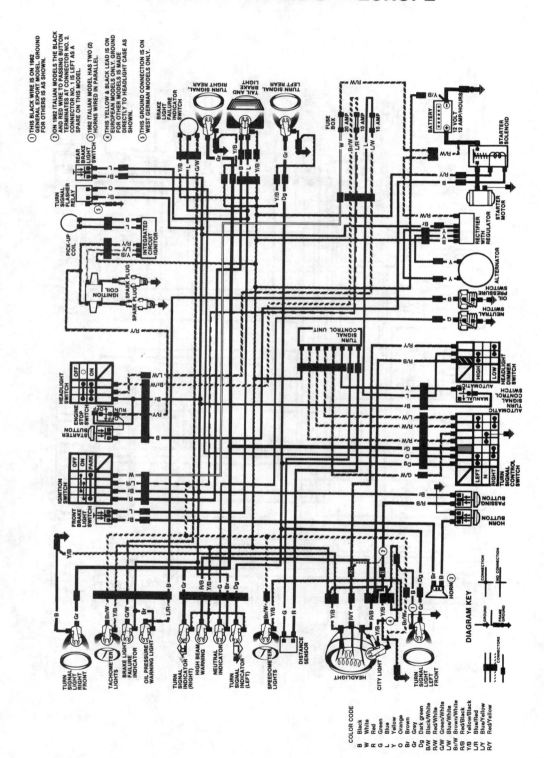

1982-1983 KZ440A AND D — U.S. AND CANADA

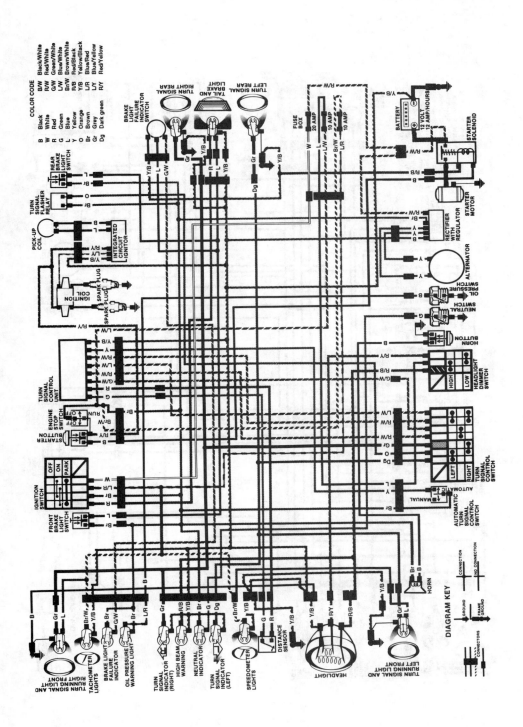

16

1982-1983 KZ440G — U.S. AND CANADA

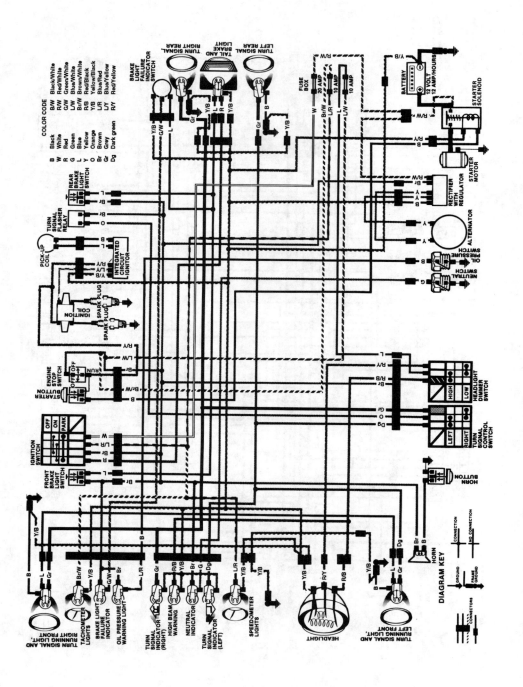

1982-1983 KZ440H — EUROPE

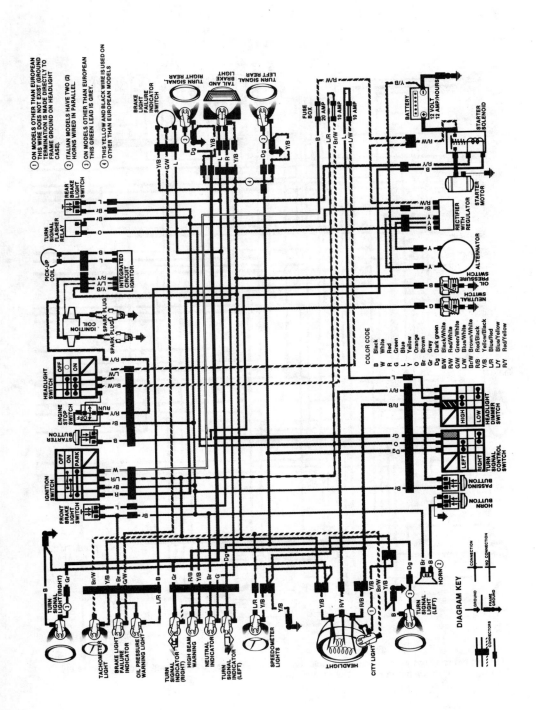

1985-1990 EN450A — U.S. AND CANADA

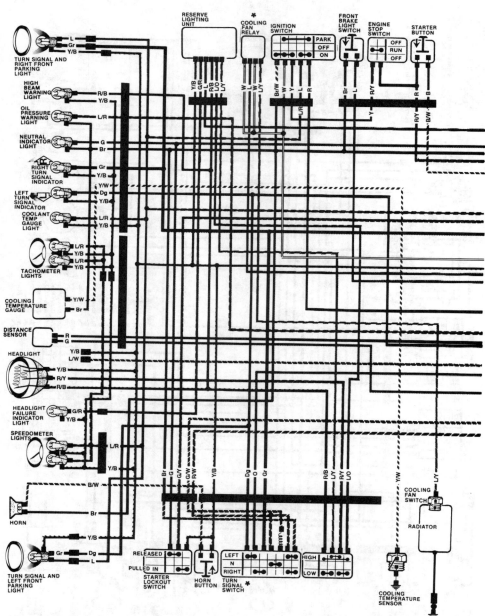

*Cooling fan relay not used on 1989 and 1990 models. Green/white, red/white and blue/white wires at turn signal switch are not used on 1989-1990 models.

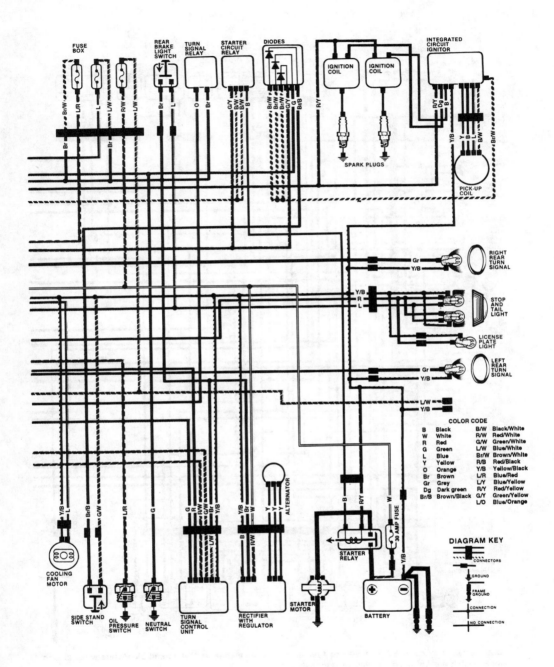

1985-1990 EN450A — EXCEPT U.S. AND CANADA

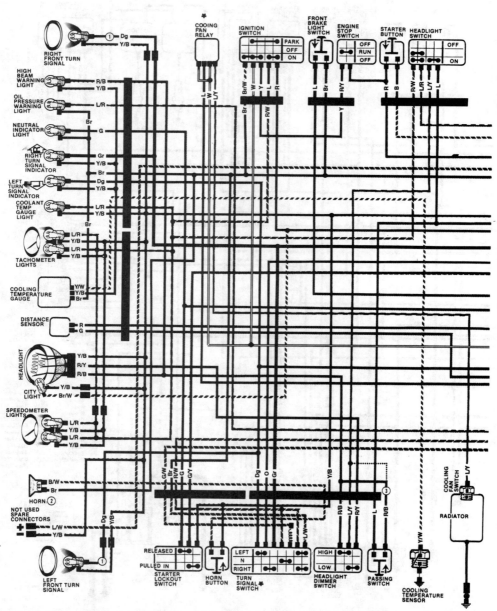

*Cooling fan relay not used on 1989 and 1990 models. Green/white, red/white and blue/white wires at turn signal switch are not used on 1989-1990 models.

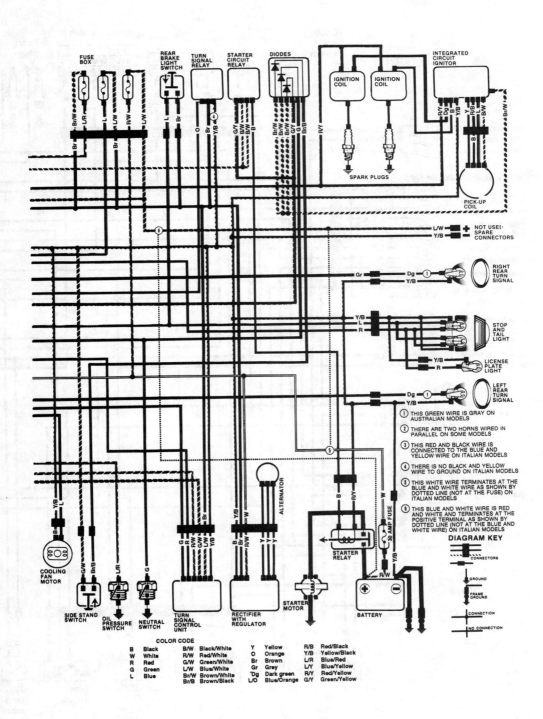

1990-1995 EN500 — U.S. AND CANADA

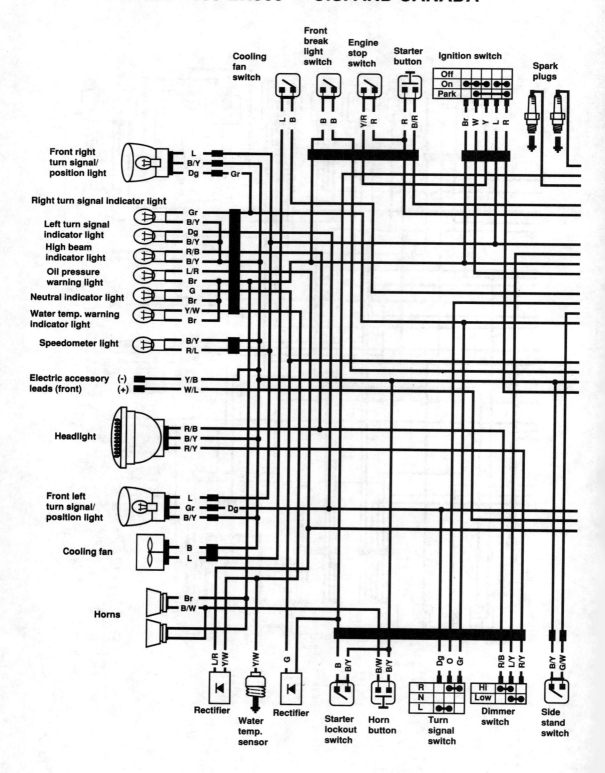

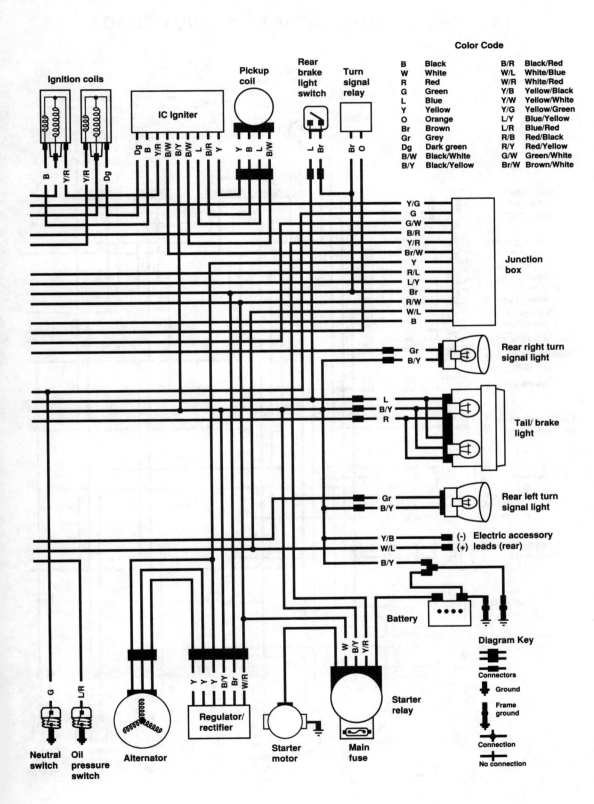

Ignition coils

Pickup coil

Rear brake light switch

Turn signal relay

IC Igniter

Color Code

B	Black		B/R	Black/Red
W	White		W/L	White/Blue
R	Red		W/R	White/Red
G	Green		Y/B	Yellow/Black
L	Blue		Y/W	Yellow/White
Y	Yellow		Y/G	Yellow/Green
O	Orange		L/Y	Blue/Yellow
Br	Brown		L/R	Blue/Red
Gr	Grey		R/B	Red/Black
Dg	Dark green		R/Y	Red/Yellow
B/W	Black/White		G/W	Green/White
B/Y	Black/Yellow		Br/W	Brown/White

Junction box

Rear right turn signal light

Tail/ brake light

Rear left turn signal light

(-) Electric accessory
(+) leads (rear)

Battery

Diagram Key

Connectors

Ground

Frame ground

Connection

No connection

Neutral switch

Oil pressure switch

Alternator

Regulator/ rectifier

Starter motor

Main fuse

Starter relay

16

1990-1995 EN500 — EXCEPT U.S. AND CANADA

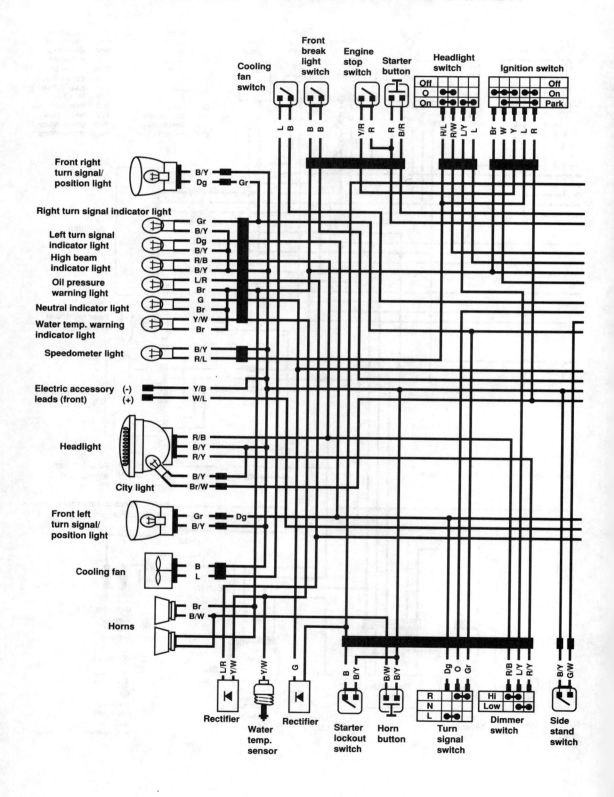

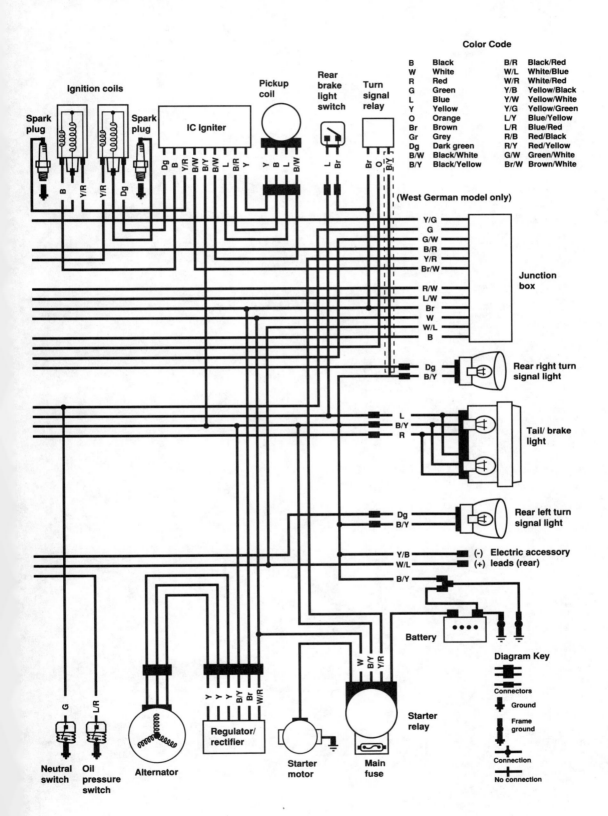

Color Code

B	Black	B/R	Black/Red
W	White	W/L	White/Blue
R	Red	W/R	White/Red
G	Green	Y/B	Yellow/Black
L	Blue	Y/W	Yellow/White
Y	Yellow	Y/G	Yellow/Green
O	Orange	L/Y	Blue/Yellow
Br	Brown	L/R	Blue/Red
Gr	Grey	R/B	Red/Black
Dg	Dark green	R/Y	Red/Yellow
B/W	Black/White	G/W	Green/White
B/Y	Black/Yellow	Br/W	Brown/White

(West German model only)

Ignition coils

Spark plug

Spark plug

IC Igniter

Pickup coil

Rear brake light switch

Turn signal relay

Junction box

Rear right turn signal light

Tail/ brake light

Rear left turn signal light

Electric accessory leads (rear)

Battery

Diagram Key

Connectors

Ground

Frame ground

Connection

No connection

Neutral switch

Oil pressure switch

Alternator

Regulator/ rectifier

Starter motor

Main fuse

Starter relay

16

NOTES

NOTES

NOTES

MAINTENANCE LOG

Service Performed	Mileage Reading				
Oil change (example)	2,836	5,782	8,601		